WOMEN: *Is the man in your life afraid to tell you the truth . . .*

- About how he views the role of male power . . . even in the most intimate situations?

- About the way y

- About his true fe

- About what he may never say so

MEN: *Is the woman in your life afraid to hear the truth . . .*

- About your resentment at the mixed messages she keeps sending?

- About your fantasies . . . including the one that makes commitment so hard for you?

- About her unrealistic expectations . . . expectations that not even Prince Charming could meet?

- About what she could do, if she had a mind to, to make your relationship *really* work?

Now, you can learn what's wrong between the sexes—and set it right in your own life!

WHY MEN ARE THE WAY THEY ARE

Turn the page for more rave reviews . . .

WHY MEN ARE THE WAY THEY ARE

THE MALE-FEMALE DYNAMIC

WARREN FARRELL, Ph.D.

BERKLEY BOOKS, NEW YORK

This Berkley book contains the complete
text of the original hardcover edition.
It has been completely reset in a typeface
designed for easy reading and was printed
from new film.

WHY MEN ARE THE WAY THEY ARE

A Berkley Book/published by arrangement with
McGraw-Hill Book Company

PRINTING HISTORY
McGraw-Hill edition/published 1986
Berkley edition/September 1988

ISBN: 0-425-11094-X

A BERKLEY BOOK® TM 757,375
Berkley Books are published by The Berkley Publishing Group,
200 Madison Avenue, New York, NY 10016.
The name ''BERKLEY'' and the ''B'' logo
are trademarks belonging to Berkley Publishing Corporation.

PRINTED IN THE UNITED STATES OF AMERICA

10   9

Grateful acknowledgment is made to the following for permission to reprint previously published material: Maine Line Company, Rockport, ME 04856, for the greeting card, "What to Look for in a Guy" by Jo Jo Waldon; material from "Pooping Out" by permission of Eve Babitz; from *Okay, Thinner Thighs for Everyone* by Nicole Hollander by permission of St. Martin's Press; *The Bride's Registry Checklist* courtesy *Bride's*, copyright © 1984 by The Condé Nast Publications, Inc.; cover photograph from *How to Get a Man to Make a Commitment* by permission of Bob Brody; for the cartoons "Handholding leads to the hard stuff" and "Have you had much experience as a human being?" by permission of Martin J. Bucella; for the cartoon "What does she need a Daddy Warbucks for?" by permission of Martha Campbell; for the cartoon "I don't need a dating service" by permission of Clem Scalzilti; for the cartoons "How do you plan on supporting my daughter emotionally?," "The Joy of Not Cooking" and "We should have brought along a man to do the cooking" copyright © 1984, reprinted with permission of Artemas Cole as seen in *New Women*; for the cartoons "My birth control device" and "Okay, okay, I'll stay on my own side" by permission of Bob Dayton; for the cartoons "Don't play house with him" and "It's not too serious" by permission of George Dole; for the cartoon "I want a perfume . . ." by permission of Lou Eisele; for the cartoon "I used to be Superman" by permission of Jules Feiffer; for the cartoon "I didn't mean actually living together . . ." by permission of Mort Gerberg; for the cartoons "If he doesn't like your rough, red hands," "You know why I'm so fond of you?," "Are you passing me because you don't like my lemonade?" and "After my breakup with Bill" by permission of Randy Glasbergen; for the cartoon "Today for show and tell" by permission of Malcolm Hancock; for the cartoon "Come off it, Daddy" by permission of Pearl Hill; two cartoons and front cover from *No Good Men* copyright © 1983 by Rick Detorie, reprinted by permission of Wallaby Books, a division of Simon & Schuster, Inc.; cover from *Men: An Owner's Manual* copyright © 1984 by Stephanie Brush, reprinted by permission of Linden Press, a division of Simon & Schuster, Inc.; "The New Etiquette" by permission of Natasha Josefowitz; for the cartoon by Bill Keane; for the cartoon "Daddy, you hafta listen with your eyes" by permission of Cowles Syndicate; for the cartoon "Doesn't your tiny little mind" by permission of Joe Kohl; for a reproduction of the cover of *The Lecherous Professor* by Billie Wright Dziech by permission of Beacon Press; for illustrations from *No Bad Men: Training Men the Lovehouse Way* by Dr. Barbara Lovehouse as told to Anna Sequoia and Sarah Gallick, reprinted by arrangement with New American Library, New York, NY; for the cartoon "Your surprise first" by permission of Jerry Marcus; for the cartoon "Oh, no! I'm finished" by permission of Tom Mason; for "Plan A and Plan B," drawing by M. Stevens, © 1983 the New Yorker Magazine, Inc.; for "Minimum Security Prison," drawing by Mankoff, © 1984 the New Yorker Magazine, Inc.; for "Here's a Turkey," drawing by Frascino, © 1984 the New Yorker Magazine, Inc.; for the cartoon "I'd like to go all the way" by permission of Delbert Polston; for January 31, 1985, cover of *Rolling Stone* magazine by Straight Arrow Publishers, Inc. © 1985, all rights reserved, reprinted by permission; for the cartoon "Your secretarial skills" by permission of Jack E. Schneider; for the cartoon "I can't remember your name" by permission of Bob Schochet; for the photograph originally appearing in *Cosmopolitan* by permission of Jonathon Taylor; material from "Why Smart Women Make Dumb Choices" by Nanci Hellmich copyright © 1985 *USA Today*, reprinted with permission; for the cartoon "Oh, nothing, it's just that you were better as a fantasy" by permission of Kimberly Warp; for the cartoon "I've decided to run for Congress" by permission of George Winners; for the cartoons "It's you I'm crazy about," "I don't remember your face," "Are you trying to be macho," and "I think this calls for a moment of silence" by permission of Bob Zahn. CATHY (Breathmints) copyright © 1983 Universal Press Syndicate, reprinted with permission, all rights reserved; copyright © 1984 Universal Press Syndicate, reprinted with permission, all rights reserved.

To Dad, Mom, Lee,
Gail, Wayne, and
Anne

Contents

QUESTIONS WOMEN ASK

To Which of These Questions Would You Like the Answer?*	Yes	No
Why are men so threatened by successful women?	☐	☐
Why are men's egos their second most fragile instrument?	☐	☐
How can I change a man—without just getting him ready for the next woman?	☐	☐
When I take initiatives, men seem to back off. Why?	☐	☐
Why won't men listen?	☐	☐
Why can't men get in touch with their feelings?	☐	☐
Why do men often say "You're special," and then I never see them again?	☐	☐
Why do so many men have so few men friends?	☐	☐
Why are "girly" magazines so big with men?	☐	☐
Why can't men ask for help?	☐	☐
Why do men spend so much time watching sports (even when they say they want more time with their family)?	☐	☐
Why can't men let a friendship develop . . . and then, if sex happens, it happens?	☐	☐
Sometimes when I'm with a man I see his open and vulnerable parts. And then when he gets around other men, he closes them off. Why is that?	☐	☐
Why are men so preoccupied with their jobs even when they're losing contact with their family?	☐	☐
Why are men so often like boys underneath?	☐	☐
Why do men seem to have contempt for women on the one hand (witness their jokes) and put them on a pedestal on the other hand?	☐	☐
If men are "just desserts," why am I willing to give up so much for a little banana split?	☐	☐
Why do men rape?	☐	☐

*Each of these questions, based upon actual workshop experiences with 106,000 women and men from all walks of life, is addressed in this book. See Index of Questions, page 386.

To Which of These Questions Would You Like the Answer?	Yes	No
Are men just interested in conquest—is that the real excitement for men?	☐	☐
Why do men always feel they have to promise love—even when they're not "in love"?	☐	☐
Why do women earn 59 percent of what men earn even when their contributions are "indispensable"?	☐	☐
Men have the power—why would they want to give it up?	☐	☐
Why can't men admit when they're wrong?	☐	☐
I'm an attractive woman. I have lots of options. Yet so many men I end up with are successful but insensitive. Why?	☐	☐
Why did my father criticize me so often?	☐	☐
Why are men so paranoid about homosexuality?	☐	☐
I'd like to be able to get lovey-dovey without it necessarily leading to intercourse. Is that too much to expect from a man?	☐	☐
When I first meet a man I often think he's wonderful—I tell all my women friends and I'm elated; then he disappoints me once, then twice . . . before I know it I think he's a jerk. Yet I'm still tempted to stay with him . . . why is that?	☐	☐
Why do male leaders get into so many wars? (Would it be different if women led?)	☐	☐
Why is it that men who aren't macho are often, well . . . wimps?	☐	☐
Why are men afraid of commitment?	☐	☐
If I could wish one thing from my relationship with a man, it would be to have more honesty.	☐	☐
Are there any men who are both sensitive and strong . . . who are not already taken up?	☐	☐

QUESTIONS MEN ASK

To Which of These Questions Would You Like the Answer?	Yes	No
Why do women often want friendships before sex and then, when a friendship is developed, say, "I don't want to spoil such a good friendship with sex"?	☐	☐
Why do women treat men like "success objects"?	☐	☐
Why do women complain that if they took the initiatives a man would back off?	☐	☐
Why do women want to have their cake and eat it too—they want to be independent, but they expect me to pick up the check?	☐	☐
Why are so many women so *angry* at men?	☐	☐
Why do women always seem to need reassurance about their place (status) in a relationship? Why can't they let a beautiful relationship just be?	☐	☐
Why does it seem as if women run when the going gets tough financially?	☐	☐
Our relationship was going fine, but she was always pressing for another level of commitment—saying she couldn't "open up" and "really give" until she had that security? I felt like a "relationship object." Why?	☐	☐
When I first meet a woman she treats me like God. I can't do anything wrong. By the end, I can't do anything right. Why is that?	☐	☐
I sometimes feel "damned if I do and damned if I don't." For example, if a woman responds hesitantly to a kiss and I *pursue*, I'm insensitive; if I back off, I'm not exciting enough; if I stop and try again I'm incorrigible. Why doesn't *she* take some responsibility?	☐	☐
Why do so many women talk behind men's backs? Why don't they confront the man directly?	☐	☐

One day a woman was totally devoted to our relationship and, I thought, emotionally connected to me. When I said, though, that I didn't want to get

---

*Each of these questions, based upon actual workshop experiences with 106,000 women and men from all walks of life, is addressed in this book. See Index of Questions, page 386.

To Which of These Questions Would You Like the Answer?	Yes	No

married, I hardly ever saw her again—she didn't seem to care about what I did and seemed able to cut off the sexual relationship without a problem. Why? ☐ ☐

When a woman is angry at me she often withdraws sexually. I don't. Why? ☐ ☐

Why are so few women at the *very* top in business? If it's male prejudice, why don't they start their own businesses? Men did. ☐ ☐

When women do "make it" in business, why do they seem to become like men? ☐ ☐

I held a door for a woman the other day, and she looked at me as if I was part of a conspiracy. Why are some women "paranoid-liberated"? ☐ ☐

Why does my woman friend get preoccupied with makeup even though I tell her I prefer her without it? ☐ ☐

Why can't more women just enjoy sex for itself—without having to attach conditions? ☐ ☐

I asked my girlfriend, "Did you have an orgasm?" She told me I was preoccupied with performance. So I didn't ask my next girlfriend, and she said I didn't care about her needs. I don't get it. ☐ ☐

Women are always complaining about the way men are, but aren't they the ones who brought us up that way? ☐ ☐

Why do so many women play victim? ☐ ☐

One day a woman's devoted to a successful engineer; the next day, to a drug-dealing artist—they're like chameleons. I don't understand. . . . . Why? ☐ ☐

Why do so many women give so many mixed messages? What do women really want? ☐ ☐

If women want something, why don't they go out and get it? ☐ ☐

If we condense women's questions about men into one question, it might be, "Why are men such jerks?" Women's questions are often complaints which center around the perception that "men can't see the forest for their egos." These complaints are well articulated.

In contrast, men's questions about women are at the pre-articulation stage: they feel that something's happening that's unfair, but can't quite put their finger on it. Nor do they try very hard to put their finger on it—they're more focused on proving themselves. Yet men seem to feel they're living in an era when women want to "have their cake and eat it too." For many men, the age-old Freud-attributed question, "What do women really want?" is still without a clear answer. And the fear of being accused of being a male chauvinist has made them afraid to ask the questions necessary to get the answers. In the process of responding to the questions women have about men, I'll respond to the concerns men have—but rarely articulate—about women.

A Personal Introduction

My mother was forty-nine. I had seen her move in and out of depression. Into depression when she was not working, out of depression when she was working. The jobs were just temporary, but, she would tell me, "I don't have to ask Dad for every penny when I'm working."

When the Christmas season ended, so did my mother's final job. Her depression returned. Tension mounted between her and Dad. Doses of medication became stronger and soon led to dizzy spells. Some of the dizzy spells resulted in falls. One fall was her last. At forty-nine she died.

Soon after my mother's death the women's movement surfaced. Perhaps because of her death, it made sense to me in an instant. I could not miss the sense of self that I saw in my mother when her work brought her both income and adult human communication, when it brought her a sense of purpose and a feeling of having some rights. I was surprised when I saw men trivialize the intent of what women were struggling to articulate. I soon found myself at the homes of emerging feminist friends in Manhattan, plopped in front of their husbands with instructions to "tell him what you told me."

The impact of these events was strong enough that I changed my doctoral dissertation topic to one related to the male-female attitude change, gave up my position as an assistant to the president of NYU, and wrote a book called *The Liberated Man*.* *The Liberated Man* explained to men the value of women's

*I will soon be revising this as *The Value of an Independent Woman (to a Secure Man)*.

independence, what independence means in everyday interaction, and the value of listening to a woman's story as a way of
loving her.

Why Men Are the Way They Are is its complement. It is men's
story. It, too, has evolved from personal experience.

My brother Wayne was approaching twenty-one. He and his
woman friend went cross-country skiing in the Grand Tetons.
Their goal: to cross the highest mountain in Wyoming.

The snows were slipping from the mountains. It was April.
They came to a dangerous pass. Both feared the avalanches.
Two of them going forward would put them both in danger, yet
would give each the opportunity to save the other. Wayne went
forward alone. The snow slipped from the mountain, gathered
momentum and tumbled its thousands of frozen pounds over my
brother. Burying him 40 feet under. He would have been
twenty-one.

Wayne and his girlfriend had just naturally agreed that it was
his life that would be risked—and in this case sacrificed—as he
and she both played out their roles. It took me years to understand how Wayne's willingness to give his life away was its own
brand of powerlessness.

Once I did, a lot followed. Every day. The day I write this is
the tenth anniversary of the end of our involvement in Vietnam.
The New York Times features a picture of the war memorial
engraved with the names of almost 57,000 Americans. All but
eight of the names are the names of men. One of those names,
near the end I imagine, is Al Zimmerman, with whom I ran the
hundred-yard dash every spring day for two years. We shared the
all-important goal of beating each other by one-tenth of a second. An Honor Society student, Al carried himself like a young
Dwight Eisenhower. We graduated together. Six months later I
returned for Christmas and called Al. His mom choked up and
passed the phone to his dad. "Al has been shot in Vietnam. I'm
afraid he's dead, Warren."

To Al, and to my brother, male power was male powerlessness. I sensed the need to listen to another story.

How could I listen to the male experience of powerlessness
without minimizing the story that led to my mother's death? Was
it possible for the sexes to hear each other without saying, "My
powerlessness is greater than your powerlessness"? It was becoming obvious each sex had a unique experience of both power
and powerlessness. In my mind's eye I began to visualize a

"listening matrix" as a framework within which we could hear these different experiences. It looked like this:

LISTENING MATRIX

Female experience of powerlessness	Male experience of powerlessness
Female experience of power	Male experience of power

As I looked more carefully at the listening matrix I saw that during the past twenty years we had taken a magnifying glass to the first of these four quadrants, the female experience of powerlessness. I saw I was subconsciously making a false assumption: *The more deeply I understood women's experience of powerlessness, the more I assumed men had the power women did not have.* In fact, what I was understanding was the *female* experience of male power. When a woman is divorced, has two children, no alimony, no child support, and no job experience—that is her experience of powerlessness; when a man is in the hospital with a coronary bypass operation caused by the stress of working two jobs to support two children his former wife won't let him see, and he feels no other woman will get involved with him because of those very circumstances—that is his experience of powerlessness. Both feel loneliness. The flip sides of the same role make both sexes feel powerless.

In visual form, the magnifying glass we have taken over the past two decades to the first quadrant—the female experience of powerlessness—gave us the following view of the world.

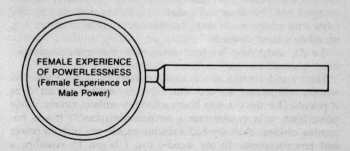

FEMALE EXPERIENCE OF POWERLESSNESS
(Female Experience of Male Power)

Instead of understanding male powerlessness we had come to understand only the female experience of male power. In fact, the greater a woman's expertise on the issue of female powerlessness, the less she tended to understand the male experience of powerlessness. Why? She assumed that female powerlessness meant male power. The imbalance would not be corrected until we held the same magnifying glass to the second quadrant, giving us the following picture.

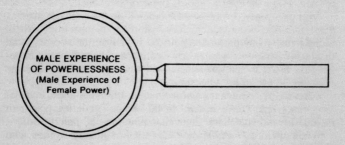

MALE EXPERIENCE
OF POWERLESSNESS
(Male Experience of
Female Power)

When I began to look carefully at this listening matrix I recalled living in Europe when I was fourteen and fifteen. The Dutch and Scandinavian women were much less into playing out the helpless or dependent female who was also afraid of her body and sex; and, sure enough, the Dutch and Scandinavian men were less into making jerks of themselves by overperforming. Later, as I traveled through Spain, Italy, Greece, Turkey, and Morocco, I saw men who played variations on a much more macho role. And women who played variations on a much more economically dependent and sexually restricted role. I began to see that sex roles were symbiotic. That we were all involved in a complex sex role dance. The listening matrix was crucial, because every time we blamed the other sex for doing something we despised we could be substituting looking within ourselves and discovering what we were doing to reinforce that behavior. Even to create it.

The more I applied this listening matrix, the more I saw the women and men I worked with develop intimacy rather than hostility. The more I saw men willing to make commitments rather than getting close to a woman only to pull back for reasons neither understood. Which brings me to a special message to women—mostly.

A Message to Women—Mostly

During the past two decades, women have been frustrated because the more they "find themselves," the more they seem to be placing their relationships with men in jeopardy. They have expressed frustration that they were the ones doing all the work in their relationships, and having to spoon-feed what they learned to men. Even the spoon-feeding created "feedback."

Over the years, I have seen women's body language alter as the frustration accumulated. They didn't like what they felt in themselves. I saw tears of hopelessness well in the eyes of more than a few women—women who were alternating between hopelessness toward men and a haunting fear that "Maybe it's me . . . maybe *I'm* doing something wrong."

Increasingly, women are finding men to be less and less lovable. Yet we say men have power. In this book I redefine power to include lovability. Which gives us a new look at male power.

When I wrote *The Liberated Man*, it was mostly women who responded positively. They felt understood. A woman would give it to a man with any excuse—Valentine's Day, Father's Day, birthdays, anniversaries—in the hope that he would understand her better. I think it is fair to say that the book accomplished that much. But I noticed that only a small number of men really changed. And those who changed the most changed defensively—because she wanted the man different. Over the years, though, I noticed women back off from these men. Their relationships became asexual. They were picking up on men's defensiveness. As one woman put it, "A man walking on eggshells doesn't have much sex appeal." Some men were even called wimps.

At first I didn't understand how a man who was more sensitive could ever be less appealing. But I came to understand the distinction between men who are *defensively sensitive* ("walking on eggshells") and men who are sensitive as a result of their own security. Only a secure man is appealing.

Women know how destructive it is when they change *for* men. Women changed so much for men that it shocks them now to learn that while they were adapting to men, men were adapting to women. Adapting in a manner that is so different from women's experience of adapting that at first it is barely recognizable as adaptation.

That's too bad—because women have done so much work on relationships. Yet the articles *on men* in women's magazines do not discuss life the way *men* experience life. So the questions they purport to answer, such as those in the opening questionnaire (about egos, listening, fear of successful women, and so on), are not answered in a way that rings true *for men*—only in a way that rings true *for women about men*. These perceptions cannot be applied to men without the men feeling uncomfortable, without knowing quite why. So it becomes easier for a man to escape via TV, sports, or behind a paper.

It has taken me much of the past seventeen years to understand that men do not become more lovable until they feel understood. Increasingly, I have altered my workshops to get both sexes to understand each other. But that understanding does not work if it is only on an intellectual level. So I started developing exercises to have each sex "walk a mile in the other sex's moccasins." That's when things started changing. I began listening more carefully to men. And as I listened, I observed some important paradoxes:

- I expected that the men who were asking—even demanding—that *their* stories be heard, would be chauvinists. In fact, chauvinists didn't think about their stories. I found that the men who understood their stories were those most in touch with their feelings. Their stories *were* their feelings.

- I noticed that men who were willing to read and discuss books on relationships were tuned into women. But if they were not also tuned into their own hurts, it was usually out of the fear of confronting women. Underneath they usually retained the attitude that women needed special protection. It was the first sign that the man was still not treating a woman as an equal. And a sign that the man was not secure enough to risk female rejection.

I found that those women who could hear men's stories—without seeing them as taking away from their own—were among the few whose independence seemed to come out of internal security, who were not turning life into a fight, and who had consistently good relationships with men. For some women, feminism had opened the whole vista of reexamining roles—including men's roles. For others, the deeper the feminism, the more closed the women were to men. Strict ideology is for women what macho is for men.

These perceptions forced me to look within myself. At first I really believed I was writing because I was just naturally sensitive. But why was I not so naturally sensitive to men? Was it possible that "understanding women" was my way of becoming women's hero? Of gaining female acceptance and minimizing rejection? If I was so secure, why didn't I apply that same sensitivity to men? What was I afraid of?

Well, I *was* afraid—of losing women who loved me, cared for me, and confided in me. Intellectually I knew that if a woman who was herself secure really loved me, she would delight in my self-exploration—no matter what it uncovered. If anything, she would relish the sense of security she knew was behind it.

But in real life it didn't work that way. Women thought I was being most vulnerable when I was discussing genuine feelings of love, mistakes I had made, and feelings about my family. Actually I was being most vulnerable when I discussed sexual desires. But my experience had taught me that if I wanted to be intimate with a woman in a way that included sex, I should mention intimacy more and sex less. Which is why it will be very difficult for men to discuss openly with a woman the portions of this book that reveal what men are willing to do for sex. It puts women off. And most men sensitive enough to make it through this book will also be sensitive enough to be aware that openly discussing what they would do for sex (with *any* attractive woman) would directly cut them off from sex or love from that woman. Women have a parallel vulnerability. Which it took me some time to be fully receptive to hearing from a woman. An embarrassing example . . .

A few years ago I was walking down the street with a woman friend. She said, "I have to admit, one reason I've fantasized being your wife is that I'd like to be Mrs. Dr. Warren Farrell—and have people know *I* got the man who wrote *The Liberated Man*." At the time I thought that was one of the most *un*liberated comments I had ever heard. My opinion of the woman dropped. I was just an object to her, I thought. And I told her that.

It took me some time to understand that I had asked her for vulnerability—and that this woman, perhaps more than any other, had really offered it. Smart enough to know both what she was saying and to predict my reaction, she acknowledged the part of her that was treating me as a *success* object. She knew that would make me feel less special as a person—and that she would risk rejection. *That's* vulnerability.

Men's equivalent vulnerability is our sexual desire. Especially the compulsive parts: because they're compulsive, they're vulnerable. Discussing the compulsive parts openly—talking about all the women a man would like to approach but is afraid to approach—requires the deepest trust and vulnerability from a man because it makes the woman he'd like to feel closer to feel less special—and therefore distant from him.

In contrast, discussing love, hinting at commitment, questioning this compulsiveness, letting our feeling side show—these are all beautiful traits. But the exhibition of them requires far less vulnerability, because they increase women's respect for us and they enhance a woman's feelings that she is special. So they increase our power with a woman, not our vulnerability. In fact, the tougher we act on the outside, the more special women feel when men let their feelings show, so feelings like these are not really the vulnerability of reasonably sensitive men. These feelings are, rather, men's way of adapting—by being ''vulnerable'' in the areas in which women want us to be vulnerable.

If you can tap into what this book triggers for a man sexually, and understand that a man who peels off his sexual vulnerability in front of you is making the deepest statement of his trust in you, you will see a part of him you will *not* like—his real vulnerability. Just as I saw the real vulnerability of the woman who admitted a part of herself she did not like. Which is why it is vulnerability. If you like something, it's hardly vulnerable.

In my personal and professional life, hearing this vulnerability from men meant another layer of hearing men differently—*not* monitoring a man's voice with ''the more you understand him, the less pro-woman you'll appear,'' *not* trying to create a rebuttal while he is talking—but rather, being willing to support him in exploring his emotions, no matter where they led.

As I tried this, I found it harder to do than I expected. For fourteen years, I had prepared convincing responses to anything sexist. But more important, my responses frequently left women saying, ''Right on—you tell him, Warren.'' I am embarrassed to admit it was not easy to substitute listening carefully to men for that response from women. And that embarrassment gave me a hint about where to explore.

First I explored the assumption I mentioned above—that understanding women's sense of powerlessness meant assuming men had power women did not have. Theoretically I had always agreed sex roles hurt both sexes. But in practice I was becoming less and less understanding of—and tolerant toward—men. I didn't realize it wasn't just sexual desires that make a man vulnerable in a world that treats sex as dirty. Little makes a man more vulnerable than "whining" (when whining means blaming a woman) in a world that says he is powerful and she is vulnerable. True vulnerability involves acknowledging the whining side, the helpless side, the blaming side. There is no sex appeal in this side of men. Which is why it requires such true vulnerability.

As my willingness to listen to men began to coincide with my willingness to listen to women, I became increasingly uncomfortable with yet another paradox: women were coming to me to change their men because the women felt understood. None of us realized that if we wanted a man to change, he must feel understood by us just as the woman felt understood by me. Here I was criticizing the fragile male ego without comprehending that *criticism rarely undoes fragility*. Especially criticism not preceded by deep understanding. Like most ideologues, I was producing exactly the opposite of my goal.

Yet as I began to share some of my new understandings of men with women, I could feel many women form a "yes, but" in their mind's eye. Which signals me to stop talking and ask what's happening. A number of women expressed fears that if they understood men, it would give men an excuse to remain the same; they didn't want to hear about men's preoccupation with sex—they just wanted men to be less preoccupied. One woman feared that if she understood men's fear of commitment, she'd be giving her man an "out."

A politically oriented friend expressed some fear that if she presented an expanded understanding of issues like rape to her colleagues, they'd accuse her of "justifying" the issues rather than really hearing her. Because she is a woman in touch with her feelings, she saw how vulnerable she was to her colleagues' accusations of being sexist, or "not a real feminist." And she saw how that vulnerability blocked her from fully hearing men— just as it had blocked me. Together we came to understand how we beg men to express feelings, but then, when men do express feelings, we call it sexism, male chauvinism, or backlash. We saw how these labels are to a reasonably sensitive man what labels like "aggressive" are to a woman first trying to assert herself. How it is like knocking down a baby who is struggling to take her or his first steps. The women I was able to delve most deeply with often said they feared that if they knew men were as adapting to women as the women had been to men, they would divert their anger away from men and toward themselves. Intellectually they knew that wasn't necessary—but in their gut, that was their fear.

And so "understanding men" created some genuine blocks. Yet the men who felt truly understood seemed to be the first to acquire the key prerequisite to change: personal security. Just as support groups gave women the additional security they needed to change.

All of this is fundamental to Eastern philosophy—that we gain power when we listen to the energy of a potential opponent and ride with it rather than dissipate our own energy resisting it. This philosophy, as manifested in martial arts like aikido, demonstrates how doing battle (as in the "battle of the sexes") leaves everyone with neither power nor soul.

I expect that more women than men will, at first, pick up this book. But I think that if you give this book to a man and listen to the stories it triggers for him—without arguing, without clamming up so that he senses he's telling each story at the expense of closeness from you, he will gain power and you will gain power, and you will discover a part of him which hears a part of you he was too insecure to hear before. You will discover a part of him you will love to love.

How Did You Research This Book?

The experiences I shared in the personal part of the Introduction made me responsive to the women's movement to the degree of serving on the board of the National Organization for Women (NOW) in New York City for three years. It also led to my forming some three hundred men's groups and a similar number of women's groups, most of which met separately for a few months, then alternated between meeting jointly and separately until the energy ran out. None of these methods of studying men and women, though, were as important as the two men's groups and the joint group (with women) that I joined. These groups helped me confront every aspect of myself.

Still more important was learning that no presentation at which I merely spoke could be as meaningful to the audience as a presentation that I transformed into a mini-workshop based on an old Indian proverb: "Don't judge me until you walk a mile in my moccasins." I asked each audience member to go through a carefully structured simulation of the socialization of the other sex. Or to play the role of the other sex in a series of role reversal exercises.

From the role reversal exercises evolved the answers to hundreds of questions I began hearing women ask about men: "Why can't men listen?" "Why are men afraid of commitment?" "Why are men threatened by successful women?" Each question also implied a complaint, and each complaint had at least a germ of truth. But how to discover *why?*

My first glimpse as to why came about sixteen years ago, when a woman asked, "Why can't men listen?" When she played the male role of asking out a "boy" and initiating kissing him, though, she found herself so fearful of rejection ("If I kiss him on the lips is that too forward? If I don't, will he think I'm a wimp?") that she could barely listen to a word the "boy" said. That gave me a first hint as to why men couldn't listen.

That also gave me some hints as to what there was in the male *role* that made a biological female act like a male even beyond the extent I had instructed. *From the scientific perspective, we had allowed for biology, which gave us insight about the impact of role*. After working in this manner with 106,000 women and men* (the number that attended my presentations which evolved into workshops) over seventeen years, *why* men are the way they are became clearer and clearer.

Simultaneously, I was also asking men to experience women's dilemmas. For example, I designed a men's beauty contest to allow the men to experience being looked at as sex objects. Normally, men love it, so they don't easily understand women's protestations. But as each man in the contest (except the winner) is *rejected* based on his looks, his emotional experience of being viewed as a sex object is altered.

The men's beauty contest also gave men a second experience normally reserved for women. For one hour a man's looks become *central* to his identity, as the criteria for his acceptance and rejection were centered around his body. So he *felt* how a woman can have a love-hate relationship with being looked at as a sex object.

*About 55 percent women.

Deep understanding of another person rarely occurs unless we participate in the other person's way of getting respect and approval. How do we do that? First, we listen to the messages they received to gain respect. This is their interpretation of the "rules of the game." Second, we see how they have assessed their strengths and weaknesses so they can win at that game—or win respect. (Some will conform, some will rebel, and some, like myself, will write social commentary.) Each of these steps is incorporated in the role reversal experiences.

Were the 106,000 women and men a self-selected sample? No. Thousands came because they had to ("IBM is requiring this for management training"); and many, like college jocks, who would seldom have been attracted to a *talk* on men, were attracted by portions of my presentation like the men's beauty contest. Audiences ranged from Kiwanis Clubs to the National Association of Architectural Metal Manufacturers to alcohol treatment centers. The diversity of the participants kept me in touch with the broad spectrum of Americans. And during workshops abroad I was able to see how Americans contrast with people from other countries—from Australia to Yugoslavia.

Why Men Are the Way They Are differs from books on men and women which are based on responses to questionnaires (such as *The Hite Report* and the *Cosmo Reports*). On questionnaires, most people respond that they are more trustworthy than most people, that they are less interested in looks and money than their actual behavior indicates, and so on. So these books understandably miss the less pleasant motivations that create the reality with which each sex contends. For example, many people claim they are fairly "free from roles." So I ask these people to simulate meeting at a party and show me how they would conduct themselves *without* playing roles. That's how I discovered how rare it is for a woman ever to take the hand of a man who had never before taken her hand, or to kiss a man for the very first time, or to take any of the 150 initiatives between eye contact and sexual contact I found are typically expected of a man if a relationship is ever to be sexual. That opened me to examining the defenses men must have formed to keep from feeling the rejection which led to the chapter on male powerlessness: "Why Are Men So Preoccupied with Sex and Success?" *Each theme in the book evolved from my examination of actual behavior—as opposed to claimed behavior.*

Once I began to understand how men and women adapt to

roles that make them acceptable to the other sex, I had to take just as careful a microscope to the study of women's actual behavior versus their verbalized behavior—in order to understand the real messages men were unconsciously receiving and therefore what roles they thought they needed to adapt to. In essence, women's desires were an important ingredient in determining why men are the way they are.

Why Men Are the Way They Are does not focus on parental or genetic influences on men. It focuses on the dynamic between men and women that can be worked with on an everyday level. Which is why the book is subtitled "The Male/Female Dynamic."

Warren Farrell
103 North Highway 101
Suite 220
Leucadia (San Diego), CA 92024

PART 1

THE WAY MEN ARE

1

Men Have the Power—Why Would They Want to Change?

Ralph was a forty-one-year-old man in our men's group. He was married, the father of two children. He had been in the group for three months, and had hardly said a word. One evening he looked up and said, "I think I'd like to speak up tonight. I'm afraid I joined this group only because my wife forced me to. She got involved in one of these women's movement operations and started changing. She called it 'growing.' About three months ago she said, 'Ralph, I'm tired of having to choose between a relationship with you and a relationship with myself.' Pretty fancy rhetoric, I thought. Then she added, 'There's a men's group forming that's meeting next Tuesday. Why don't you get involved?'

"Well, I kind of laughed her off. But a week later she started again. 'The group's meeting next Tuesday. As far as I'm concerned, if you're not doing some changing in *three* months, that's the end.'

" 'The end! For the sake of a *men's group?*' I asked.

" 'It's symbolic, Ralph,' she said.

"So I figured I'd join this symbol and see what you fags were talking about! But the problem was, you didn't fit my image, and I began identifying with some of the things you were saying. Well, anyway, last night Ginny reminded me the three months were up tomorrow. So I think I'd like to speak up tonight."

We laughed at Ralph's motivation, but encouraged him to continue.

"Well, what struck me was how each of you chose different careers, but you all worried about succeeding. Even you, Jim— even though you're unemployed and have a laid-back facade. That started me thinking about my career.

3

"All my life I wanted to play baseball. As a pro. When I was a sophomore in high school I was pretty hot stuff, and my uncle came and scouted me. Later he said, 'Ralph, you're good. Damn good. And you might make it to the pros if you really work at it. But only the best make good money for a long time. If you really want to be good to yourself, make use of your intelligence, get yourself a good job—one you can depend on for life.'

"I was surprised when my folks agreed with him. Especially Dad. Dad always called me 'Ralph, who pitched the no-hitter.' Dad stopped calling me that after that conversation. Maybe that turned the tide for me." Ralph hesitated, as if he were piecing something together, but he quickly withdrew from his introspection.

"Anyway, I was proud of myself for making the transition like a man. I'd always liked reading and learning, but just hadn't focused much on it. But I figured just for a couple of years I'd 'play the system': borrow friends' old term papers, take a look at old exams, focus my reading on the questions different teachers tended to ask, and so on. I never cheated. I just figured I'd 'play the system' for a couple of years, raise my grades, then when I got into college, I could really learn—I could do what I wanted after that.

"Well, 'playing the system' worked. I got into a top-notch university. But it soon became apparent that a lot of people graduated from good universities—if I wanted to really stand out it would help to 'play the system' for just a few more years, get into a good grad school or law school, and then, once I did that, I could do with my life what I wanted after that.

"I decided on law school—but to become a social-work lawyer, so I could make a real contribution to people who most needed it. But about my second or third year of law school—when my colleagues saw I was taking what they called this 'missionary law' seriously, they explained that if I really wanted to be effective as a social-work lawyer, I'd better get some experience first in the hard-knocks, reality-based field of corporate law rather than ease into the namby-pamby area of social-work law right away—if I didn't I wouldn't get the respect to be effective. Frankly, that made sense. So I joined a top corporate law firm in New York. I knew I could work there for a couple of years, and then really do what I wanted with my life after that.

"After a couple of years in the firm, I was doing well. But the whole atmosphere of the corporate legal community made it clear that if I dropped out after two years it would be seen as a sign that I just couldn't hack the pressure. If I continued for just a couple more years, and became a junior partner—junior partners were the ones marked with potential—then I could really do what I wanted with my life after that.

"Well, it took me seven years to get the junior partnership offered to me—with politics and everything. But I got it. By that time I had lost some of the desire to be a social-work lawyer—it was considered a clear step backward. In other ways I maintained that ideal—it seemed more meaningful than kowtowing to rich money. But I also knew the switch would mean forfeiting a lot of income. My wife Ginny and I had just bought a new home—which we pretty much had to do with two kids—and I knew they'd be going to college. . . . Ginny's income was only part-time now, and she was aching to travel a bit.

"By that time, I also realized that while junior partners had potential, the people with the real ins in the legal community were not the junior partners, but the senior partners. I figured I had a pretty big investment in the corporate law area now—if I just stuck it out for a couple more years, I could get a senior partnership, get a little money saved for the kids' education and travel, and *then* I could really do with my life what I wanted. . . .

"It took me eight more years to get the senior partnership. I can remember my boss calling me into the office and saying, 'Ralph, we're offering you a senior partnership.' I acted real calm, but my heart was jumping toward the phone in anticipation of telling Ginny. Which I did. I told Ginny I had a surprise. I'd tell her when I got home. I asked her to get dressed real special. I refused to leak what it was about. I made reservations in her favorite restaurant, bought some roses and her favorite champagne.

"I came home real early so we'd have time to sip it together; I opened the door and said, 'Guess what?' Ginny was looking beautiful. She said, 'What is it, Ralph?' I said, 'I got the senior partnership!' She said, 'Oh, fine, that's great,' but there was a look of distance in her eyes. A real superficial enthusiasm, you know what I mean?''

We nodded.

"So I said, 'What do you mean "Oh, fine"—I've been working since the day we met to get this promotion for us, and you say "Oh, fine"?'

" 'Every time you get a promotion, Ralph,' Ginny announced, 'you spend less time with me. I guess I just wish you'd have more time for me. More time to love me.'

" 'Why do you think I've been working my ass off all these years if it isn't to show you how much I love you?' I said.

" 'Ralph, that's not what I mean by love. Just look at the kids, Ralph.'

"Well, I did look at the kids. Randy is seventeen. And Ralph, Jr., is fifteen. Randy just got admitted to college—a thousand miles from here. Each year I keep promising myself that 'next year' I'll really get to know who they are. 'Next year . . .' 'Next year.' But next year he'll be in college. And I don't even know who he is. And I don't know whether I'm his dad or his piggy bank.

"I don't know where to begin with Randy, but a few weeks ago I tried to change things a bit with Ralph, Jr. He was watching TV. I asked him if he wouldn't mind turning it off so we could talk. He was a little reluctant, but he eventually started telling me some of what was happening at school. We talked baseball, and I told him about some of my days pitching. He said I'd already told him. He told me about some of his activities, and I spotted a couple of areas where I thought his values were going to hurt him. So I told him. We got into a big argument. He said I wasn't talking with him, I was lecturing him . . . 'spying' on him.

"We've hardly talked since. I can see what I did wrong— boasting and lecturing—but I'm afraid if I try again, he'll be afraid to say much now, and we'll just sit there awkwardly. And if he mentions those values, what do I say? I want to be honest, but I don't want to lecture. I don't even know where to begin."

Ralph withdrew from the group. He had struck so many chords it took us more than ten minutes to notice that he was fighting back tears. Finally one of the men picked up on it and asked, "Ralph, is there anything else you're holding back?" Ralph said there wasn't, but his assurance rang false. We prodded.

"I guess maybe I am holding something back," he said hesitantly. "I feel like I spent forty years of my life working as hard as I can to become somebody I don't even like."

When I heard that sentence fifteen years ago, I was twenty-seven. It's been perhaps the most important sentence I've heard in my life: *"I feel like I've spent forty years of my life working as hard as I can to become somebody I don't even like."* Even as I heard it, the ways it was threatening to be true in my own life flashed through my mind.

Ralph continued: "I was mentioning some of my doubts to a

few of my associates at work. They listened attentively for a couple of minutes, then one made a joke, and another excused himself. Finally I mentioned this men's group—which I never should have done—and they just laughed me out of the office. I've been the butt of jokes ever since: 'How are the U.S. Navel Gazers doing, Ralph boy?'

"Suddenly I realized. Ginny has a whole network of lady friends she can talk with about all this. Yet the men I've worked with for seventeen years, sixty hours a week, hardly know me. Nor do they want to."

Ralph withdrew again. But this time he seemed to be taking in what he had just said as if he were putting together his life as he was speaking. Then his face grew sad. A few of us who might otherwise have said something held back.

"I guess I could handle all this," Ralph volunteered, fighting back the tears again, "but I think, for all practical purposes, I've lost Ginny in the process. And maybe I could handle that, too. But the only other people I love in this world are Randy and Ralph, Jr. And when I'm really honest with myself—I mean *really* honest—I think for all practical purposes I've lost them too—."

We started to interrupt, but Ralph stopped us, tears silently escaping his eyes. "What really gets me . . . what really gets me *angry* is that I did everything I was supposed to do for forty years, did it better than almost any other man I know, and I lost everyone I love in the process, including myself. I don't mean to be philosophical, but the more I did to stand out, the more I became the same. Just one more carbon copy. Oh, I got to a high level, okay. A high-level mediocre.

"In some ways, I feel I could handle all that, too. But look at me—paid more than any two of you guys put together, supposedly one of the top decision-makers in the country, and when it comes to my own home, my own life, I don't even know how to begin."

Ralph cried. For the first time in twenty-two years.

Ralph is with me almost every day of my life. Every time I am appreciated or applauded, the image of Ralph makes me wonder whether the applause is seducing me into saying something that is popular but less honest than I want to be. Sometimes, of course, I just forget Ralph and take the applause, but the image of Ralph is there as a resource when I'm in my more secure moments.

After that session, I started looking at my life and Ralph's life differently. I had always assumed power meant having status and access to income, influence, and external rewards. Ralph had all of them. Yet up close he didn't seem very powerful. I started asking whether power meant, rather, the ability to control my own life. And that made looking at power much more compatible with looking within myself.

Most men feel much less powerful than Ralph. Ralph is a winner among men—and women. Compared to him, millions of men are losers. If you are a man, powerlessness is hearing a bomb go off and watching your only buddy's head spurt blood before you told him you cared. Powerlessness is returning with agent orange from a war that you were thought of as a fool or a murderer for fighting, having your government refuse to take responsibility for the agent orange contamination, passing it on to your daughter and looking at her deformed arm every day of her life, paying taxes to support the war, and then being told, "You make the rules." From his perspective, that's blaming the victim. At eighteen he did not make the rule to subject himself to death while his sister stayed at home, received an education, and married a survivor. He didn't feel powerful when women had an equal *right* to join the armed forces for money, but not an equal responsibility to be drafted.

On the Nature of Power

If we define power in traditional terms—the ability to gain access to external rewards—Ralph had it over all the men in the group. And almost all the women in America.

Cathy Guisewite, *A Mouthful of Breathmints and No One to Kiss*, p. 47.

Yet if we redefine power as *the ability to control one's own life*, Ralph probably had less power than anyone in the group. Ralph had given up the ability to control his own life by spending his life doing what he was programmed to do. Most of us were questioning at least some of the things we were programmed to do. *Ralph had lost real power by trying to gain the appearance of power. He was a leader. But he was following "a program for leaders"*; therefore, he was really a follower. He had reached a high level, but had done so by adapting to his boss and his boss's boss. He was, as he put it, a "high-level mediocre."

The Five Components of Power

By redefining power as control over our own lives, we can see exactly what Ralph gained and lost, and what women who imitate the male model gain and lose. I define control over one's own life as first, defining our own expectations and then meeting them in five areas. Looking at these five areas, we can see that Ralph had power almost exclusively in the first area, even when he was "succeeding."

1. Access to *external* rewards and resources (e.g., income, status, possessions) equivalent to the level of a person's expectation or desire.

2. Access to *internal* rewards and resources (e.g., inner peace, the capacity for emotional release, positive self-concept, alignment of overall values with daily activities, spirituality). Access starts with the awareness of the importance of these rewards, and becomes real with the time and ability to experience them on a level equal to one's expectation or desire.

3. Access to *interpersonal contact* (attention, affection, and love and respect from others, whether family or friends) equivalent to one's expectation or desire.

4. Access to *physical health, attractiveness, and intelligence* equivalent to one's expectation or desire.

5. Access to *sexual fulfillment* in a form that meets one's expectations.

By redefining power as control over our own lives, we can ask questions that illustrate the limitations of our traditional view of power—as status, income, and control over others.

Does a company president who has never known how to be intimate have power? Does a thirteen-year-old Olympic gymnast who has never known whether she is loved for herself or for how she performs have power? Does a boy who must register for the draft at eighteen, or who is shot through the face in Vietnam, have power? Does a beautiful woman who marries a doctor have power, when she never discovers her own talents? Does her doctor husband have power when he is forever the slave of his beeper?

Which of these people has control over his or her own life?

When we call people "heroes" we encourage them to replace real power with an image. When we say "men have the power," we reinforce the assumption that income, status, and control over others are more important than assessing our values internally.

Women who feel men have the power are also the most likely to reinforce the male acquisition of the image of power by marrying the men with that image. In the process, they adapt to these men, often losing their identities and therefore their own power.

With the accusation "men have the power," women enforce the belief that external reward power is all there is to power. The more they see the limits of external reward power, the more they will stop saying "men have the power."

The phrase "equal to the level of one's expectation or desire" is important. For example, John gains income and loses inner peace. Did he gain or lose power? *We cannot tell* until we know John's expectation or desire. If he expected or desired that his income produce inner peace, then, from his perspective, he has *lost* power, since his real goal was inner peace, not income. From the perspective of an outsider who saw only John's income soaring, John gained power. But if John never even considered the option of inner peace, he can be considered cut off from power in this area.

Each component of power can be feigned, which usually gives a person just the appearance of power. For example, if a marriage that everyone thought looked happy is not at all happy, it makes the couple more powerless every day. They are forfeiting power in the area of human contact—the very power they are feigning. To say nothing of inner peace.

So why do people stay unhappily married? Take Ralph. His "family man" image is part of an executive package that gets him promoted to more external rewards. Nelson Rockefeller's divorce is often thought to have cost him the presidency. And John F. Kennedy is widely believed to have persuaded Jacqueline to remain married to him so it would not cost him the presidency. Generally, if the external rewards are significant, people discount the internal rewards of a happy marriage. External reward power is the most common "bribe" for both sexes to give the appearance of power.

On the other hand, a job, or other external rewards, *can* bring internal rewards such as inner peace, which in turn can reduce stress and improve physical health.

Do men have "power"? And why would they want to change?

1. In the area of *external* rewards, a man's socialization is still to be able to provide for a woman as well as himself. Women currently learn three options to get external rewards: through marriage, through their career, or through some combination of both. So men earn the most power through external rewards; married women share most of the money and a portion of their husband's status. Never-married women earn 91 percent of what never-married men earn.[1]

2. Conversely, in the area of *internal* rewards, a man becomes dependent on a woman for emotional support. The competition to supply external rewards for himself and others encourages a man to devalue internal rewards, and his need for emotional support is intensified by the fear of failing to support more than himself.

Up to this point, male and female power is about equally incomplete. This is the first step that tempts both sexes to call something "love" that is really just the process of completing our incomplete parts.

3. In the area of *access to interpersonal contact* (attention, affection, love), each sex experiences about an equal amount of deprivation, though in different ways.

4. In the area of *physical health*,* women fare far better than men. On the average, women live 7.8 years longer than men; men suffer over 98 percent of the major diseases.[2] Some of this may be biological. But since the gap has increased in the United States by almost 700 percent since 1920[3] (from 1 year to 7.8 years), and since many causes of death have high sex-role-related characteristics,[4] from war (the all-male draft) to the 600 percent higher incidence of work-related accidents among men (including over 2 million disabling injuries and 14,000 deaths per year),[5] we can see that a good portion of this difference is due to sex-role assignment. It is in the area of physical health and longevity that men's power—control over their own lives—begins to fall considerably short of women's power. There can be no greater loss of power than loss of life.

Our reaction to the fact that men die earlier than women might be viewed as the quietest response to genocide in the history of humankind. It might be called "androcide." More empathy is directed toward widows who cannot find men than toward the men who have died.

KILL AMERICAN MEN . . .
THEY'RE ASKING FOR IT

If this were an American billboard, it would probably be ripped down overnight. But sex roles systematically assign men a shorter life. Men are told they "ask for it" by playing their role of hero.

5. In the area of *sexual fulfillment*, both sexes feel frustrated, but for different reasons. Both ideally would like sexual contact with someone to whom they are attracted, for whom they have respect, and with whom they feel an emotional and intellectual connection. How do they both end up feeling sexually powerless? Here's how, for starters.

*Physical attractiveness power is dealt with in Part 2.

Her Nine Conditions; His One Condition

Women are still taught to be sexually cautious until two, three, or all four conditions—attraction, respect, emotions, and intellect—are met. Many women add fifth and sixth conditions: singleness and status/success. And many add a seventh, eighth, and ninth: the man must ask her out; he must pay; and he must risk rejection by initiating the first kiss, being the first to hold hands, and so on. (If he doesn't risk kissing her, she is likely not to kiss him.)

Men are socialized to want sex as long as only *one* condition is fulfilled—physical attraction. For each sex, the demand is so great in relation to the supply, each perceives himself or herself as sexually unfulfilled, and therefore powerless in this area. But by being cautious until more conditions are met, *women gain enormous sexual leverage power over men. They can use this power to get the external rewards of which they feel deprived.* An example is "marrying up."

Women ideally would like more than external rewards from men. But men are so busy competing for the external rewards women feel deprived of, they are often never even *aware* of internal rewards. Communication, intimacy, love, and commitment have different meanings for each sex. Both sexes feel powerless, but men are less in touch with their powerlessness because they know less about what it is they are missing.

Women end up finding few men who have the *combination* of qualities that leads to their total sexual fulfillment, which makes them feel sexually powerless. Men feel as if their expectations are so much lower than women's—there's only one condition—and they can't even meet that. And so men feel sexually powerless.

But how can I say men feel sexually powerless when few men admit they feel sexually powerless? In my work with men I have found that men don't articulate these feelings for one of two reasons. First, they have internalized their lower expectations. Not many a man ever expects an attractive and successful woman to whom he feels intellectually and emotionally connected to ask him out the first time, pay for him, and keep making advances until he responds. Many women expect these conditions, which are beyond the limits of men's fantasy lives. A man often feels subconsciously that a woman's minimum requirements are greater than his wildest fantasy.

The second reason a man rarely articulates his sexual powerlessness is that he has become so much of a performer—meeting the nine conditions—in our society, which has brainwashed us into calling that performance "power," that he can't imagine that much of his performing is a compensation for his sexual powerlessness. More on that later.

A man experiences a dilemma when he finds that the most beautiful women have the least incentive to become well integrated in the other areas of power. He knows intellectually he should choose a well-integrated woman. But he feels torn between attractive women, whom he notices are choosing "supermen," although he realizes supermen are often not well integrated themselves, and less attractive women, who have had more incentive to integrate all five areas of power. So he is caught between giving up his first and only condition for sex (attractiveness) and getting the condition met at the price of sacrificing the other areas in the woman.

What does a man do before becoming a Superman? He goes to a party and hopes merely to achieve sexual contact. He may call it sexual fulfillment, but in reality he is subconsciously redefining sexual fulfillment as merely getting to the stage of sexual contact.

The gap between a woman's desire for the conditions she would like fulfilled—such as emotional connections—and the conditions she actually gets fulfilled is reflected in compensatory mechanisms such as "women's magazines," romance novels, and soap operas, all of which hold out the fantasy of the integration of sex with the right conditions. The male gap is reflected in a man's compensatory mechanisms like pornography and prostitution: pornography gives him attractive women vicariously for little money, prostitution directly for more money. Both help him avoid being rejected for not meeting the nine conditions.

For women, learning to depend on the power of youth, beauty, and sexuality turns beauty and sexuality into power tools rather than internal sources of fulfillment, which thereby denies a woman the very integration within herself she was socialized to desire for both herself and her men.

Men's first incentive to change, then, comes with redefining power; it comes with understanding their experience of powerlessness (while not denying the female experience of powerlessness). Men do not change by being persuaded that one component of power means "men have the power." That just keeps men blind to real power.

PART 2

WOMEN HAVE CHANGED—WHY AREN'T MEN CHANGING TOO?

Introduction to Part 2

Christine and I had "dated," if you will, between fifth grade and twelfth grade. Then I went off to college and graduate school and underwent a radical transformation in the way I looked at the world. Each of us got married—but not to each other—and here we were, some ten years after high school, sitting with each other's spouses in Christine's New Jersey home.

In my heart of hearts, I was hoping Christine would have a deep respect for the changes I had undergone. As we walked across the wall-to-wall carpeting to take our leave, Christine slipped her arm through mine and tugged me to the side. In a stage whisper she summarized her observations: "I am thrilled to see you again. You're *exactly* as I remember you."

Devastated by the "compliment," I was too innocent to know I had just experienced what I now call "the reunion phenomenon" —the belief, as we each return to our reunions with our microscopes focused on ourselves, that *we* have changed and everyone else has remained the same.

In the past two decades many women have had the strong belief that they have changed and men have remained the same. This has made many women feel, "I've done my part—now it's his turn," or ask, "Why am I always the one giving so much to a relationship?" While many women feel lucky to be born a woman in an era when women are so vital, they also feel cursed being born a woman in an era when men are so mediocre. The result has been an increasing resentment of men, or what I call a "bad rap against men."

The "hopelessness" of men has made many women feel hopeless—and angry, lonely, and self-righteous. I have seen the

17

hurt slowly turn to cynicism and withdrawal. It is impossible for me to have started three hundred women's groups, listen carefully, love women, and feel that women *want* to feel either hopeless or lonely.

How can we change this hopelessness? I find change starts most effectively with the understanding that men adapt to women just as much as women adapt to men—and why it doesn't appear as if they do. What exactly do men adapt to? I'll discuss this issue in more depth throughout the book, but let's start with an understanding of the male and female primary fantasies.

The Male Primary Fantasy Versus the Female Primary Fantasy

Playboy and *Penthouse* outsell all men's magazines. They represent *men's primary fantasy*: access to as many beautiful women as desired without risk of rejection. Women's primary fantasy is reflected in the two best-selling women's magazines: *Better Homes and Gardens* and *Family Circle*. Security and a family.

Female Primary Fantasy		Male Primary Fantasy	
Magazine	Circulation*	Magazine	Circulation*
Better Homes and Gardens	8,041,951	**Playboy**	4,209,324
Family Circle	7,193,079	**Penthouse**	3,500,275

*All circulation figures and comparisons are based on listings in *The World Almanac 1985*, whose source is *FAS-FAX* (Schaumburg, Ill.: Audit Bureau of Circulation, 1984). Based on total paid circulation over a six-month period.

Both sexes ideally would like to "have it all": an intellectually and sexually exciting partner who provides security; a partner who is a "10" but who is not self-centered; a partner who offers unconditional love, yet pushes our boundaries; a fulfilling job, yet time with the family; income and plenty of time to spend it; and so on. What distinguishes the sexes are our different fantasies of the most important thing the other sex can provide to help us get what we feel we're missing (the primary fantasy) and our second greatest desire from the other sex (the secondary fantasy). The primary and secondary fantasies represent compromises both sexes make with our hidden "have it all" fantasy.

If checkbook stubs reflect values, the *traditional* female values are the strongest. Romance novels comprise 40 percent of *all* paperback book sales. Six of the eleven top-selling magazines are traditional women's magazines *(Better Homes and Gardens* outsells *Playboy* and *Penthouse* combined). *None* of the eleven top-selling magazines are men's magazines. And none are the "new woman" or "working woman" variety of magazine. The more a magazine sells to women, the less it focuses on working.

The primary fantasy magazines all require their readers to work—to work at the role they must play in order to entice the other sex to fulfill their fantasy. *Family Circle* gives a woman recipes to make it worthwhile for a man to keep her and her family secure; *Playboy* gives a man recipes about how to be successful at making women more interested in having sex with him.

After working with 106,000 women and men from all walks of life, I have found that any medium read or watched almost exclusively by one sex creates a remarkably accurate springboard to that sex's world view. I could examine any of the media, but magazines provide the easiest vehicle to study, given the limitations of the book format. An overview of the second-rank best-selling magazines for each sex gives us a view of the differences between the way women and men approach the achievement of their primary fantasies—or, put another way, their *primary means* to their primary fantasies.

The chart on the next page shows that the female primary *means* to her primary fantasy is glamour/beauty *and men*. Over 90 percent of ads in women's magazines focus on glamour, fashion, and beauty. The articles are divided between glamour/ beauty and men: how to get men, and what to do with them. Next to nothing on careers.

To men, the second rank of best-sellers illustrates *men's primary means* to their primary fantasy: heroism—or performance. If he wants *part* of his primary fantasy *(one* beautiful woman), he must be at least a successful performer. If he wants his entire primary fantasy (access to many), it helps to be a hero. His magazines are *American Legion* (war hero), *Sports Illustrated* (sports hero), *Forbes* (business hero), and *Boy's Life* (the childhood preparation to perform). In the table on the next page we see there is no alternative to heroism for a man to reach his *primary* fantasy—

Female Primary Means to Primary Fantasy: Beauty and Men		Male Primary Means to Primary Fantasy: Being a Hero*	
Magazine	Circulation	Magazine	Circulation
Cosmopolitan	3,038,400	American Legion	2,507,338
Glamour	2,275,743	Sports Illustrated	2,448,486
Seventeen	1,688,954	Boy's Life	1,452,201
Teen	1,022,552	Forbes	719,908

*The four male magazines represent the four major categories of being a hero. Riflery magazines sell very well, but they are a bridge between the categories of sports and war (*American Legion*) and are therefore not listed separately.

many beautiful women—and no alternative to performing to reach a part of his primary fantasy. At least, that is the male perception, reflected by his purchases.

In the past two decades, with the increase in divorce, the female primary fantasy often came tumbling down. Without a man guaranteeing security and a better home, a ''new woman'' needed to emerge to supply some for herself. To supply an *alternative* means to her primary fantasy. So during the late sixties and seventies, a new group of magazines, the ''New Woman'' magazines, emerged.

The Male Reality Versus the Female Reality

As we can see from the circulation figures, the greater the emphasis on independence, equality, and working, the lower the

Female Alternative Means to Primary Fantasy: New Woman		Male Alternative Means to Primary Fantasy: None
Magazine	Circulation	
Self	1,091,112	No
New Woman	1,055,589	alternative
Working Woman	605,902	to
Ms.	479,185	hero/performer

circulation. In all of these "new woman" magazines, what women buy (reflected in the full-page ads that run repeatedly) is remarkably similar to the offerings in the ads in magazines like *Cosmo, Glamour,* and *Seventeen.* They have almost no overlap with the ads in men's magazines. This is important insofar as it reflects the gap between the female and male realities, and the gap between conscious and unconscious messages.

There are more computers, financial services, and large office systems advertised in one issue of *Esquire* than in issues of all the top selling women's magazines combined—including *Working Woman, New Woman, Sex* and *Ms.* And if we substitute *Forbes* or *Fortune* for *Esquire,* the gap is even wider.

Is this because women read both types of magazines? Only 5 percent of *Forbes* subscribers are women—about 35,000.* Over 8 *million* women subscribe to *Better Homes and Gardens.*[1] Thirty-five thousand is less than half of one percent of 8 million.

The gap between male and female realities can be seen by looking at other contrasts. There's *Bride's Magazine*; no *Groom Magazine.* No ad in *Sports Illustrated* touts a wedding as "The Most Important Day of Your Life," as *Bride's* does. In *Fortune,* Max Factor is an investment opportunity. In a woman's magazine it's a different type of investment opportunity. In *Forbes* an article on slimming down is subtitled, "A Nifty Way for a Banker to Get Smaller";[2] slimming down in *Good Housekeeping* means "How I lost 283 Pounds."[3] Even when men and women appear to talk the same language, we mean different things.

Determining whether someone has changed means delving under the surface. Both sexes have made surface changes. Under the surface, the underlying values are remarkably unchanged. For example, fifteen years ago boys wouldn't be caught dead with dolls. Now many boys have dolls. Yet when we look more closely at their dolls, we see most of them have just expanded the repertoire by which boys can either perform or kill. G.I. Joe's gun and tank help him fight "an international paramilitary terrorist force," according to the promotional literature. The He-Man doll is muscle-bound, and Luke Skywalker and Lord Power differ "ever so slightly" from Strawberry Shortcake, who comes replete not with a tank but a thank-you postcard. Blithely citing the extraordinary rise in doll sales for boys ignores how

---

*According to *Forbes* offices in New York City, 95 percent of *Forbes* subscribers are male, as of 1985.

boys are just playing out their traditional role with one more medium—cowboys and Indians have switched turf to Star Wars.

Is the same true for the "new woman"? Women's *situation* has clearly changed in the last two decades. But has *what women want from men* changed? Or is more expected of men, because women feel they are giving more?

Do these questions imply that I think men are the way they are merely because of what women want? No. But if a woman, his parents, his peers, and his boss reward a man for success in ways they are unaware of, he gets a very clear message. The only group *overtly* telling men, "Stop—we want you to be different" is women. Most women do want men to be different and honestly want to know if their message to men is more mixed than they realize. They are not as concerned about what a man's parents or peers did—they want to know what *they* can do—and whether they have a role in perpetuating problems about which they are complaining. These issues are what I will address in this part of the book.

I'm an Independent Person . . . Ads Don't Influence Me

Examining the articles and ads in women's magazines, as well as romance novels, rock stars, soaps, movies, and *Dynasty*, can prompt the objection, "But ads and popular culture don't influence me." That misses the point: whether or not a woman is influenced by them is not as important as the fact that they reflect her values; they could not exist without her financially supporting them. *Her financial support is her choice and therefore her message*, just as *Playboy* and *Sports Illustrated*, which reflect male values, could not be best-sellers without men's financially supporting them. Women's choices create women's magazines. We will see in the next two chapters how their choices get conveyed to men.

It is a mistake to assume that we are not influenced by ads. When I buy a Coke I don't consciously say to myself, "I'm being influenced by ads." But there's a reason I buy Coke more often than "Brand X." At $16,000 per second for some television ads no advertiser can afford to operate only on the conscious level. No advertiser will have a pimple-faced, fat woman selling perfume (even in a scratch-and-sniff ad). If we say "*I* don't pay attention to these commercials,'' we play right into the advertiser's hands—by not admitting we would be less likely to buy perfume from a pimple-faced, flabby woman. In the process, we also miss the most fundamental message being sold in almost every ad with a woman selling a product: the power of the thin, beautiful, made-up, young-appearing female. So let's look at what women's purchases say about what women value—the real signals men are hearing from women.

What is the reward for understanding all this? Once the female primary fantasy is understood, women begin to understand how men adapt to it. They then gain something far more valuable to men than beauty is: an understanding of men.

Many women are beautiful. An understanding of men—from a man's perspective—is rare. And men? Most men aren't quite sure what ''getting in touch with feelings'' means. Sometimes they ask, embarrassed, ''What feelings am I not in touch with?''

In the next chapters we'll see what messages create which feelings.

What Women Want: The Message the Man Hears

We can best tell our values by looking at our checkbook stubs.

Gloria Steinem

Women's magazines have one thing in common— self-improvement.

Patricia Carbine,
Publisher, *Ms.* magazine*

The Female Primary Fantasy and How Men Fit In

To gain insight into the values of the most articulate and independent women in America, let's glance at some ads in America's largest feminist publication, *Ms.* magazine, remembering that a look at our ads is a look at our checkbook stubs and therefore our subconscious values.

Start with two diamond ads. One in 1982[1]; one in 1984.[2] They are by the same company, with the same picture and the same copy. Or are they? Look *very* closely.

The picture is identical in both ads except for the woman's hand. A new hand has been photographed over the old hand! Why? The diamond on the new hand is twice as large. And

*Telephone interview, February 1985, confirming statement quoted in several women's magazines.

Ms., April 1982

Ms., March 1984

there's three times as much gold. In the 1984 ad the ''spending guideline'' at the ad's bottom right eliminates the one-quarter carat option and adds a full-carat diamond. In the meantime, women are educated about the importance of the 4 c's: *cut, clarity, color,* and *carat size.* It's important to have a diamond of *fine* color or clarity. But the $11,000 price shown buys only *medium* color and clarity.*

So let's see what happens when Ms. Equality takes a man to the jeweler for a spending guideline. If she expects the respectable diamond he spends about $14,000. If that's two months' salary, that means he's making $7,000 per month *after* taxes. If he's earning that income he's paying about 50 percent in taxes, meaning he's earning about *$168,000 per year.* For the poorer man, a three-quarter-carat diamond of fine color and clarity will do—so he need make only about $100,000 per year.

Ms., November 1984

*This is indicated after the asterisk in the 1984 ad.

Engagement rings have a history of male-to-female giving. I assumed *Ms.* would feature other gifts women could give to men, such as wallets, colognes, books, jewelry, and calculators, especially in issues before Father's Day and Christmas. I checked the full-page ads of each issue from July 1983 through January 1985—nineteen months. Not one full-page ad for one gift a woman could give a man appeared in any *Ms.* magazine for all nineteen issues—including two Christmas issues.*

Wait . . . there's one exception. One issue of *Ms.* magazine does include an ad with a gift for a man: a subscription to *Ms.* magazine. The ad below suggests thirteen categories of people to whom the reader can give the gift. The first male mentioned is "your brother, who wouldn't mind if they sent it in a brown wrapper." The second is "your best friend's future ex-husband."

Of the thirteen categories, note that there is no subscription mentioned for a boyfriend, none for a husband, none for a lover. What subliminal message does a man who wants a woman of "equality" receive when there is no full-page ad for any gift for any man with whom the woman is "romantic" in any of the nineteen issues? Yet he is giving her $14,000 worth of diamonds. Is the hidden message that the only thing worth giving *any* man is a *Ms.* subscription—but if he is a husband or lover, well, he's getting her body and isn't that enough?

If marriage means a diamond without equal financial reciprocation it also means a honeymoon without equal financial reciprocation and a home that a man making $100,000 to $168,000 can afford—and expectations that he handle the mortgage.

The De Beers Transfer

How does a woman who genuinely feels she believes in equality rationalize such inequality? Here's how. Check out the difference between a De Beers diamond ad that did *not* appear in *Ms.* and the two that did.

Note that in the *Time* ad, the man gets the credit for working all those nights to earn the diamond. In the *Ms.* ad, *he* spends $14,000 and *she* gets the credit for taking him to the jeweler for a spending guideline! *Her belief in equality forces her to deny him credit for what he does for her.* She transfers the credit to herself. She may even say, "He is buying this big diamond because of his

---

*All ads referred to in this book are full-page ads.

Time, October 12, 1981

ego needs"—which may also be true. In either case, the credit
gets transferred away from him, so the contradiction with equality
can be avoided. The part of him that provided still gets clues to
provide, but by denying him the credit for it she can ask him to
provide even more and also tell him he is a chauvinist for picking
up the tab. This is the first of two parts to the "De Beers transfer."

The second part? Ask "If men are doing the buying, why are
there so many diamond ads in women's magazines?" Experience
has taught the De Beers Company that if a man is to spend
money on a woman, the woman should be sold—she decides, he
pays. This is part two of the "De Beers transfer." The De Beers
transfer is a first example of how women's choices and values
get transferred into male behavior, and how men adapt to the
female primary fantasy. The transfer is implied in the title for
this chapter: "What Women Want: The Message the Man Hears."*

*Women have their own experience of adapting to men. In a book entitled
"Why Women Are the Way They Are" an appropriate chapter title would be
"What Men Want: The Message the Woman Hears."

There's an even more powerful difference between the *Time* ad and the ads in *Ms*. The *Time* ad is almost the only example I saw of a beautiful adult woman looking lovingly at a mechanic—or at any working-class man. *Ms*. magazine occasionally discusses such attractions in articles. But, as we shall see, this image does not appear as an image in the advertising of any women's magazine unless the woman is portrayed as wealthy and using the man purely as a sex object. But for now the mechanic learns he must earn his way to equality with the attractive woman—he has to buy her a diamond. But with the above exception, men learn a mechanic is never enough to make it to an attractive adult woman's heart. No matter how sensitive, loving, and warm he is. Even if he has a diamond.

Cinderella—or Superwoman?

Have women changed? Yes. The changes that represent real progress—from assertiveness to work status—have been widely discussed. Many fundamentals, though, remain remarkably the same. Why do we think the progress has been greater than it is? Because what is the same doesn't make the news. Superwoman makes the news. Cinderella is old hat. But almost every women's magazine has articles talking about Superwoman next to ads focusing on Cinderellas. Even in *Working Woman*, *New Woman*, and *Ms*.

Did the ads in *Ms*.* feature "liberated dolls" of Elizabeth Cady Stanton or Golda Meir? No. Instead, in *Ms*. we find a full-page ad (pictured on the top left of the next page) for a *Cinderella* doll—standing on top of a bell-shaped clock. The hands on the clock point to 12:00—is time running out for the *Ms*. reader? This is a *Ms*. reader's exclusive for only sixty-three dollars, to keep her company while she and Cinderella wait together for the prince. No wonder she feels there is a male shortage.

Is this an isolated example? The previous month's issue of *Ms*. advertised the Eliza Doolittle Doll of the "My Fair Lady Collection," then Amy of *Little Women*. Many men credit feminists

---

Ms. has a greater variety of full-page ads than any of the other best-selling (400,000 or more subscribers) women's magazines. The ads mentioned are not meant to be a random sampling of *Ms*. ads, but do represent the mixed messages even the more independent woman buys and therefore sends to men.

Ms., February 1984   *Ms.*, October 1983

with teaching them that to call a woman "little woman" is a quintessential example of condescending male chauvinism. I agree. Yet *Ms.* readers pay over $150 for this "little woman." And what can we make of articles condemning the bound feet and subservience of the female in traditional oriental culture when we see *Ms.* readers buying a piece of porcelain glorifying a traditional oriental woman (see ad above, at right)? Only $120. Somehow, amid articles on the feminization of poverty, a mixed message emerges.

Cinderellas are rarely portrayed so directly. Most Cinderellas in women's magazines are selling another product, such as cigarettes. In a varied series of Benson and Hedges ads one theme dominates—all the women are Cinderellas of sorts. In one the woman is pictured running through the archway of a mansion, beneath a grand chandelier, onto a patio overlooking a massive garden of flowers resembling Louis XIV's Tuileries in Paris. How does she get into this setting? By buying the right product and being beautiful. The product can change. But she must be beautiful. If she is, she can be portrayed as having the wealthy surroundings without earning them herself.

Why is the man often not present in these "beautiful woman" ads? The implicit message is that if she is beautiful he will find her, and that she can choose from a variety of men, a variety of kingdoms.

How do these images differ from that of the Marlboro man, who is also attractive? *He is portrayed doing the type of activity it takes to earn possession of his environment.* Why are women often not present in these "master your environment" ads? The implicit message is that if you cannot master your environment, a beautiful woman will look right past you. If the man is a master, the beautiful woman is implicit.

If the story is the same in every women's magazine, then why start with *Ms.*, the only best-selling women's magazine to treat women as if they have political opinions? Because it claims to be beyond this and looking for men who are "as liberated as we are." For example, in May 1984 *Ms.* devoted two full pages to an ad for itself: "We've changed so much. We changed the world." This is what throws men off. They have bought the line that they're far behind. Yet, if ads focusing strictly on female beauty power are considered sexist by treating women only as beauty objects, then there are more sexist ads in the first eleven pages of the May 1985 *Ms.* magazine than in the entire May, June, and July 1985 issues of *Fortune* magazine combined.

Who's changed?

Why Do Men Say They Feel They're Getting Mixed Messages from Women?

Open up a *Self* magazine (the best-selling female self-improvement magazine). I reviewed the June 1984 issue. In the first twenty-seven pages of full-page advertising, *all twenty-seven pages* were devoted to female-beautifying products—not just beautiful females advertising other products. The role of men in these pages? In the first twenty-six ad pages the males are implicit; they are not shown; nor are they shown in the non-ad pages. In fact, in the first seventy pages of *Self*, only three men are pictured anywhere. Two of the three are buying women something. One is buying a diamond; the other is buying a woman a wardrobe from a catalog on impulse at two a.m. She calls the spontaneous wardrobe buying "crazy" and "wonderful." When a man says, "I love her because she's spontaneous and crazy," he doesn't usually mean she bought him a new wardrobe. The third man is pictured being lured to a beautiful woman's diamond-studded ear by the fragrance of her perfume.

Many men hear women saying they'd like a man who shares the housework. "Is this true?" the men ask. Yes. Women *do* want men who share the housework, but only if it is in *addition* to being successful enough to buy the wardrobe and diamond.

Does this increased expectation of men happen because women's magazines are preparing women to buy men wardrobes and diamonds too? No. But suppose we look beyond the ads—do the articles focus on self-improvement or preparing women to share the responsibility with men for earning the income? About 10 percent do. The other 90 percent focus on subjects like the body ("The Quickie Diet"), "desire dullers," "passion prompters," or heroines under stress.

Back to the ads. Do any of the products in *Self* address the issue of women sharing responsibility for earning the income? The entire issue features *no* ads for computers, office equipment, or financial services, which comprise approximately 80 percent of the ads in *Forbes*. Instead, we have ads for hairstyling mousse and hairstyling systems; hydrating fluid and contouring body cream; eyeliner and eye fix; super nails and hair removal systems. A woman can choose cold wax hair remover, which presses on and pulls off in strips, or some other hair removal system. Which would you use? Whichever you choose, put it down when you get to your face—use facial hair cream remover. If this confuses you, you can just bleach your hair with Sally Hansen's Creme Bleach. Of course, there's extra strength bleach or the bleach for facial hair only. Which would you choose? And this is just one issue.

How can a woman focus on her career?

Are there any women's magazines easily available to women without these ads, and which include articles that treat women like career-oriented adults? Yes. *Savvy. And very few women buy it.* *Savvy* has fewer than *one-third* the subscribers of *Mother Earth News* or *Workbench,* and fewer even than *Bassmaster* magazine.*

Is it just among women who seek equality that there exists such a gap between what men hear women saying they are after and what they actually are after? Let's compare (see illustrations on the next page) an ad for *Cosmo* against the actual issue of *Cosmo.* Contrast the overt message of the ad and the real message,

---

*All subscriber figures used here are listed in *The World Almanac 1985,* based on the Audit Bureau of Circulations' FAS-FAX reports. *Savvy* does not make the list of the top 140 magazines and is therefore not part of my analysis.

COSMO'S REPRESENTATION OF ITSELF*

READ THIS:	*THE REAL THING*

Billboard, December 15, 1984	*Cosmopolitan*, September 1984

OVERT MESSAGES	*REAL MESSAGES*
"Don't play games."	Play games: "Preserve the *Mystery* . . . Love the Old-fashioned Way. Make Him *Earn* It."
"Play your career for all it's worth."	No articles on career. No career-related ads (computers, office systems). Eighty percent of ads on cosmetics and beautifying products.
Career for career's sake.	Career as a way of getting him to commit. "[First] I got the noncommitment speech . . . [then] I went on a business trip to France . . . [now] he's the most attentive man I've ever known."

*In an ad for *Cosmo* in *Billboard*, December 15, 1984.

represented by what the magazine actually features. First read the copy on the ad on the left. Then look for the articles on careers on the cover of the magazine on the right.

What is happening? The woman is learning two ways to play hard-to-get: She can play sexually hard-to-get—the old-fashioned way. Or career hard-to-get—career is being used as the newest way to get a man to make a commitment. Or, more accurately, since no articles on career appear in the issue, the *appearance* of a career is used to get a man to commit. Or could it be that the appearance of a career is being used to get a man to commit so that the woman will never, in fact, have to worry about a career?

There is in this new formula a no-win situation for men. If he commits, it is because she played hard-to-get in either the modern, career-oriented, way or the old-fashioned way. If he doesn't commit, it is reasoned that men are threatened by successful women.

No wonder one of the *Cosmo* reader's most satisfying relationships is with a magazine.

What Are Boys Good For?

What does a teenage girl learn to give to a boy? Let's look at a thirteen-page spread in *Teen*—the Christmas 1984 issue. Approximately seventy presents are mentioned, with an average price of about thirty dollars (over two thousand dollars' worth of presents). Only one is for a male—pajamas for a baby boy. As with *Ms.*, no presents for boyfriends.

There are several teenage boys shown in the pictures. One admires a girl while she admires herself in the mirror; another is towing a girl's brand-new car. The same use of men as in *Self*.

Is the girl in the *Teen* spread helping the boy who has attached her car to a tow truck? No. She drapes herself over the tow truck. And how does she learn to handle a stressful situation? The caption explains: "If a stressful situation causes complexion concerns, keep skin under control with Noxzema Acne 12. And pass the time in an easy-to-wear wardrobe!"

All twelve days of Christmas run the same pattern: "Keep tabs on your weight," "File your nails . . . ," "Massage your hands," "Massage your feet," "Turn heads in your direction by keeping lips lusciously lubricated. . . ." What does he get? Nothing is mentioned but her beauty. What lessons does he learn? Admire and rescue. In *Teen*. In *Ms*. In *Self*.

Do teenage boys' magazines show a girl towing *his* brand-new car, while he drapes himself over her tow truck and worries about his acne? Hardly.

In men's magazines there are only a few gifts for men to buy women. Remember the principle of the De Beers transfer. She chooses the diamond and chooses among the men her beauty power can attract to buy it. Which is why his ads are for how to become successful enough to buy whatever she chooses; hers are to become beautiful enough to be able to make the choice of both the gift and the man to buy the gift. Men's magazines do not feature many gifts for women because men are expected to do the buying after consulting the women, not the magazine, and to concentrate their energies on making the money.

The Princess and the Patron: The *Flashdance* Phenomenon

Who are among the women appearing most frequently on the front covers of women's magazines? Princess Di, Jackie O, and, until her death, Princess Grace. Each married a prince or a president.

Prime-time television fantasy gets a bit more complex. *Dynasty* features two types of women—Joan Collins as Alexis, the empire-builder/scoundrel; and Linda Evans as Krystle, the traditional lady/goodprincess/stenographer-who-gives-up-working-upon-chance-of-child. What is common to both the traditional "lady" and this scoundrel? They both created their options by marrying wealth.

In *Dynasty* some things *have* changed. It now makes no difference whether the husbands are older and about to die or half a woman's age—as long as they've already made it big. When good, sweet Krystle becomes pregnant after marrying the owner of the oil company for which she was a secretary, he gives her a Rolls-Royce as a pregnancy present. After several years' leave of absence she returns to work. As secretary? No. As head of the multimillion-dollar corporation's public relations department. What training did she have between being a secretary and being head of public relations? She married the boss. This is the Flashdance Phenomenon—finding the right patron. Qualifications? Look like a princess.

In real life, Linda Evans exclaims that for the right man she'd "quit acting and stay home all the time."[3] Which was, in fact, what she did. Career by option and wealth by marriage. Which have made her the fantasy woman of millions of women who would like to have it all—including softness—by marrying a man who has it all but has become hard in the process of earning it.

People, May 13, 1985

We don't like to admit that the fantasy still silently implies men kill each other off so that the survivor can be eligible to "flashdance" a woman into a princess. The fantasy is marrying in a minute what he earns in a lifetime.

The two "different" images in *Dynasty* are really two methods of achieving the same end: marrying one's way to options. But which patron should a woman choose? Both the Krystle and Scoundrel images are now encapsulated in perfumes, so millions of women can try out both scents for themselves.

Magic Think: The Unicorn, the Princess, and the Hero

"Makeup Magic," the cover feature of the December 1984 *Seventeen*, promises to turn the average girl into a beauty and a potential star—like magic. *Dynasty* promises a "flashdance" to fame, Rolls-Royces, and oil barons. Like magic. The Elizabeth

Seventeen, December 1984

Arden Salon's Red Door made its reputation promising it could transform *any* woman into a beauty like magic.

And if a girl herself fails to make the effort, the horoscopes promise that success with boys is in the stars anyway. The January 1985 *Seventeen* devotes thirteen full pages to horoscopes—almost every one of which has some version of "Coming up for you in '85: *Boys, boys, boys,* particularly in June and July—you'll practically have to fight them off!"[4]

What about the girl who's nine or ten and is just experimenting with beauty, but isn't quite ready to experiment with boys? She experiments with unicorns. Look at the *Seventeen* ad (pictured above) for Magical Musk perfume. While a boy begins to leave unicorns behind at the age of nine or ten, a girl—even a seventeen-year-old girl—can still be wooed to a product by the magic of unicorns. While a boy is trained that he must earn his pot of gold, a girl continues to search for the rainbow. The rainbow symbolizes the promise of the pot of gold—to be delivered as soon as the wonder diets and magic makeups can create a magical transformation to attract some male to provide her that pot of gold.

The magical unicorn becomes the magical man; the gold at

Ms., June 1985

the end of the rainbow becomes the diamond at the beginning of commitment.

Does the independent woman shed the expectation of magic—of being given to or provided for? Look at the similarity between the *Seventeen* ad, on the previous page, and the one from *Ms.*, above.

Note the description of the unicorn as "The Messenger of Love." But how is the love attained? Its "*elusive* soul can only be *tamed* by a *maiden's magic power*" (emphasis added). "Elusive soul," as opposed to a man who expresses feelings directly; "tamed," as opposed to a gentleman with nothing more than equal passion; tamed by a "maiden's magic power," as opposed to "encountered by an independent woman with a career commitment." This is *her* fantasy. In *Ms.* A fantasy *Ms.* readers supported? So much so that by 1986 it became a full two-page ad.

The expectation of being "given to" is understood so well that there is no box for a payment option; instead, a woman will be billed "when my sculpture is ready to be sent to me." That is, she buys the illusion it will be created just for her: we also read, "Each sculpture will be *individually hand-cast and hand-finished,*" and *"Limit: One sculpture per order."* Love, as part of her primary fantasy, must be faithful to her alone. (The unicorn is an ancient symbol of fidelity.) So as a woman gets older, her "Magical Musk" from *Seventeen* becomes her magical power, with which she can *tame* the sexuality of a beast—rather than *be* sexual with the beast—and transform it into faithful love. The primary fantasy. In *Ms*.

Imagine an ad in *Forbes* for a $120 porcelain unicorn. For the male executive's desk. With no option to pay directly. Men learn they cannot get love by exercising their inborn "magic power," or by spraying some on; they must *earn* love. In *Forbes* the ads are for computers and office systems. *Forbes* teaches men what they must buy to *earn* a woman's love.* *The more she believes in magic, the more he must create the miracles.*

Virginal Sex

Each Christmas and birthday I debate between two types of presents for Megan, the daughter of my woman friend: those I think she should have and those I know she'll love. When she was eight to twelve years old there were two things I knew would make it in the "I love" category: unicorns and posters of heroes. This was true of her girlfriends as well. It's taken me all this time to understand the connection. With neither the unicorn nor the male star on the wall did Megan have to deal directly with her sexuality. It was not like having a picture of one of the boys in her class on her dresser. None of the boys in her or her girlfriends' classes could make it to this star status, so Megan and her girlfriends did not have to deal directly with their sexuality.

Of course, there were different types of male heroes on Megan's wall—or different images representing how her sexuality might eventually be channeled. In the same manner, for boys, different types of performing—sports, scholastics, or stealing—are different kinds of experiments to become heroes, to be wanted *by* different types of girls.

Why is it that so many girls' first posters on the wall are male and boys' first posters on the wall are also male and only later female? And why are boys' male heroes also male performers? Because a boy must learn to perform—to earn a female. For him, the more attractive the female the less likely she is just

*Forbes reports its readership as 95 percent male.

magically to come along. He must earn his way to equality with her. So his posters are of male role models: the role he must play to have access to his fantasy female.

When can a boy make the transition to the female on the wall? When he has tried his hand at performing and is ready to make the relatively short transition between fantasizing and being directly sexual. At that point, he usually changes to nude or seminude posters of women. Similarly, a girl's male-performer posters reinforce her unconscious notion that it's fine for the man to do the performing for her. That ideally she can skip the performance stage herself and can "magically musk" or "magically make up" her way to his performance, tame it, and call it love.

She is deciding the type of performer she should be sexual with; he is deciding how to perform to get sex. The bodies a boy puts on the wall are Miss June, Pet-of-the-Month, etc. Not names of real people. Rather they are interchangeable parts. A girl's heroes do not *appear* like interchangeable parts; they have real names. But the moment Michael Jackson fell out of favor with the press, he came off Megan's wall. Her heroes actually *are* interchangeable parts. Their interchangeability is simply better masked, which makes us think better of the female, that "women don't exploit and objectify." Underneath, it's his sex object and her success object.

What is the relationship between the horn on the white horse, the prince on the white horse, and the hero on the wall? They all offer the female child the *ideal* of skipping sex itself, skipping a career, and being "flashdanced" magically to security, adventure, and fame by a male performer.

What are some alternative gifts or posters I consider healthy? What do I buy Megan that I think she should have? Posters of female Olympic gymnasts to tie into her gymnastic interests, a baseball bat, a soccer ball. But more important than buying the baseball bat is using it with her—setting up games with rules that allow her a 60–40 chance of winning if she really tries. So she can become her own hero.

Falling in Love within a Framework

Item: *Good Housekeeping,* February 1985: Fifty "eligible" bachelors chosen. Only two sentences describe what makes them eligible: their exact salary, their title, their source of power, their availability (if they were rich enough they could be engaged and still qualify as "eligible").

In the film *The World According to Garp* we can observe how little Garp's future wife was interested in him during his first overtures. Then he told her of his plans to be a serious writer. She showed *some* interest. So off he went to prove to her he had what it took to be a *great* writer. He proved it. She read it, was overwhelmed with what he had proven. *Then* she fell in love with him. She did not go off to prove anything to him. His interest in her came on first glance and evolved toward love as they got to know each other; there was no test of her greatness.

I call this "falling in love within a framework." A man's experience teaches him a woman is more likely to fall in love *once he makes it within a certain framework*. And since sex comes much more easily with love, "making it" also seems to open her up sexually. "Making it" means getting love and sex. *"Not making it" means rejection, less sex, and tenuous love.* Once Garp's future wife loved his manuscript she fell in love and *then* they fell in bed.

How does falling in love within a framework work from the woman's point of view? Here is an example from a woman in Texas.

"Who are some men you could easily fall in love with?" I asked a community audience in Waco, Texas.

"My husband . . . all over again," was the first reply—to applause.

The next day Mary, the woman who had so replied, came to a workshop. This time she was talking among women only, the men watching silently from a distance. I repeated the question. This time Mary's answer was, "Well, *ideally*, Phil Donahue." The other women were hotter for Tom Selleck and Paul Newman. I asked her to fantasize being single and bringing Phil home to her parents for the first time—assuming Phil were single again.

She answered: "I watch the shock on my father's face. His newfound respect, barely concealed. I giggle with delight. No, with pride. I have 'made it' in his eyes. He doesn't say much, but, oh, can I feel it. And my mother? Well, she is beside herself. Just beside herself. I imagine her, well, I shouldn't say this, but I imagine her—metaphorically speaking—peeing in her pants. I can feel her look us over with disbelief as I introduce him to her. I can feel her eyes direct a shocked-with-pride stare as he plays with my fingers, as *he* plays with *my* fingers—right in front of my mother's eyes. Wow! My mother is Catholic. Bringing Phil Donahue home would be like, 'Goodness and mercy shall follow you all the days of your life.' ''

"What about your friends?" I asked.

"Oh, my God! The high school prom queen would turn queen . . . er, green with envy. I wasn't exactly *the* most sought-after girl in school."

"Phil Donahue falls in love with you. Do you fall in love back?"

"You must be kidding . . . wouldn't you?" The group laughed.

After some discussion, I chimed in. "Let's look at part of what love meant for Mary. Mary felt a terrific feeling. She felt this feeling even though the 'love' consisted of her receiving *approval*—it wouldn't be the same if he didn't like her—and the promise of a *secure attachment*—it wouldn't be the same if she brought Phil Donahue home for a one-night stand—to someone who fit her *ideal*. For Mary, love involved receiving approval and security from an ideal image. Most of the approval did not even come from Phil—it came from others, others who knew little about their real relationship."

"Image?" a woman piped up.

"Yes. The ideal was in fact largely an image. It had nothing to do with her interaction with Phil: how they talked together, whether he spent time helping her define her goals in life (as opposed to running off and producing shows), or whether he was receptive to her input about *his* goals in life. It had little to do with their chemistry. Little to do with mutuality of tastes, attitudes toward child-rearing, or how they listened to each other. Little to do with *love*."

"Why do you think women do this 'hero selection'?" a woman asked.

I replied, "Let's look at the pressures on Mary not to look carefully at love. For example, imagine her parents preparing for Phil to come over for Christmas. The special cakes being baked. Telling the neighbors. The local paper running stories. Photographers calling the house. Excitement coming into the life of this 'average' family.

"Now suppose Mary realizes that she's fallen in love with an image. And she finds Phil doesn't have the time for her that she needs. She needs someone to need her more. She calls her parents and tells them she's decided to ask Phil not to come over for Christmas until she can 'get herself together.' Imagine Mary's parents calling their friends. Calling their neighbors. Calling the paper. Facing how many special things they had baked for Phil to eat. These are the pressures—masked as support—for Mary to commit without falling in love. Her pressures to confuse love with her primary fantasy. And to confine her search for love to the framework, so that at best she falls in love within a framework.''

How can we determine whether we are falling in love within a framework in the reality of everyday life? Take this test:

Case 1:   You are a single woman. You are about to bring home to your parents a man you are about to marry. He is tall, handsome, articulate, warm, tender; he listens carefully, understands you thoroughly, and expresses his feelings. He works as a night watchman in a local junkyard.

How do you feel your parents would react to your marrying him?

Enthusiasm level on a scale of one to ten (one is lowest):___

Would you, in fact, seriously consider marrying him?

___Yes ___No.

Enthusiasm level:_____

Case 2:   You are a single woman. Your friend would like you to meet and go out with a short friend of hers. She explains he has had plastic surgery four times, often wears makeup, and has a high, squeaky voice. Some people think he is gay—but she is fairly sure he is not, and he has taken an interest in you. He does have some odd habits, like watching some movies as often as sixty times. It seems he may even have a glove fetish. Interested?

___Yes ___No. His name is Michael Jackson.

How to Marry Money

In New York City a therapist and author teaches a popular course called ''Marrying Up.'' She has written a book of the same name.[5] In San Diego there is a highly popular course called ''How to Marry Money.'' Note that the marriage is to money—not to a person. I inquired about the percentage of men attending. ''Oh, I have to warn men,'' the instructor replied. ''They're welcome to attend, but the course is really for women. I mean, it's not relevant to men.''

HOW TO MARRY MONEY

North Park   **University / I-15**

"It's as easy to fall in love with a rich man as
with a poor one." The fantasy can come true if
you're willing to pay the price in planning,
patience and persistence. We'll look at where the
wealthy are and how to decide if you have what
it takes, prepare for the search, develop your
strategy, make connections, and enjoy the whole
process.

Barbara Jones *is a human relations and com-*
munication consultant, a researcher into
upwardly mobile marriages, and an astute
observer of the social scene. She directs Human
Potential Unlimited.

Fee $25.   one meeting   class size 6-15
Sec. A: Mon. Jan. 14   6:30-9:30 pm
Sec. B: Thu. Feb. 21   6:30-9:30 pm

Access to Learning Catalogue (San Diego, 1985)

Both courses are taught by women involved in self-improvement—one is a therapist, the other the director of Human Potential Unlimited. There is no course for men called "Marrying
Down." But what would a course parallel to "How to Marry
Money" be for men? Would it be "How to Find Great Sex"?
No. Because men also give sex—in fact, sometimes they beg to
give it. (Women attending "How to Marry Money" are not
begging to give money equally.)

Would it be "How to Pick Up Girls"? No. "How to Pick Up
Girls" describes the work a man must do to get someone *equivalent*
to himself. It implies he is not equal until he does this work. A
legitimate equivalent for men would in fact be "How to Marry
Money." But that *is* the title. And almost no men attend.

What if they gave sexism and no one came?

The Back to Home Movement

Ladies' Home Journal (September 1984) runs a cover story:
"I'm Sick of Work: The Back to Home Movement." Imagine,
on the front cover of *Playboy*, "I'm Sick of Work: The Back to
Home Movement." And yet we think of the playboy as not

being commitment-oriented, as wanting to keep his options open. In *Working Woman* (November 1984) there is a cover article called "How to Work Part Time Without Smashing Your Career." Imagine in *Forbes*: "How to Work Part Time Without Smashing Your Career." This attitude makes some men wonder whether work is a right women want, instead of a *responsibility* women realize they must share.

Has there been a marked switch in mental attitudes among women who work away from soap-opera-as-fantasy to equal sharing of all roles? With some women, yes. But there are more and more evening soap operas, and daytime soaps are now recorded for evening viewing. In fact, the Nielsen surveys[6] disclosed that in 1984 the most frequently recorded TV program was "All My Children." The second most frequently recorded was "General Hospital," the third, "Days of Our Lives," then "As the World Turns," "Guiding Light," and "One Life to Live."

What is the message to men? The soaps do not show an admired male hero caring for the children and housework while a woman supports him. None shows a woman focusing on a career with the expectation she will support a man from her career earnings. The men she fights with other women over have incomes large enough to give her the option to quit work, as in *General Hospital*. There is no *General Custodian*.

Prepare for Greatness

In five recent issues[7] of the three best-selling magazines for teenage girls there was *not a single article on careers*. And there was just one ad entitled: "Prepare for Greatness!" Finally—real equality! What will make her great? A career in hairstyling with a Redken certificate. Where can she prepare to be great? Try Aura School of Beauty in Texas, or Allure Career College of Beauty in Arizona.

Are there smaller ads offering more options? Yes. Tucked away in the classifieds are columns of smaller ads for careers in fashion, retailing, and modeling. One of the largest is for the Barbizon Schools: "Train to be a model (or . . . just look like one)."

If there is no encouragement to pursue careers, how is a woman expected to survive?

How to Get a Yale Law Degree with a Pair of Jeans

The Zena jeans ad offers diverse career options—for the price of jeans and a ski vacation.* Note that the Zena teenager finds herself plowing into a Yale Law School grad. By wearing the right jeans she can search for the right career. So her options *are* more diverse than twenty years ago: there are more ski slopes.

Seventeen, December 1984

Zena Jeans

Fit for the Way You Live

"Sue . . .

"There I was, on top of Mt. Snow, trying desperately to avoid a mogul, when I found myself plowing right into this hunk from New Haven.

"I'd say he was a cross be-tween . . . uh . . . Sting and my beagle.

"He has those sad puppy dog eyes . . .

"So we shook hands and by the time we disentangled our legs, I knew everything about him I needed to know.

"Law School grad from Yale. (Brains.)

"Likes his mother. (Hope.)

"No steady girlfriend. (Whew!)

"Hates French films. (Ditto.)

"Sue . . . you'll love him. *Absolutely* die for him.

"I know you hate my taste in men, but this one's an ex-ception.

"Do you know what his opening line was when I ran into him?

" 'Those jeans sure are dangerous.'

"Sue . . .

"I'm in love."

*The Zena ad is one of the most popular in the best-selling girls' magazines.

Note that the Zena girl plowed right into the hunk from New Haven—he finds women by performing; she finds men by messing it up. She did not do it purposely—she *found herself* plowing (she learns never to admit responsibility). Note that his graduation from Yale Law School is called "brains"—a euphemism for money, status, security, and ambition. And he even looked powerful, intelligent, and famous, like the rock and movie star Sting—yet he was gentle, like a beagle. Of course, *he* created the opening line, and he had to be uncommitted to warrant any further attention. "By the time we disentangled our legs I knew all I needed to know . . . I'm in love." So *that's* love.

It took the hunk a lifetime to prepare for and get through Yale Law School. It took her a pair of jeans and a pair of legs to get his law degree. With those and a Redken certificate she can "Prepare for Greatness." What's the message to him? Yale Law isn't enough. He must be a hunk, have the potential for fame, and be gentle. *Then* she might take her jeans off.

Now suppose this ad were in a teenage boys' magazine. A boy whose career ambition is a Redken certificate from Aura School of Beauty stumbles over a mogul and plows into a woman. He writes his boyfriend:

"Bob . . .
"There I was, on top of Mt.
  Snow, trying desperately to
  avoid a mogul, when
  I found myself plowing
  right into this chick from
  New Haven.
"I'd say she was a cross between
  . . . uh . . . Madonna and my poodle.
"So we shook hands, Bob, and by the
  time we disentangled our
  legs, I knew everything I needed to know.
"Law school grad from Yale.
  (Security.)
"Likes her father. (Hope.) . . . .
"Bob . . . you'll love her.
  Absolutely die for her.
"Do you know what her opening line
  was when I ran into her?

'' 'Those jeans sure are
  dangerous!'
''Bob . . .
''I'm in love.''

There is another path to greatness featured in *Teen* (in the
December 1984 issue): ''Announcing *Teen*'s Great Model Search
1985! . . . Here's Your Chance to Achieve Your Dream.''

Are there any articles or ads extolling inner values? An article
in *Teen* on soap opera star Catherine Hickland tells us how
self-confidence was important to her. But we discover she gained
this self-confidence in a week or so—after years of downgrading
herself. How? She ''happened to be'' working for National
Airlines when they were looking for an employee to be a ''Fly
Me Girl'' (remember ''Fly Me, I'm Cathy,'' the campaign the
feminist movement protested as sexist in the early seventies?).
To her surprise, she was chosen, and she suddenly lost her
self-denigrating image. Is this beauty-based self-confidence presented by *Teen* in magical terms? Judge for yourself. Here's how
the article opens: ''Once upon a time in the faraway land of Fort
Lauderdale, Florida, there lived a young maiden named Catherine Hickland. . . .'' Later it continues: ''. . . she met a handsome prince charming named David Hasselhoff. They fell in
love and were married. Now they live in a castle of a home—
high above the glittering kingdom of Hollywood.''

Seventeen does have a feature called ''Most Likely to Succeed.'' Is it about a young, entrepreneurial woman or teenage
girl? No. It is about a man.

So a girl can prepare for greatness by a career in beauty—or a
man's success. What's changed?

Must the Zena woman rely only on falling over ski-slope
moguls to fall in love with male moguls? No. It is clear that her
jeans and his Yale Law School degree are only symbols. But
symbols of what?

The Hint of Sex Brings the Lenox of Love

''Gettin' into Mischief'' is the hint thrown out in *Seventeen* (see
ad at the top of the facing page), the best-selling magazine for
twelve- to nineteen-year-old girls. If a girl gives a hint of ''mischief''
she will be in demand among the boys. When she chooses a boy,
do she and he get into mischief together? No. She gets ''love.'' As

Seventeen, December 1984

symbolized by the large heart into which all three boys have been drawn, and by the small heart on the T-shirt to which the mischief points. If the mischief actually led to the type of mischief to which all the boys were drawn, the arrow might point to a silhouette of two lovers. So a girl subliminally learns that the sexual *tease* buys her both boys and love. And the purpose of this love? Why, "Love leads to Lenox." As Zsa Zsa Gabor put it in a diamond ad: "If I were good, why would anyone want to give me a diamond . . ."[8]

The Commitment Dodgers Versus the Commitment Giants

It's a race to the finish—for the Olympic Gold Medal. The ad shows a black man in uniform number 31 and a white man in another uniform, a tuxedo. The tuxedoed white man wins! He has gotten married. Turn the page. Now the white man is number 17 and the black man is in a tuxedo. The tuxedoed black man wins. He has gotten married. No racism here. But the message? Gingiss formal wear makes it clear (in *Bride's Magazine*,

Seventeen, January 1985

October/November 1984) that the man who commits is hero for a day—a hero who can beat anyone—if only he commits himself.

Commitmentism as a form of sexism?

Throughout the women's magazines men are called names—"commitment dodgers,"[9] commitment phobic, and fearful of marriage—the "M word."[10] In contrast, if the man commits, he is a hero—at least for a day. This dichotomizing, like the division of women into madonnas or whores, is a form of sexism I call "commitmentism."

When it comes to commitment, men and women, like the old Dodgers and Giants, are pitted against each other in a battle to the final inning. Men are freely branded Commitment Dodgers; but commitmentism is such a deeply ingrained form of sexism no one even thinks of calling women Commitment Giants.

Perhaps *Bride's Magazine* can help us understand one aspect of commitment, the way going shopping helps us understand an important aspect of Christmas. The October/November 1984 *Bride's*, which might be called the "catalogue of love," features four pages (two of them are reproduced on the following pages) of purchases a woman might wish to consider as part of the ultimate commitment. Not including the diamond. But including microwaves,

BRIDE'S

REGISTRY CHECKLIST

This checklist is the perfect helpmate for keeping track of your wedding gifts. First, read down the columns and mark the number of items you "want." Then clip and take these pages to the Wedding Gift Registry at your favorite giftware or department store—to list your preferences. (Remember, that store is filled with everything from measuring cups to jogging gear, so do list all "other" gifts that you want—but don't see listed—in the empty spaces at the end.) When friends come in to shop for your wedding gift, the Wedding Gift Registry Consultant can offer perfect suggestions from your form on file, and mark off what's purchased, to avoid duplications. Meanwhile, you keep these pages, and mark the number of items "rec'd" in the boxes to the right. It will keep you and your consultant up-to-date!

FORMAL FLATWARE	Want	Rec'd
Pattern:		
Manufacturer:		
Dinner fork		
Dessert/salad fork		
Cocktail fork		
Tablespoon		
Soup spoon		
Tea/dessert spoon		
Demitasse spoon		
Iced tea spoon		
Dinner knife		
Steak knife		
Butter spreader		
Serving fork		
Serving spoon		
Cold meat fork		
Gravy ladle		
Pie server		
Cake knife		
Sugar spoon/tongs		
Butter knife		
Lemon fork		
Carving set		
Salad set		
Silver chest		
Other:		
CASUAL FLATWARE		
Pattern:		
Manufacturer:		
No. of settings:		
Other:		
FORMAL DINNERWARE		
Pattern:		
Manufacturer:		

	Want	Rec'd
Dinner plate		
Luncheon plate		
Buffet plate		
Dessert/salad plate		
Bread/butter plate		
Soup/cereal bowl		
Cream soup bowl		
Rim soup bowl		
Fruit bowl		
Teacup/saucer		
Coffeecup/saucer		
Demitasse/saucer		
Egg cup		
Serving bowls		
Platters		
Gravy boat		
Teapot		
Coffeepot		
Sugar/creamer		
Salt/pepper		
Other:		
INFORMAL DINNERWARE		
Pattern:		
Manufacturer:		
Dinner plate		
Salad plate		
Bowls		
Mugs		
Serving pieces		
Cups/saucers		
Other:		
HOLLOWARE/SERVERS		
Water pitcher		
Serving bowls		
Tea service		

	Want	Rec'd
Coffee service		
Serving platters		
Trays		
Tureen		
Compote		
Salad bowl		
Trivets		
Salt/pepper		
Condiment dish		
Cream/sugar set		
Gravy boat		
Bread tray		
Dessert dishes		
Candlesticks		
Service plates		
Napkin rings		
Chafing dish		
Other:		
FORMAL GLASSWARE		
Pattern:		
Manufacturer:		
Goblets		
White wine		
Claret		
Champagne		
Cocktail		
Brandy		
Liqueur		
Iced tea		
Other:		
CASUAL GLASS-/BARWARE		
Pattern:		
Manufacturer:		
Goblets		
Wine		

BRIDE'S

REGISTRY CHECKLIST

Item	Wanted	Rec'd
Iced tea		
Old-fashioned		
Highball		
Beer glasses		
Fruit juice		
Cocktail		
Other:		
BAR/ENTERTAINMENT NEEDS		
Wine cooler		
Cocktail shaker		
Ice bucket		
Wine rack		
Corkscrew/opener		
Decanters		
Jiggers/tools set		
Punch bowl set		
Coasters		
Ice crusher		
Cheese board		
Other:		
GOURMET-/KITCHENWARE		
Toaster/toaster oven		
Coffeemaker		
Coffee grinder		
Microwave		
Microwave cookware		
Juicer		
Food processor		
Mixer		
Blender		
Pressure cooker		
Steamer		
Can opener		
Electric skillet		
Deep fryer		
Cookware/non-stick		
Slow cooker		
Bakeware		
Ovenware		

Item	Wanted	Rec'd
Hot tray		
Tea kettle		
Cutlery		
Spice rack		
Mixing bowls		
Kitchen utensils		
Cutting board		
Wok		
Cannister set		
Other:		
HOUSEWARES		
Fire extinguisher		
Carpet cleaner		
Storage systems		
Iron		
Other:		
ELECTRONICS		
TV/video system		
Stereo		
Telephones		
Clock radio		
Smoke alarm		
Camera equipment		
Security devises		
Calculator		
Other:		
LINENS		
Formal cloth/napkins		
Informal cloth/napkins		
Place set		
Lapmats		
Runners		
Cocktail napkins		
Potholders/dish towels		
Aprons		
Bed sheets		
Blanket		
Electric blanket		

Item	Wanted	Rec'd
Comforter		
Bedspread		
Mattress pad/cover		
Pillows		
Jumbo bath towels		
Bath towels/face cloths		
Guest towels		
Bath mat		
Rug/lid cover set		
Shower curtain		
Accessories		
Other:		
DECORATIVE		
Vases		
Lamps		
TV tables		
Mirrors		
Area rugs		
Baskets		
Clocks		
Window treatment		
Louvered blinds		
Accessories		
Other:		
GENERAL		
Furniture:		
Closet/storage:		
Luggage:		
Exercise/Sporting Equipment:		
Stationery:		
Hobby:		
Other:		

lapmats, bar *needs,* televisions, stereos, and video systems, in addition to the traditional silver and china.* As I have said, there is no *Groom Magazine* to develop an equivalent primary fantasy for men.

In *Cosmo* the "Commitment Dodgers" article is subtitled, "If Your Lover Ducks and Hedges, Can You Possibly Pin Him Down?" Note that the underlying assumption is that he's the problem. If an article in *Playboy* were titled "Commitment Dodgers: If She Won't Commit to Sex When You Want It, Can You Possibly Pin Her Down?" it would be considered male chauvinist and verging on rape. If we were labeling women "Commitment Giants," *Fortune* might feature an article like "Commitment Giants: If She Tells You She Loves You, Don't Take It Personally—She Just Wants Your Bank Account."

Commitment to an exciting career man whose income can allow a woman to have the luxury of choosing a career by option is still prevalent as the female primary fantasy in almost every medium that sells best to both girls and women. It would be unfair, however, to suggest that women are attracted only to men who fall within a success framework. We can find in what sells to women and in women's actual behavior a secondary fantasy.

What makes it secondary, and how does the primary fantasy and secondary fantasy relate to intimacy and love?

The Secondary Fantasy Versus the Primary Fantasy

A Woman's Secondary Fantasy

Sometimes a woman will recall affairs that were purely sexual: "They had nothing to do with commitment, attachment, his status, or whatever—I just liked our chemistry and his body and I wanted a good time. If anything, he was the one who wanted commitment." As she says this, she convinces herself she is free from the primary fantasy, that she loves sex and ideally would like more of it—both in quality and quantity. If this man does

---

*The female fantasy, like silver and china, also serves men, just as the male fantasy of sexuality also serves women. The difference between a primary and a secondary fantasy is the difference in importance attached to each fantasy by each sex.

not meet her primary fantasy *in addition to* her sexual fantasies, though, rarely will she consider commitment to him. Which is why this is her secondary fantasy. And why she can legitimately say "if anything, *he* was the one who wanted commitment."

The Club Med Syndrome

> *"One day she tells me, 'I can feel my sexual openness to you will increase if I just feel more secure—if I have a commitment.' Yet she told me once about the time she went to Club Med and had passionate sex with four different men in a week."*

Hank, thirty-two

Why is it, Hank wanted to know, that his future wife, Linda, didn't need commitment to really open up at Club Med, but needs it with him? I call it the "Club Med Syndrome." Consider the woman's side of this.

Many women approach Club Med wanting to experience what it would be like just letting it all go. No reputation, no expectations. "This time *I'm* going to experiment . . . even use men. I've never had a surfer boy before." As a result, many report they are as orgasmic and sexually open as they've ever been. But when a woman returns home and meets a man she is interested in for a long-term commitment, and he is less certain than she, she finds herself less open than she was with a Club Med stranger—yet she honestly knows she would open up should he commit.

The woman is caught between two cultures. The first is her natural self, which the Club Med "island-no-money-primitive setting" is calculated to tap into; the second is her socialized self, which was taught to associate sex with love, and in the context of which she may consciously or unconsciously use sex to gain commitment.

She tries to achieve this commitment by being "all-out" one day to "show him how good it can be," as one woman put it, and by withholding the next day so he'll be tempted to commit to "get it good again." These "all-out" and "withhold" feelings may appear manipulative to a man who's had enough experience to know the pattern. But for a woman, they may be so built-in that they accurately reflect her inner conflict of cultures—one day she may genuinely feel "all-out" and the next day hurt by his not wanting more. Women's socialization keeps these feelings very much in tension; men's does not. Rather than assume it is conscious manipulation, it is important for a man to understand a woman's conflict in cultures. Mixed socialization produces mixed messages. Conversely, it is important for a woman to understand how a man can feel manipulated by her alternating behavior—even if manipulation was not her intent.

Let's take a look at what happens when primary and secondary fantasies fall short of reality.

When the Primary Fantasy Tumbles Down

Women's primary fantasy is of marriage to one man who is able to provide security, in which she has the option to devote energy to work, home, children, or a combination thereof, as she chooses. Ideally she wants her secondary fantasy as well: excitement, passion, respect, attention, romance, gentleness, and firmness from this one man. Often, however, the man is too busy providing her primary fantasy to fulfill her secondary fantasy. She fears that if she expresses this dissatisfaction, her primary fantasy will also come tumbling down. So, both disappointed and depressed about repressing her dissatisfaction, she resorts to female "pornography" (romance novels, soaps, and *Better Homes and Gardens* centerfolds), or she has affairs with someone more exciting. If that doesn't work, she may sharpen her work skills and gain advanced degrees while she is still married.

Then, she can reassess her options. If her disappointment has leaked out and her primary fantasy has been dissolving, she may work on ways to achieve for herself what he did not provide for her. Rarely, though, will she have developed the financial tools he has developed. Instead, she has developed a different set of tools: self-improvement tools. And yet self-improvement tools by themselves don't guarantee big bucks in the job arena. So always lurking in the background is the old magical tool: the man on the white horse.

A blend of the old magic and her new self-reliance prompts a new search: The "yellow brick road to self-improvement." "Self-improvement" seems to imply a new role for the man. The yellow brick road—or magic—seems to imply the old role for the man. Let's look.

The Yellow Brick Road
to Self-Improvement

What is common to the following "self-improvement" articles in women's magazines? "How You Can Lose 10 Pounds in 10 Days (Without Dieting)"[11]; "Big Money Careers, M.B.A. Not Needed—Financial Jobs in Which Women Can Out-Fast-Track Men"[12]; "Low Calorie Gourmet Cookbook"[13]; ". . . How to Win People Over in Seconds Without Saying a Word (. . . a little paint, properly applied on a woman's face . . .)"[14]; "I Lost 283 Pounds"[15]; "Conquering Your Shyness: At 23, 35 or Even 55"[16]; "Essential Career Readings: Business Buzzwords."[17]

The common denominator is the "do it without work," the magical quality to these articles, which imply "You can have it all." Imagine *Esquire* printing an article, "I Lost 283 Pounds." Or *The Wall Street Journal* promising the ability to create fundamental personality changes—"Conquering Shyness"—no matter what the executive's age. Or *Forbes* telling men they can lose 10 pounds in 10 days without dieting. Or *Fortune* suggesting buzzwords as career readings. Such articles would not be subscription grabbers, but rather subscription stoppers. They are comparable to a greasy snake-oil salesman's offering bottles of cure-all serum from the back of a truck. What he promises he cannot deliver.

Perhaps the greatest harm to women comes when these magazines, one and all, including *Cosmo,* are called "self-improvement magazines" by people who should know better—like the publisher of *Ms.* magazine. By offering a woman the illusion that she has improved, such claims cause her to become impatient with a man who "does not improve." She does not understand that for many men "those who can do, do; those who cannot do, talk." Many men respect other men who shut up and act, so when women talk about self-improvement they cringe—they are reminded of men who are "all talk and no action." And when this gut reaction on a man's part combines with her criticism of him for not improving himself, he withdraws from her—the same way he withdraws from his braggart male friends.

The male-female tension about self-improvement is best illustrated by a couple I met in 1976, the year after *The Liberated Man* was published. Wilma had come to my workshop after reading the book. She felt she had been "helped beyond belief." What had actually happened was "the workshop illusion."

What is "the workshop illusion"? Feeling she had changed so much, Wilma now wanted Raymond to change "just as much—to keep up with me." It sounded like a reasonable request, so Raymond tried. From Raymond's perspective, though, Wilma had changed very little. He felt that Wilma's major change was that she was more demanding of him. As a result he felt *his* response to her new demands was the biggest change that had actually taken place.

The belief in magical, overnight change is not a harmless fantasy. Rather, it raises expectations of our partners, makes us more demanding than our own real change warrants, and makes us self-righteous. The combination wreaks havoc in relationships. And workshop leaders who play into it are letting their egos interfere with reality.

What Does *Romance* Really Mean?

If a woman has security but lacks excitement, she can turn to "female pornography":

Item: Forty percent of all American paperback sales are romance novels.[18]

Item: Seventy-one percent of romance novel readers have jobs outside the home.[19]

Item: Between 98 and 99 percent of romance novel readers are women[20]—a total of approximately 25 million women.[21]

The number of women who read romance novels—25 million—is almost fifty times greater than the number of *Ms.* readers. *Romance novel readers are the real women's movement*. The 98 percent female readership represents the real gender gap.

One of America's most respected and popular romance novelists is Danielle Steel. Let's look at the message to men reflected in the role of males in her books. The following descriptions are taken from the sales brochures, which are what initially sell the novels.

In *Now and Forever,* heroine Jessica has an extramarital affair with Ian. Ian soon has another affair and is charged with "rape!" The exclamation point is there in the sales brochure. Does she leave Ian and return to her husband in remorse? No. After the rape charge Jessica finds herself "only beginning to learn the power of her love" for Ian. The point is not whether Ian committed the rape—it is that "rape!" with an exclamation point sells to a female audience.

In *The Ring,* the male hero is a Nazi officer whom the heroine, Ariana, falls in love with and marries despite her anti-Nazi family's disappearance as a result of the Nazi activity. She is described as "saved by" the Nazi officer.

In *Remembrance,* Serena is rescued by a "wealthy American officer" after her aristocratic family has lost its fortune in the "turmoil of post-World War II Italy."

In *Remembrance* and *The Ring,* being an officer is primary fantasy material—but only when the setting—the stage—is war. What type of message does this give military men about the value of peace?

In *To Love Again,* Isabella "finds herself in love with the man who wants to destroy all she has left of her husband." In *Thurston House,* Sabrina falls in love with the fiercest rival of her late father. In *Crossings,* a wild and impulsive love for an American steel magnate destroys the heroine's "devotion" to her husband.

What is the message to men? Once a woman has her security needs met, she'll be off with someone else who is really exciting—a steel magnate or a "rapist." And someone who will destroy her love for the man who was devoted to her.

How do men pick up these messages when it is women who read the romances? By the distance they feel when they are not exciting enough, or their rejection by women if they don't have their success act together—not rejection or distance from *all* women, but rather the women they are taught to want most—the women who have options.

In *Thurston House,* Sabrina is flashdanced to control of a mining empire at her father's death. Because of her education, experience, and savvy in the mining field? Hardly. Sabrina is eighteen. In *To Love Again,* Isabella is flashdanced to become the sole head of a successful fashion business when her husband is killed by terrorists (which makes his death glamorous). We see, then, a fantasy of male death bringing female fortune; male death flashdancing women to power and status.

Of course, the fantasy parallels real-life examples. In real life, almost all of America's one hundred wealthiest women made their personal fortunes on their husband's or father's death, and many women with power flashdanced to it on their husband's death, such as Helen Copley, who quit her job as a secretary when she married the president of Copley Enterprises and flashdanced to president of Copley Enterprises on her husband's death, or female U.S. Senators such as Muriel Humphrey, elected with no prior experience upon the death of Hubert Humphrey; or Margaret Chase Smith, elected after the death of Senator Smith; or Katherine Graham of the *Washington Post*, or Joan Kroc of McDonald's.

Reality is one thing. But what will men think romance is when they learn 25 million women are reading these as their have-it-all fantasy every year?

Is this fantasy of the romances or soaps, that male death equals female power and fortune, any better than *Hustler* magazine's infamous front cover that processed a woman through a meat grinder? *Hustler* claims the picture was not fantasy, but rather a self-denigrating mockery of their own meat-market approach to sex. But suppose the image served both purposes? Both images involve death—hers through a meat grinder for male pleasure, his via terrorists for female pleasure. Yet the woman's death is rightly condemned as the worst category of pornography. The male death at the hands of terrorists is called romance, akin to love.

Sexual Harassment Versus Sexual Flashdance

Item: Harlequin Enterprises is an old company, but until the early seventies it was only moderately successful. In 1970, the net earnings from sales of Harlequin Romances were $110,000. By 1980, they were over $21 million.[22] An increase of 20,000 percent.

What created the sudden 20,000 percent increase in Harlequin's profits? The working woman's romance formula. The formula? A heroine who holds a dull to moderately creative job is "come on" to by her older, wealthy, handsome, and powerful employer (or financial equivalent). She repeatedly resists him. Then he confesses the depth of his love, his desire for happiness ever after—marriage.

As in the movie *Flashdance*, the male employer comes on to the female employee. In lawsuits, such "coming on" is considered sexual harassment; by definition, it is considered a misuse of his power. When she resists and he persists, as in both the movie and the Harlequin formula, it is an even clearer form of sexual harassment.

Why is sexual harassment the subject of a lawsuit in one case and a female fantasy in another? When a woman buys a Harlequin romance, the male employer, after a battle of wills, as in *Flashdance,* eventually becomes the man on the white horse (or black Porsche) who flashdances her to a more exciting career, tossing in marriage and love to boot. Since she is married to wealth, she now has the option to quit.

The female reader may well have faced the reality of divorce. Her fantasy must now put her in a better position than the pain of her last divorce. The Harlequin formula does just that: *she has been flashdanced by him to independence of him.* She has the option to quit the relationship in wealth, not poverty—with top-notch job experience, not secretarial experience.

Does the Harlequin fantasy of the working world include a woman's being valued as a person in her own right? Often. How? By being applauded for her performance on a tightrope—showing her independence, daring, and talent—but there is a safety net underneath that few notice. Her safety net is still his underlying financial support. Since she does not view it as a safety net, she feels justified in criticizing him as too preoccupied with his work. Her fantasy never involves having to support him financially.

The Harlequin romance doesn't stop here. Its formula allows a woman the *fantasy of real power—excitement, independence, and security—without having to work so hard for power that her femininity gets lost in the process.*

If femininity got lost in the pursuit of independence, a woman would lose power (because real power means having control over one's life), which is having the option to work and not to lose one's gentler side. Protection from tragic outcomes—like the loss of femininity in the pursuit of independence—and safety and stability are what Harlequin romances are about.[23] Even much of their cover art—borders within borders—reflects this protection.

What does the female reader fantasize she will give in return for these options? Sex and perhaps beauty. But in her fantasy she gets sex, and *always* gets male beauty (she never fantasizes ugliness). She fantasizes getting more than she gives. For example, it is never a reader's fantasy to give a man the option to quit. And it is never her fantasy to work hard to get to the top, then have an affair with a male employee whom *she* flashdances to the top, then marries and protects while he quits work to care for their child.

How can she justify this gap? By an underlying belief that her body is worth more than his. As is her sexuality. Especially if she is beautiful.

Does the more ''sophisticated'' woman outgrow these attachments to this flashdance to independence? Some do—some do not. *Playgirl* did interviews with professional women who are ''Hooked on Romance: One Out of Three Women Reads Over 50 Romance Novels a Year.''[24] The interviewer asked one woman who read between forty and fifty romance novels per *month* if she had ever found a man she thought she could love. Her answer was one word: ''No.'' In response to ''What do you do for a living that gives you so much time to read?'' she answered, ''I am director of securities [naming a Fortune 500 company], corporate vice president.''[25]

''Did You Ever Think You'd Be So at Ease in a Man's World?''

Repeatedly, when women are pictured ''making it'' in a man's world, there is a hint of sexuality and almost always a hint of beauty. For example, note the position of this Calvin Klein woman in the *New York* ad below.

New York, April 4, 1984

Note that her legs are spread open; she is on her back. Her face does not appear focused on management decisions. And now for the copy: ". . . so at ease in a man's world."

Falling into Bed within a Framework

What do the ten sexiest men chosen annually by *Playgirl* from 1983 to 1985 have in common? All thirty have wealth, status, and "power." There's Boy George and George Bush; Bob Hope and David Bowie. Would George Bush be picked out from a crowd of men for his sexiness were he not vice president? Pets-of-the-Month and *Playboy* centerfolds do not have to be famous. Or powerful. They can be, but they don't have to be. The framework is different. Imagine *Penthouse* or *Playboy* choosing Betty Friedan and a famous female transvestite as two of the sexiest women of the year?

Look at the subtle ways this message is run throughout videos and movies. Rent a videotape of *Reds*. Observe how Diane Keaton breaks up with Warren Beatty, then agrees to go on a trip with him to the Soviet Union purely as a professional colleague. She retains her professional distance every second—until he gives a speech and is hailed by the Soviet audience. Her eye contact changes. The next scene they are in bed together.

Does this hold true for the younger generation? Let's look.

Would You Give Up Your Boyfriend for a Star? Or What Does the Rock Star Symbolize to Your Son?

Somehow boys are still not getting the message that sharing the housework turns women on. Instead they hear the message that *the best foreplay is success*. Here's how they hear it. . . .

In a promotion for the rock group Motley Crüe, a San Antonio rock station (KISS-FM) asked listeners to answer the question "What would you do to meet the Crüe?"[26] The winners would get free concert tickets, and some would meet the Crüe. Be warned. The responses are X-rated; to be honest, I was shocked.

We'll start easy . . . sort of. A fifteen-year-old wrote, "I really like Vince Neil's body. When he's on stage he wears a bunch of spikes and leather pants." She explains she would have sex with Vince Neil's best friend to meet the Crüe— "even if it would mean losing my boyfriend." She would also do "it" with "the ugliest, fattest, most disgusting guy in the world" if it took that to meet them.

The interviewer called the girl, as he did the other respondents, "Are you for real?" Her response: "I meant what I said. I know they're grown men and I'm only fifteen but so what?"

One thirteen-year-old girl volunteered to spread whipped cream all over her body and have Vince lick it off. When she was called, she said, "I wouldn't make the same offer to my boyfriend I made to the band. It just wouldn't be the same with him."

One mother, who described her sixteen-year-old daughter as a "very Christian girl," read and mailed the letter in which her daughter wrote, "I would tie you up, spread-eagle and naked, with leather straps. Then I'd shave all the hair off your chest, and if I should nick you, I'll suck up all the blood."

A fourteen-year-old boy offered his thirty-four-year-old mother. The mother was called. "Yes. I approved of his letter." Why did the boy offer his mother? Even at the age of fourteen the boy sensed he did not have access to men in power—but a woman might.

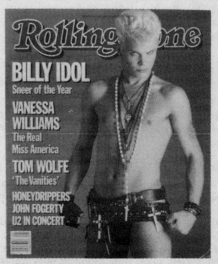

Rolling Stone, January 31, 1985

What makes these men so appealing to enough women between thirteen and thirty-four to gain the Motley Crüe millions of dollars? What makes a fifteen-year-old girl say, "They're like God, but even better"? Is it the sadomasochistic elements of whips, chains, leather, and spikes? Or, to mention other rock stars, is it Ozzy Osborne's biting off a dove's head, Alice Cooper's tearing chickens to pieces on stage, or Billy Idol's (subtle last name) gold crucifix earrings and phosphorescent rosary beads?[27] Hardly. *If these men tore poultry apart in their family's chicken coop, they'd get ostracism, not sex.*

It is only if these acts translate into publicity and if the publicity results in an audience (it helps Ozzy Osborne's career if he almost dies of food poisoning from eating a live dove), that their perpetrators become stars and get women. Then Billy Idol can walk into a restaurant, be surrounded by groupies (or, as he prefers—"dodgey birds"), look at the most beautiful, say "Let's go down to the men's toilets," and one minute later have her follow him through the men's room door.[28–29]

It is only if publicity succeeds in creating the star that a sixteen-year-old girl will want to suck the star's blood. This is what I mean by "falling into bed within a framework." Or, in the case of the women wearing white wedding dresses to Billy Idol concerts,* falling in love within a framework.

A boy gets the message, then, that though looks are ideal, if he is successful, he can be the "ugliest guy in the world" and his fantasy woman will have sex with him just to *meet* him. The message is that women may miss male gentleness, but only because it is missing in the men they choose—men who bite off doves' heads. He learns that if he develops gentleness but not success, he'll probably get rejected by the girls to begin with, and if he doesn't get rejected, they'd leave him for a success at a moment's notice.

The Female Frontier: Forbidden Love

What is the appeal of "forbidden love" in both preteen romances and award-winning adult romances?† For the *most* at-

---

*The wedding dresses commemorate his video "White Wedding," in which the bride drives away in a gleaming black Rolls-Royce.

†*Forbidden Love* is the title of a Sweet Dreams preteen romance and a dominant theme in *Rangoon* (New York: Avon, 1985), by Christine Monsoon, who won the 1984 Romantic Times Award for "Best New Historical Author."

tractive girl in the Sweet Valley High romances, no *boy* is enough of a challenge. Just as no frontier on earth is enough of a challenge for the modern male hero. In *Too Good to Be True*, Suzanne, a newcomer, is more attractive than any girl anyone has ever laid eyes on. Even the cool, sought-after Bruce Patnam is turned to putty by her charms. Suzanne has clearly never had a challenge—a real frontier. So she challenges herself by hugging, then kissing, the school's best, most respected *teacher*, Mr. Collins, described as a "Robert Redford look-alike." He gently but unequivocally refuses to go further. Suzanne has never known rejection. She is determined to make Mr. Collins pay, so she retaliates by accusing him of molesting her. Fortunately, Suzanne is caught stealing, and soon the truth is found out.

If this is the Bad Girl way of conquering forbidden men, what is the Good Girl way? In *Deceptions*, Elizabeth "would never cheat on Todd, her steady." But along comes "fabulously wealthy and extremely handsome" Nicholas. So Elizabeth says, "Well, just once . . ."

In such story lines, there is a positive morality: the power of beauty can be taken too far; it can be misused. The eleven-year-

Working Woman, November 1984

old girl learns how she can both use and abuse her body and her beauty—and what prices and costs different types of uses and abuses have. But she also learns that *unless she is beautiful she is not even a player*. At least, not for the most competitive and successful boys. And she learns that the most beautiful girls, like the most powerful boys, are always conquering new frontiers: if not a Kennedy, then an Onassis. The distinction is between the good and bad ways of getting heroes—the off-limits and within-limits heroes. But no one questions the primary fantasy—conquering the hero. Nor the primary means: beauty. Or that the *best* beauty can venture into frontiers not reachable by ordinary beauties.

Power Tools

Does the new woman dance her part in the sex-role dance with new steps—or the old ones? Does she focus on internal beauty and find that men do not respond? Does she use honesty rather than flirtation, and find she has no men to be honest with? Does she hope to be loved for her independence and search for men who can express dependence? And if she hopes for all these things, are her messages to men consistent with that hope?

Let's start with what happens behind her locker room door—the development of "beauty power."

Beauty Power: The Three Career Opportunities

Why does advertising for beauty products and fashion occupy approximately 90 percent of the full-page ad space in at least a dozen of the best-selling women's magazines? What *is* the power of beauty power?

Beauty power provides three types of career opportunities. First, Max Factor explains, it helps her succeed in business. "That great career look—from sassy to sophisticated, here's how to show you mean *business*." A detachable eight-page "career booklet" in *Cosmopolitan* gives the woman her "Make-Up for Success Guide."

There are four rules for success (see reproduction opposite). Three of the rules involve "making sure your lips always look and stay luscious." Examples:

- Rule 1: *Outline your plan of attack. Line lips with a Lip Contour Lining Pencil. . . .*

- Rule 2: *Make sure your beauty lasts through the day. . . .*

Cosmopolitan, September 1985

A woman also gets "secrets" for success—she needs a "well-stocked briefcase" with tools to be "in control" at the board meeting. What tools should be in her briefcase? The tool of "Unshine® 100% Oil Free Blotting Powder." Does this mean she should have just the superficial appearance of control? Oh, no, a good foundation is important. What type of foundation? The type over which she can put Maxi-Fresh Blush.

Is this just the "hype" of the ads? No. Check out the only article on "Getting Ahead at the Office" in the same issue. Is the image (see illustration below) one of intense work-consciousness?

Cosmopolitan, September 1985

Isn't this woman just "putting her legs up, as any man would do"? Why does it have to imply flirtation if a woman does it? Isn't that sexist? The power of "studied casual" beauty and body language is the power of sending off multiple messages and claiming innocence. As Jontue perfume puts it, "innocence is sexier than you think." Studied innocence can be an effective cover-up. What we see in both the articles and ads is how pervasive is the training to use beauty and the hint of sexuality as tools in business success.

Back to the career guide. How is a woman instructed to show she's done a good job? Here's how: " . . . whether you're making a point at the podium or holding a coffee cup, your hands will show you're doing a beautiful job." Only if she uses the correct nail enamel. She is told this look "turns business into pleasure."

And so we begin to see the connection between a career in business and a career in men (husband as the source of income).

The career guide shows pictures of men touching a woman at business meetings. And her eye shadow (see illustration below), called "eye for success," features names such as Lavender Kiss, Goldilocks, Silver Fox, and Stormy Weather that are not in the Harvard MBA curriculum.

Cosmopolitan, September 1985

A career in men might be called "custom eyes for custom home." In a different ad, Revlon explains what a woman's "custom eyes" are designed to achieve. Look at the names of the colors from which she creates her "Custom Eyes": Billionaire Blue, Prosperous Plum, Society Mint, Black Diamond. How does she get these billions? Well, she can choose Shy Brown. . . .

If she perfects her beauty, a woman can enter the business of beauty—the third career opportunity—which can mean (as with Christie Brinkley) both becoming a multimillionaire and marrying a multimillionaire.

Sociologist Jacque Lynn Foltyn has found that despite our focus on female achievements in areas other than beauty, the most common denominator for women appearing on the cover of

Time magazine is the woman's status as a professional beauty.[30] Is this changing? Yes. Between 1975 and 1985 beauty has been a *more* important factor than it was previously. One front cover of *Time* chronicled a major feminist convention, headlined "After Houston." Did *Time* select an acknowledged feminist leader like Betty Friedan or Bella Abzug? No; they selected a very attractive unknown blond woman. Why? Covers with attractive females sell best to *both* sexes.

If beauty offers women so much power, why don't women have their own equivalent of the Super Bowl, which exemplifies the competition for power? They do . . .

The Female Super Bowl

The Super Bowl is watched by about 75 million Americans, mostly men. The "female Super Bowl"—the Miss America contest—is also watched by about 75 million Americans, about 75 percent female.[31] The Miss Universe pageant is watched by *600 million* viewers—in fifty-one countries. Beauty is an international passport.[32]

Are beauty contests dying out? Hardly. In the United States alone, there are 750,000 beauty contests for women each year.[33] The fact that the number entering the Miss America contest at all levels has almost doubled in recent years, to 80,000, tells us of their endurance.

Why are more women watching these beautiful women than are men? Because both sexes are careful observers of the contests played out by their own sex. Each sex studies the tools that bring us our primary fantasies. So a man watches the Super Bowl and a woman watches the beauty contests. Most men don't know the meaning of the Red Door (Elizabeth Arden's salon) and can't tell a hairstyling mousse from a hairstyling gel. And most women think the ERA is just an amendment and that Montana is just a state. We all pay closer attention to our own power tools.

The Birth of Beauty

Bert Parks emcees the International Kiwanis Little Miss Peanut contest, offering $10,000 scholarships to eight-year-old winners. And *Newsweek*[34] reports four-year-old Mandy Bennet crying for an hour when she lost the Little Miss Pink Tomato contest in

Hooper, Utah. But what could be expected—she lost to a girl in her prime, Mandy Rankin, age two. And then there are baby and toddler pageants . . . based on talent, of course. Some of these girls—still children—have three hundred crowns and two hundred trophies.[35]

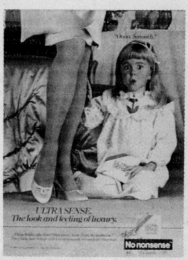

Ms., January 1985

The babies entered into beauty contests are not the only ones with parents who teach them beauty power. Studies show mothers hold, kiss, and cuddle attractive babies more than less attractive babies and, more important, tend to limit their attractive baby's development in other areas by neglecting, for example, to offer such stimuli as challenging toys.[36]

The Female "Line"

What is the subliminal message female makeup delivers to men—a message men reinforce by choosing "beautiful" women? From eleven to seventeen years old, a girl learns in a million ways to "look natural by being artificial." A boy is learning, subconsciously, that her makeup is the female "line"—what she "says" doesn't ring true. Makeup is her lie, her deception, the equivalent of his bragging or exaggerating. The sexes learn not to trust each other. Which is one way sex-role training becomes divorce training.

The Female Locker Room: The Red Door of Vulnerability

A 1985 study found that "if they had to do it over," 97 percent of women would spend as much time as, or more time than, they do on appearance.[37] Appearance was only one of twelve areas of life about which they were asked this question. No other area ranked even close in importance to appearance. The study, reported in *Good Housekeeping*, gives us a hint about the connection between appearance and achieving the primary fantasy of better homes and gardens.

Suppose a woman isn't naturally beautiful. Can she "makeup" the difference? She is told she can.

In women's magazines we find two female equivalents to the male locker room: woman-to-woman talk about men, and women applying makeup and face masks, in the process of "becoming beautiful." Men are absent in the full-page ads of women applying makeup. One female equivalent of the male locker room is "Behind the Red Door," the symbol of the Elizabeth Arden Salon—the home of female secrets, where the competitors let their hair down. Female vulnerability is pimples, curlers, bags, and sags. A woman's techniques for obtaining her primary fantasy are hidden from male eyes, just as men hide their strategies for obtaining their primary fantasy of having sex with attractive women.

Exactly what happens behind the Red Door? Although it features eighteen steps, the Elizabeth Arden ad on the following page only scratches the surface. The eyes are not even mentioned—and for the eyes alone there are not only eyeliner, mascara, and eye shadow, but numerous double-page Elizabeth Arden ads devoted to one eye product alone, such as Eye Fix Primer with Primilin III (see *Self*, June 1984), which serves the sole function of preserving the eye shadow.

Where does the working woman get the time for this? And where does the nonworking woman get the money for this?

Vogue, October 1984

The Female Western

The Female Western is the battle between the good and evil methods of getting the men who perform best. But whether good or evil, the top female players are all beautiful. Whether Alexis the Scoundrel or Krystle the Almost Pure; or in the preteen romances, Jessica the Ruthless, or Suzanne the False Accuser of Mr. Collins. In both scenarios, from evening soaps to preteen romances, inner values are for losers. Unfortunately, the only game in town is still beauty for women and performance for men.

Among the teen romances there are almost no positive images of girls who think, who are intellectual, who question the larger system, who run for student body president, or who mow lawns or babysit a few extra times for the purpose of affording tickets to take a boy out. Perhaps most sad, even the good girls rarely understand anyone who deviates—either in looks or in attitude.

"Beauty Power"? Bull—All This Emphasis on Beauty Makes *Me* Feel Inadequate

The irony of power is that both sexes often see themselves as powerless in exactly the area in which the other sex sees them as powerful. Why? A woman sees the inadequacy of her breasts next to ideal breasts. Commercials bombarding her with the ideal weight, rear, hair, and skin keep her aware of her imperfections even as she is actually making herself thinner, firmer, and more "perfect." A man is exposed to commercials of the ideal female as well; if he meets a woman who approximates that ideal, his mind calls up images from millions of commercials, making him feel nervous and unworthy. Most men around a very attractive woman feel the way a fan feels around a movie star—grateful for a second of attention. And they sense they must prove themselves before they can be expected to be treated as equals.

Women see male external rewards as power. When confronted with images of male success power, the average man sees his comparative inadequacy next to these powerful males and feels powerless. The average man does not feel more powerful because of Michael Jackson's power. The fact that it takes six Grammies in one night to get Brooke Shields to fly across the country to be his escort does not leave most men much hope of gaining the acceptance of the most attractive women unless they produce more than they already have. A man may in fact have more money, or a higher position, than the woman, but he may also feel powerless next to his "movie star" ideal male image.

How does this happen? When *Playboy* takes 6,000 shots* for each centerfold spread, and when movies substitute pictures of a different actress's buttocks so we won't see the imperfections in the rear of the star, we get some idea how every woman who looks at a centerfold feels inadequate next to the airbrushed best of 6,000 photos and replaced rears. This faked image is true with hairstyles too. Remember the hairstyle on the "career-for-commitment's-sake" *Cosmo* woman? Notice how little has changed from the hairstyle of this *Vogue* model (opposite) from May 1967. *Vogue* was kind enough to show us how the hair got that way!

On the one hand, female checkbook stubs are a clear statement

---

*The Canadian National Film Board cites 22,000 snapshots. The *Playboy* photo editor, Gary Cole, could not confirm that number. Based on information from him, my estimate is 6,000 snapshots.

Vogue, May 1967   *Vogue*, May 1967

of the value women as a group place on the power of beauty. Yet
for any given woman these constant images of beauty only make
her feel more inadequate—powerless. And they make any given
man feel powerless next to her—unless he compensates by earning his Grammies.

If a woman values the leverage beauty can gain for her, can't
an increase in beauty give her more self-confidence—and make
a man feel like "more of a man" pursuing her?

If Beauty Gives a Woman Self-Confidence,
Why Should That Bother a Man?

The beauty-focused woman who depends on men to "tow my
car," "pick up my presents," and pay for the dates pays a high
price for her dependence on men. Her life cycle is often one in
which she feels less happy the older she gets. With the woman
less focused on beauty the opposite life-cycle pattern occurs: she
learns to depend more on herself, often getting happier as she
gets older.

Beauty *can* offer self-confidence. Anything that offers approval can offer self-confidence. Gang leaders gain self-confidence
from approval. (*West Side Story* is the story of the search for
approval.) But to channel children into gaining self-confidence
by making them dependent on something they will have less of
with age (gangs or facial beauty) is self-destructive. To say

nothing of its shallowness. The impact on men is to be married to women who become more dependent with age.

"The beauty-focused woman has the most sexual problems and simultaneously most denies her sexual problems," Dr. Gwen Leavesley, a gynecologist who directs Western Australia's Family Planning Association, says. "When I ask her if she has orgasms, she is the most likely to say, 'It's not relevant.' She has the most difficult time opening her legs for vaginal exams, and tends to find problems with each type of birth control as an excuse not to be sexual. Among beauty-focused women, the one who has the most difficulties opening up is the one who sees her beauty as essential to her climb to the top—such as an ambitious fashion model."[38]

If beauty-focused women are the most likely to close off sexually, and if most men learn to desire sex with whatever version of beauty is being competed for most, we have the perfect lose-lose symbiosis. The most beautiful women feel the most objectified—because they are—so they close off. Other women feel left out.

For men the gap between desire and fulfillment creates a pressure cooker. And the man's role of taking initiatives and receiving rejection puts an aggressive anger (as opposed to her passive anger) in his pressure cooker. If there is no outlet, the ultimate explosion can be violence, one form of which can be rape.*

Isn't It Wonderful That Older Women Are Models Now Too?

Dynasty's Joan Collins, fifty-one, and Linda Evans, forty-one, and *Dallas*'s Linda Gray, forty-four, are considered role models. But for what? For the dream that beauty can get diamonds and oil barons for twice the number of years as they could before. If a woman marries the right oil baron, she has two power options: to be homemaker with oil baron's money, or to be an empire builder with her husband's or ex-husband's money. If she is the latter, soon no one will ask how she got the money originally any more than we question the original source of the money for the Nobel peace prize. Now, beauty can get her indirect status or

---

*See Chapter 8, "Why Did the Sexual Revolution Come and Go So Quickly?," for the stages that lead to rape.

direct status, indirect power or direct power—as long as the oil baron flashdances her past the hurdles. This reinforces beauty power; I predict it will create even more hurt, disappointed, and frustrated women who will postpone even longer preparing themselves for financial independence from a man and dream instead of independence *through* a man.

Can we develop alternative images? Yes: women who are attractive yet make it *from scratch* (sometimes supporting a man along the way, other times not); women who are sometimes with a man, sometimes without one, and just as happy either way—and sometimes with a woman, without its being a big deal. Other alternatives are women who are not so attractive, who do any of the above. I am not talking about Eleanor Roosevelt, whose *initial* credibility as a national figure came via her association with a man. I am speaking more of the Shirley Chisholms, Mary Lou Rettons, and Bella Abzugs, the Cathy Guisewites, Betty Friedans, and Ursula Fairbairns; also of women who are internally happy without ''making it,'' the unsung heroines. None of these women signal to men the need to be oil barons.

Power Tools: Love and Money—or the Appearance of Love and Money

Love as a Power Tool—Or Falling in Love with Love

If love can lead to Lenox and diamonds, it is potentially a power tool.[39] Would love ever be used so cynically? Let's see. In *Working Woman* Silences perfume advises ''Live like you're in love and you will be.'' Is the woman learning to give the appearance of love rather than real love—as a way of getting a man to ''love'' her? *If she does not really love him, what is the purpose of this love?* Is the appearance of love a power tool to get security?

In men's magazines women are pictured looking adoringly at men, while the man is looking away from her, indicating that the man is in control. In women's magazines, the man looks at the woman and the woman looks away, indicating she is in control. Both get their control by offering something. We saw this in Chapter 2 in ''The Hint of Sex Brings the Lenox of Love'' in *Seventeen*—in which a girl is offering the appearance of mischief to get love. If we look in *Working Woman*, we can see how this message gets refined as a woman becomes older and works—she now offers a more explicit hint of sex (half-naked nymphs and a half-naked self), but since the sex is more explicit, it should attract male wealth (tuxedo). As an adult she offers the imagery of love (just as the girl offered the appearance of sex), to attract a man. The hint of sex and the appearance of love together lead to control.

Working Woman, November 1984

In both ads, he looks at her; she looks away. And in neither does the man serve the purpose of companionship alone. He leads to the Lenox of love or the tuxedoed wealth of love. *Which is why men are both women's primary fantasy—and also part of the primary means to her primary fantasy.*

The White Shoulders ad is no coincidence. It is one of the longest lasting and most widespread of ads. Check for it in *Cosmo* or *Working Woman*. The primary fantasy is the same.

So while in men's magazines success is a power tool to get sex and love, and therefore the ''look of success'' is crucial, in women's magazines love and sex are power tools to get success—

and therefore both the "look of love" and the sexual tease/ promise are crucial. If a woman gets the formula down, she is promised a life of "love"—meaning total security and wealth— via a man. In this way love becomes a power tool and a woman is taught to fall in love with security— euphemism "love."

Love and Money—or the Appearance of Money

The Cosmo Cat . . . with a Moneyed Voice

The *Cosmo* article title: "Pass Yourself Off as a Woman of Wealth." The subtitle: "Longing to Mingle with Moguls and Millionaires . . . ?"[40] How is the woman instructed to look wealthy in order to get wealth? She can:

1. Take a limo to the airport when meeting a rich, *eligible* out-of-towner. "He'll love your thoughtfulness and the 'fact' that you're a woman of means." (Funny, weren't men supposed to be threatened by successful women?)

2. When you're short of money "say you're *not* going to Rio or Seychelles as planned." *Cosmo* discusses how valuable it is to drop the names of various places a woman is *not* going.

Among the other pieces of advice? Here are some of the section titles: "Develop a Moneyed Speaking Voice," "Be a Client of Big-Name Professionals," "Have Fascinating Friends," "Talk about Mummy and Daddy" ("They travel a great deal and are thinking about buying a house in Sardinia"), "Use Britishisms" ("I know an awfully nice little man who repairs zips"). The final section: "Watch Out for Fortune Hunters."

Sandwiched within the article is a box, saying: "Read Your Fate in Tea Leaves." Within the box is the *Cosmo* symbol, a cat. The article on tea leaves explains how tea leaves that fall into the symbol of a cat indicate treachery. In my opinion, reinforcing the stereotype of woman as treacherous is not the sign of—in *Ms.* publisher Pat Carbine's words—a "self-improvement magazine." Nor does it meet *Cosmo*'s own standards of "We don't play games."

Vulnerability—or the Appearance of Vulnerability

She Gets Love by Messing It Up; He Gets Love by Performing

LOVE IS ALWAYS
FULL OF
SURPRISES.

Love's Baby Soft
Nothing feels as good as Love.

Seventeen, December 1984

How does Love's Baby Soft woman (see ad above) fall in love? She falls. Literally. It used to be "she drops hankie; he picks hankie up." Now she just drops herself and he picks up the whole hundred pounds. As she falls and he rescues, she falls in love. Or perhaps she fell in love first and then fell. . . . Either way she "falls in love" by messing things up; he gets love by performing. She is like the Zena jeans woman who plows into a Yale Law grad and gets *love and status* in one fall. The competition to mess it up is fierce. How to succeed in business by falling—in love.

"How to Turn a Crush into the *Real* Thing"

Seventeen[41] gives women three steps to "turn a crush into the real thing": (1) Smile. (2) Become a master of eye contact. (3) Learn where he works or what his schedule is so she can create an "accidental meeting," such as buying aspirin if he works at the pharmacy. Never is she instructed to initiate by beginning a conversation. Only if all else fails should she add a "hi" to her smile.

Is this because a young girl cannot absorb anything too complex? Hardly. Two full pages of detailed steps tell her how to apply makeup. No steps tell her how to take *direct* responsibility for a conversation. Direct responsibility makes a person truly vulnerable—to rejection. Creating "accidental meetings" allows her to *appear* vulnerable to his "come-ons"—and claim to be pestered by "the employee at the pharmacy." So if it works well, she can have her man; if it doesn't work well, she can report him to the head of the pharmacy.

Suppose a crush doesn't turn into the real thing by saying nothing? When she grows up, she can be a "new woman." *New Woman* magazine features an alternative: "The Power of Seduction at Your Fingertips."[42] But suppose flirting, accidental meetings, and seduction all fail? *New Woman* poses the hard question: "Should You 'Be Yourself'? (or Will Taking on Another Personality Make Your Life Terrific or Even a Little Better?)"[43] That's the "new woman"?

How to Think

"Making it in a man's world" without depending on sex or beauty power requires a complex blend of conformity and independent thinking. While some of the articles, especially in *Ms.*, encourage this, a common denominator of women's magazines is the quiz—from *Redbook* to *Self* to *New Woman* to *Playgirl*. Quizzes are fine, except there is almost always, in examining the answer choices, a correct selection. *Ms.* rarely, if ever, presents "right answer" quizzes to its readers. Articles, rather than quizzes, provide the "right answer" in *Ms*.

How does this relate to men? Women often accuse men of being dogmatic. People who look for the "right answer" find people who are dogmatic.

The Victim Dictum: "I Found Myself . . .";
"It Just Happened . . ."

The Zena jeans teenage girl *"finds herself"* plowing into a Yale Law School grad. The Sweet Valley High girls "find themselves" in dangerous positions with men with whom they "find themselves" going too far; *Ms.* women find themselves in dead-end careers, blaming male chauvinism, male patriarchy, the male system, and even male mentors—but never their own Cinderella ads—for holding them back.

For how long are women taught to use this "victim dictum"? Joan Collins teaches women that if they do the job of setting themselves up to be "come on to," they can sit back and "watch something happen" well into their fifties.*

In men's magazines such phrases rarely "find themselves" into print. Instead, phrases like "find a way" or "make it happen" happen to appear. The first phrases, when used frequently, are signs of victim dependence; the second, signs of independence.

Power Tools: Sex—or the Hint of Sex

Are our daughters subject to pressures to use their sexuality artfully and indirectly—or honestly and directly? Are they encouraged to take sexual initiatives if they desire sex, *so that even the absence of any initiatives is an implicit no?* If women say no and mean no, why aren't men listening?

The male misuse and abuse of sex has become *the* emotional topic of the eighties. Let's see if the women's magazines can give us a hint about the message men hear from women about sex.

Sex for Security

What message does the married woman receive about sex? Or should I say, what is the message the married woman *chooses to purchase* about sex? Claiming she only receives these messages is part of the "victim dictum." It is also condescending to women. Look in *Woman's Day:* "Can We Still Have Sex?:

*See "The Art of Building His Fire," page 87.

Don't Let a Heart Attack Ruin Your Marriage."[44] It does not say, "Don't Let a Heart Attack Ruin Your Enjoyment of Sex." The concern is more with a source of security, marriage. Imagine *Esquire* featuring an article, "Can We Still Have Sex?: Don't Let a Heart Attack Ruin Your Marriage." If *Playboy* concerned itself with marriage, it would be, "Will Marriage Ruin Our Sex Life?" The difference in priorities points up the difference between the male and female primary fantasies.

If sex is secondary to security, how does that account for *Playgirl*? What is most significant about *Playgirl* is how few women read it. *Playgirl*, like *Savvy*, has fewer subscribers than either the *Mother Earth News* or *Workbench*[45] and with *Playgirl*, half of the subscribers are not women.[46] No wonder *Viva*, formerly *Playgirl*'s only competitor, went out of business.

Ninety thousand women responded to Ann Landers's question, "Would you be content to be held close and treated tenderly, and forget about 'the act'?" The 70 percent of women who said "yes" would seem to be content without sex.[47] Notice how the word "sex" is not used to describe sex. What most surprised Ann Landers was that 40 percent of the women who would be content without sex were under forty.

Most men don't read even popular findings like this. They don't read "women's columns," "women's magazines," or "women's romances." These messages are transferred to men only indirectly, as in the De Beers Transfer. So a wife's "sex for security" feeling may be picked up by her husband subconsciously, but neither the sports pages nor the front pages articulate these feelings, so he soon skips over them. The price of men getting in touch with these feelings will be a series of new questions, like "Is our lovemaking her way of keeping her security blanket?" Or "Does she want me for me as much as I want her for her?" That is, "If we weren't married would her sexual interest in me suddenly drop off more than my sexual interest in her?" These are "male questions." But then again these are male feelings.

How to Flirt

"Getting ready for a social event without thinking about how you're going to flirt, or if you're going to flirt, is like ironing a dress and then not wearing it."[48] So advises *Glamour*, the second-best-selling magazine in the fantasy-not-yet-fulfilled category, in an article on flirting.

Guess what the setting is in this article on flirting—would you believe a business convention? Featuring Cheryl, a woman described as "average-looking," but who has three great-looking men pursuing her at the business convention. Because she knows the fine art of flirting. Which is . . . ?

First rule: "Picture a moth near a flame, as it dances in and out." That first move (dancing in) is "when you are as assertive as you are ever going to be." So much for assertiveness training. The second move? "A complete back-off." The next rule is to alter her normal rhythms of behaving; for example, "in that split second before you pass the salt . . . lock eyes for a half beat." The key to all this? "Keep all your actions a little ambiguous . . . be a bit evasive."

What is the attitude a woman should hold if she is to flirt effectively? At first, she is told: "Flirting is child's play" (after all, she is only dealing with a man). Later, it gets more serious: "You should think of flirting as you would a job interview." Of course. It *is* a job interview.

What is confusing to men at Cheryl's business convention is that they are told Cheryl's primary focus is work. A man can be sued, demoted, or not promoted for failure to recognize this. Yet Cheryl is portrayed in the article as using business as merely one more arena for getting a man. Remember that identical message from *Cosmo?* These are the two best-selling magazines to women in the fantasy-not-yet-fulfilled category.

Wife Beating Versus Violence as Sexy

Looking for Mr. Goodbar catapulted Richard Gere to stardom and made his name synonymous with erotic violence. Yet the two movies that put him on the front cover of *Newsweek*[49] as *the* symbol among male sex symbols involved another portrayal of sex, violence, perpetual life-risking, and, finally, insane self-destruction *(Breathless)* with the actor's ability *also* to be *An Officer and a Gentleman*. Gere was able to pull off appealing to both fantasies. Most men find it hard in real life to kill women *(Goodbar),* be an officer and a gentleman, self-destruct *(Breathless)*, and still make the front cover of *Newsweek*. In real life there are shelters for men who batter women—jails. Yet most men would not protest the female approval Gere generates. By 1986 that approval was coming from *Ms*. magazine,[49a] which also featured Gere on the front cover. He was interviewed by Gloria

Steinem and touted as the possible new male hero of the late 1980s.

Male violence is declared sexy not only by box-office sales, *Newsweek* covers, and Danielle Steel romances of Ian the Rapist, but by serious nonfiction, like that of feminist writer Rosemary Daniell, whose popular *Sleeping with Soldiers* was published in 1985. The macho man, the man who kills (as in soldier), who "sometimes displays a *brutal* brand of male chauvinism," is found to appeal to such feminists. Appeals sexually—as in *sleeping with* soldiers. The book was promoted under the headline "Is the Macho Man Today's Prince Charming?"

On the one hand, I condemn this attitude in that it glorifies behavior which is punishable as rape. It is one more way of saying, "Risk your life for me—be a man." On the other hand, here's some honesty, finally—acknowledgment of the conflict within women about men, an honesty that allows men to acknowledge the conflicts within themselves. Both sexes must begin by acknowledging their internal conflicts before we unravel our society's rape socialization.

Nowadays, Girls Don't Have to Worry about "Reputation" and Things We Worried about When We Were Young—Do They?

The plots of preteen romance novels say a great deal about female sexual socialization—and the roles expected of men. Girls read all this much more systematically than boys. In *The Wrong Kind of Girl*, another Sweet Valley High romance for eleven- and twelve-year-olds, "Easy Annie" learns only one thing can ruin the power of her beauty, talent, and spirit: a bad reputation—meaning the same thing now as it did in 1950 and 1850. "Easy Annie" will be kept from becoming a cheerleader because, if she gives it away too easily, it will ruin the other cheerleaders' images. The eleven-year-old female reader learns not too subtly that if her body is not kept in scarce supply, she will be psychologically killed (the teenage definition of not being accepted). She learns about the existence of the "female mafia," without its ever being labeled as such.

Are the sought-after boys in the Sweet Valley High romances those boys who are respectful of the girls' more cautious attitudes toward sex? Do the girls reward the boys who pay attention to their messages of caution by paying more attention to those boys? Hardly. The most sought-after boys are boys like Scott and Bruce. The burning question in *All Night Long* is "has Jessica gone too far with Scott?" In *Playing with Fire*, it is "has Jessica gone too far with Bruce?" *The boys the girls seek out pay the least attention to the girls' nos*. They are willing to challenge the female mafia's stronghold—they "play with fire" and challenge the girls to stay out "all night long."

While male adventures pit man against nature and death, Sweet Valley High romances pit girl against male and sex. Any boy who doesn't create this tension is not worth being sought after by a female heroine. Keeping boys coming after her body and keeping them from going too far is the age-old game of *Playing with Fire*. The game the eleven-year-old girl is excited about enough to keep some of the country's best publishers churning out competing thirty-volume series of these romances by the multimillions of copies. It is a game that starts at age eleven. Does it continue in college? And how long does it last? Let's look at the female mafia in college years and Joan Collins's version of "how to build a fire" at fifty-one years.

The Female Mafia

Item: *Cosmopolitan*, September 1984. The lead cover story: ". . . Make Love the Old-fashioned Way. Make Him *Earn* It!"

Isn't this concern about reputation outgrown, at least by college? It appeared that way in the sixties. And it seems that way today, when many female college freshmen go on a sex spree. But a research assistant of mine, Michie, explained that when she engaged in just such a brief spree shortly after entering a prestigious Eastern university, she was quickly labeled a slut and therefore backed off. I began to inquire whether this was also true out West. I heard stories of women publicly chastised in open forum meetings for being too promiscuous—not by administrators, but by the most popular and attractive women and their henchwomen: the female mafia. I began to see that the spree was a brief period during which women were acting on the rhetoric of sexual freedom, believing it was only their "awful parents" and the closeness of the high school female mafia that confined them, but soon discovering that in the absence of their parents a new female mafia had formed at college.

There is a male mafia that fuels the female mafia. Paul, a summer intern who had just completed four years in the dorms, described how the boys on his floor would pass judgment on certain women as "too unattractive" or "too not with-it." A scholarly type, Paul had felt attracted to two "girls" in this category. The male mafia put pressure on him to stop dating one "girl," although he sacrificed the mafia's approval in that case; in another case Paul admitted he had never even asked Sharon out because it was not worth the disrespect, mockery, and cold shoulders of the guys on his floor. Note that the male mafia censures men who choose women who are not attractive enough, because the man would be giving away what he has to offer for too little in return. Both sexes' mafias control their own kind by not letting a person give away what he or she has to offer without getting some of the primary fantasy in return.

The Art of Building His Fire

Want to be a Scoundrel? Revlon hires Joan Collins to instruct. A woman is told implicitly that, even at age fifty-one, if she thrusts one shoulder forward and lets her dress fall off the other, wears the right perfume, the right diamonds, and gets high on a magnum of champagne, she can build his fire, sit back, and "watch something happen." This is the receptive initiative: because she is teaching women to be passive and to lead all men to be active—so that she can reject all men except the one with whom she chooses to be active—this is the perfect formula for "leading him on." Does this ad appear in *Cosmo?* No. In *Working Woman.*

Joan Collins is considered a role model. What profession is she training women for? Of course, no one's quite sure whether the game is "how to keep a reputation," "how to build a fire," or "how to make a fortune." Or whether they're all the same game: access to men who compete the best and perform the best. That means the future lawyers and doctors.

Reputation as caution. Caution as fortune. Packaged as morality.

"No" Means "Maybe" Means "Yes" . . . Maybe

Go to your local video store and rent a few movies for a rainy Sunday. In both *Body Heat* and *The Verdict* observe a woman being approached by a man. She makes it crystal clear she is not

Working Woman, September 1984

interested. Eventually they go to bed. Is that the point? No. We later find out that in both movies, she was after him even before they met—even while she was saying "no." So we learn no means maybe means yes. In both cases she could say no only because she was beautiful, sexy, and indirect, and because he could be counted on to pick up subliminal cues and keep initiating—with no awareness of how his socialization to initiate made him vulnerable.

How early do girls learn this message? Open up *Seventeen*.[50] Or *Teen*.[51] Coty's Nuance perfume puts it into words. "Nuance always says Yes. But you can always say No." Does the message stop at *Seventeen*? Take a look at *Glamour*'s Nuance ad.[52] "Nuance always says Yes. But you can always say No." Same message, older woman. Judges are called male chauvinists if they suggest a woman gives mixed messages. Yet *Seventeen*, *Teen*, and *Glamour* are paid for by over four million girls and women (or their parents) each month—females learning to make their nuances say yes while their words say no.

Why can't Nuance find a market among *Forbes* readers with an ad saying, "Nuance always says Yes. But gentlemen can always say No"? What do men have to offer that might have an

Seventeen, December 1984

equal impact, if they promised it and withdrew it? Commitment. Imagine an ad saying, "Remind her of commitment with a Zirconian diamond. You can always tell her later it wasn't for real." Or "Zirconian always says Yes. You can always say No."

Social Rape

Rape socialization? When twelve-year-old girls are taught to let their nuance say yes while their words say no; when violence is sexy; when the boys who get the most attractive girls' approval are the ones trying hardest to break through the barriers erected most successfully by the most attractive girls in the name of morality and reputation; when "rape!" carries an exclamation point because it increases the sales of Danielle Steel novels; when *New Woman* advises on the power of seduction and *Cosmo* on the power of making him earn it; when eleven-year-olds call *Playing with Fire* a sweet romance . . . when all these are part of our everyday socialization, is it any wonder that a large UCLA study found that 54 percent of boys and 42 percent of girls felt it was okay to force a girl to have sex under certain circumstances?[53] Or that *Cosmo*, after promoting seduction, then cries "Social Rape: When Seduction Turns to Horror."[54] Who are we kidding when we act confused about why America has one of the highest percentages of rape of any country in the world? The instructions for it are sitting in most American living rooms at any given moment.*

*See Chapter 8, "Why Did the Sexual Revolution Come and Go So Quickly?"

3

The *Flashdance* Phenomenon

In tribal myths and Greek mythology, as scholars such as Carl Jung and Joseph Campbell have documented, some themes are enduring. One is the theme of men competing to get a woman's attention and avoid her sexual rejection. In American society, movie stars are the equivalent of the Greek gods, and these themes are played out in both the conscious story lines and the subliminal messages of the most powerful and popular movies— whether it's Fred Astaire pursuing a resistant Ginger Rogers in *Top Hat*, the boss in *Flashdance* pursuing a resistant Jennifer Beals, Superman performing his way to Lois Lane, or Madonna's boyfriend *Desperately Seeking Susan*.

If this theme has been with us so long, why question it now? Because, in the course of evolution, this theme meant that men competed with each other, often killing each other off, and the survivors and heroes produced offspring with the women considered most desirable by that society's criteria. Nuclear technology has made this system outmoded almost overnight, because the process that formerly allowed the fittest to survive and breed now would kill off everyone.

The "enduring theme" of male competition and female competition for the hero/survivor has taken us from the fittest surviving to the brink of no one surviving. Sex roles have gone from functional to dysfunctional almost overnight. That is why the enduring theme must be questioned now.

In the last chapter we saw about fifty examples of how the female participation in this theme is still with us (e.g., falling in love within a framework).* But how do these themes work together as a whole, in the context of one male-female relationship? Let's look at America's most enduring myth, *Superman*, and a current adaptation, *Flashdance*, to tap into how the theme operates on the conscious and unconscious levels in male-female relationships.

One caution. We are told fantasy gives us hope. But when fantasy leads us in the wrong direction it dries up hope, which creates depression.

The Flashdance to Liberation

Both *Flashdance* and *Superman* involve working women. Theoretically this should reduce men's performance pressure. Does it? Let's start with *Flashdance*. *Flashdance* features the mid-eighties version of the liberated woman. The film catapulted Jennifer Beals from an unknown to what *People* magazine called "the image of her generation."

Beals lives alone (with a dog) in a Pittsburgh loft. She bikes to work, weaving fearlessly among cars like a Jedi among trees. She holds a second job by night—as a dancer in a sleazy nightclub. Somehow she works out in between. And somehow, she choreographs her complex and brilliant evening acts between her welding, dancing, and working out. The urban single version of Superwoman.

Yet our welder/dancer dreams of performing as an art—as in formal ballet. Dancing for the critics and wine sippers, not the beer guzzlers. She has never taken a lesson, but her talent at disco dancing is raw and real.

How does Superwoman achieve her goal? By giving up her welding job and taking formal training? No. By keeping her welding job and saving her money to train? No. Her handsome, black-Porsche-owning, mansion-dwelling boss sees her dance. The man on the white horse is replaced by the man in the black Porsche. He pursues her. She turns him down. Quickly. Curtly. He pursues repeatedly. She insults him. Why? "I can't go out with the boss!" she claims independently. In mock frustration

---

*For the male participation, see Chapter 4, "Why Are Men So Preoccupied with Sex and Success?"

the boss responds, "Have it your way. You're fired. I'll pick you up at eight tomorrow evening."

Now, here's the rub. She's *not* fired. Nor did she for a second respond to his declaration with the look of someone who thought she was fired. So she goes out with him after all, and keeps her job. We discover that a man unwilling to take no for an answer will ultimately get the woman who may, in fact, have been willing all along (of this we're never certain—being certain would spoil the mystery). Her beauty and talent allow her to be successful at playing harder to get. As her black woman friend points out, letting the man do all the pursuing, playing hard-to-get, playing pseudoindependent, never risking rejection directly— that's "the honky way."

If she had really given up her job to go out with the boss, we could appreciate her sticking to her principle. If she had kept her job and refused her boss, we could appreciate that. But when she keeps her job and dates the boss, her constant rejection of him is not independence, but rather performance pressure to see just how long and hard he will pursue, to see just what a fool he will make out of himself for her.

It is one more condition. She can avoid responsibility for the potential conflict of interest by passing it on to him. The probability that they both do this unconsciously makes it all the worse—unconscious behavior must become conscious before there's hope of stopping it; performance pressure is only exacerbated by a lack of consciousness or perspective about what one is doing.

Of course, this never would have worked were she pimple-faced and plump. And he would not have stood a chance had he not been recognizable to her as "the man who signs my paycheck." But it wasn't just that he was successful and wealthy. He had become successful and wealthy precisely because he never took no for an answer. Whether it was her no or the nos of the work world. So, the more attractive and sexy woman isn't always conscious of choosing only successful men. But if she's beautiful she often unconsciously protects herself with a certain aloofness to keep away "every male welder."

Which man gets past this aloofness? The one whose name appears on her paycheck, the one who is unwilling to take her nos seriously. So, unwittingly, she selects a man who has developed a combination of status and a willingness to hold her nos in contempt.

Why, then, should she expect him to be the type of man to listen to her in any other area?

Men who watch this movie learn unequivocally that ignoring women who make their lack of interest crystal clear is self-defeating. That they'll miss a beautiful, tender, and powerful romance with a gorgeous and sexy woman. In other words, a sexy woman will reward you if you ignore her nos. Sound like rape training?

Our pseudoliberated heroine still dreams of dancing. She finally goes for an application. But when she sees the competition, she runs away. When she finally returns, she is handed a ten-page application and asked to fill in her years of experience and training. She is competing not for a job, but merely for the audition, with hundreds of others. It is obvious she stands no chance.

However, the man in the black Porsche once again appears (a device developed by Greek playwrights—"deus ex machina"). He secretly calls a contact on the arts council. He gets her an audition. But she discovers his interference. Outraged at his insensitivity to her need to "do it for herself," she jumps out of his black Porsche in the middle of a tunnel as he begs her to return, cars swirling and screeching all about them.

If she in fact went on to pursue the dancing career by herself, it would be independence, not pseudoindependence. The struggle would be slow, involving years of training at the ballet barre not the corner bar. *She would have to confront every priority and value in her life.* She does none of this. Instead, she puts on a charade of independence and then takes the audition arranged by the man with the right contacts. And, magically, she does marvelously.

Now what message does this offer? Simply, *if you do take the help of "the man in the black Porsche," be sure to let him know he's putting you down by helping you, then you'll be able to take the miracle he's created, and retain your pride.* This miracle will come to you if you're beautiful. Beauty is the credential that attracted him. Then, because you've been a good girl and worked hard at other things, like welding or barroom dancing, without any formal education or training, without years of work like hundreds of other women and men—you will overwhelm everyone. After all, you deserve it—the other women don't.

But we have numerous new twists to this "liberation." In the process of "refusing" to take the arranged audition, the level of his insult to her integrity justifies her slapping him, throwing a high-heeled shoe in his face, and slugging him. How often? Eleven times. Count them. This does not count the brick she throws through his mansion window.

Imagine Alan Alda dreaming of getting a Ph.D. A lover offers him a way to get it quickly—through her help. He slugs her for the insult. And then slugs her again. And again. And then he accepts the Ph.D.

This sham independence is an insult to every woman who has worked to "make it big." I was married for ten years to a woman who is now a vice president at IBM. Working until 5 A.M. and getting up to return to work at 7 A.M. was not unusual for her. For years. In the process, she was supportive of my work—or she felt conflicted when she was not. But sacrifices were made. Her dance to the top was a slow dance, not a flashdance. And as every woman who has ever slowdanced to the top knows, when another woman snatches up a position via her sexual connections to a man, she forces everyone else to work that much harder to get the remaining positions. If there are any. Flashdancing is discrimination against the working woman; it is also discrimination against the working man on the basis of his sex. It makes people feel hopeless. Yet we call *Flashdance* a fantasy. For whom?

All of this creates one more pressure on men—now we must provide not only for ourselves, we must make miracles happen for our women's egos as well.

A woman's becoming successful overnight is like expecting a man to become sensitive overnight. Yet the *"Flashdance* phenomenon" reinforces the ethic of magic without work repeatedly. At eighteen Beals is a welder. There is no hint she is a novice. Exactly when did she have time to get her apprenticeship? *Flashdance*. The poster headlines: "Take Your Passion and Make It Happen." Yes. Pull your sweatshirt off your sexy shoulder. And wait for the One Minute Manager in a black Porsche. Take your passion and *let* it happen.

The Return of Superman, or Clark Kents Finish Last

Perhaps the most prevailing expectation of men is our Superman expectation: the fear we are merely Clark Kents who won't be accepted unless we are a Superman. This myth is usually looked at only from the perspective of how the man puts this pressure on himself—as if that pressure were in isolation.

Has the pressure to be a Superman diminished now that women are working and don't need rescuing? The answer is made clear in *Superman II*, in which, as in *Flashdance,* a man encounters a working woman. Is the working woman attracted to a warm, sensitive, vulnerable man like Clark Kent, a good, solid reporter who's as handsome as Superman, but without the invulnerability? No. While that might have been good enough for a woman who *didn't* work, the working woman can expect more. We see her condescending to Clark Kent, a symbol of the normal man, a bit bumbling, mocked when his back is turned. Lois Lane is portrayed as having no sexual interest. The message to men is: If she's attractive and working, he'd better be even more successful to awaken her sexually. (Also a message to—and a pressure on—women.)

How successful should he be? Well, for starters, he should fly. His body should be bulletproof, but his mind sensitive. He should never let on about these talents, but should be so brave at just the moments her world is falling apart (as symbolized by earthquakes, for example) that his hidden talents will be discovered despite his attempts to cover them with phone booths.

But he must do more than expose himself to assorted telephone directories before disasters. He must:

- Have intergalactic ESP that focuses on Lois's needs despite all impending disasters, always managing to handle *both* Lois' needs and the disaster (Lois is not selfish).

- Have eyes *only* for Lois, rather than all those beauties who don't know the weak, namby-pamby Clark Kent parts of him—which she accepts only when she knows he is also Superman (when she tells him his gentleness is endearing, he feels accepted by her, which gives her power over him).

- Be unafraid of commitment—commitment to Lois, of course—giving up all fantasies of other women (the other career women back at the office will be so envious). Of course, this is for his own good—*they're* only after his stardom. "Keep saving me, Clark: should my career fail, should we have children, should those nasty earthquakes come back again. . . . Oh, a white horse would have been so insufficient. . . ."

No wonder women are disappointed in men. Even angry at men. Next to Superman, there's a lot to be disappointed in! I made note of my feelings on a napkin when I left *Superman II:* "On the one hand, want to fly through the air/save world—other hand, feel strangely incompetent."

There was never a hint Lois would fall in love with just the reasonably competent career man, Clark Kent. And if she had, would Lois ever have suggested using her income to support him—even for a year—while he took care of the children and did the housework? And if Lois had gotten a commitment from Superman himself, can we imagine Lois having a *fantasy* of financially supporting Superman while Superman retrained to become a sensitive, underemployed artist?

All of this, though, is just entertainment if it doesn't translate into reality. Let's look at reality. Christopher Reeve, who is bland enough to play Clark Kent, becomes a national sex symbol, which he never had been before. And the image faded as he played other parts. But as long as he was attributed Superman-like qualities in fantasy, he became a sex symbol in real life. In other words, we can say, "Oh, Superman's just a childhood fantasy—no one takes it seriously." But, if that were the case, Christopher Reeve would not have risen and fallen as a sex symbol in direct proportion to the degree of his association with Superman. Fantasy does become reality, but in the cruelest of ways—leaving women unfulfilled by real-life men, and men who become heroes loved more for the fantasy they fulfill than for who they are.

Women's depression about real-life men has many outlets—from withdrawal from men to the female versions of pornography—romances and soaps. When reality reveals a man is not a Superman/rescuer after all, the romance novel rescues a woman instead. The romance novel does not force her to choose between her primary and secondary fantasies. It says, "You can have it all." If, in real life, you only have your primary fantasy—*Better Homes and Gardens* and *Family Circle*—you can feel okay about having an affair with an exciting man who, by the way, happens to be the man who will give it all to you, even though at first he might appear like Ian the rapist, a Nazi officer, or a Clark Kent.

How can deserting a male security blanket be justified? In some cases, via disappointment and anger. But in many romances, as we have seen, the man's leaving can be justified only by death. And if he dies, it is core to the romance that his death bring her a fortune; her husband's disappointing her Superman fantasy justifies her death wish.

(Jules Feiffer, *Explainers*, pp. 12, 13.)

Note that the woman still marries the man who rescues her. But now she protests his role (as in *Flashdance*) prior to marrying him for his role. In the final frame, note who has, in fact, made the change.

The consequences for men? His performing will ultimately lead him into fights over limited resources, or even into fights over being a better hero than another man ("My religion/ country/ race/ideology/team/theory is better than yours"). His need to be the Superman will lead him into making promises he cannot keep. In politics, Jimmy Carter was very much a Clark Kent, Ronald Reagan very much a Superman, who promised to "make America great again." The electorate, both male and female, very much a Lois Lane. Just as both sexes vote for the beautiful woman, so both sexes, like Lois Lane, vote for Superman.

Are These Images Changing for Younger Men—and Women?

Young men have not had a chance to earn their way to career success, and ten- to fifteen-year-old girls are not into worrying about how they'll finance their lives, via their own efforts or men's. So how does a teenage boy earn his access to an attractive girl? We can check that out by looking at some popular younger females' actual reactions to perhaps the only movie ever produced at the request of and with the cooperation of a high school, *The Outsiders*. The hero of *The Outsiders*, Matt Dillon, became the heartthrob of teenage and prepubescent females of all socioeconomic backgrounds.

What role made Dillon such a heartthrob? A modern version of James Dean as he appeared in *Rebel Without a Cause*. He's introduced as the handsomest of the greaser crowd (from the wrong side of the tracks), his hair is greased back, he is the escaped convict type, eligible for "Most Likely to Be Psychopath."

We first see Dillon coming on to a beautiful cheerleader type, from the "society side of the tracks," at a drive-in movie with her girlfriend. A gang of greasers sits menacingly behind them. Dillon spots the beautiful one. He comes on. She resists. He comes on stronger. She pulls away. He puts his face and body in "her space," pushing her menacingly, putting her down every time she gets turned off. She's trying to keep her cool, but the viewer can cut her fear with a knife as she anxiously scouts for a way out.

How scared was the cheerleader? She reveals the depth of her fear to Dillon's buddy. "Keep that guy away from me, you hear? You hear? I don't ever want to see him again, never . . ."

"Why?" Dillon's buddy asks.

"I'll fall in love . . ."

I saw *The Outsiders* with my woman friend, Anne, and her daughter, Megan, who was ten at the time. Megan had not yet learned to cover up her feelings with what's ideologically correct. Two days later a poster of Matt Dillon appeared on her bedroom door (Megan's, that is!). Alongside it went a poster of Scott Baio, who looks like Pat Boone with Latin blood: warm-eyed, tender, handsome.

The next day, Megan and her twelve-year-old girlfriend were giggling next to the posters of Baio and Dillon. I joined in their kidding, and asked, "If Matt Dillon and Scott Baio wanted to kiss you, and you could only kiss one of them, who would it be?" Without a second's thought, they both shouted, "Matt Dillon!" I pursued. "If they both wanted to marry you, and you could only marry one, who would it be?" Not even a second's thought: "Scott Baio."

Anne and I rolled our eyes, and then broke up with laughter. The ultimate irony—two "egalitarian-oriented over-thirty adults" with two preteenagers already desirous of the delinquent hero for a kiss, and the tame hero for marriage.

"What are you laughing at?" Megan asked.

"It makes so much sense," I laughed, with a twist of sadness.

"Tell us why we said it . . ." Megan's friend asked.

Oh, boy, I thought. Now I've done it. How do I explain *that* to a ten-year-old? (Meaning: a two-sentence explanation, the last sentence being a joke.)

"Well," I attempted, "you know how when we play hide-and-seek, and the tension builds up, the more difficult I make it for you to find me, the more you dislike it at the time—but later you want me to do it over? Well, in a way, that's what Matt Dillon's like—he gets girls angry, that's like tension—and that makes for excitement sometimes. So a kiss from him might seem exciting, like hide-and-seek. But you saw in Scott Baio a type of gentleness you want to live with. So you chose to marry Scott Baio. . . ."

"Oh—Can we go for an ice cream after lunch . . . ?"

Conclusion to Part 2

What has and has not changed in the past two decades? Reality has changed. The reality, for example, of divorce. As marriage no longer provided security for a lifetime, it appeared women adjusted by "getting into" careers. But when the fantasy—of a career created by one's own efforts—collided with the reality of what had to be sacrificed for a career, it faltered. Yet career was an important safeguard and a highly successful career a wonderful fantasy. So "man as flashdancer of woman to success" began to be an alternative fantasy a man could fulfill for a woman.

The teenage girl's fantasy hero, whether a male hero on the wall, a magical unicorn, or another combination of male and magic, such as a guru, all have yet another advantage to the girl: the association with a successful male image without having to *be* sexual with the everyday man. Sex, like love, was to be saved for a framework—a framework in which magic could occur.

The female primary fantasy, then, changed in only one respect: the women expects more of a man. Different types of women have different expectations: for Ms. Equality, bigger diamonds and salaries, while the man shares housework and exudes gentleness; for the more traditional woman it is four pages of wedding gifts plus income for a lifetime; for the teenager it is Lenox and a Yale law degree. The range is from man as wallet to man as a financial safety net.

What is the best means of attaining this fantasy, as presented in traditional magazines like *Family Circle* and *Better Homes and Gardens?* Always a man. That is, a husband/man. Men and marriage are the means as well as the fantasy. They become the fantasy because they are the means.

Woman, New Woman, Self, Playgirl, Working Woman, and *Ms.* are all creations of the past seventeen years. All are magazines whose primary market is women who do not have men providing the major paycheck. These magazines contain the most anger toward men.* The more the orientation is toward women working and women as independent, the greater the anger. And the greater the orientation toward independence and equality, the lower the sales. In the "new woman" magazines, articles like "That Jerk Wouldn't Commit" portray men as both the primary enemy and the primary fantasy. In the process, the tone of the "new woman" magazines becomes "Marry the Enemy."

The central problem in the fantasy-not-yet-fulfilled magazines becomes how to get a man who is willing to commit to earn her the home, garden, and family. The four best-sellers in this category, *Cosmopolitan, Glamour, Seventeen,* and *Teen,* all answer the same way, as do the romance novels and soaps: femme-fatale it all the way, baby.

How Do Men Adapt to Women?

Every time female beauty is flashed before a man, it raises the value of the slender, made-up, beautiful female. And value raises price. Just as any ad is designed to raise a *product's* price. A perfume ad with a seductively dressed, beautiful woman is also an ad for the female body. The more something is worth, the less likely we are to give it away for free. So why should a woman be "free" with her body when it and a Redken certificate can be traded for a Yale law grad?

Selling a body outright is called prostitution. So euphemisms must be developed: "I don't feel it's moral to have sex *until*: I'm in love . . . I feel secure . . . feel a commitment. . . ." For the male these become the conditions to which he feels he must adapt—since they are not his conditions. The more sex is placed in opposition to morality, the more morality can be used (or, rather, misused) as an excuse to withhold sex. Which turns "morality" into an excuse to have a man earn sex by providing a woman with security. In Chapter 8, "Why Did the Sexual Revolution Come and Go So Quickly?," we will see how this attitude, which seemed to be on the wane in the sixties, has returned in full force in the eighties. And why.

*See Chapter 7, "The New Sexism."

All of this is no easier for a woman, who learns to build security by keeping her body beautiful, only to find herself sacrificing other priorities in the process. She may find herself open with her sexuality when she is with a secondary-fantasy man, and fluctuating between sexual openness and closedness with a primary-fantasy man who is doubtful about commitment.

From the male perspective, when commitment is associated with diamonds and mortgages, promises of love can feel like promises of payment.

Our advertising has assigned the attractive fifteen-to-twenty-nine-year-old-appearing female more power than her mother and more power than most men are ever likely to have. The latest twist is to suggest this power can last into a woman's fifties. Which makes the investment in beauty an even more "worthwhile" investment. And therefore increases beauty's importance as a way of taking a receptive initiative, as in "how to build a fire" and "watch something happen."

Enough beauty may allow a woman to reject *every* man. At every party. Except one man, at one party. Which keeps every man wondering whether he's succeeded enough even to stand a chance should he approach her. Will he, despite his human qualities, be unable to treat her to a ski vacation like the man she met last week? This dynamic creates a devastating impact on the woman as well.

When women are at the height of their beauty power and exercise it, we call it marriage. When men are at the height of their success power and exercise it, we call it a midlife crisis. The wedding is held in a church; the crisis in a therapist's office. "Sow your wild oats," for a man, means "get your primary fantasy out of your system." The equivalent, for a woman, would be "sow your domestic oats"—get married. Marriage usually commits a man to a woman's primary fantasy, though, longer than a one-night stand commits her to his. That's a lot of adapting—from his fantasy to hers.

Is This Men's Fault? Or Women's Fault? Or Are We All Victims of Capitalists?

This dilemma is no one's fault; we are all innocently born into a system in motion. It is also everyone's fault, because men continue to cater to beautiful women, so women continue to buy the cosmetics and diet formulas; women continue to choose from among successful men, so men continue to compete to be within the range of female binoculars. Capitalists will not stop advertising to appeal to the unfulfilled needs of both sexes until women and men stop buying products on the basis of such an appeal. Every time we buy a product we vote for the ad that sold it.

It's easy to blame the capitalist; the top capitalists are almost 100 percent men—all with external reward power—the perfect enemy. *But we forget that* since only 13 percent of top male capitalists' wives work *at all* outside the home,[1] *the capitalist is also a male feeding a female*.

How do men compete to be within the range of female binoculars? Is male competition partly an adaptation to get within her range? I think this consideration helps us understand why women feel there are so few good men—the "Great American Man Shortage."[2]

Where Are All the Good Men?

Dr. Donald Symons found that, cross-culturally, men judge women primarily for attractiveness while women find men attractive only if social, economic, and political status criteria *as well as* looks are met.[3] Women, he found, often perceive a "man shortage" much larger than is warranted statistically—because far fewer men meet their greater number of demands. The graph on the opposite page has been helpful to some women and men in explaining what appears to be the great shortage of "good" men. In future chapters we'll look at how to solve this problem.

In this graph we see a woman's binoculars focused on approximately 10 percent of men: those who come closest to meeting her multiple criteria for her primary fantasy. In the meantime the men, willing to start out by considering any woman who is attractive for a "one-night relationship," focus their binoculars initially on a much larger percentage of women—women meeting that one criterion of attractiveness. So, for example, a woman might warn her friend, "Don't get involved, he's married," meaning she is likely to make that a reason not even to consider him in her "binoculars." Conversely, a man will rarely not go to bed with a willing and attractive woman just because she is married. His binoculars take in a wider number—initially. In part because his initial goal is more limited. For exactly that reason, the more serious things get, the more likely he is to be the one to back off. *He and she become selective at different*

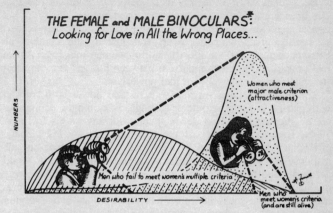

THE FEMALE and MALE BINOCULARS*:
Looking for Love in All the Wrong Places...

Women who meet
major male criterion
(attractiveness)

Men who fail to meet women's multiple criteria

Men who
meet women's criteria
(and are still alive)

NUMBERS →

DESIRABILITY →

*My version of this chart is an adaptation of a combination of Symons's and its adaptation in *Success*, October 1984.

points: she can be selective when he wants his primary fantasy—sex; he can be selective when she wants her primary fantasy—commitment.

The graph can also help us see how male competition can be male adaptation. Men learn they will get rejected less by competing in business and getting within the view of women's binoculars than they will if they ask women to turn their binoculars around, begging, "Consider me—just for a moment. I'm a part-time house painter, but I'm a wonderful human being." Work rejection hurts less than personal rejection. But more important, men feel better able to *earn* work approval than personal approval: "If I meet the quota, I'll make it; if I don't, I should have worked harder." This is one reason men are so preoccupied with success.

Many women have noticed that men often go out with a movie star and marry a plainer woman. Why? We shall see in the chapter on commitment the shift in what becomes important to men once the basic attractiveness criterion is met. But if this is so, why do women put so much focus on substituting hair mousse for chocolate mousse? In part because, like the male focus on work, it is what women can control. Women can play with hair mousse in front of a mirror rather than risk rejection by calling a man.

Both sexes work on their "lines" before they appear onstage. His lines are a lifetime of work; her introductory "line" is her appearance—or her lack of lines. Just as careers give men power, so beauty gives women power. But just as the comparison between herself and the most beautiful women makes a woman feel powerless, so the comparison between himself and the most successful men makes a man feel powerless.

The process it takes for men to earn their power is in conflict with getting in touch with their feelings. Becoming a "computer whiz" did not help Bart get in touch with any of his feelings. When Bart saw pictures of male movie stars on his teenage girlfriend's wall, he used to feel a bit uncomfortable; but his response was just to work harder at the one thing he knew would get him respect: being a "computer whiz." Which was his way of dealing with his feelings—skipping past verbalizing his feelings of powerlessness in front of the movie star, and "solving the problem" by digging in deeper. With his head in the sand, furiously digging to earn respect, he missed the second, third, and fourth components of power: internal, interpersonal, and health power.

Women's *underlying* fantasies of men, then, have not changed. But *both* sexes now expect more of themselves and the other sex than ever before. As the preteen's unicorn is transformed into the man on the white horse, whose current form is the man in the black Porsche, it becomes important to remember that the fantasy, which is often considered harmless, can ultimately destroy both sexes. The twelve-year-old's fantasy that Mischief will bring love in the form of Lenox, and the fifty-year-old's fantasy that "building his fire" will bring "love" in the form of diamonds and mansions, are both setups for a lot of disappointment and anger among women. And setups for men who work to make it as computer whizzes or owners of black Porsches, and who are then confused when they're told they are not vulnerable enough. We can't fall in love with men who appear invulnerable and expect vulnerability. Why did he want a black Porsche? Because he never saw an ugly woman get out of one.

PART 3

WHY MEN ARE THE WAY THEY ARE

4

Why Are Men So Preoccupied with Sex and Success?

"Encore! Encore!" Sixty thousand people stomping their feet, flooding the aisles. Entranced. Enamored. The man focuses the microphone before his powerful lungs. But there is no song. "Here I am, Kathy. The pimple-faced boy who sat behind you in seventh grade. . . . Here I am. Neil—who wasn't good enough to kiss you after class . . . the class frog. . . . Well, your frog has turned into a Prince, Kathy. Kathy, wherever you are—they're eating out of my hands, Kathy . . . eat your heart out now, Kathy . . . eat your heart out . . . wherever you are . . ."

Neil Diamond in live concert
Phoenix, 1976

Like millions of men, Neil Diamond has learned to perform. Most men spend their lives performing—in sports, at sex, on the job—"proving ourselves" in one form or another. Most women sense how often this masks a deep insecurity. Why is male insecurity so great that men will perform to the point of killing—for money, for status, for "power"? Kill themselves and others for what ultimately amounts to only one of five components of real power?* Why do even men working for a "good cause" become furious if the cause is achieved and they are not the ones credited with the achievement? Why do they become attached to supposedly ideological differences as if their personal identities

*See the end of Chapter 1, "The Five Components of Power."

were at stake—turning both Marxism and religion into holy wars?

There are literally dozens of answers to those questions, from genetic to environmental. Here I will focus on three important stages, which are mostly environmental, and which women and men can change more easily than they can genetic and parental influence. These stages relate to the dynamic between almost every man and woman, of no matter what class background or sexual orientation. I will start with the five messages men hear during Stage 1: The Genetic Celebrity.

Stage 1: The Genetic Celebrity

Male Message 1: She's a Genetic Celebrity; I'm a Genetic Groupie

Let's start with Male Message 1. Billions of dollars' worth of subliminal advertising is flashed into the prepubescent boy's unconscious, before his "age of consent," subliminally building his desire for the fourteen-to-twenty-nine-year-old model-type woman—literally advertising *her*. This creates in his young mind the seeds of a fantasy stronger and more powerful than any other. A primary fantasy. We employ every means of technological sophistication to plant this in his unconscious. So that by the time he is fourteen, any girl in his class who looks anything like her feels to him like a movie star, a genetic celebrity next to whom he, a fourteen-year-old, pimple-faced, bumbling adolescent, feels as nervous as a groupie.

The fourteen-year-old boy notices something about the genetic celebrities in his ninth-grade class: They are going out with the eleventh-grade boys. He does not feel equal to the most attractive girls in his class. He feels unequal to his peers. Unless he stands out as a performer. The genetic celebrities might be willing to go out with him if he earns his way to their attention by performing as a football player or class president. He feels desperate. Why? *The girls he has been socialized to desire have beauty power before he has performance power*. This socialization is so powerful that the genetic celebrities in his class can influence boys like a drug. He becomes addicted to an image; anything less feels like an inferior fix.

For decades marketing researchers studying men have found

that *the only common denominator that can appeal to men of all classes is their desire to achieve acceptance by the culture's most "beautiful" women.*[1] Or, conversely, the common denominator is their anxiety about being rejected by these women. (From the marketing perspective, the greater a man's anxiety, the more likely he is to buy the product promising to make the anxiety go away.)

Exactly what makes the beautiful girl/woman image so much more powerful than other products that are also advertised? Other products, like cars or beer, occupy only a tiny portion of our subliminal seduction; the beautiful woman exists wherever a woman is pictured. Why? Because the marketing researcher knows the male does not feel worthy of her. And if the marketing researcher can make the man feel that buying the product will give him hope of being worthy of her, he will buy the product. This is so much a part of our unconscious that we will see, in Male Message 2, how the woman does not even have to be pictured to restimulate his feeling that he will be worthy of her if he does something.

Each culture has a different but overlapping standard of beautiful women. And in most cultures powerful males fight each other to have access to them. Have we made progress in more "civilized" societies? Not quite. In technologically advanced cultures there is an advanced tension: on the one hand, the rational mind has more information to fight this socialized and genetic propensity; on the other, technology is better able to penetrate the rational mind's unconscious. In fact, the desire to think of ourselves as rational often only increases our denial (*"I'm* beyond that . . ."), which puts us more off guard.

Somehow these ads never suggest to the adolescent boy that he search within himself. The boy does not see a model-type woman standing next to a product any man can afford as she is watching a warm, sensitive man reading *I'm O.K., You're O.K.* in an unemployment line. No matter that the man may just have dropped out of a position selling something he didn't believe in and is now struggling to bring integrity into his life.

Male Message 1 is subconsciously experienced by the boy like this: *"Some girls in my class already look like movie stars. If they wanted me as much as I want them, then I'd know I was okay. They are genetic celebrities. I am a genetic groupie."*

How can a woman be expected to believe this about men when she has never heard a single man say, "She genetic celebrity; me genetic groupie''? Remember how, in the 1950s, no man ever heard a woman say, ''*I* feel like I'll lose my identity when I get married''? Yet when the feminist movement articulated it, millions of women felt it rang true for them. In my work with over three hundred men's groups from varied backgrounds, these three stages—and the five male messages—have passed the ''ring true'' test with men. Women can legitimately say they haven't been articulated. If they had been articulated, men would be in touch with their feelings. Instead boys enter Stage 2 unaware.

Stage 2: The Male Search for Equality, or the Way Boys Compensate for Feelings of Powerlessness

How does a boy learn to bridge the gap between the genetic celebrity's power and his feelings of powerlessness? To make him feel less like a puppy dog begging for a morsel? He learns Male Message 2: *''I must do something—perform—to earn my way to equality with the genetic celebrity's first natural resource— her attention. I must defend against the genetic celebrity's rejection by performing to attract her respect.''*

How does he learn to perform? For starters, if she's a genetic celebrity and does nothing, people say she's beautiful; if he's genetically gifted in *any* way and does nothing, people say, ''What a waste.'' No matter how ''powerful'' a man becomes— whether a Neil Diamond, a Henry Kissinger, or a Woody Allen, he started out as a boy, drooling over a Kathy.*

Male Message 2: Perform for the Genetic Celebrity's Attention

I can recall my first three or four girlfriends during grammar school and junior high school. They watched me perform athletically with a special attentiveness. I remember how, as captain of a small summer camp team, I assigned myself the pitcher role. After a few innings I decided it would be nice to give some of

---

*And if he did not, he lived in fear of being rejected by both sexes, his parents, and even himself. Each message that only heterosexuality is normal leaves boys who discover they are gay between a rock and a hard place.

the other boys a chance. I exchanged positions with the second baseman. His eyes lit up. After the game my girlfriend Joann said, "Why did you give up pitching?" I explained. "That's nice," she said, but disappointment flooded her eyes. "The girls thought it was great when you were pitching." I could feel Joann's disappointment, not just in me but in the loss of her status with her girlfriends as "the girl the pitcher liked." I can remember feeling, at age eleven, the pull between the human parts of me and the part that wanted to maintain that look of admiration in her eyes.

A boy learns to perform years before he learns what the performing is for—years before he knows anything about the genetic celebrity, peer-group approval, or parental respect. Both parents teach boy babies to perform rather than cry by picking up the male less frequently than the female infant when he cries.[2] The result? By the age of thirteen months, boys who are picked up less are already more likely to "tough it out" and refrain from crying.[3] By the time the boy child subliminally absorbs the *purpose* of these messages, he is already more comfortable with behavior such as solving his own problems or "doing" rather than complaining or crying.

But now for the tricky part of Male Message 2. If he's learning to be a "doer," what does he do? The surface answer is "look cool and tough." But looking cool is a consequence. If he looks cool and stubs his toe, he's a fool. The real answer? Choose an environment; become its master. Whether in Marlboro territory or sales territory, becoming a master makes him successful enough to buy the car *next to which a beautiful woman stands*. And from success all other forms of respect are derived—from parental approval to peer approval.

All of this could be dismissed as "aren't those ads stupid" if they were not, in fact, reinforced by his reality. By junior high he is observing the most attractive women—called cheerleaders— paying attention to the most successful performers—football and basketball players. When a football player loses his position on the team, he seldom sees a cheerleader run off the field, saying, "Wait, I'm still cheering for you—I love your openness and vulnerability." He notices, instead, that *she cheers for his replaceable part*. He learns, on some level, that *all heroes are replaceable parts*. And so even if he makes it as a hero in his field, he feels insecure—should he lose his position, his loved one will cheer for his replaceable part. She senses this insecurity and wonders how a man can be such a child.

In the process, he is learning many things. He learns it is not popular to verbalize feelings, which he therefore keeps secret, even from himself. He is learning, subconsciously, that *female support, nurturing, is conditional—it goes to the men on the playing field.* Therefore her *support* is really *pressure* to keep performing.

Nor does he ever verbalize the subconscious feeling that the cheerleaders are a socially sanctioned group of females using their bodies to cheer on twenty-two males to their self-destruction. Cheerleading is the socially sanctioned female encouragement of male molestation. The message is that the molested survivor gets the female. It is organized practice for a girl to learn how she can get someone else to take life's risks—preparation for financial dependency.

Not all boys earn attention via sports. For a different type of woman a different type of boy might earn attention by becoming newspaper editor or student-body president. That was my route. For others, it might be speeding in a flashy convertible. Marc, a man in our men's group, verbalized some of his own decisions during a meeting.

The topic was the first crush that we never told anyone about. Marc started: "In the eighth grade I had a crush on Janice. She had a sweet, innocent face, gorgeous hair, and great breasts. At basketball games, I'd watch her cheer. I fantasized approaching her . . . even kissing her. I still have images of looking at her from a distance. I mean, I knew there was no way I could really get Janice to consider me—and if I did, not for long enough to admit I wanted to touch her all over her body. Other girls, maybe, but Janice, no."

"Did you ever try?" Jim asked. "You should have 'gone for it' " was implicit in his tone of voice.

"Nobody in *our grade* was worthy of Janice. She dated Jeff—a tenth-grader and basketball player, I think from a rich family; he got a new car as soon as he could drive. The older I got, the more I noticed who these beautiful girls went out with. Maria was Italian, from a poor family—she was so impressed when Tony became a Green Beret. She fell in love with him. But in college, some of the prettiest girls would hang out at the med school and law school libraries. Or they'd somehow get invitations for weekends with the guys from the prestigious private schools. They'd fall in love with one of them. I was doing pretty well, but I didn't know if I could keep up. I didn't know whether to give up—marry Marge who wasn't so beautiful but loved me and didn't expect all that or hold out and try to make it . . . until I could prove myself to one of those girls.

"Everything I considered to 'make it' had its problems—acting might leave me waiting on tables; politics corrupt; engineering might leave me a bore; the military dead; sports might turn me into an insurance salesman at thirty. It was so overwhelming . . . so lonely. I guess I felt if I married Marge we could make it as 'a team.' "

Marc observed two types of compensations for his perceived powerlessness. Or two types of defenses against rejection from women: short-term and long-term. *Short-term*—like getting on the basketball team, buying a flashy car, or building a muscular body—attract attractive women, but usually only for a short time; *long-term*—like doing well in school, preparing for a profession, or apprenticing for a union job—last longer. When short-term defenses run out and the long-term ones don't look possible, he may try *desperate defenses*—like gambling, stealing, or dealing—hoping to "make it big" quickly. Or he may try a combination of long-term and desperate defenses; if he is caught, it results in a John DeLorean, a Watergate, or an Abscam—all replete with males.

None of these, of course, is necessarily a defense. All can involve multiple motivations. And they can all offer internal rewards, excitement, and respect from parents or peers—just as being a cheerleader can for a female. But all these "male choices" have a different meaning for the male than for the female—even today. A woman is rarely motivated to be a doctor to minimize her rejection from men. Or to assure her of the money to support a man.

This is a boy's perception of what it takes to earn attention. Girls are also desirous of male attention and feel they have to earn it by being attractive enough. Most girls do not feel they are attractive enough to get easily the boys they want for what they want them for. The more attractive a girl is, the higher she sets her sights. For her, there's also a gap. She feels her other options—like becoming student-body president—will not have the same impact on her as on a boy. They may make her respected, but not necessarily more attractive to boys. The girl learns she can fill the gap in a different way.

An ad for cottage cheese says it best. The camera zooms in on the body of a beautiful girl/woman. The old fifties song plays:

She has an itsy-bitsy-teeny-weeny-yellow-polka-dot-bikini . . .
That she wore for the first time today.

How did she finally get into this bikini? The song continues:

She got into this bikini when she ate cottage cheese . . .
So get yourself a body that'll bring the boys to their knees.

Like the average girl, the beautiful girl, or genetic celebrity, also has her own experience of powerlessness. "This guy keeps pestering me," she may complain. "He follows me to my locker, waits for me after school, asks me out, makes comments about me to his friends. . . . I wish he'd just drop in a ten-foot hole." She experiences this as harassment if she's not interested. The average boy looks at this harassment, sees it as attention he would have to work all his life to get. For him, this is just the price of her being a genetic celebrity. Her complaints sound to him like the complaints of a Princess Diana.

Male Message 3: Paying for Female's Sexuality

Both sexes have the desire for attention in common. His first experience of inequality is how much less he feels she has to do to get attention at age fourteen. The big gap starts when he subconsciously feels that he and she want attention for two different reasons—to fulfill two different primary fantasies. Girls want male attention to lead to "dates," going steady, a gold bracelet, or other symbols of her primary fantasy. Boys want the attractive girl's attention for a different reason—physical intimacy.

Boys' primary fantasy—the exchange of physical intimacies—is free for both sexes. The female primary fantasy requires male payments—dinner out, an engagement ring, "better homes and gardens."

When a man hears women speak of "getting a man," the connotation is somehow different from when men speak of "getting a woman." "Getting a man" often connotes getting a relationship; "getting a woman," especially when said among men, usually connotes getting sex ("I got laid last night . . .").

So he begins to learn sex isn't free. He'll give his away for free, but on some level, she charges for what he gives away. So, on the physical level, as well as with attention, he learns: *"I must earn my way financially and/or by making myself a hero to gain equality with her second natural resource—her sexuality."* This is Male Message 3.

Isn't it a woman's company that men pay for, not her sexuality? Think about it. Sue and Linda went to Grey Rocks, Canada, for a ski trip with their two male suitemates, Jeff and Joe. They were each looking for *other* partners; no one paid for anyone's dinner. Then Sue and Jeff found partners with whom they had a *sexual* relationship. Once Sue found a man, her dinner and drink expenses dropped to $11. Jeff's went up to $108. During this period Joe and Linda's expenses totaled about $60 or $70 *combined*. If it was a person's company that was being paid for, Jeff's woman friend would have been paying for his company too.

Playgirl, November 1979

"Today, for Show and Tell, I've brought Uncle Wilbur."

Men spend billions of dollars to expose women's bodies. When they expose their own, they're called exhibitionists. So men learn to fulfill conditions under which their bodies can be exposed without imprisonment.

I showed this paragraph to the woman friend who had asked the question "Isn't it her company that is being paid for?" Her first half-facetious reaction was, "Where can I find a Jeff?"

The degree to which men desire sex is kept secret—since to be open only creates the opposite result. In her measurements of male sexual response, Dr. Shanor found *men between twelve and forty think of sex an average of six times per hour.*[4] Between twelve and nineteen, it is *twenty times per hour.* Or every five minutes. But even between thirty and thirty-nine, it is four times per hour. I'm glad I'm forty-two.

Male Messages 2 and 3 combined create the basis for the male search for equality, what I call the "oil crisis of male puberty."

Item: 1973. The oil crisis hits the United States. Huge lines form for access to short supplies of gas. Everyone is preoccupied with how best to solve the problem: "Where do I go for the shortest line to get the gas?" "How can I beat my neighbors to the pump?" "What time must I get up to do it?"

Boys enter puberty in an "oil crisis." Just as U.S. citizens felt powerlessness when they had a high demand for a short supply of OPEC's natural oil, so boys feel powerless when they have a high demand for a short supply of women's attention and sexuality. The more attractive the girl, the more the boy feels he needs to prove himself to have access to her. At puberty, he may not earn a penny more than the girl. So the more desire he feels, the more insecure he feels.

Every day as he grows up his crisis is reinforced by little giveaways in his vocabulary. Just as the words "men" and "girls" for people the same age give away an unconscious difference in our respect for men and women, women talk of "giving him sex." Meaning men must do something to earn the "gift." As he listens to *what* he can do, he hears phrases like, "I'd feel better about *giving* a man sex *if . . .*" Phrases that subconsciously teach him what to do to meet women's *conditions*.

Whether sexuality is more conservative, as in the fifties, or more liberal, as in the sixties, is not the issue. Both have advantages and disadvantages. The issue is whether both sexes learn to sexually desire each other *equally* and for the *same* reasons, or with *similar conditions*. Oil crises are not created when two countries consider their equal amount of oil of equal value, with both desiring each other's oil for similar reasons.

Men rarely talk about what we feel we must do to earn women's "gift." And least of all do we speak of what we directly or indirectly feel we have to pay for her sexuality. Which is why we decided to break the taboo during discussions in one men's group. We started talking about high school and moved to married years.

"I still remember taking Donna to the senior prom," Bob started. "I took her to dinner at Elario's beforehand and a formal Italian waiter handed me a wine list. I was so insecure, I ordered a ten-dollar bottle I had heard my dad talk about. Ten dollars . . . that meant mowing our lawn once a week for a month. What with dinner, dessert, coffee, tax, and tip, the whole thing ran over forty dollars—three more months of lawns!"

"What about the corsage?"

"I got her an orchid; then there was the tuxedo, prom tickets, and gas for the car. Another forty dollars. Oh yeah, and drinks after the prom at some place she wanted to go that had a view of the city. God, the whole thing must have been a hundred dollars. And that was 1960 money."

"That's over three hundred dollars in today's money," Larry, our group economist, calculated. "Were you pretty serious about her?"

"*I* was. I don't think she was. She never wanted to do much more than kiss. And then we both went to different colleges. I haven't seen her since."

Myron volunteered: "I didn't meet my first love until I was a sophomore at Lehigh. She was a sophomore at Montclair State in New Jersey. I'd take a bus to New York City and the De Camp Lines out to Upper Montclair almost every weekend. At that point, the time was more a bother than the bus fare. But our relationship got more expensive each year. Once a month we'd meet in New York or Philly and do a round of theater, dinner, and drinks. That would usually run about eighty dollars, including the cab fare and buses. Until our junior year, when I'd rent a hotel room on Friday and Saturday and we'd spend a weekend together."

"How'd you afford that in college?"

"I had to work twenty hours a week at Lehigh as night manager for a supermarket to save enough for that. Then she'd be angry when sometimes I'd have to study during our weekend together."

"What happened to you two?"

"She met some guy from Princeton, invited him for some big weekend we had talked about going to together, and we broke up a month or two after that."

"Were you hurt?" Bob asked.

"Well, you know . . . I could quit my job at the supermarket!" Myron laughed, avoiding the question.

"Ski trips used to wipe me out," Glenn recalled. "Rent a lodge, rent a car, rent a slope, consume a drink, devour a meal . . . and then I remember one girl thinking she was real independent because she treated me to one dinner and rented her own skis. Sometimes those weekends ran three hundred dollars . . . I could only afford one or two a year. I guess I paid about 90 percent. But then Mary would be able to afford another weekend with her girlfriends, five or six girls to a lodge. They'd meet a bunch of guys who'd buy them drinks and half their meals."

Al chimed in: "You guys seem to find women without children. I've been involved with two women who have children, and there was always this sense I felt that I'd be a real nice daddy/uncle if I paid for their kids at the movies, or dinner, or at a carnival. Fun at a carnival meant financing the kids and trying everything. Being a good sport meant doing it until they won a prize. A weekend with Madeline and the kids could run into hundreds without batting an eyelash. It's like I have to figure out a career that'll pay for all that."

"I have only myself to blame," Norm started. "I'm a sucker for taking women I'm serious about on European vacations. *Then* buying them fur coats, lingerie, dresses, and once even a Mercedes in Europe. Fortunately, the woman I bought the Mercedes for became my wife!"

Of course, all of these "payments" for a woman's sexuality are symbols of how effectively a man will be able to handle the better homes and gardens, and the $140,000 per child in the family circle. A man's consciousness of having to pay often makes him avoid the humanities in college and enter the higher-paying sciences; take hazardous construction, coal mining, or welding jobs, and the jobs in cold and isolated regions like Alaska.

In the process, he somehow senses that the word *love* may cost him. So professing love creates a built-in tension: on the one hand, it is a way of reducing rejection—promising her primary fantasy to get his (he may not know about love, but he's beginning to learn about politics); on the other hand, love may mean a lifetime of payments.

Cathy Guisewite, *A Mouthful of Breathmints and No One to Kiss*, p. 49

Male Message 4: 150 Initiatives, or 150 Ways to Lose a Lover (Before Getting Started)

All this gets worse as puberty progresses. Paying is a cinch compared to initiating. A boy learns he's supposed to want sex before he knows what it is, and now he learns he's supposed to initiate before he's even seen what he's reaching for. He only knows that the girls he most wants sex with seem to want it the least, even if they do want his attention and Saturday-night treats. A boy is actually in a worse position than being willing to give his body away for free—every other boy is trying to give his away before he does. He has to earn the "privilege" to be the one to give it away.

It's actually even worse than that. He's so anxious to give it away, no one even thinks of it as a gift! He has to add something to it to make it palatable. He has to compensate by working for her body. How? He has to initiate everything that has anything to do with her body.

The pubescent boy rarely knows what he's doing. The assumption that he should initiate as if he knew sends the fear of looking like a fool shivering through every cell of his nervous system. Do girls appreciate his risking rejection? On the contrary. Risking rejection could be seen as an act of giving—taking the pressure off the girl. If it were seen in this way, girls might be expected to compensate—to pay for the boy's dinner, or whatever. But it is not seen this way because everyone's bought the line that *he*'s getting the sex—it's for him, not for her. So he's told he must pay for dinner, too. As if he had to *compensate* for the rejection he risks.

It's not just that a Neil Diamond starts out drooling over

Kathy. He learns he has to risk rejection by asking Kathy out. And if she accepts, it is he who has to reach out to put his arm around her for the first time. I can remember, in sixth grade, it took me all afternoon to work my hand from my side to around Joann's shoulder. By that time, my parents had come to pick me up. On my way out, Joann's dog rushed up to her and she gave it a big kiss.

If a woman is receptive to hand-holding, he thinks: "Should I caress her fingers a little, rather than let our hands get like two lumps of clammy clay—but suppose I caress her fingers too soon, and she thinks I'm forward and I lose everything?" If she's receptive again, he may try to crack a joke so he can hug her during a moment of laughter, thereby reducing his risk of rejection; he may whisper something in her ear and see if she keeps her ear there; then kiss her on the lips and wonder, "How long? How hard? How much passion?" If her lips aren't closed tightly, does that mean her tongue is receptive? Or would pursuing turn a kiss of affection into an act of intrusion? If she is kissing him passionately, should he rub his chest against her breast? Is it the right time for his hands to run over her breast *over* her clothes? And now, under her blouse? Should he move his leg between hers just a little? Or a little more? If she responds, does that mean she wants more, or is enough enough?*

He soon begins to piece together the first of three commands in the most devastating of all male messages—Male Message 4: *"If you don't initiate, women won't—and what little there is will go to those who ask for it. So be prepared to risk rejection about 150 times between eye contact and sexual contact."* Start all 150 over again with each girl. The more attractive a girl is, the more she can afford to reject you and know some other guy will pursue her. The more attractive she is, the longer your period of rejection. So compensate by becoming a star.

The "first time" is the important time, when the risk of rejection is by far the greatest. Girls have greatly improved about reaching out to a boy once a relationship has begun. But few girls ever reach over to kiss a boy who has never before kissed

---

*In the first draft of this book, I followed one couple through all 150 stages of sexual initiatives—from laughter to fears. But the chapter entitled "The Anatomy of a Sexual Initiative" became a mini-book unto itself and had to be cut. Or at least saved for a next book. The examples above and below will serve the purpose here.

them. The girl usually knows the boy is interested or he wouldn't have asked her out. But the first time, the boy doesn't know whether she just accepted because she didn't know how to say no, or wanted something to do on Saturday night, or wanted to look sought-after to some other boy she was *really* interested in, or just felt sorry for him. With all these fears, which every girl will recognize as often valid, he then risks rejection by reaching out to hold her hand—"Will she reach for a Kleenex in her purse, and if she does, is it because she sneezed or to give me a polite hint to lay off?"

All of this may seem like a bit much to many women. "Why not just let it happen naturally?" women often ask. "Why is he so compulsive—it takes the romance and spontaneity out of it. If it's going to happen, it happens." This is like a man saying, "Why are you so compulsive about keeping the house clean?" He likes a clean house; she likes good sex. They both like the outcome, and they both want the other sex to take care of it so it looks as if it "comes naturally." We both want it to look like great service at a great restaurant—so we never even notice it's happening. She learns it's her job to make it *appear* as if it came naturally. And he learns it is his job to make it appear as if taking the initiatives comes naturally. And then both wonder why they're not appreciated.

As with housework, unshared responsibility for the taking of initiatives can turn a broad-minded human being into an obsessive-compulsive. It has a way of transforming consciousness. *When women's consciousness was raised, women ended up seeing housework as their "shit work"; when men's consciousness is raised, sexual initiatives will be seen as the male "shit work."*

How does a boy learn this ultimate initiation rite—to plan it right, to time it right? By trial and error. Mostly error. Always on trial. *All the "locker-room bragging" just increases a boy's insecurity—each boy knows he's exaggerating but he's uncertain if the other guy is.* The underlying message of locker-room conversation is: "What's wrong with *me*—I tried the same thing with Susan and she rejected *me*."

The female perspective is different. A woman may feel she says yes to male initiatives even more often than she'd like. And that if she didn't slow down the process, he'd often rush from a kiss to intercourse like a railroad train. She'd like some time to savor the process. Let's look at what happens to him when, to savor the process, she says yes at the beginning, by, say, responding to a kiss, and no shortly after, by cutting off the kiss, to slow down the process.

He sees her slowing down as a possible no. He feels he has been left holding the bag; he must choose whether to give up or try again. Why? Because he's never seen a woman say no and then later reach over to start again at the point where she stopped him. He had never, for example, had a woman stop him at her genitals and then, later, start kissing and touching his genitals before he attempts again. Yet they may eventually have sex and she may tell him she had a wonderful time sexually the very evening she said no.

The male then learns a *second command* in Male Message 4: *discover which nos mean no, which nos mean maybe, and which maybes mean yes.* (He doesn't even consider the possibility of saying no himself. That's a luxury that comes from abundance.)

How does he do this? Joan and Harold are kissing for the first time on a couch. Joan slows down the process by withdrawing her tongue. Harold senses the withdrawal. Should he back off? "If I do, maybe she'll feel I'm sensitive. But maybe she'll feel I'm a wimp." Should he pursue? "If I do, maybe she'll feel I'm overbearing. But maybe she'll feel I'm exciting."

Harold chose to be sensitive. But now, he wondered, "Should I turn the lights up or turn them down? Make the music lower or change the music? Should I ask her questions about herself, or tell her more about me? Should I give her a foot massage or back rub, or just sit on my hands? Will more wine relax her or put her to sleep? If she's sleepy, will coffee awaken her or just make her less relaxed? If I kiss her again, should I kiss her on the cheek or lips? If she withdraws again, should I back off again, or this time should I pursue? . . ."

Cutting off is part of what creates the 150 initiatives between eye contact and sexual contact. In a typical first-time encounter, some of these initiatives are recycled with a twist. Starting to kiss again after a sign of sensitivity is different from starting to kiss again with no prior sign of sensitivity. So the ego goes back on the line. This means he has to do more than *guess* which nos mean no. It means there is a *third command* in Male Message 4: *Take responsibility for turning nos into maybes and maybes into yeses. Discover afterward whether you're right or a rapist.* He feels he must do this because if he waits for her he will miss out on the sexual passion in his life—even much of the "love" (which can be catalyzed by sexual passion). And besides, wimps get rejected even more than men who don't take no for an answer.

The core of this male neurosis comes not from taking the initiatives, but rather from overcoming all the nos; from the fear that if he asked a woman if she'd like to participate in his sexual fantasy as soon as he was willing, he'd get almost 100 percent nos; from the feeling that when he's first willing, there's no word in the female vocabulary for yes, but if only he is good enough, polite enough, persistent enough, successful enough, romantic enough, gentle enough, if he earns enough, spends enough, cares enough, commits enough—*if, if, if* . . .

How he takes this responsibility determines whether he is a hero or a jerk. (They are two sides of the same coin—a jerk is often a potential hero who messes it up along the way.) From a woman's perspective, this may seem a bit exaggerated. Many women say: "I make my cues pretty clear. Men don't have to take such a great risk." Or "One thing that makes women mad is when we're giving off cues that we're not interested and the man keeps coming on." I've discovered, though, that *a woman's set of cues can be clear to the woman. But every woman is an individual, and to a man each woman's set of cues is as individual and unique as the woman herself.* He is expected to discover just the right formula to determine which cue means what to which woman at whichever stage of development in their sexual relationship. When we multiply the options by 150, we have full-blown obsession, which makes becoming a jerk quite easy.

For example, a woman might say "I know the moment I meet a man whether I'm interested." So she may give off receptive, excited vibrations immediately. For most women "who know immediately," though, it is not okay to act immediately. Therefore the man may feel positive vibrations at the beginning of the evening and varied vibrations as he spends more time with her. From his perspective, he feels her slipping away while he's paying for dinner.

While some women "know immediately," others say, "With most men I really don't think much about sex until the man starts coming on. Once he starts coming on, how he does it makes a difference about whether I'm receptive or not." A lot of women identify with that sentiment. But it contradicts the expectation that a man shouldn't come on until he feels receptive cues. On the one hand, he should wait for receptive cues; on the other hand, she won't give them until he comes on. If he waits too long, he finds he's often told "You're such a *nice* man . . . I'd like us just to *be friends.* . . ."

Let's look at the female perspective. Women feel they help ease this process for men by protecting men's egos. In the short run, it does that. In the long run, *the extent to which a woman protects a man's ego is the extent to which she preserves ambiguity about the real meaning of her signals*.

Still more confusing is the enormous range of "sexual morality" attitudes a man experiences among women. Ranging from "no sex before marriage" to "I'm as interested in making love as you are . . . I expect a few orgasms and no questions about whether I had them." A statement like "I'm interested in you" may mean, from one woman, "I liked your gentleness; please ask me out again," and from a second woman, "So initiate already." They are both receptive cues. But receptive to different things despite the fact that they are the same words.

Even when women are clear about their own sexual desires for a man, they often don't feel free to make their cues as clear as their desires. A frequent admission from women is: "I'm afraid I have to calculate whether 'holding out' will excite him or whether appearing too interested will turn him off." A man may pick up both receptive and "calculating" cues simultaneously. The assumption that a woman's cues are clear, "so why do men keep coming on anyway?" does not acknowledge conflicts within a woman, and therefore the conflicting messages a man receives.

In all these ways, cues that are clear to a given woman may be unclear to a given man. But even cues that are crystal clear to a man can be tricky. Barry was a man for whom "no means no." In a workshop setting he explained, "If a woman says no, I wait until the next date before I try again. I thought that was only right. But a few months ago I went out with two women and the same thing happened. They were both receptive to kissing, but gave a no signal before intercourse. And they both told me they liked me more than anyone they'd met. But then I heard via the grapevine that they were both having sex shortly after with guys I knew didn't mean that much to them. Now they're both serious with these guys. I must be doing something wrong. . . ."

Paula responded. "I'm married now, Barry, but when I used to date, sometimes *the clearer my no was, the more I would feel released from guilt—I had fulfilled my obligation by saying a super-clear no*. Do you understand? I mean, like it was right after I said that clear no that if a guy persisted, he'd get somewhere. Then I'd convince myself I really liked him—or loved him. That's the way I got pregnant my first time and ended up marrying the man who got me pregnant. I don't like to admit that, but it's true.''

Paula's honesty helped us understand the extent of men's dilemma in reading signals from women with different backgrounds. For Paula, the clearer the no, the clearer the release from guilt. In essence, the clearer the no, the clearer the yes. For some men, this is confusing.

Many women feel this may all be true for *other* women, but that personally they take lots of initiatives. As they explain in greater depth, though, we discover they have mostly taken *receptive* initiatives. For example, if a woman is at a movie with a man, she might place her hand on the arm of the chair common to both of them. If her intent is to make it available, I call it a *receptive initiative*. If her intent is for her to pursue further, I call it an *active* receptive initiative; usually, though, such an act is to make it easier for *him* to take the next step; I call this a *passive* receptive initiative.

The hallmark of a receptive initiative, in either case, is the lack of an ego on the line. Since she could have been resting her hand there merely to rest it, nothing is risked. The difference between the passive and active initiative is the intent. If the intent is to leave the risk to the man, it is passive.

Men take receptive initiatives too, but usually only to put themselves in a better position to take *probing* or *direct* initiatives. A woman's receptive initiative is usually a way of making it easier for the man to take probing or direct initiatives. How? To return to the movies, a man might place his hand for half a second on hers as he asks her if she'd like some popcorn. He is probing to get a feel for whether her hand relaxes or tenses up a bit. He does it lightly and quickly enough that it could be mistaken for getting her attention. *Probing* initiatives test the waters: ''Does she pull away; appear nervous; appear receptive and relaxed?'' But probing initiatives leave doubts: If she's relaxed, it could mean she's physically receptive. Or it could mean she's just relaxed!

All these distinctions may seem ridiculous. But they are no more ridiculous than the distinctions between Wisk and Woolite, labels that come with the responsibility for housework. Men have not had labels for their initiative-taking because no one wanted to admit the work needed doing.

After the probing initiative, there is a greater level of risk: *shifting the intimacy level*. For example, when Phyllis and Bill meet at a party and are discussing their jobs, Phyllis will almost never be the first one to shift out of that level of intimacy by volunteering: "*I* like your eyes." She may say, "*I* like your curly hair" *after* he says, "I like your eyes," but rarely will she say it after a conversation on their respective jobs, before he has taken the first risk to shift the intimacy level.

The biggest risk is the *direct* initiative, as when he takes her hand directly for the first time. He risks total acceptance or total rejection. In one respect, though, all these direct initiatives are not direct. For many men, a direct initiative might be "making mad, passionate love *immediately*."

Male Message 5: Homophobia

As the adolescent boy learns that attention from attractive girls and female sexuality are in short supply, he learns Male Message 5: *Being attracted to other boys is off limits*. Any hint of it will leave him ostracized as a "queer," beaten up; he will forfeit his status as a human being in the eyes of other boys. Male Message 5 tells him to put all his eggs in one basket—sexual response from girls. The intensity of the fear of sexual contact with boys also makes him withdraw emotionally from boys lest he be "suspect"—like a liberal in the McCarthy era—which makes him dependent on emotional response from females as well. This combination, called homophobia, forces boys to be female-dependent. The fear of emotional contact with men out of fear of being a "sexual suspect" makes boys, ironically, *even more powerless before girls. Homophobia is like telling the United States it will be a "sissy nation" if it doesn't get all its oil from OPEC.*

It is the progression of the male's "oil crisis" from sexual dependency to emotional dependency.

These five messages are what a boy typically experiences during puberty. None of the messages denies the fact that a girl feels powerless too, especially if she is not attractive; if she is attractive, she may have doubts about what she is valued for. As with the boy, she hears messages that create double binds. The pressure on her to enhance her attractiveness often leads to her developing a love-hate response to the attention she gets to the attractiveness she's worked so hard to enhance.

Parents can feel as powerless as their adolescent. Raising a boy's awareness, they may fear, would relegate him to the "queer group" of his peer group. Parents who persuade a boy to be conscious risk turning him into a "guinea pig of consciousness," isolated among his peers during the years when conformity is desperately sought as a way of setting his foot securely on the ground. Of course he does not understand that this "security" will become the core of his insecurity.

In the conclusion we will look at some alternatives. Any alternatives, though, need to incorporate an awareness of the defenses men use to compensate for their feelings of powerlessness—defenses that can lead to male crimes. We'll start with the sexual defenses.

Stage 3: Sexual Defenses against Feeling Female Rejection

The male's feelings of powerlessness before a genetic celebrity—the feeling of having to beg like a puppy for every morsel of her attention and sexuality by performing, paying, risking rejection, and being told he's dirty or akin to a rapist—make his ego fragile and his self-concept vulnerable. *Vulnerability creates defenses.*

How does he defend against this vulnerability? In the sexual arena he discovers the *first defense* of Stage 3: *It hurts a lot less to be rejected by a sex object than it does to be rejected by a full human being.* So if a male can turn women into objects and sex into a game (and call it "scoring"), he will be able to treat rejection less seriously. He will hurt less.

No sooner has a boy learned "When the going gets tough, objectify" than he learns that objectifying by itself isn't enough. His second defense can best be understood by a quick glance at the male internal dialogue when a boy sees a girl he finds attractive. "She's beautiful. It would be great to go to bed with her. Yum, yum. . . . *but if I tell her that directly, she'll say no.*" He learns that if he is *honest* with his sexual feelings the moment he is in touch with them,* and tells her his desire directly, he'll get the reaction Dustin Hoffman got in *Tootsie* after he was direct with a woman who had told him how much

---

*To the degree he is compulsive about sex he is really not in touch with his sexual feelings in the fullest sense of the word.

she craved directness—a drink in his face. For a man, expressing his sexual feelings as soon as he's in touch with them will get a refusal almost 100 percent of the time—especially from the women he most wants.

The *second sexual defense* of Stage 3 is to *suppress sexual feelings and replace the feelings with dishonesty*. Honesty guarantees rejection. Dishonesty becomes a defense. He learns sexual politics.

Needing to be dishonest and suppressing sexual feelings team up to block any distant thought a boy may entertain of asking a woman to share the responsibility for taking initiatives. Most boys never even consider it, because they observe that *the boys having the most fun are not asking girls to share initiatives*. They begin to observe how sensitive behavior is not only "deviant" but also extends the period of potential rejection.

What does he substitute for asking girls to share sexual initiatives? *A third sexual defense: railroad sex. Railroad sex is getting from eye contact to intercourse as quickly as possible.* To what end? The faster he gets from eye contact to intercourse, the shorter the period of potential rejection.

Why don't men just let a friendship develop with a woman, and then, if sex happens, it happens? Because, similarly, the longer the friendship, the longer the period of potential rejection.

Will this change? Not until both sexes share the responsibility for all sexual initiatives—and therefore sexual rejection.

Boys move through three significant stages, then, in their relationships with girls. During these stages they hear five major male messages, which might be summarized like this:

THE MALE SEARCH FOR EQUALITY OR THE
GENETIC CELEBRITY CRISIS

Stage 1: The Genetic Celebrity

Male Message 1:   Some girls in my class already look like movie stars. If they only wanted me as much as I want them, I'd know I was okay. They are genetic celebrities. I am a genetic groupie.

Stage 2: The Male Search for Equality—the Oil Crisis of Male Puberty

Male Message 2:   I must perform for the genetic celebrity's attention.

Male Message 3:   I must pay for female sexuality.

Male Message 4:   I must risk rejection about 150 times for female sexuality. Do not assume her nos mean no if her nuances say yes.

Male Message 5:   I must focus all sexual and emotional energy on females. Homophobia is better than being a "sexual suspect."

Stage 3: Sexual Defenses against Feeling Female Rejection

Defense 1:   Turn women into sex objects. It hurts less to be rejected by an object than by a full human being.

Defense 2:   Suppress sexual feelings and replace them with dishonesty—politics work better than honesty.

Defense 3:   Practice railroad sex. Do not stop at friendship. The longer the period of friendship, the longer the period of potential rejection.

Is there an alternative to male feelings of powerlessness and vulnerability? Sort of. A male senses only one thing that addresses every need and every defense. It is called success.

Success as Panacea and Trap

How does the male adolescent avoid being a genetic groupie? By success on the playing field. A few years later, when he is successful at work, he can afford ski trips and theater tickets, dinners, drinks, and rental cars. A few drinks after dinner and a day of skiing tend to reduce his risk of rejection. Success reduces the number of initiatives and increases the likelihood that an attractive woman will be interested in accompanying him. It seems like a panacea.

In each way that success is a panacea (it pays for the dinners and makes him more ''interesting'') it is also a defense against female rejection. And a compensation for his feelings of powerlessness (''Why can't she want me without my paying?''). And if a man gets too much female rejection despite his success (or is not interested in women to begin with) success serves as the perfect alternative. He can fall in love with success. It has its own rewards, both inherently and externally. And it can be a cover-up. If a man is successful enough, few people question him about anything—from women to gayness.

Am I exaggerating all this? Let's do a reality check.

Think of women under thirty who are attractive enough to be models—the women with the most options. Write down their names if they married men they felt had little financial potential:

1._____

2._____

3._____

The reader will doubtless find a few women who married men who are supportive but less successful than themselves, like Bella Abzug. But Bella Abzug fits neither the age category nor the highly attractive category. She has fewer options. And besides, her husband is still successful enough to support them both, should they desire that. So cross off names of such women. If no one is left, we can add people we don't know—but know of. How many are left?

If anyone remains or appears in the "know of" category, is it a woman under thirty driven to be a success in a highly risky field who has married a man with the contacts and style to manage her talents? That is, a man still playing a financial role?

Remember Marc? He married Marge, who wasn't his fantasy woman, but she loved him. Some men like Marc team up with women like Marge in the hope that they'll "make it"—only to face a male mid-life crisis if they do make it and a male mid-life crisis if they don't. The more he makes it, the more attractive he becomes to another woman, the more he is tempted away from Marge. During the mid-life crisis, even happily married men often feel that now that they've made it to the point where they're successful enough to attract the women in the ads, they're married to a woman who doesn't fit the image. Few marriages are strong enough for long enough to withstand the Kathys who once rejected the Neil Diamonds when they were the class frog, but now that the men are class princes, are eyeing them.

The more Marc is tempted away from Marge, the more he feels guilty about betraying the woman who supported him, so he would become, ironically, more attractive to "other women."

If he does find a younger woman, often he's never quite sure whether she loves him for who he is or for what he has. (I've seen few men secure enough to give up their success or refuse to spend their savings to find out.) So he still feels empty inside. He loses if he wins, and he loses if he loses. Now that he has "power," he loses if he uses it.

Perhaps the astronaut Gordon Cooper knew what he was appealing to, as he feared losing his wife before he was selected to try out as an astronaut. Millions watching *The Right Stuff*, based on the astronauts' real-life experiences, saw Cooper trying to keep his wife by pleading, "Who's the best pilot in the world?" When he received no answer, he'd volunteer the answer: "You're looking at him." Subtle. But he was simultaneously moving her into a drab, plain, run-down house; bragging about his potential was all he had. Holding out hope. He hadn't proven himself. The house and hope, while good enough for him, weren't good enough for her. She left him. Then he made it as a finalist in the astronaut program. She considered his plea to return.* Then he made it as an astronaut. She returned.

Perhaps it was Gordon Cooper's "bravado personality," his male chauvinism, that alienated her. But that wouldn't account for her returning without anything changing but the *proof of his bravado*. Called status. Nor does it account for the fact that 84 percent of top male corporate executives are married to their first wives, compared to 53 percent for the total male population,[5] even though the male executive is often emotionally cut off from his wife, his children, and his feelings.

In another socioeconomic class, men who drop out of officer training also find the women who love them dropping out of their lives. I live near Camp Pendleton, one of the largest military bases in the United States, just north of San Diego. One man after another has told me that there is "no way personality is as important to a lady as my rank." They identify with the man in *An Officer and a Gentleman*, who lost the love of his life the moment he followed his integrity and dropped out of officer training.

---

*It appears his plea was based on the fear that he would not make it into the program if he wasn't married. Would he have pleaded with her to return if he felt he could make it without her? Or would he have held out for all the women he knew would come his way once he made it? Were they *both* using each other as objects?

Sam, a salesman in a Chicago men's group, put it this way: "When I was selling, my wife complained, 'I'd like you to be home earlier, to be more sensitive, to develop some of the creativity I know you have.' So I went into part-time sales and set up a studio in our home. We both agreed I have lots of potential as an artist. But my sales income is one-third. And my art barely breaks even. Our marriage suddenly started deteriorating even though I was acquiring everything she had said I was missing. I feel confused and, I guess, angry."

All this may remain on a subconscious level for most men, who (like the women of twenty years ago) have not had their consciousnesses raised. Once a man *has* raised his consciousness, he slowly understands that *Alan Alda is loved not because he's sensitive, but because he's successful and sensitive.* I call this the Alan Alda Syndrome.

Each sex strives to attain from the other sex the type of power it is most discouraged from attaining itself. The more a person expects from the other sex, the more trapped he or she becomes by the expectations on himself or herself. *The less a man is willing to give up a sex object, the more he will be trapped into becoming a success object.* As he drops the hope of becoming a Kissinger, a Woody Allen, or a Dustin Hoffman he may lower his sights from the starlet. But *if he still desires the female model, he'll find himself becoming the medical model.* Or a star. As the five-foot-six-inch Dustin Hoffman put it, "When I was in high school, women wouldn't touch me with a ten-foot pole. Now I can't keep them away with a ten-foot pole."

This distinction between the impact of success on men and women helps explain why men are so compulsive and competitive about their pursuits. Either consciously or unconsciously, the adolescent boy observes how much each option will help him solve his "oil crisis" by getting him to the pump before his neighbors. It takes a rare teenage boy not to need the approval these options supply—to turn in isolation to questions of the spirit, introspection, sensitivity, and love. (People who were trying to beat their neighbors to the pump rarely found themselves focused on questions of love.)

For each man who makes it to the top of a pyramid, there are a thousand who do not—a thousand who live at least in part vicariously through the "superiority" of "my" sports team, "my" children, or "my" country. They get their women vicariously too—through *Playboy, Penthouse,* or pornography. It's neither men's fault nor women's fault. They are adult men still playing out their "oil crisis"—getting their rewards vicariously to the degree they earned them vicariously.

Before we delve more deeply, I'll do some clarifying. The difference between the desperation felt by men and that felt by women as they pursue external reward power lies in men's having to prove themselves worthy recipients not only of women's attention and sexuality but also of the approval of parents and peers. We mistakenly tend to see these as three separate contributors to male pressure. They are not.

Take parents, for example. Most parents want to help their child live compatibly with the other sex. Even when they don't like what they see they consider it their duty to prepare the child for hard reality. They don't tell their daughters, "When you grow up you should support your husband." A career woman's expectations are to support herself. Not her husband. *Since men observe that career women often "marry up," a woman's career can actually increase the pressure on a man to perform to earn his way to equality with her. By preparing boys for this reality, parents unwittingly increase the pressure on boys.* And it makes proving ourselves to our parents not very different from proving ourselves to girls.

I am increasingly impressed by the degree to which so many men risk their lives, investments, and careers for an attractive woman's attention, especially her sexual attention. Think of the men willing to risk their careers with charges of sexual harassment for an affair with a secretary or student. Think of the men who risk years in prison, total humiliation, and the destruction of career and family for the attention of or sex with an underage female, the one female they believe they can have access to—a child.

Think of how often we read of men throwing themselves into cold rivers or hot fires to rescue a woman. We hear of women performing such heroics for the sake of a child—but try to recall one example of a woman doing that for a man, even her husband. It is not inherently good or bad to risk one's life for another. But when men risk so much to be a hero or to get sex, it makes one wonder about the limits of male sexual vulnerability.

Item: Look at the praying mantis or the black widow spider. The male and female are "making sex." The male gets so involved he cannot undo himself. The female satisfies herself, then bites off the head of the male. The male is so locked into the sexual act that he cannot prevent himself from being consumed. The ultimate in vulnerability.

Like the praying mantis and black widow spider, a man may feel so vulnerable and powerless that, for the sake of visibility and respect, he will risk his "head being chopped off" as a war hero or boxing hero; as a fireman; as a president or an astronaut; as the person who creates the master race or destroys the human race—or gets the Nobel Prize to save it from destruction. Or, if national heroism is out of reach, as a volunteer fireman in his hometown. It's all the same. In the process of gaining his family's respect, peer group respect, female respect, and his own respect, a man may forfeit his family, sacrifice his wife, destroy his body, and lose his soul.

The male training to overcome sexual rejection also turns out to be valuable for success. Both at work and with women, *not taking no for an answer creates the core of male strengths and the core of male neuroses*. Women are attracted to men's success; they hate men's defenses. They hate men who don't take no for an answer; they love men who don't take no for an answer. Both are ways of dealing with female sexuality: *changing nos into maybes with women is direct; changing nos into maybes at work is indirect. Success is the most respected defense against rejection. It is the male insurance policy. Success is preventive medicine.* But the characteristics it produces do not always make the male lovable at home, or keep him alive for the one he loves.

The Larger Implications

What are the deeper implications of these messages to women and men? These messages say, "Make yourself *attractive* to the other sex by making yourself *opposite* from the other sex." The problem? Opposites attract; they just can't live together. Sex-role training becomes divorce training.

Is this just the way it is—biological and natural? In the 1860s, Darwin documented how sexual selection—the most powerful males mating with the most attractive females—was a key element in the survival of the fittest. Yes, it is probably deep within our genes that the most valued women choose the most competitive and surviving men. And vice versa. But genetic evolution has also created technology—and the ability to adapt to what our technology creates. And technology has made male competition into a lose-lose game on the level of genetic survival. What was genetically functional is now genetically dysfunctional.*

Has technology made sex roles dysfunctional in relationships as well? Yes. (Women are more inclined toward computer technology than hunting bear.) And in raising children? Yes. (Once either sex can work, either sex can raise the child.) Technology has made sex roles unnecessary. In the future, the "fittest" relationships will be the ones that adapt to a new reality—the higher expectations of good communication, not mere survival.

How did this happen? First, let's look at the impact of technology. Technology's obviation of the need for brute male strength made the workplace amenable to women at the same time that technology's birth control led to smaller families and medicine to longer life, which meant that a woman no longer needed to spend her entire life at home.

But it is human nature to *raise expectations* once mere survival is no longer the issue. So as we no longer required the division of labor to survive, we raised our expectations and saw how division of labor was leading to division of interests—divorce training.

Sex roles, then, have quickly been made dysfunctional on the survival level (nuclear war), the relationship level (divorce training), and the raising of children level (absentee fathers) by the part of our human nature that both created technology and raised our expectations. All of which is in battle with another part of our human nature: women choose the most performing man.

What will the future bring? Sex roles *were* functional. A species always adapts to a new reality until it ends itself.

The Male Search for Equality: In Summary

Both sexes can enjoy sex and success for healthy reasons. But men are so preoccupied with sex because: First, they're subliminally socialized to be addicted to a drug in short supply—the genetic celebrity. Anything "less" feels like an inferior fix—but the "inferior fix" meets so many needs at so much less cost, they'd take it rather than go cold turkey. Second, they are socialized to risk constant rejection to get this short supply.

*See Chapter 3.

Third, they're told to overcome the rejections by women to their compulsive initiative-taking. But they do not experience women sharing these initiatives. To defend against this rejection they turn women into sex objects. Which further alienates women from sex with men. So men become more desperate. All of which creates preoccupation with sex.

Why are men so preoccupied with success beyond the intrinsic rewards, peer group and parental approval of success—to the point of forfeiting life itself? Success is the form of power women feel most deprived of. While women *desire* sensitivity in men, men sense women are in *need* of their success. So men also work to get what *they* feel deprived of—women's respect, attention, sexuality, and love. Men don't feel great about spending their lives overcoming potential sexual rejection directly, so they do it indirectly as well—through success.

Success is preventive medicine for the cancer of rejection. It is the male form of power, designed to compensate for the male form of powerlessness; it is the most respected defense against vulnerability. In part, it is men earning their way to equality with women.

5

What Makes a Man Successful at Work That Makes Him Unsuccessful at Home? Or Why Can't Men Listen?

If men earned incomes, came home, solicited their loved ones' feelings, listened attentively, and played with their children, few women would complain. Put another way, if becoming a millionaire didn't have its price, few women would object to the income.

Many women sense that the more successful a man becomes at work the more *un*successful he is at home. That the "bottom line" conflicts with love. As women are becoming successful competing in the male framework, some men find these traits emerging in women as well. Yet until now very little attention has been paid to exactly what makes a man successful at work that makes him unsuccessful at home. We may be aware that while playing "goo-goo" with our one-year-old is appreciated at home, goo-goo training is not part of this year's curriculum for top management. But what about adult communication? Why, for example, do so many men have so many problems listening? Let's return to Ralph.*

Self-Listening

Alan is making a presentation at a department meeting. Ralph listens for a few seconds, picks up the gist of what Alan is saying, then, while Alan is still talking, Ralph is formulating in his mind's eye a contribution he can make the second Alan pauses. As he rehearses his contribution, he may still listen to

*See Chapter 1, "Men Have the Power . . ."

139

Alan peripherally, so he doesn't appear like a jerk, but he's mostly listening to himself—or *self-listening*. Once he's satisfied with the contribution he's mentally created, he makes eye contact with Alan, nods a knowing yes, and inadvertently pressures Alan to a pause. The second Alan pauses, Ralph interjects with his well-rehearsed contribution.

Both sexes self-listen, but men self-listen to prepare contributions, to solve problems. Why? *Ralph senses that the more he listens to himself rehearse his contribution, the more likely his interjection will command the respect that will shift his boss's attention from Alan to him.* And that is behavior for getting ahead.

Experience has also taught Ralph that if he finds the flaw in Alan's presentation ("That's good in theory, but *realistically*—"), his boss might perceive him as having critical faculties and perceive Alan as having critical flaws. And *that* was functional behavior for getting ahead. But is it functional behavior for loving his wife, Ginny? Let's follow Ralph home.

Ginny has had a difficult day at work and a bad encounter with their older son. Ralph listens for a few seconds, picks up the gist of what she is saying, then forms in his mind both a solution to her problem and a flaw in her approach. He nods his head with a knowing yes and interjects at the first pause. He feels proud of how he's "helped" her.

But Ginny hears a different message when it takes Ralph only a few seconds to solve a problem that she may have been working on all day. What's help to him is a put-down to her.

What does Ginny want? She wishes he would just listen—with receptive, unrushed body language—that he would let her make her own discoveries—perhaps noting a couple of things she had done well during the day, possibly with his hand lightly caressing (not controlling) her knee—that he would just draw her out.

But suppose Ralph uses this "drawing-out" listening back at work. First, he listens to Alan by being receptive and unrushed. Consequence? Ralph never even gets a chance to speak—the self-listeners, who rehearsed while Alan was presenting, speak up first. Second, suppose Ralph does speak, and points out what Alan did well. The result is that *Alan* gets recognition for his discoveries. Third, Ralph gives Alan support by touching Alan's knee. The result? Ralph has gotten his last promotion!

What Makes a Man Successful at Work That Makes him Unsuccessful at Home

Why was getting promoted so important to Ralph? In his adolescent "work" of basketball, success made rejection by women less likely. Now, in his adult work as a professional, Ralph can't help but feel Ginny would lose respect for him if he "plateaued out." But the very traits that were keeping her respect were losing her love.

Men's incentives to self-listen extend beyond the work arena. For example, Jeff reaches out to kiss Amanda for the first time. Amanda's interested, but he's moving too quickly. So she stays with the kiss for a few seconds, then carefully withdraws. To reduce Jeff's burden, Amanda starts the conversation again.

As Amanda is talking, Jeff is running an inner dialogue: "If I try kissing her again immediately, while there's energy in the air, maybe my persisting past her resistance will excite her. . . . On the other hand, maybe I'll mess up my chances altogether. Or maybe I should turn the stereo up, or turn it down, or massage her feet, or rub her neck, or ask her a question, or mention my last accomplishment—"

In the meantime, Amanda is still talking. Jeff hasn't heard much of anything. He's been listening to himself prepare his next move—self-listening.

Why doesn't he just relax? Build some trust from which sex can become meaningful? Or let Amanda return the kiss if and when she's ready, rather than compulsively testing the waters? Because, as I discussed in the last chapter, he's rarely been with a woman who did initiate a kiss she had cut off. And, as happened with Fran, if too much "friendship" time elapses, he's afraid he'll get the line about not wanting to spoil a friendship with sex. But most important, as long as he's expected to take the initiatives and therefore to risk rejection, *the longer he listens, the longer his period of potential rejection*. The sooner he has intercourse, the faster the period of potential rejection is over.

Are women better listeners? Overall, yes, but women also self-listen in their own way. When I studied women in mixed groups, I found that they often listened for a few seconds, picked up the gist of what was being said, and then formed in their minds a *question* they could ask while the conversation was in process. If they were interested in a man in the group, or if there was a man of influence in the group, they often asked the question with eye contact on that man. *Even if they already knew the answer*.

While men self-listen by problem solving or faultfinding, women self-listen by pseudo-questioning.

Why this difference? A woman knows that if a man is drawn into the center of attention by her questions, he's more likely to notice her—more likely to feel secure enough to initiate asking her out. Her questions, however, often lead men to think they have answers women don't have. The man rarely understands that a woman who asks a question may have her own version of the answer—that the awe in her eyes at his response may be flirtation or female "awe training," not enlightenment created by a Professor Henry Higgins. *It is ironic that the very process that makes a man secure enough to risk initiatives with a woman is the same process that creates his contempt for her.*

In the meantime, a man is often uncertain to what extent a woman's questions reflect an interest in him, and to what extent they reflect an interest in the content of the question. The confusion reinforces his inability to separate his occupational identity from his personal identity. No wonder he defends his substance as if it were his soul.

The misunderstandings resulting from the female training to ask pseudo-questions and the male training to solve problems often amount to divorce training—if not legal divorce, at least psychological divorce. Yet another way in which sex role training is divorce training.

Couples are frequently disappointed in each other because "my therapist listens to me better than you do" or "Sally understands . . ." or "John and I don't even have to discuss this." The comparisons are false. *Listening is easy when the person we're listening to is not complaining about us;* when we don't have to live with the outcome; when we don't have to negotiate the everyday terms of life; when we don't have an emotional and financial history and an emotional and financial future. In contrast, when all these circumstances are combined, our listening skills are tested.

What should we do when a loved one is complaining about us? The following are the steps I use when I listen most effectively. When I follow these steps I am consistently amazed at how almost any complaint can turn into a deeper love connection. It is as if the complaint becomes an opportunity. When I don't follow these steps, the complaint remains and a new complaint arises (that I have not listened).

Guide to Listening When Someone Is Upset

The Complainer

• Don't complain too often.

• Don't ask the listener questions ("Tell me why you did that?") if you want the listener to listen.

• Ask the listener to listen. Tell the listener you have a complaint and ask the listener if he or she is willing to follow the steps below.

The Listener During a Complaint (No One Does This Perfectly!)

• Listen by using supportive eye contact and drawing out; for example, "Tell me more . . . ." "Yes, I see . . . ." "Explain. . . ."

• Do not correct distortions. Instead, reach inside yourself to understand the complainer's best intent and her or his underlying hurts.

• Allow time after the complainer finishes (30 seconds to one minute).

• Offer your understanding of the complainer's complaint from the complainer's perspective only.

• Ask the complainer to clarify anything that you misinterpreted or omitted.

• When the complainer clarifies, restate the clarified complaint.

• Allow more time.

• Now, it's your turn to bring up your perspective—objections, misinterpretations, etc. If you followed the first seven steps, the complainer should now be ready to be a mini-listener.

• If the complaining process has stimulated your need to register a separate complaint, make an appointment to take care of that some *other* time. Have some fun first.

What Makes a Man Successful at Work That Makes Him Less Successful as a Father?

THE FAMILY CIRCUS   **by Bil Keane**

Copyright 1985
Cowles Syndicate, Inc.

"You hafta listen to me with your eyes,
Daddy. Not just your ears."

Los Angeles Times, April 28, 1985

Item: As a boy I prided myself on playing soccer. When I moved to a new school and they had no soccer ball ("soccer—that's European") I persuaded the PE director to buy one for the school. I then went out and "taught" my eighth-grade class how to play. To illustrate I took on all the boys in the class. Of course, I wasn't illustrating, but attempting to garner respect. When I beat them and quickly discovered I had isolated myself, alienated my classmates, and made few, if any, of the boys interested in the game, I was learning you don't create enthusiasm by defeating others.

My training to win, though, was strong enough that I had a déjà vu experience as I was teaching Megan, the daughter of the woman I live with, to play soccer. Megan was ten, and it was she and I against two boys who had been playing since they could walk. The score was even, I had a clear shot at the goal, and I took it, for "us." When I saw Megan's face I realized I had taken it for me. That's when I had the déjà vu. I started employing whatever kicking ability I had to pass more balls to Megan. By the end of the game we had lost. But Megan had won. And therefore, so had I.

Item: Mr. Polhemus was our principal at Midland Park High School in New Jersey. As one of my classmates saw me come out of his office, she came over to me and asked, "You just came out of Mr. Polhemus's office?"

"Yeah," I said.

"Do you think he's a bit strange?"

"Not especially. Why?"

"Well, I'll tell you," she said confidingly, "he just moved into our neighborhood in Midland Park, and a few days ago I passed his house—and you know what he was doing? He was doing somersaults *all over the lawn* with his daughter! Going peekaboo through his legs and chasing her all around the house. He didn't see me watching but I saw him in these funny shorts, and a T-shirt—he was so skinny without his suit! It was just like he was a little kid. Can you imagine—and *he's* our principal! Weird, huh?"

At the time I was thinking about becoming an educator myself, so I guess that's why I registered her expectation so clearly. I was learning: "If you're going to have the respect of the community, stop playing around like a child." I didn't realize I was also learning how *not* to be a good dad; how *not* to play at a child's level, on a child's turf. Hopefully, I learned badly.

It is theoretically possible for people to maintain two sets of behaviors—one at work and one at home. But after a while, the executive who is not only dressing for success but also behaving for success begins to develop body language that carries over to the home setting and makes the daddy who used to go "goo-goo" feel increasingly awkward. The conflict can occur with either sex. Dorothy Schiff, former publisher of the *New York Post,* showed how work influenced her personal life when she remarked, "Most people to me are nothing but personnel problems."[1]

How does this occur? Behaving for success means developing behaviors that are so natural and integrated with a person's personality they create a uniform and consistent image on which people can depend. As with great actors, most successful people begin to "live" their parts at home. But behind the image often hides a neurosis. For example, men professionally diagnosed as neurotic earn 23 percent more than "normal" men.[2] Dozens of written and unwritten rules exacerbate a successful man's neuroses. No men's room ever features either a couch or a comfortable chair. Coffee yes, couches no. And naps—no, no, no. We can drug up and drug down, but not lie down. Not if we're on the way up. And so when the children of a man on the way up take a break, he tends to see them as lazy rather than well-paced. Especially if they are sons.

When Gary Hart was being discussed as a vice presidential possibility after Mondale was nominated, he commented, "I would not make a good second man. I don't follow very well." Many men, though, find themselves accepting positions for which they are suited like a round peg in a square hole in hopes of positioning themselves for "two jobs down the road." When men do this, studies show they are especially likely to have "spillover stress"—stress that spills over to the home environment.[3]

Many men I have worked with report themselves during these periods as "more critical than I want to be. . . . The kids get into a little quarrel at the dinner table and I eat them up. We all leave the table with indigestion." Other men confess, "It's a tough world out there, and when I see my kids being lazy, I can't stand it. I criticize out of love, but I'm overly critical."

Among the hundreds of women's groups I've started, one of the most common issues women deal with is self-concept. Almost all the women with this problem also report having critical fathers. Spillover stress makes many fathers far more critical and stricter disciplinarians than they want to be. This seems especially hard on daughters. Why? To a certain extent, sons can take the criticism as role preparation—this is reinforced by what boys do to each other all day in play groups. Girls, not preparing themselves for toughness and criticism as part of their femininity, tend to take it more personally.

With sons, the effect is often like that portrayed in *East of Eden*. One son becomes the good boy, following in Dad's footsteps or excelling in a different but compatible field. The other son (James Dean), seeing he cannot compete, rebels. Neither son is his own person: one imitates, the other reflexively reacts *against*.

Item: Frank is a top sales rep for a midwest region of Xerox Corporation. It is his turn to give his quarterly sales report. He announces he just lost his main account—meaning the entire branch loses its rank as number one in the district and they all lose the Caribbean trip with their families. Bob goes over to Frank, puts his arms around him, brings his head gently to his shoulder, and tenderly allows Frank the opportunity to cry. As tears fall onto Bob's jacket, Bob holds Frank affectionately and says gently that he knows the loss must hurt, that he would have lost the account too, and that they're all supporting him.

Obviously, the above "item" is fictional. Had it been true, both Frank and Bob would be suspect as the office's "gay squad." But imagine this item.

Item: Bob's son, Steve, has just gotten his first D—in his junior year in high school. He had hoped to get into the University of Michigan's honors program. Now, he fears, there's no chance. Bob goes over to his son. He puts his arms around him, brings his head gently to his shoulder, and tenderly allows Steve the opportunity to cry.

Most of us would agree that it is desirable for Bob to go over to his son and comfort him. Such behavior may or may not be desirable for him in an office setting. This is not the issue. The issue is that what is desirable behavior at home is considered totally inappropriate at work. Again, there are two conflicting sets of behavior expected of the same successful man.

We shall see that the more successful a man, the less likely his wife is to work. And therefore his daughter is more likely to have as a role model a mother who does not work full time. To compensate for a lack of attention, some successful fathers give things to their daughters, creating the message that "men give money, you don't have to earn that yourself."

One danger of a man succeeding is that it teaches his wife and daughter not to worry about success.

In the effort to become successful at work, then, self-listening and finding the flaw are rewarded; to be successful with our wives and children, listening is helpful—and a dose of "awe training" doesn't hurt. To be successful at home, it helps to hug and hold; holding at work can lead to gossip. Saying "oh, boy" is great for daddy at home; it provokes stares if said by a male executive at work. At work, defeating an opponent is top priority; at home, helping a child win is top priority. At home, it helps to roll on the floor, play peekaboo, go goo-goo; at work, well . . .

Men try to make themselves attractive to women by the very process that ultimately alienates them from women. And women find themselves most attracted to men who have the most training in distancing, then wonder why they cannot find sensitive, vulnerable, intimate men. The very process that creates male distancing leaves an intimacy vacuum. Which means men approach commitment with a deep need for intimacy. So why are men afraid of commitment?

6

Why Are Men So Afraid of Commitment?

Why are men so afraid of commitment? Chapter 2 explained how most men's primary fantasy is still, unfortunately, access to a number of beautiful women. For a man, commitment means giving up this fantasy. Most women's primary fantasy is a relationship with one man who either provides economic security or is on his way to doing so (he has "potential"). For a woman, commitment to this type of man means *achieving* this fantasy.

So commitment often means that a woman achieves her primary fantasy, while a man gives his up. Commitment, then, means almost exactly the opposite to a woman as it does to a man. And legally, once a man commits to marriage, if he tries to achieve his primary fantasy he breaks the law (adultery). Women's primary fantasy *is* the law.

Because commitment means a man must forfeit his primary fantasy, a man may need to be more *in love* to commit. Let's look at that one more closely.

We know that we cannot assume a man is in love by his willingness to go to bed with a beautiful woman. Similarly, we cannot assume a woman is in love by her willingness to commit to a man who provides a security blanket. She could be falling more in love with the security blanket than with the man—or rather with the image of the freedom that blanket will give her to do what she wants with her life; with the image that her parents consider her mature for choosing a man who is "mature"; with the image of her children in good schools; with the image of living in a good neighborhood; or with the image of trying a fantasy career that will leave her independent, fulfilled, and a respected role model. If a man provides security, commitment can be her way of saying, "I want that security locked in for life." For a man it can mean forfeiting his fantasy for life. So he'd better be *really* in love.

None of this means commitment is bad for men. In fact, married men live longer and are often happier than single men. One of the reasons commitment is generally good for men is precisely because it takes away their preoccupation with a destructive, often no-win, fantasy. But it is often as hard for many men to break with the fantasy as it is for a woman to marry an unemployed house painter because it will make her shed her Cinderella complex.

From a man, "I'm not interested in marriage" is the equivalent of a woman's first "I'm not interested in having sex." Just as a man often tries to turn the sexual nos into maybes and the maybes into yeses, so the woman often tries to turn "no commitment" into maybe, and maybe into yes. But the woman who discounts the man's warning finds herself hurt when he is still not committing two years later.

In the area of commitment, the man is in the power position—to grant or deny a woman access to her primary fantasy. Just as the woman is in the power seat with sex. Yet most women want to have sex. And most men want to commit. So what is the underlying meaning of both sexes' nos? It is *"you don't meet my conditions."*

Most women are quite good at supplying those conditions—from supportiveness and attractiveness to devotion and sex, and now, even income. But men have begun to tune into the likelihood that her income will decrease after marriage, her weight will increase, and, eventually, devotion, intimacy, and sex will diminish. So why commit?

This places a different slant on "the male fear of commitment." Behind that phrase is generally an accusation: "He's a typical man—he doesn't know how to get close. I know he loves me, but then he runs away as soon as we get close. . . ." Both sexes have difficulty with intimacy. But commitment does not require intimacy. In fact, *if a man doesn't know how to be intimate, why, exactly, would a woman want to commit?* Accusing a man of a fear of commitment is sometimes accurate. And many men have difficulties with intimacy. But a woman cannot suggest that she honestly want intimacy from a man and then say she wants commitment from a man who is not intimate.

Cathy Guisewite, *A Mouthful of Breathmints and No One to Kiss*, p. 14

The Pressure to Commit

Do men in the mid-1980s still get pressure to commit? Yes. Men who are "afraid of commitment" are called "Peter Pans"—men who never grow up—in articles such as "The Peter Pan Principle" in *Esquire*[1] and even in the only book on male psychology written by a man ever to make *The New York Times* best-seller list: Dan Kiley's *The Peter Pan Syndrome: Men Who Never Grow Up*.[2] By February 1986 the Literary Guild's portrayal of a book, *How to Get a Man to Make a Commitment*, played on a woman's fear of a commitment's being broken by showing the man removing the diamond.

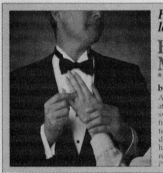

For those women who are looking for "Mr. Right"!

How to Get a Man to Make a Commitment*
*Or Know When He Never Will
by Bonnie McCammon Barnes and Tisha Clarke

Are you tired of a full day at work and an empty evening at home? Authors Barnes and Clarke may have the answer as they give their advice on avoiding "Mr. Wrong," finding "Mr. Right," and winning a commitment. They tell you: • Where to go to meet eligible men • How to develop your own style and self-esteem • How to get him to make a commitment, or discover for sure if he never will, in a two-week, day-by-day program.
Pub. Ed. $12.95   Mem. Ed. $9.79 ②   #052571

The *Esquire* article throws light on what underlies the pressure to make men commit. The author interviewed women about men who could not commit. They all gave him examples of such men and wanted to know what was the matter with them. The examples, though, were, to a man, all very successful professionals. The women were *not* complaining about *unsuccessful men who were afraid of commitment*. They were complaining about men who were very committed to work but not committed to them.

These men were committed enough at work to get the necessary advanced degrees (Harvard M.B.A.s, M.D.s, etc.). They had committed their lives to becoming the success they felt these women now wanted overnight. They learned that creating fantasies and achieving them requires perseverance, commitment, and postponed gratification (as opposed to being a *Playboy*). For most, it also meant minimal time spent pursuing women.

Some men were doing more than developing social lives for the first time; they were exploring the values their parents may never have had the chance to explore, and asking themselves, "Now that I have the option to make $100,000 a year writing ad copy, do I want to spend my life actually doing it?" For these men, the exploration of such values means growing up.

In my own life, I explore my values best in a committed relationship—whether it's marriage or living with a woman. Some men do not. When Barry considered committing to Meg and Meg's two children, he knew the added expense would make him less likely to give up writing ad copy. For Barry, holding off on commitment was a sign of maturity. Nor did he want to commit and be resentful of Meg.

Men who "won't commit" are often condemned for treating women as objects—hopping from one beautiful woman to the next. Many men hop. But the hopping is not necessarily objectifying. Men who "hop from one beautiful woman to another" are usually looking for what they could not find at the last hop: good communication, shared values, good chemistry. These men are pursuing what we all want, although most of us stop short out of fear we cannot get it. Men who have enough security to demand all these things learn they are as difficult to find with one woman as they are to find with one man. Hopping is the male equivalent of her saying, "I can't go on this way any longer—I need a commitment." She is hopping to a commitment. He is hopping until he finds someone he wants to commit to.

If a man cannot expect a perfect woman, what is he willing to give up? Almost anything, if he gets enough. Including beauty. But the process of learning he may have to give up beauty is a hard one, especially if he is giving up his primary fantasy of a *variety* of women and the one woman he chooses is not even beautiful. In that case, commitment for a man is harder than it is for a woman, who is achieving part of the female primary fantasy merely by the act of marriage.

Some women who believe men can't commit may feel a need to hold on to that position. As one woman confessed, "He rejected me. For a year I preferred to say, 'He couldn't commit.' Now I'm ready to look at why." *When a woman complains about "men's fear of commitment," she may also be avoiding looking at why she was rejected.* An understandable defense for a while, to be sure. But if "He was afraid of commitment" becomes a defense against looking at what created his fear, the new men in her life will quickly sense her unresolved anger toward men.

In fact, if a woman brings that anger to her next relationship, it may well get off to a *worse* start than her last one. This may prevent a relationship from happening at all. She will line up at the starting block handicapped with the pain her body language exposes to the man from the outset.

Commitment valued for its own sake, then, tempts "falling in love" to *commit* rather than genuinely falling in love. This encourages a fragile family life. A parallel pressure occurs for women when we call women selfish if they choose to not have children—we generally recognize this now as unenlightened.

I have discussed how a single woman who supports herself is called a career woman, while a single man who supports himself is called a play*boy*. *He may pay for her play as well as his own—but he hasn't "grown up" until he pays for her life.* Ironically, a woman who commits and becomes financially *de*pendent is considered more mature than a man who does *not* commit but is financially *in*dependent.

When we pressure a man to commit by implying he has not grown up, we become like the coach who calls a man "sissy" to egg him on to perform. Maybe commitment is just the modern word for pressuring men to perform.

Women also get pressure to commit. The part of this pressure that comes in the form of a fantasy is often not recognized for what it is—pressure. Just as a man who fantasizes being a war hero is discouraged from questioning the purpose of war or the possibility of his death—and he does not realize that the fantasy of being a hero is actually pressure on him not to question—so a woman's fantasy of better homes and gardens is actually pressure on her not to ask herself, "Is marriage for me?" "Is he for me?'' or ''Are children for me?'' Both sexes' fantasies deprive them of power.

A woman's commitment fantasies make her ''commitment compulsive'' just as a man's work and sexual fantasies make men workaholics and sexually compulsive. As one woman in a women's group put it, ''Why did I rush into a twenty-year sentence of children and housework?'' Her fantasy camouflaged the pressure.

The Politics of Commitment

Why Does He Say He Loves Me . . . Then Backs Off from Commitment?

In a group I worked with in Stevens Point, Wisconsin, a woman named Elena asked, ''Why do men hint at commitment if they don't mean it? It's not to get sex, because that's already happening.'' Her boyfriend Bob was standing next to her; and, to her surprise, he volunteered an answer. ''When we started going out I'd say things like 'Next month it would be great to take off a weekend and go skiing—if we're still together.' Elena would sulk and say 'Why do you always add, *''if* we're still together''?' So I stopped adding it. Now she says I shouldn't have held out promises I couldn't keep.''

Bob played into the system. He was fearful Elena would break off the relationship or sexually withdraw if he said no rather than maybe. So when Elena asked him his opinions about favorite months for weddings and favorite styles of homes and Bob answered, Elena translated his answers into ''He's interested.'' He may have been aware she was going down a different path, but he was afraid to confront her out of fear she would withdraw. Both sexes were behaving identically in one underlying respect— each was trying to feed the other sex's fantasy just enough to get more of its own.

Do Women Have Fears of Commitment?

Many a woman is committed to a man who approaches her, rather than to one of the hundreds of men she may have seen during her life whom she might have approached had she been socialized differently. This socialization to veto (I call it ''veto power socialization'') may have left her committing to a man who would have been her fifth or sixth choice had she initiated with some of the hundreds of men who caught her interest. Her socialization to veto or say "Isn't he cute" to a woman friend—but not to work past the barriers to initiate a conversation with him, ask for his phone number, and get him to take out his calendar for a follow-up dinner—means she may have missed many men who did not pursue her indirect cues. All this may leave her ambivalent about the man she is committed to even though she is not ambivalent about the *idea* of commitment.

Other women, like Jan, approach men who excite them. But Jan married a man who was "good" for her. She told me that she often fantasized about the one man who had "broken through to the real me."

During undergraduate school, I rented a room from a couple who had been married for twenty-four years. Mrs. Levinson was fond of telling me how much she had been pursued while she was in college, and how two of her "suitors," as she called them, later went on to become well-known and wealthy. As she would watch one of them on the news she would mention to me repeatedly, sometimes in front of her husband, how she had dated the celebrity. There was remorse in her voice: "And I gave up John for Barney. . . ." I remember that the evening she and Barney celebrated their twenty-fifth anniversary, she told him, unconvincingly, "I could have married John, but I'm glad I married you."

While theoretically symbolizing the "female primary fantasy fulfilled," a couple's twenty-fifth anniversary can be built on a deeper foundation of ambivalence for the woman who accepted a man who pursued her, who was *safe*, or who didn't reach his potential, than for the man who was able to get up the nerve to at least ask his second or third—if not his first—choice.

Do men sense this ambivalence toward them? Yes. They hear ambivalence when phrases like "You're always late for dinner" coincide with "I need more time to myself." Among working-class men, many of whom work close to home in mines, factories, stores, or gas stations, for whom coming home for lunch is a possibility, a favorite motto is, "I married him for better or worse—but not for lunch." This makes some men wonder exactly what they are wanted for. The fantasy may be intimacy, but when it comes to the reality of a husband . . . well, not for lunch, thank you.

Women, then, are much less likely to have fears of the idea of commitment; they are quite likely to feel ambiguous about the actual man to whom they are committed.

Afraid of Being Afraid

Women sometimes get men to commit by accusing them of being afraid of commitment, which can work—but for the wrong reason—to prove he's not afraid. A man who can be manipulated into proving that he is not afraid to commit can eventually be manipulated into proving that he is not afraid to have a child, and not afraid to try for a promotion he doesn't think suits him. This manipulation comes with the price tag of eventual withdrawal—whether at the bar or in front of the TV. The price tag is the lack of intimacy. Yet another reason willingness to commit may have little to do with intimacy.

The man who admits he is afraid of being manipulated into commitment by appeals to prove he is "not afraid of commitment" is a man who is in touch with his feelings. He may not be able to articulate what he is fearing, but he is at stage one—in touch with the feeling that *something* is wrong.

What About Women Who Have No Trouble Finding Men Who Want Commitment?

Younger women are the least likely to say that men are afraid of commitment. In fact, for women in their early twenties it is often the reverse; they find that men are "easy," "easy commits." (If our attitudes toward commitment were as negative as our attitudes toward sex, a man who was *not* afraid of commitment would be called an "easy commit.") Why? In all age groups prior to age thirty, men outnumber women.[3] Including single men. So women in their early twenties have more options—and people with options worry less about commitment.

Like young women, highly attractive women have little trouble getting men to commit. But what about women who are neither young nor Charlie's Angels? Do some of them have men knocking down their doors to commit? Yes. They also often have relationships that leave them and their men happy. What distinguishes these women from the ones who have trouble?

In my work with some three hundred women's groups, I have found significant differences between these two groups of women. One is the difference in the attitudes they have about men. If I were to apply this difference to how women might read this book, the women who have men banging down their doors—even at the age of fifty, when they are rarely part of the male primary fantasy—are likely to have read everything preceding this chapter rather than skipping to this chapter. She is less concerned with the *goal* of commitment than with how men like Ralph hurt or feel powerless. Second, as she reads she is much less likely to be thinking, "But he doesn't understand how *I* feel." She reads to find the germ of truth rather than to find the flaws.

Third, women with little trouble with commitment only occasionally call their mothers or their women friends when they have a criticism of their men. They use their energy first to consider his perspective and second to confront the man directly with what is still not understood. When they receive criticism in turn *they don't make a big thing out of it*—whether it's direct criticism ("I don't like the weight you're gaining") or indirect ("I found myself fantasizing about another woman"). Fourth, they don't focus on the verbal excesses of anger, whether it's name-calling or "I hate you," but are more likely to look at the anger in the entire context of the argument. They do not focus on the excess of anger as a way of sidestepping the issues that led to the anger. As a result, the men in their lives rarely resort to anger. In brief, people who feel heard rarely explode. *These four distinguishing characteristics seem to attract men with the same four characteristics.*

In the work arena, these women like their work and have no plans of forfeiting it after a man commits. She enjoys sex for its own sake, not just commitment-related sex; she possesses a *joie de vivre*. In the process, the men in her life sense the potential for the fulfillment of their primary unfulfilled *need*—intimacy—as well as a good sex life. And they bang down the door. And the one who gets admitted rarely feels tricked or trapped, but rather grateful.

Is Conquest More Important Than Commitment for Men?

The male "conquest" mentality does exist. In the process of turning women into sex objects in order to handle rejection, some men prevent themselves from really getting to know women as persons. And whenever either sex is getting its primary fantasy fulfilled there is a tendency toward conquest—getting it fulfilled—rather than truly understanding the person. But the importance of conquest to men is greatly overemphasized. When a man has sex, two things happen: first, the quality of the sexual connection tells him a lot about whether his partner could be Ms. Right; second, after sex there is less preoccupation with how to get sex without getting rejected in the process. After sex, his preoccupation is reduced, which allows him to make a shift in priority—to determine more clearly whether all the time he spent with a woman before sex has made her a candidate for Ms. Right. It is less that a conquest has happened than the fact that, if the woman isn't Ms. Right, other women still hold the potential of being Ms. Right. Since commitment isn't his fantasy, he doesn't fantasize commitment with her unless she meets his other needs—so he keeps on searching, especially if he senses strings will be attached should he stick around.

We often say men are just after sex and conquest, as if they were one and the same. *If men were just interested in sex, they'd stick around for the sex they've invested all that time, money, and potential rejection to get.* Of course, most men *will* stick around if the sex is terrific. But then we can't accuse them of being just interested in conquest. The quality of the sexual connection is an important ingredient of commitment. Sex itself is not.

Why Do Men Commit?

The meaning of commitment changed for men between the mid-sixties and the mid-eighties. Commitment used to be the most certain route to sex and love, and to someone to care for the children and the house and fulfill the "family-man image." Now men feel less as if they need to marry for sex; they are more aware that housework can be hired out and that restaurants serve meals; they are less trapped by family-man image motivations, including the feeling that they must have children. Increasingly, that leaves men's main reason to commit the hope of a woman to love. Which is why the changes stimulated by the women's movement have contributed so much to the potential for love.

Do men feel as if they get love from commitment? When more

than six hundred couples were asked, "Do you love your spouse?" only 11 percent were able to respond with an unhesitating yes.[4] Men are increasingly hesitant about commitment because when they forfeit their primary fantasy they increasingly do so in exchange for *intimacy and love*. Since the odds are almost 9 to 1 against their getting intimacy and love, they are hesitant. On top of this, if a man is committing for love but is also successful, he may wonder whether the woman has fallen in love or risen in security.

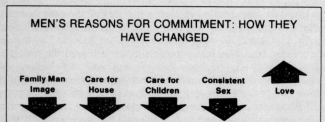

MEN'S REASONS FOR COMMITMENT: HOW THEY HAVE CHANGED

Family Man Image	Care for House	Care for Children	Consistent Sex	Love

Down arrows mean these reasons are less important than previously; up arrows indicate increased importance. "Women's Income" is a new reason some men commit, but is not listed because it was not previously a reason for a man committing to a woman. As children become less a programmed assumption of male maturity, a man's need to "find a mother for his children" becomes secondary to finding a woman he loves and then deciding whether or not he wants children. There is less of a need to look for a good mother; more of a need to find a good woman.

The Male Commitment Shift— Primary Fantasy to Intimacy

When a man commits, a crucial shift occurs. I call it the "male commitment shift." He trades in his primary fantasy and hopes to receive his primary unfulfilled need: intimacy, respect, and appreciation—in essence, love. Survival and security are the primary needs of all human beings,[5] but male socialization succeeds in training most men to take care of security needs for themselves; female socialization leaves many women expecting men to fulfill their primary need of security. *So for many women security is the primary unfulfilled need; for most men it is intimacy or love since he expects himself to handle his security needs. This frees more men to commit for love only.*

Does woman's primary fantasy already incorporate intimacy? No. Her "have it all" fantasy does. But she does not tend to fall in love within an intimacy framework (such as with an intimate male secretary), but rather within a success framework. Which is why her *primary* fantasy is security.

How can I call security a woman's primary *fantasy* if I am saying it is also her primary *need*? Because the fantasy is that her primary needs get taken care of by someone else. Or at least that a man has the responsibility to take care of them and she has the option to take care of them.

Why do so many women focus so much more than men on intimacy? Because within the framework from which they have chosen their men intimacy is often the single biggest missing ingredient. And because these men, by taking care of much of their primary need, allowed them the luxury of focusing on the neglect of intimacy.

Given the male pull between his primary fantasy and his primary unfulfilled need, it is interesting that, after a marriage ends, a man usually has more of a desire to return to fulfilling his intimacy needs by remarrying than to reactivate his primary fantasy of many women. Statistics show that a man is likely to remarry much faster, especially if he is widowed, than a woman.

The extent of the male commitment shift can be appreciated if we compare Dr. Shanor's finding that the average man under forty thinks of sex six times per hour[6] to the fact that the average married couple has sex 1.5 times per week.* So a man thinks of sex over 600 times for each time he has it. Men in their forties think of sex 336 times per week and have it 1.5 times per week.

The great majority of married men (three-fourths even in Kinsey's time) want extramarital relationships, but few men enter a commitment with the intention of having them. *Given the extraordinary stimuli idealizing a variety of women and more sex within a relationship, men's willingness to shift gears upon commitment is perhaps the most unappreciated adaptation in all human behavior.* Almost as unappreciated as men's desire for intimacy and for being understood and loved.

---

*Couples married under two years have sex slightly more frequently; couples married over ten years slightly less frequently (*American Couples*, pp. 195–196).

It also tells us much about how men change: slowly, but deeply. Men may be slower to commit, but when they do *(even if they have outside affairs once a month)*, the change in relation to their fantasy is enormous. Especially if a man was living out the fantasy in reality prior to commitment.

The meaning of commitment for men cannot be appreciated until that change of behavior is fully appreciated. Or until we understand what the nature of intimacy is to a male.

A man often puts all his intimacy eggs in one basket: those of his wife or woman friend. A woman distributes hers among the children, her women friends, and him. Since a man is likely to have fewer close male friends, and since after divorce he gets the custody of their children only 10 percent of the time, when he loses his wife *all* his intimacy eggs are cracked. When she loses him, her women friends support her, women's magazines support her, her ties with her family often improve, and her children need her; her intimacy network may get stronger. Since intimacy with one woman often means risking everything, it gives a man caution about the woman to whom he entrusts himself. Yet once he has admitted his need for intimacy, a woman's compassion and nurturing become a more potent drug than even his primary fantasy. He can become so dependent that the woman resents his desire for "a mother."

How dependent? In a nationwide study, widowers were found to suffer mental breakdowns, commit suicide, contract diseases, and die in accidents at a much greater rate than widows.[7] The financial security a woman often gets from a man is generally partially preserved by life insurance (if he dies) and by community property laws or alimony (if he leaves). *The intimacy men often receive from women is not at all preserved by insurance or alimony.* The "male power structure" does not save a man from the complete loss of intimacy. When he needs it most, his "power" is powerless.

The solution? Men must take the primary responsibility for developing emotional intimacy with other men and women. The best women can do is to support this process and understand it may mean forfeiting the power of his emotional dependency on her.

When men make the male commitment shift, they often fail to get the things they committed for—intimacy, being understood, and feeling needed. The need they are most likely to have fulfilled is the need of feeling needed—although sometimes they are not aware that this can mean being financially needed.

Researchers at the University of Chicago and the National Institute of Mental Health have pinpointed ten "life strains" that increase men's stress. They discovered three were related directly to marriage, two to parenthood, and the other half to work traumas (being fired, demoted, etc.). Married men are almost twice as likely to live longer than single men,[8] despite the fact that all ten of men's major life strains are exacerbated by commitment. Work failures obviously become more significant to a man who is committed to supporting a family. And so, men's ten greatest life strains are *all* increased during marriage. This can help us understand both the male fear of commitment and the extraordinary importance to men of an even partial fulfillment of their need for intimacy.

Just as many women are now taking a conscious look at their mothers' lives to see if they want lives like that, so men look, although less consciously, at their fathers' lives when deciding if they wish to commit. Buzz grew up in the suburbs of Detroit before attending Wayne State University. Buzz's dad had spent his weekdays working at the Ford plant, his weekends mowing the lawn, fixing up the house, and watching TV. The only excitement in his dad's life, it seemed, came from the tension of two teams clashing on a remote screen.

When Buzz was sticking his high school graduation pictures in the family album, he asked his dad if he had any pictures of himself from high school. His dad took them out and dusted them off. Buzz was shocked. He saw the leanness of his dad's body, the glow in his eyes, the little-boy-devil carefree smile on his face. "I had a German girlfriend at the time," his dad reminisced. "She loved to call me *Teufel*—that's German for 'devil.' " Buzz had all he could do to keep from crying as his dad rested the album on his beer belly. Gone was his dad's glow. He just wanted to put his arms around his dad and say, "Was it my fault, Dad?"

Buzz was afraid that if he told this to his fiancée Kerry, she would take it personally rather than see it as something they both had to work on consciously to prevent. He was afraid she would claim it was part of his fear of commitment, that he should "grow up." But if that's what commitment and growing up was about, Buzz thought he should search for a woman who would search *with* him for a meaningful alternative.

Her Juggling Act, His Intensifying Act

As some women began to see their fantasy of better homes and gardens as drudgery (Cleaner Homes and Housework), they made shifts in their fantasy. But they expected men to pursue the remaining housework and child care *as if it were part of men's fantasy.* It was presented to men not as a fantasy, though, but as "you'd better do it or you're a chauvinist." Men became fearful of committing to a fantasy that was never theirs.

Many women's fantasy shift actually was a fantasy expansion, to include work but not exclude the original fantasy. This led to the female "juggling act"—juggling children, home, and work. But once men committed and had children, they underwent an "intensifying act"—they intensified their commitment to work.

If a woman works, she is forty-three times more likely than a man to take off from work for six months or longer for family reasons.[9] Which means men are about forty-three times more likely to intensify their commitment to work even if they have a

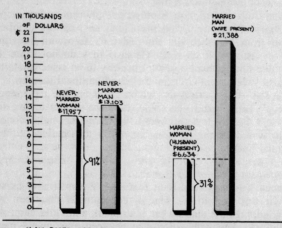

HOW MARRIAGE AFFECTS WOMEN'S AND MEN'S DECISIONS RELATED TO EARNINGS ✻

✻ ALL RACES, AGES 25 to 64. AVERAGE ANNUAL INCOMES

Source: Author's Graph, based on Current Population Survey, Bureau of the Census, series P60, #146 (July 1985), Marital Status

working wife.* The expense of children's clothes, doctor bills, and home expansion forces a man to work more and work at jobs which have more pay. The preceding graph explains the income shift that occurs upon commitment, a shift that creates his intensifying act.

During a speaking engagement in Atlanta, one man said to me: "Hilda and I are talking marriage. This weekend we went looking at homes in a nice Atlanta suburb. Hilda feels it would be a good place to bring up children. Well, she fell in love with a $165,000 house. But at 13.5 percent interest that was over a *half million dollars*. Then I read kids cost $140,000 per, and I figured, two kids times $140,000 equals $280,000. *After* taxes! Shiiiit . . . then I got to figuring utilities, cars, gas, insurance, clothes, and, oh yes, eating. That was enough to send the acid through my stomach. I got so preoccupied with *how to do it* I couldn't get in touch with my feelings until tonight. Well, my feelings are that I'm scared. Real scared. Hilda says I'm afraid of commitment."

Women's magazines acknowledge women's problem—with words like the "Superwoman Syndrome."[10] Women at least feel some empathy. But *Forbes* and *Fortune* do not include stories called "The Male Intensifying Act—Are *You* Feeling Helpless and Out of Control? . . . Read about Other Gentlemen Who Share Your Frustration." Women read ads, cartoons, articles, and books on "How to Get Your Man to Help with the Housework," which call men Neanderthal if they do not share it. It took going back almost a quarter century to an issue of *Playboy* for me to find a parallel critique of the traditional woman.[11]

Such one-sided portrayals, which leave out the never-ending demands of traditional women's work, are similar to one-sided housework articles that do not fairly portray the male economic burden. The ad does portray, however, the burden felt by a traditional man upon commitment that is almost never vented in "men's magazines" like *Forbes, Fortune, Esquire, Sports Illustrated,* or *Popular Mechanics*.

Women who expanded their fantasies, therefore also expanding their responsibilities, were quite resentful that men were merely helping, not sharing the housework and child care. Articles did not clarify the difference between a woman's merely

---

*Statistically, a woman is still "a married woman who works" if her leave is only six months.

helping with the breadwinning—as opposed to her sharing life-time responsibilities for earning a half million dollars per decade, no matter how unfulfilling it becomes. The parallel was undefined, and women were becoming angry at men for not doing their share.

TIRED OF THE RAT RACE?
FED UP WITH JOB ROUTINE?

Well, then . . . how would you like a chance to make $8,000, $20,000—*as much as $50,000 and more*—*each year*, working at Home in Your Spare Time? No selling! No commuting! No time clocks to punch!

BE YOUR OWN BOSS!!!

Yes, an Assured Lifetime Income can be Yours *now*, in an easy, low-pressure part-time job that will permit YOU to spend most of each and every day *as you please!*—relaxing, reading, watching TV, playing cards, socializing with friends! All this, *plus* a Lifetime Security Package that includes *free* Medical Care, Insurance, and All Retirement Benefits! A *free* Home of Your Own Choice! A *free* Late-Model Car, with All Expenses Paid! *Free* Food, Clothing, Telephone and Utilities! *Free* Vacations, Travel, Entertainment!

NO EXPERIENCE NECESSARY!!

Act NOW!
This Offer May Never Be Repeated!!!

Can men justifiably expect anything but anger if women are playing Superwomen while men are playing the same old roles? The recent nationwide study by the University of Michigan's Survey Research Center combining all of men's and women's contributions to the family and home shows that there are only two significant gaps between men's and women's total contributions to the family. These can be seen in the first two pairs of columns in the chart on the next page.

WIFE'S vs. HUSBAND'S TOTAL TIME WITH HOUSEWORK,
CHILDCARE and WORK OUTSIDE OF HOME*

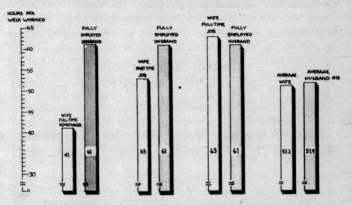

*ALSO INCLUDES COMMUTING. HOUSEWORK INCLUDES OUTDOOR GARDENING, REPAIRS, AND MAINTENANCE AS WELL AS COOKING, CLEANING, ETC. CHILDCARE INCLUDES GENERAL OVERSEEING OF CHILD, PLAYING, TEACHING, READING, TALKING TO AND TAKING CHILD PLACES. IF OVERSEEING CHILD OVERLAPS WITH HOUSEWORK, ONLY ONE GETS COUNTED.
** INCLUDES UNEMPLOYED HUSBANDS

Source: Author's Graph, based on U. of Michigan Survey Research Center data by Martha S. Hill, *Patterns of Time Use in Time, Goods, and Well Being,* ed. by F. Thomas Juster and Frank P. Stafford (Ann Arbor: Institute for Social Research, Univ. of Michigan, 1985), Table 7.3

The career woman who supports only herself is like the bachelor who cooks for himself and cleans his own apartment. If this bachelor claimed he understood what it was like to cook and clean *for a wife and children,* we'd laugh at him. We would claim he did not understand what it was like to pick up after someone else's laziness, to be a servant to his partner, to take on the burdens of a large home, to do it every day, and to be expected to do it as part of his long-term role.

Similarly, the career woman may claim she understands what men go through, but she does not really understand what it's like to pick up the financial needs of a spouse with an income one-quarter of her own (which would be the case if roles were reversed). The career woman who supports only herself does not understand what it's like to take on the extra bedrooms of a larger home needed for her, her husband, and a growing family. To say nothing of the mortgage, utilities, property taxes, second car, clothing, and children's needs. The career woman who supports herself alone is the equivalent of a bachelor in terms of understanding the other sex's burdens.

The career woman who also has full custody of her children, in a home her own earnings have built, and without child support or alimony, is the equivalent of a man in that position. We call her Superwoman. Interestingly, many men are now arguing for such a privilege—the privilege of custody in a home their own earnings have built, without asking for child support or alimony. We do not call those men Supermen.

Why Do Women Work? And How Does That Relate to Their Enthusiasm about Commitment?

For both sexes work can enhance self-concept and serve many needs other than financial. Yet two-thirds of women who work also do so because they have *no choice*. In a 1983 study by the National Commission on Working Women in Washington, D.C., 26 percent of working women had never married; 19 percent were widowed, divorced, or separated; and 21 percent were married with husbands earning less than $15,000 per year. That amounts to two-thirds of all working women—women who work out of necessity.

Of the remaining third, two-thirds have husbands who earn $35,000 or more per year,[12] giving them the option of either choosing fulfilling work or stopping work if it becomes unfulfilling. Work for married women, unlike work for married men, does not mean supporting a spouse (unless it's temporarily supporting his schooling so he can become a better breadwinner). Marriage retains its primary fantasy content because, in reality, it often means a woman no longer has to work out of absolute necessity (46 percent of married women still do not work at all[13]), but that she may work as long as it is fulfilling and feels good.

When we picture a working woman, we picture a woman who has outgrown the primary fantasy that a man will support her. In fact, *the woman who works because she has no husband may actually strengthen her primary fantasy of how wonderful it would be to be relieved of her burden by a man*. The divorced woman with custody of children and a poor job may have an even more pressing primary fantasy. And the married woman who works because her husband earns too little only strengthens the fantasy of a husband who earns more. The woman who works for fulfillment still often wants to marry up. So the increase in the number of women who work has, for every socioeconomic class, only increased the pressure on men to be more of women's primary fantasy. It has given us the illusion of "independent-woman-not-interested-in-a-man-supporting-me." In fact, the "independent working woman" may be looking that much more desperately for a man to support her.

Neither poor women nor wealthy women *choose* to provide for their husbands—or even the family. The socialization to take on financial responsibility *"for better or worse"* has not shifted.

When men are able to support women well, the statistics about women working change drastically. In a survey of newly promoted male executives, 87 percent of these men's wives did not hold paid jobs.[14] In general, *the more successful a woman's husband, the less likely the woman is to work*. This is not the woman's fault. It is a couple's decision.

The Female Commitment Shift

Item: Trial marriage, the *American Couples* study found, differs from the *institution* of marriage in one major respect: "A woman who intends to quit her job will not do so until the marriage has occurred."[15]

Item: Forty-five percent of single women (vs. 23 percent of single men) live with their parents. For women, commitment often means going from their parents to a man. And should they break up with a man, their relationship with their parents is ten times more likely to improve once again.[16]

Both of the above "items" reflect aspects of the "female commitment shift." They are perhaps best illustrated by Colette Dowling, author of *The Cinderella Complex*. Dowling recalls how when she made a commitment to a man by moving in with him, she found herself sliding from being a full-time professional writer who supported herself and her three children before moving into "letting" her new living partner become the sole supporter of her three children, herself, and himself. He resented her shift. She recalls, "I hadn't anticipated the startling collapse of ambition that would occur as soon as I began sharing my home with a man again,"[17] and moreover, "I didn't even seem to be *aware* of the inequity."[18]

How much of an inequity does this commitment shift create? Imagine a woman telling her woman friend: "When we moved in together I supported him, his three children by another woman, and myself. I didn't even seem to be *aware* of the inequity." It would be impossible for any woman to be unaware of the inequity of moving in with a man and immediately supporting him and his three children—without even a marital commitment. Impossible because the woman's mother, father, and women friends would let her know in no uncertain terms: "He's *using* you. Are you sure he really even loves you?" If she defended him with "But he cooks the meals, makes the beds, and cares for his kids," she would be met with "Did you marry your housekeeper?" They would both know the children were his, not theirs, and that housekeeping could be hired; they would suspect that he was at best a charming gigolo—that is, *if* he were charming.

A man's commitment to a woman can mean her shifting from working out of necessity to working for fulfillment, *thereby postponing his ability to make the shift himself.*

If a man wants to commit to an independent woman with a blossoming career and believes he has found her, should he be fearful that once he commits she will become pregnant to avoid career anxiety? Drs. Ruth Moulton, of Columbia University, and Judith Bardwick, author of *The Psychology of Women,* suggest that he should. Even highly talented women, Moulton finds, often "become pregnant to avoid anxiety about their blossoming careers."[19]

Suppose, though, the woman already has children and a career and, as soon as the children get a year or two older, plans to return to her career? Should he worry that she won't? Moulton says that among her patients, at least half the women who were about ready to return to work had another child to keep from facing the outside world again. In what she calls the "pregnancy-to-avoid" syndrome, Bardwick explains that college-educated mothers complain about boredom and claim to want to return to work: however, "It's easy to talk, but difficult to face potential failure and loss of self-esteem. As their children grow older and the possibility of entering into a profession becomes a reality, their interest declines. The logical and salient mechanism for prohibiting entrance into the occupational world is an accidental pregnancy."[20]

Do Women Commit Desiring Equality, While Men Commit Desiring Dominance?

Item: The largest study of singles in the eighties found that women earning high incomes are almost twice as likely to want to remain uncommitted as are women earning low incomes.[21]

Item: The authors of *American Couples* found that lesbians were more likely than other women to claim that income and status were irrelevant. However, the authors found, to their surprise, that the high-income and high-status partner in a lesbian relationship was almost always the one to leave.[22]

Taken together, what the items reveal is that the more income a woman makes, the less willing she is to commit. Which makes her just like a man—and therefore helps us understand why men (who earn more) commit more cautiously. Item two reveals that among lesbians the female primary fantasy of desiring someone with more income and status—marrying up—is still the controlling issue. The study found this an important factor in lesbians having the highest breakup rate of any group investigated—higher than gay men and 400 percent higher than heterosexual couples.[23]

Once a woman is committed, income affects her decisions about leaving in a way that is opposite from men. Men who earn more are *less* likely to leave—or be left. As mentioned above, 84 percent of top male executives are married to their first wives, compared with 53 percent of the total male population.[24]

So if women commit in part to benefit from someone else's income and break commitment when that income is not forthcoming, is it mostly because it is in "the nature of men" to want dominance? A look at gay men gives us some hints. Men in gay relationships resent it if their partners do not contribute equally.[25] Gay men, the same research shows, have no problem sharing housework equally, keeping their homes clean, and preparing a variety of good-quality meals.[26]

Men are much more likely to provide economically for women in marriage than in cohabitation.[27] And women are 40 percent more likely than men to prefer marriage over cohabitation.[28] Once married, though, both sexual quality[29] and sexual frequency decrease.[30]

In brief, the greater the level of commitment, the more the man supports the woman, the less frequent the sex, and the poorer the quality of sex.* This occurs *not* because women are tricky. Both sexes are doing the same thing—fulfilling role expectations. But the more a man fulfills the role expectations of commitment, the less he fulfills the role expectations of his fantasy; the more a woman fulfills the role expectations of commitment, the closer to her fantasy.

The "Just in Case" Syndrome

When men see women exercising more options when they are married, they sometimes wonder whether they are being married "just in case": just in case her career fails and she needs a security blanket; just in case it gets too exhausting, or she wants to switch careers or become a mother—the "Just in Case" Syndrome. As a ten-year-old boy, I used to wonder what God would feel if God felt I were going to church on Sunday "just in case." Would God be afraid of committing to me?

Why Does Commitment Usually Mean Less Sex? The "Marital Incest Taboo"

What happens to reduce sex between married couples? Hundreds of reasons fill thousands of books. An interesting one that I have not seen discussed, though, is what I call the "marital incest taboo." I have found that, for many couples, if they go for about a month without making love, and then one night either partner contemplates initiating sex, he or she confronts a type of taboo—almost like reaching out to a brother or sister. I call it the "marital incest taboo." Our real incest taboo taught us not to feel passion toward the people with whom we take out the garbage—our family; not to feel passion toward the familiar, or those who know intimately our burps, snores, and curlers. Not to feel passion toward the people with whom we survive. The taboo on incest teaches us, rather, to direct our passion outwardly—toward those we can romanticize and idealize. Married sex is sex

---

*Less frequent and lower-quality sex is a deprivation to both sexes. But studies show that the sexual frequency of gay male couples is about twice that of lesbian couples; this gives us some idea about which sex might feel more deprived by a cutback in frequency. See *American Couples*, pp. 195–196; Karen Shanor, *The Shanor Study* (New York: Dial Press), p. 253.

with the familiar. Which may be part of the reason sex between married couples becomes almost taboo.

Few men understand why sex diminishes (the taboo is only one reason), but they do sense something about the familiar that makes sex less likely; they fear it will happen to them once they become day-to-day familiar with, or commit to, a woman. Men articulate this indirectly—by turning up their noses at station wagons and eyeing the Porsche with envy.

If the marital incest taboo helps make familiar sex taboo, what is it about the first vacation, shortly after a couple meets, that makes sex so passionate? Take Orin and Hope, who made passionate love twice a day in the Caribbean shortly after they met, but who, when they returned to the Caribbean four years later to renew their vows, were more concerned about the night life and the quality of the hotel.

What creates this Caribbean passion that no longer exists after commitment? In the Caribbean, Hope had the fantasy of commitment in the wings, which gave her a kind of permission to open up. Orin's fantasies of passion and frequency were nurtured by Hope's openness. And Hope was a new lover for Orin; her newness represented the "variety of partners" aspect of his primary fantasy. In the Caribbean, Orin's and Hope's primary fantasies meshed, and what emerged was passionate sex.

The Real Double Standard

It does not work to a man's advantage to have the primary fantasy of a variety of women and an ideal of marriage that excludes that fantasy. Nor does it work to his advantage that marriage fulfills a woman's primary fantasy and requires him to forfeit his. *The fact that we create different fantasies for each sex and use marriage to fulfill one sex's fantasy but not the other's is the real double standard.**

Male Intuition and the Secret Agenda

"A woman marries a man expecting that he will change, but he doesn't; a man marries a woman expecting that she won't change and she does." This colloquial observation rings all too true.

---

*For a careful explanation of why the double standard (men can have sex more than women . . .) is a myth, see Chapter 8.

When a woman hopes that a man will change, she is keeping a secret agenda. Here are two I've overheard recently:

"Tim says he doesn't want to get married—just live together. So we'll live together—*for now*."

"Oh, yeah . . . Vince says he doesn't want children, but you know how Vince is . . . once we have one he'll love it."

Men who "suddenly" stop calling a woman sometimes have tapped into that secret agenda on a gut level. The woman is angry that he cannot articulate why he "suddenly" wants to "back away from intimacy"—why he is unwilling to tell her directly what's wrong. The man only has an intuition; he's not comfortable telling the woman he "senses" something for which there is no concrete evidence.

The man senses the secret agenda, but he also senses the secret behind the secret agenda—her contempt for him. The contempt reflected in the phrase, "You know how Vince is . . ."; the contempt reflected in her willingness to make a life-altering decision (children) behind his back as if she knows what is good for him better than he does. The contempt in planning for the short term with the long term in mind ("We'll live together—*for now*"). This contempt gets reflected in the woman's body language; few men have developed the skills to do more than feel uncomfortable without being able to say why.

Sometimes a man who breaks off a relationship without articulating why knows why he is doing it and is just being a coward. Rather than rationalizing with "I don't want to hurt the fragile female ego," he just keeps quiet. Other times *intimacy has brought him closer to sensing her secret contempt,* but not close enough to articulate it. And if she is pressing for commitment, he gets out rather than in.

The fact that a man cannot articulate what creates his fears of commitment does not mean little things don't register on some level. If he's a man who really does want an independent woman, the first sign of whether she is independent or wants it both ways comes with the first restaurant bill. The first time Lois and Craig went out, when the check came, neither Craig nor Lois picked it up. When Craig finally did, Lois asked, "Can I help?" Craig responded, "If you'd like." Lois responded in two ways. Verbally, she said, "How much do I owe?"; nonverbally, a look of negative surprise crossed Lois's eyes. Despite her behavior of volunteering to share the cost, her look of disapproval made Craig feel like a cheapskate for agreeing.

Craig was not able to put his finger on this cheapskate feeling until a man in a men's group happened to describe an almost identical scene. For Craig, it was like recalling a dream. He remembered feeling like the boy who believed his mother when she said, "I don't want anything for my birthday." Craig was not aware that an accumulation of mixed messages made him suspicious that committing to Lois would mean taking care of Lois, even though Lois was proud of her work and the independence it brought her.

Men who get in touch with their feelings begin to be able to apply them to the contradictions they see around them. If they are honest, they will confront the woman with these contradictions. That's the price of men getting in touch with feelings. The reward is that when the contradictions are even partially resolved, the path to commitment out of love becomes that much clearer.

The Special Fears of Men Who Have Had Children

"Once we had children our sex life deteriorated. I was told we had to wait till the kids were sound asleep; I couldn't make too much noise; she was tired; had to get up early. Do you think this motherhood stuff is an escape from sexuality?"

Brian, forty-six

"Once we had Sammy, it seemed she and Sammy were the family and I was an outsider, just 'Daddy the Wallet.' When Sammy would ask for something, she'd be so quick to say yes I felt Sammy was getting spoiled. So I became 'Mr. Discipline.' I don't want to be 'Mr. Discipline' again."

Harvey, forty

"At best, I admired my ex's ability to love the kids; at worst, it felt not like her love, but her neediness . . ."

Tom, thirty-eight

The very real fear of commitment for many men who have had children comes from the memory of their first wives becoming childaholics, escaping from their husbands and the world through their children. Some men feel children have the effect of forcing them to distance themselves by having to become workaholics to support them, making the home not his castle, but hers. As one man put it, " 'A man's home is his castle' is bull; I came home to my wife's rules. It was *her* castle, my mortgage."

Many men recalled that the biggest shift in their marriage occurred when children arrived. The wife gets paid for intimacy with the child. The husband loses pay when he takes time out for intimacy. Intimacy, which is the job of the woman at home, becomes a distraction from his job for a man. But intimacy is what he committed for. So if he has already had children, the thought of commitment to a second woman's children can make him wonder whether he'll be forfeiting the very intimacy he traded in his fantasies to attain. He experiences the "intimacy take-away."

The men who seem to experience the greatest intimacy take-away are those who were married to women who felt children were "part of a program"—sort of the next stage in her primary fantasy. At first these men are unable to let themselves admit they feel used. They feel replaced by the child just as the Velveteen Rabbit felt replaced when the boy substituted it for the newest toy in his developmental stage. Men react not by getting in touch with these feelings, but rather by withdrawing; not by renegotiating the balance between her juggling load and his intensifying load, but by increasing his intensifying and paying for her intimacy.

For a man, not a scrap of his primary fantasy of *Playboy* and *Penthouse* is met by having to provide for a home with additional rooms, higher utility bills, baby-sitters, cluttered floors, and dirty dishes, with rejection by the children and a woman who feels pulled between him and someone else thrown in. Only if she and he arrange their relationship to prevent the intimacy take-away will he find his main purpose for committing—intimacy—satisfied. And she will find herself with an identity beyond their children.

As Frank, who had two children and was considering marrying Judy, who had custody of her three children, half-joked, "Every time I say 'I love you' to Judy, I think of seven mouths." For Judy, commitment to Frank meant less responsibility for feeding four mouths. There are plenty of joys in being a new parent. There is a great deal of learning. Frank loved Judy's children. They were just not what he set out looking for.

If a woman has been "father-hunting," she may not even let herself be open to a man who does not fulfill his role. For her, commitment and love to a role-fulfiller come more easily. For him, commitment and love come less easily because of the role he must fulfill.

The New Fear: Stepfathering

Fourteen million children in the United States now live with only one parent. *Because over 90 percent of these children live with their mothers, men are approximately nine times more likely to become stepfathers than women are to become stepmothers.*[31]

Stepparents of either sex (instead of saying *step*, I will use *new*—as in "new father," "new mother," and "new parent") face realities that previous generations rarely faced when married: they must deal with their new partner's children, visiting privileges, several sets of grandparents, and the relationships among the new siblings. Into this complexity are blended the adults' conflicting theories of child rearing and the balances between discipline, love, everyday schedules, fairness of treatment, and egos. This all requires such a change from the single life that it might give pause to a single person of either sex.

On the one hand, it is amazing that these "blended family" relationships last an average of almost five years.[32] On the other hand, a relationship likely to last only five years can help us understand the special fears faced by men—the sex most likely to make a five-year investment in children who are not his to begin with and whom he may never see again should the commitment end.

New Dad as Rejected Dad: The Two-Year Syndrome

The nine-times-greater likelihood of women to have custody of children after divorce means that a man is much more likely than a woman to experience the "two-year syndrome": the almost constant rejection of him by his new children for approximately two years (experts say this is the average length of time it takes for a new parent to be accepted by the partner's children). For the hundreds of thousands of these men who have never before been fathers, the "two-year syndrome" means that their introduction to fathering is two years of rejection. And no one can reject more subtly and powerfully than a child.

I have gained a special feeling for the hurt experienced by a new father during my three years of living with Anne and her daughter Megan. When I met Anne five years ago, Megan, before meeting me, thought of me as "the man Mommy stayed out with longer than she said she would—the man who made Mommy keep the baby-sitter waiting." Megan picked up on her mom's special interest immediately.

The result? When I first met Megan, her three main responses to me were "I don't know," "I don't care," and "It doesn't make any difference." She and Mom had been alone together six years. The first time her dad had remarried, his new wife showed very little affection to Megan. And Anne had fallen in love only once before during those six years (to a man who lived five hundred miles away); Megan saw that as "Mom was gone a lot more often. . . . If Mom falls in love again, I'm going to be deprived of her love again."

So I was to be rejected before Megan got rejected.

To casually say that it took four or five months to move out of this stage is to minimize the extraordinary pain I felt with every overture that was unresponded to: the unspoken "get out of here—you're just trying to be nice to me because you want to take my mother away from me"; the distrust in the eyes of an eight-year-old who seems to be saying, "I know what you're *really* up to"; the kiss good night with the cheek turning the other way and the hands preparing to wipe away the residue of any possible contact; the present received without a thank you; the response to the offer to take time away from writing to pick her up from a friend's when her mom was too busy—"I want *Mommy* to pick me up [not you, Warren]."

Each rejection made each day of deeper commitment a day in which I wondered whether I was setting myself up for years of rejection. Each day eroded my image of myself as a loving, giving man with enough patience and creativity to develop a balanced and loving interaction with a child. Was I inadequate, was I a masochist, or was this a stage? It was easy to know intellectually that it was a stage, but calling it a stage feels like telling an army private who has just engineered his way through his first minefield—every second knowing that one careless step could destroy everything he's worked for—that what he just moved through was "just a stage."

I know that while I was in the midst of this minefield it would not have helped if Anne saw my caution and told me I was afraid of commitment in an accusatory tone. Yet it would have been equally off-putting for Anne to have said, ''I'm glad *you're* not afraid of commitment like most *other* men are.'' That would have been an ''ego bribe'' to deny my feelings. What I wanted was that my feelings of fear be acknowledged and the *reasons* for them understood. I felt caution was a sign of maturity—and of respect for myself, Anne, and Megan. When I felt understood on that level, I came to trust that I had met a woman who understood my feelings even when they were feelings she would ideally prefer I not have. *That* told me a lot.

In turn, it would have been unreasonable for Anne to do this if I were not understanding her minefield in the process: attending to the fragility of her new relationship and the fragility of her child; the bind that if she understood me, Megan might interpret it as proof that my inclusion meant her exclusion (which would only force Megan to reject me longer); and the haunting fear that if she didn't take my side, she would lose a man she loved and resent Megan for it. I guess the more she understood me, the more I understood her, the more she understood me—but most of all, I felt good about commitment growing out of the cycle of understanding rather than pressure.

The child's understandable adjustment period can create another fear for the new father: Is the child's mother really in love with him, or in love with the fact that her child has a male role model, and a nicer home than they could afford without him?

For most fathers, all this happens in a vacuum, without the support groups women have developed over the past fifteen years, an outgrowth of women's communication style. Instead of support, magazines and newspapers announce, ''Incestuous fathers are often stepfathers who married the mother to have access to the daughter. . . . There is no identifiable profile of these men. . . . They can be the community's most respectable church-goers.'' In essence, every father is suspect. This doesn't help the new dad as he reaches out for a likely-to-be-rejected hug.

The Female Shift at Commitment's End

''My lady and I just broke up. But our sex was always terrific—the electricity was so strong we never got utility bills. I guess you could say we were sexually 'hooked.' But the moment we

broke up, she was 'unhooked.' I could understand if she needed to stop having sex to get unhooked. But it seems she got unhooked from the sex itself. That makes me wonder. . . ."

Jonathan, twenty-nine

"Before I was God; now I'm the Devil."

Ned, forty-four

Millions of women and men who are now considering commitment are "experienced." (Society calls it "divorced.") Both sexes make shifts at commitment's end. During four years of attending NOW (the National Organization for Women) meetings and fourteen years of starting hundreds of women's groups, I heard many legitimate complaints about the shifts men make after divorce—from not paying child support to physical abuse to disappearing. Out of these experiences many women developed a wariness toward men, although they still retained their fantasy about commitment. Do men have any special hurts or bitternesses that make them especially hesitant about committing again?

When I attended a meeting of recently divorced men, no hurt was more bewildering to the men than the shifts they felt their former wives had made after commitment was over: "Yesterday she was devoted to me; today she's devoted to getting every penny from me." They couldn't fathom the *suddenness* of the shifts. Or their totality. One man said, "Only when it was over did she tell me the things she had hated about me all along—if I hated her half that much, I could *never* have lived with her."

The men shook their heads in recognition when Chuck said, "First she told me what a shit I was—as a human; then she told me how helpless *she* was. It was like a one-two punch, and it worked. I felt so guilty and shitty, I promised her everything."

A few men also said Ned's experience rang true for them. "I felt that if I recommitted, I'd be wonderful again; if I didn't, I'd confirm my status as a terrible human being." These shifts make men feel like "relationship objects." And wary about committing themselves again.

Of course, neither sex corners the market for the terrible things they do to make the other sex pay when commitments end. Especially if he or she is the rejected party. Whether or not one sex pays more is impossible to measure. It is possible to say only that men often report a shift at commitment's end, from "lovely lady" to "vicious woman," whereas women often say, "I *always sensed* this side of him." Men report feeling kept in the dark longer and exposed to the sudden light when they are most vulnerable. The female shift at commitment's end is one that hurts. Ironically, though, it is one reason men scamper to another woman: to assure themselves all women won't see them the way their last partner did; to lick the wounds that feel both out of reach and too deep to heal alone.

If a man experiences the female shift after commitment's end, it can encourage a quick remarriage, particularly if the new woman enthusiastically joins his negative view of his former wife. This is a danger sign: the more unnecessarily suspicious the second woman is of the first, the more she is likely to demonstrate a huge shift should the new commitment end—for the same reason that the person who gossips to you will be the first to gossip about you.

A Mouthful of Breathmints and No One to Kiss, by Cathy Guisewite, p. 25.

Women often feel their devotion is misused—that it is being used to make a man secure enough to pursue his primary fantasy. In the second frame, Cathy, by attempting to close off Irving's "misuse" of her devotion, hopes to use it to achieve commitment. From some men's perspective, this is also a misuse of devotion. It makes insightful men feel devoted to women not for who they are but for what they provide, reinforcing their fears of being replaceable parts, or relationship objects.

Why do some women seem to objectify the very men they seemed to love so deeply even a few days previously? The more the woman fears the world, the more she will make a shift by objectifying the man who "forces" the world upon her. Her devotion came when he protected her from those fears; the man who provided protection can expect her objectification to be as strong when the protection stops as her devotion was deep when the protection was provided.

Devotion in exchange for financial support disappears when financial support disappears. How can a man sense whether a woman will react that way? A hint comes in a survey of women married to doctors published in *Medical/Mrs.*, which indicates that the doctors' wives, by their own evaluation, wanted security from marriage more than anything else. According to Colette Dowling in *The Cinderella Complex*, "the conflict and hostility they exhibited toward the men who provide them with all this security is stunning to behold,"[33] yet many of these wives were considered devoted.

If we apply the same understanding to women who fear rejection by the world as we have for men who fear sexual rejection ("it hurts less to be rejected by an object than by a full human being") we can gain some feeling for the immense fear behind the woman's sudden objectification. Her devotion was not really to him, but rather to his commitment. The shift after commitment is merely a shift in objectification.

How can a man distinguish devotion out of fear from devotion out of love? If a woman can support herself financially and is not attached to the *idea* of marriage, it is a good bet she is devoted out of love. A man cannot tell whether a woman is in love with him or his security blanket until she is financially and psychologically independent enough to leave.[34] *Until a woman has learned how to leave, even she cannot be sure she has learned to love.*

Isn't There a Great American Male Shortage— At Least When It Comes to Commitment?

I mentioned above how women, who focus their binoculars on 10 percent of men who meet nine conditions, perceive a much greater man shortage than actually exists.

Let's look at whether men would perceive a woman shortage if they imposed some of the same nine conditions. Suppose a man were looking for a woman who was more successful than he is (so as not to be threatened by his independence and career goals), and who was willing to use her income to support him should his career fail. Would this limit his choices? But suppose from among these women he were only interested in the attractive ones, and waited for them to call him and offer to take him out and take sexual initiatives. Might he perceive a "Great American Woman Shortage"?

What's the Solution? How Can I Be Sure I'm in Love?

A woman or a man can be truly in love with someone who also meets her or his primary fantasy. But if we see a man confining his search to beautiful women or a woman confining her search to men with more financial potential than she has, we can almost guarantee that if the man loses his financial potential, or the woman her beauty, the love would wane. Otherwise why would they have limited their search to that framework?

For a woman, financial independence is a prerequisite to her being able to say, "Now that I don't *need* money, I can focus on my strongest remaining needs—a man who really understands and supports me. From among these men, I can now look *not* at whether they are successful, but at the impact of their work on their lives." She can tell herself that *if his work is exacting a price on him, it will exact a price on us*. This contrasts with becoming financially independent and marrying up, which restricts her access to sensitive men.

When I was discussing this in an Oregon workshop, a woman asked, "Suppose I already love a man who's quite wonderful, but his success *is* exacting a price on his life energy? Can *I* do anything about it if I'm earning a good salary?"

"Yes. You can ask yourself this: 'Can I use my money to *help him make a transition to work which may make him less successful financially, but which would create more life energy for himself and for us?'* "

Few women use their money this way. In my opinion, *that's* using money to create love. It's very different from waiting for Mr. Eligible Successful to gallop along. Mr. Eligible Successful may have made it by himself (which is why he's eligible, but also why he's a loner), or with an ex-wife (he's paying alimony), or he may have made it among the wolves. But some of America's finest men do not fight so well among the wolves. And some who do have chosen not to.

With All This Work on Relationships, Why Are There More Divorces?

All the work men and women have put into understanding the other sex has definitely led to improved relationships—but relationships in the eighties feature both greater complexity and higher expectations, which has led to higher divorce rates.

Complexity first. Second marriages, for example, often involve blended families. And the presence of children, former spouses' attitudes, and legal custody are all factors with which first marriages did not have to contend. Were there not some improvement in the ability to communicate, forget it.

Second, expectations. In every revolution, the expectation created by the possibility for change outpaces the ability of many individuals to achieve it. For example, in the Industrial Revolution, prior to the harnessing of electric power, no one expected electricity in their homes. Soon, people were disappointed if they didn't have it. Men felt inadequate if their incomes could not provide it.

The Relationships Revolution is similar. Formerly, if men

New Yorker, December 1984

provided income and women raised a few children and gained a little weight, not a lot more was expected. Now there are blended families and multiple orgasms; dual careers and shared housework, hyphenated names and communications seminars.

Twenty years ago, a father was barred from most delivery rooms. Now he is expected. A family man was basically an absentee father. Today a family man is expected to be a working father. Twenty years ago, millions of married women didn't think beyond "giving a man sex." Today sex is also for women. Twenty years ago a woman may not have known what an orgasm was. Today she expects multiple orgasms, simultaneous orgasms, sensitivity, and sensuality. Expectations have changed. And in the process, yesterday's bonus can become today's disappointment.

The Industrial Revolution was called the "revolution of rising expectations."[35] Its fallout was disappointment, stress, suicide. The Relationships Revolution is also a revolution of rising expectations. Its fallout is anger, hurt, divorce. But the Industrial Revolution improved our standard of living; the Relationships Revolution is improving our standard of loving.

PART 4
THE NEW SEXISM

The New Sexism

The cover of a best selling book on men:

A comprehensive guide to having a man underfoot

• What they're for • How they think • Where to take them
•Whether to keep them• What to call them • How to spot a lemon

by Stephanie Brush

Stephanie Brush, *Men: An Owner's Manual* (New York: Simon & Schuster/Linden Press, 1984)

Would we recognize this role reversal version as sexism?

Author's role reversal

Introducing reality—the new sexism:

Original cover.

No Good Men consists of almost one hundred cartoons depicting one hundred despicable aspects of men—published by one of America's most successful publishers (Simon & Schuster).

Did we laugh at this violence against men?

Barbara Lovehouse, *No Bad Men* (New York: New American Library), p. 66

Author's role reversal

Would we consider this reversal as violence against women?
If this were a real ad, would this product be worthy of boycotting?

Author's role reversal

Consider the actual ad, which no one boycotted:

Vogue, October 1984

Cartoons like these are examples of the new sexism.

"Doesn't your tiny little mind get lost in your big fat head?"

Playgirl, July 1983

"It's not too serious—he just has delusions of adequacy."

Playgirl, February 1982

Introducing the New Sexism

Sexism is discounting the female experience of powerlessness; the new sexism is discounting the male experience of powerlessness.

Reversing cartoons like these is consciousness-raising, one of the most important aspects of the feminist movement and the civil rights movement. People who do these reversals to raise people's awareness of the new sexism can be called "masculinists." The goal of each of these movements is to eliminate the ways we objectify a group of people. Joking that a woman has "delusions of adequacy" would be considered sexist, as we can see in the cartoon below (a reversal of the last cartoon):

"It's not too serious—she just has delusions of adequacy."

Author's role reversal

In the past quarter century we exposed biases against other races and called it racism, and we exposed biases against women and called it sexism. Biases against men we call humor.

Human beings have always had the need to find an enemy. As

black pride diluted racism, and as women raised consciousness, men became the new enemy. We claimed men's egos were fragile and yet attacked men as if they were invulnerable.

Something becomes racist or sexist when some truth gets distorted to fit a preconceived image. *The Hite Report* found that *men* prefer intercourse more than women; the *American Couples* survey by Schwartz and Blumstein found that *women* prefer intercourse more than men.[1] Hite interpreted her findings to mean that men preferred intercourse because intercourse is male-centered, focused on penis pleasure, an outgrowth of male dominance and ego gratification.[2] Schwartz and Blumstein interpreted their findings: "We think women prefer it because intercourse requires the *equal* participation of both partners more than any sexual act. Neither partner only 'gives' or only 'receives.' Hence, women feel a shared *intimacy* during intercourse. . . ."[3] The findings are diametrically opposed, yet both interpretations could only consider the possibility that women favor intimacy and equality, and men favor ego gratification and dominance. This is distortion to fit a preconceived image—or, when it is applied to men, the new sexism.

How great is the need to distort when it comes to men? Suppose the interpretations were "Women's preference for intercourse means women prefer domination"; or "Women's preference for clitoral stimulation over intercourse means that women are focused on female dominance and self-centered ego gratification." There would have been an uproar. *That* is the real issue. The real issue is not that three scholars both condemned men and praised women no matter what their findings, but rather that hundreds of millions of us watched them on television, or read of their findings in *Time, Newsweek,* or local papers and *did not protest.* In fact, they gave us the interpretations we wanted to hear, as researchers throughout history have always done—whether they were advertisers or research scientists. And the more we hear them, the more these interpretations appear the only plausible interpretations, no matter what the findings.

Perhaps the only "study" to receive more publicity than these two was the Ann Landers postcard poll from ninety thousand readers. When she found 70 percent of women would be content without "the act" as long as they were cuddled, the interpretation was that men were so bad at sex and so deficient at talking and cuddling that women's deprivation was acute enough to make them content with cuddling and tender talk. Now suppose the findings were that 90 percent of women would *not* be content without "the act." We would have heard how women were now sexually liberated and initiating.

Have women developed a deep-seated anger toward men? Yes. I mentioned above how that anger at men is especially strong in the fantasy-not-yet-fulfilled magazines like *New Woman, Woman, Playgirl, Ms.,* and *Cosmo.* Below is one example from *Cosmo,* the best-selling magazine in the fantasy-not-yet-fullfilled category.

"My birth-control device."

Cosmopolitan, September 1984

One of the most common put-downs of men in these fantasy-not-yet-fulfilled magazines is the cartoon depicting a man approaching a woman. Below is one such cartoon from *Woman* magazine, a fast-growing women's magazine.[4] Next to the real cartoon is an example of how an equivalent cartoon might appear if it were about a woman.

"Are you trying to be macho or just stupid?"

Woman, February 1985

"You haven't said much. Are you trying to be feminine or just stupid?"

Author's role reversal

Marry the Enemy

In the next cartoon, also from *Woman*, I've kept the headline intact—since the cartoons often illustrate articles that also put down men. Note that the headline not only calls the man a jerk, but the section title is "Hooked On A Heel."

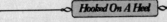

How To Wipe That Jerk Right Out Of Your Mind

...And make him wish he was back in your heart.

"Have you had much experience as a human being?"

Woman, October 1984

Observe the revenge factor: it is not enough for her to get "that jerk" out of her mind—she must make him wish he was back in her heart. It's a perfect example of the "marry the enemy" theme. If a men's magazine ran a title "How to Wipe That Jerk Right Out of Your Mind . . . and Make Her Wish She Was Back in Your Heart," no one would refer to it as a self-improvement magazine. Such titles cannot be found even in current issues of *Playboy*—which is labeled not self-improvement, but pornography.

In the article accompanying the preceding cartoon, the man is first condemned as incapable of commitment and later condemned because he committed to *another* woman. It is easy enough to see that the real issue is that the woman feels hurt and rejected. Yet aren't women supposed to be good at getting in touch with their feelings?

What provokes this denial of feelings, this viciousness? The woman felt not just rejection from a man; the rejection tapped into her fear that she would never achieve her primary fantasy. Are men any better when their primary fantasy is rejected? No. Which is why putdowns of women and violence against women are so often found in pornography—whose readers often feel their primary fantasy is not yet fulfilled. Similarly, when the female primary fantasy is threatened (as with the man who flirts, as shown earlier in the illustration from the book *No Bad Men* [page 191]), we see the man with a knife in his stomach.

Suppose a woman constantly rejects men but does not wish to look at her fear of intimacy? How might she avoid looking at her fear? She can group all men into categories, making each into a different type of loser. Here's one example: the back cover of the book *No Bad Men:*

HUMOR • Z5502 • $4.95
CANADA • $5.95

HOW TO RECOGNIZE YOUR MAN'S BREED

One crucial aspect of the Lovehouse training method is selecting the breed of man that's right for you. Here is a sample of a quiz that will help you determine what category of man you are dealing with:

You go to a party. He immediately:
(a) Starts eyeing other women.
(b) Starts eyeing other men.
(c) Is approached by people who want his advice on the stock market.
(d) Is asked to tell some funny jokes— everybody loves his sense of humor.
(e) Is asked to leave.

ANSWERS:
If your answer was:

(A) YOU HAVE A WOLF. This one will never give up the hunt; he may never learn the command "Down, boy."

(B) YOU HAVE A POODLE. These have their uses, but don't expect them to learn passionate bedroom tricks.

(C) YOU HAVE A GREAT DANE. Reserved, well-bred, and self-disciplined, this man is *proud* of the fact that he hides his emotions.

(D) YOU HAVE CAUGHT A ST. BERNARD. He is big-hearted and cuddly, but tends to leave the toilet seat up even after earnest training.

(E) THIS ONE IS A BASSET HOUND. He's the type of guy you meet on a blind date—not handsome, not sexy, not rich. Of course, he does have one thing going for him: *No one* will ever try to steal him away from you.

DISCOVER THIS AND SO MUCH MORE IN—
NO BAD MEN

0-452-25502-3

Barbara Lovehouse, *No Bad Men*, back cover

Men as Poodles, Wolves, and Turkeys, as Sharks, Worms, and Guppies

In the last two decades, we have stopped merely categorizing men—we now blatantly objectify men into inhuman categories of worms, turkeys, and wolves. Objectification of a group is a prerequisite to not caring if the members of that group are hurt or killed. Objectification of women is a prerequisite for the rapist; objectification of Vietnamese as ''gooks'' was a prerequisite for dropping bombs on them. *Until recently, we have objectified men more subtly—by bribing them. We told men that if they killed themselves, we'd call them heroes.*

The new sexism is more like the ''Vietnamese as gooks'' type of racism than hero objectification. It prepares us not to care whether the *average* man is hurt or killed. To do this, contempt must be developed for these ''dogs'':

CHAPTER 2

Men vs. Dogs: Some Clear-cut Comparisons

"YOU HEEL!"

Barbara Lovehouse, *No Bad Men*, p. 11

"I don't need a dating service when I look for intelligence, loyalty and protection. I usually find all that at the dog pound."

Playgirl, June 1980

Contempt for men ends up hurting women. Note that the women in the *Playgirl* cartoon are giving each other an excuse not to take responsibility for searching out the men they want ("I don't need a dating service . . ."). They are supporting each other by complaining rather than doing. Yet the image is of competent working women.

How is this categorization of men as losers really a fear of intimacy? It creates a support system: "We women all recognize that men are the problem." So the woman who gets into a conflict with a man *never needs to look at herself*. The institutionalized put-down of men is a careful out for the most difficult prerequisite to intimacy—looking at our own part in contributing to conflict. This fear of looking inward *critically* is the real fear behind the fear of intimacy.

Few people are afraid of intimacy per se; they are afraid of the challenge to their self-centeredness that any relationship requires. Looking inside does not necessarily challenge self-centeredness. Looking inward *critically* does. Categorizing all men as losers provides a 100 percent foolproof escape from looking inward critically—the perfect escape from intimacy.

I was surprised to see a whole section of a local bookstore

devoted to cards that categorized men and put down men. The bookstore buyer volunteered that it was her best-selling group of cards. Here is one of the cards:

MainLine Cards

If categorizing and objectifying can be done in the framework of self-improvement magazines and books, one can avoid looking within and be self-righteous about it at the same time.

Why smart women make dumb choices

By Nanci Hellmich
USA TODAY

In *Smart Women*, the authors separate these men into types of "rascals":

■ **The Don Juan.** Women consider him challenging and exciting. He makes a woman feel cherished for a time, but eventually goes off to make another conquest.

■ **The Elusive Lover.** He has the ability to create and somehow maintain a level of promise and hope, but he never comes through. He demands his freedom while holding out a vague promise for the future.

■ **The Married Rat.** He possesses the critical element for intrigue: He is off limits. He promises to leave his wife, but has no intention of doing so.

Besides the "rascals," there are other types who make women want to scream.

■ **The Clam.** His tough mystique covers up a basically selfish, withholding and guarded nature. The woman thinks he is the strong, silent type who just needs to be brought out, but she's never able to penetrate his shell.

■ **The Pseudo-Liberated Male.** Disarmingly attractive to women, he seems sensitive and vulnerable, but actually he uses his new freedom to whine about his problems.

■ **The Perpetual Adolescent.** He seems charming, but actually has shallow views and interactions with women.

■ **The Walking Wounded.** Recently separated or divorced, this man is still recovering from the hurt, bitterness and rejection, and his self-pity eventually becomes tedious.

Shown above are some examples drawn from an article based on a best-selling self-improvement book, *Smart Women, Foolish Choices:*[5]

By the mid-eighties a New Sexism formula had emerged for getting a book on "relationships" on to *The New York Times* best-seller list. Women had to look wonderful, as in *Women Who Love Too Much*[6] or *Smart Women: Foolish Choices;* or men had to look like the problem, as in *The Peter Pan Syndrome,*[7] *The Wendy Dilemma,*[8] *Smart Women: Foolish Choices;* or at best, peripheral, as in *Men Are Just Desserts.*[9]

While every one of these was a *New York Times* best-seller, books whose titles ignored the New Sexism formula, like *Mirror, Mirror,*[10] failed miserably. And books with reverse titles, like *Smart Men: Foolish Choices,* do not exist. Why?

Smart Women: Foolish Choices implies that women are the smart ones; it's just that they make bad choices—and since almost any man a woman can think of can fit into one of the "bad choice" categories, it is not the woman who is the problem—it is him. The book becomes the perfect complement to her horoscope: in a horoscope a woman can find herself in almost any of the descriptions—all of which are about 90 percent positive; in *Foolish Choices* she can find a description for any man with whom she is having a problem—about 90 percent negative.

The reverse title, *Smart Men: Foolish Choices,* would immediately be seen as a self-righteous and sexist put-down of women. No book with a title like that has made the *Times* best-seller list in the seventies or eighties.

Why did *Mirror, Mirror,* published by the most commercially successful publishing house of the early eighties (Simon & Schuster), do so badly—although it was a thoughtful and extremely well-promoted book (e.g., the subject of full-page B. Dalton ads)? Its title recalls a woman who is vain—therefore implying a criticism of women's vanity. Along with the subtitle, *A Fear of Aging,* it implies a need to reexamine beauty power as the basis for a woman's power. So it failed, while diet books sold.

Women Who Love Too Much shared *The New York Times* best-seller list with *Smart Women* in early 1986. Imagine a book titled *Men Who Love Too Much.* And a man reading that book claiming to be introspective. When we saw he was defining his one problem as loving too much—implying that the real problem is women's inability to handle all his love—we would call it "male self-aggrandizement," not self-improvement.

The problem is not always with the book itself. Some of these books have many valid points. The point is that they cannot be sold on that basis. When they are, as with *Mirror, Mirror*, they fail.

Peter Pan

In the mid-eighties, books that criticize men for not committing, like Barbara Ehrenreich's *The Hearts of Men: The American Dream and the Flight from Commitment* and Dan Kiley's *The Peter Pan Syndrome*, have appealed to both academics and lay persons. Imagine how reverse titles would have been received: *The Hearts of Women: The American Dream and Women's Flight from Earning a Living*. ''Peter Pan'' was discussed in the eighties as a man who had never committed and, therefore, never grown up—that is, he failed to fulfill the female primary fantasy of ''better homes and gardens.'' What would an equivalent ''self-improvement'' ad look like if it criticized women for not fulfilling the *male* primary fantasy of being a woman who desired him sexually?

Redbook, September 1984

We were led to believe that *The Wendy Dilemma* was the balance to *The Peter Pan Syndrome*—that it confronted women. But it was, actually, the continuation of the attack on men, with the focus on how a woman can stop being victim to an immature, self-centered boy-child. The subtitle (''When Women Stop Mothering Their Men''), and the promotional copy (''Do you have to tiptoe around his temper, apologize to others for his behavior, take on his neglected responsibilities at home . . . a drama in which you get stuck with the worst end of the deal?'') reflect the emphasis. The woman is portrayed as putting on his slippers. Nowhere in the promotion is the man viewed sympathetically. His dilemmas remain misunderstood.

The ''I Wish He Were Dead'' Fantasy . . . and the Twenty-first-Century Dilemma

Women's feelings of condescension, anger, contempt, and ''disappointed dependency'' have led to objectification and the no-longer subtle ''I wish he were dead'' fantasy toward men. How does this happen? It starts with the fantasy of total control. Look first at this ad in *Vogue:*

Vogue, October 1984

The ad symbolizes the female twenty-first-century dilemma. A woman's fantasy has expanded to the point of expecting not only wealth, but *enough wealth and control over her own life to have sex on her own terms.* The dilemma is that the fantasy has expanded faster than has women's preparation to provide it for themselves. The ad appeals to the pull between the traditional part of many women, which wants a man to provide success, and the independent part, which fantasizes control over her own sexuality, his sexuality, and even him. The traditional part of her is so furious at him for not providing success and sweeping her away (hence the anger in the "independent women" magazines) that his meager gifts must be met with her "I wish he were dead" fantasy.

"I want a perfume that says to a man 'Go to hell!' "

Woman, April 1985

"Your surprise first!"

New Woman, March 1985

I have discussed how the "I wish he were dead" fantasy is also acted out in romance novels. The photograph from *No Bad Men* showed a woman stabbing a man. In that case, the death fantasy was directed toward a man who threatened to disappoint a woman as a provider by flirting with another woman.

What Can We Reasonably Expect of a Man?

In those four cartoons, note that the women are not asking for men to give up any of the traditional male roles in exchange for adopting female roles. Instead they demand that the man *adopt the female role as well*. This makes us think of two liberated women:

"We should have brought along a man to do the cooking!"

New Woman, May 1984

But the reverse makes us think of two lazy men:

"We should have brought along a woman to pay for this!"

Author's role reversal

This would seem like a reasonable expectation:

"How do you plan to support my daughter emotionally?"

New Woman, August 1984

But would this reversal?

"How do you plan to support my son financially?"

Author's role reversal

Notice there is no indication that the woman is a working woman:

New Woman, July 1984

So the reverse must be a nonworking man:

Author's role reversal

The actual cartoon . . .

"If he doesn't like your rough, red hands, let HIM do the dishes."

New Woman, June 1983

. . . and the role reversal:

"If she doesn't like your competitive, insensitive manner let HER support the family."

Author's role reversal

Why Are Men Such Jerks?

Note the distinction in the Cathy cartoon between the three bad guys and the one good guy. Each bad guy failed to fulfill the female primary fantasy in different ways—Phil was a betrayer, Tony a life-ruiner, and Nick, just stupid, a jerk. Frank, who fulfilled the woman's primary fantasy, is the hero.

Cathy Guisewite, *A Mouthful of Breathmints and No One to Kiss*, p. 55

Once we understand how objectification is often a group's way of handling rejection by its primary fantasy, the objectification of men becomes more understandable. We can then see it immediately in cartoons like this "Suddenly Single" in *Woman* magazine:

"After my break up with Bill, I told myself there's plenty of other fish in the sea. But so far all I've found are sharks, octopuses and helpless guppies!"

Woman, December 1984

We can see the rejection by the primary fantasy man in the cartoon title, "Suddenly Single." In this light, the practice of calling men "wormboys," a current national craze, becomes understandable. In the *Washington City Paper*'s article entitled "Wormboys," Deborah Laake describes wormboys as men who shrink from marriage and even hesitate to ask a woman for dinner because that implies more commitment than a drink. Again, the insult toward men is a clear reaction to being rejected rather than being asked out, paid for, and paid for "as much as she deserves" (dinner, not drinks). But it is also anger about equality and *the name-calling is a way of avoiding equality*. A woman doesn't get as much help from name-calling as she would from an article encouraging her to be truly equal by calling a man herself and paying for his dinner rather than complaining that he is too cheap to buy her dinner. Or an article encouraging her not to label as "fear of commitment" what may be his desire to avoid another one-sided paying situation.

If real equality and intimacy are avoided via such objectification, and hopes for intimacy are repeatedly dashed, then new relationships start through a filter of suspicion and mistrust.

"I want a turkey I can trust."

The New Yorker, November 19, 1984

The woman in *The New Yorker* cartoon may be consciously asking for a "turkey she can trust," but her *mis*trust will create a lack of intimacy—who can be intimate with a turkey?—and a lack of equality—a turkey had better do something *extra* to prove himself equal to a human, the essence of *in*equality. If he can do all this, he'll be wanted by everyone else, too; he will therefore probably commit to someone else, and she will be looking for another turkey she can trust.

There is hope, though. If the turkey can't be trusted, we can tell ourselves *Men Are Just Desserts*. Whenever we cannot handle rejection, turn it into something less serious, into an object. As men do with sexual rejection by turning sex into a game and calling it scoring. Games are less serious. So why not turn men into turkeys, and if they still seem too serious as a main course, treat them as just desserts!

Why Women and Men Both
Experience Themselves as Powerless

The accusations about men giving "lines" are so frequent, cartoons on the subject practically repeat themselves.

*"I can't remember your name, but
your phrase is familiar."*

New Woman, December 1983

"I don't remember your face, but your line is familiar."

Woman, October 1984

In these cartoons, the men obviously want the women, and yet the women are still rejecting the men. Why? Because *each man is treating the woman in a way that indicates to the woman he wants her for his fantasy but not for hers*. A woman who gets treated this way feels powerless; after all, she needs *a* man— somehow, somewhere—but damn it if she is going to be treated like a piece of meat. She'd rather have self-respect than *that*.

To himself, a man's lines feel like the lines of a salesperson. As a salesperson, he feels in the powerless position. It is the person in the power position who can do the put-down. (''I don't remember your product's name, but the claim is familiar.'') The more attractive the woman, the more likely she is to not even give him the time of day.

By looking at examples in which both sexes give lines we can tell when both sexes are feeling powerless. The men in the cartoons are giving lines prior to sex. The power begins to switch after sex, and the lines start to become hers: ''I don't usually do this.'' The closer we come to commitment, the more likely a woman who fears not getting a man to commit may give a line like ''No woman will ever be able to love you the way I do.'' Both are giving lines when they fear not getting their primary fantasy. Their lines are promises designed to tap into the other's real needs. *When we give lines, we promise what we perceive as the other person's real needs—or their Achilles' heels.* When a woman says ''No woman will ever be able to love you the way I do,'' she is unwittingly recognizing how much a man commits in order to get love.

An outgrowth of male line-giving is male bragging, the equivalent of female makeup. Both are attempts to present a bit more than a person has. Both male lines and female makeup are compensations for feelings of powerlessness.

Can I Be an Independent Woman and Expect a Supportive Man?

Although studies of women ''making it'' in the work world show the extraordinary dependence on and generosity of male mentors, among the hundreds of cartoons reviewed in women's magazines there were no women playfully putting themselves down for this dependence, or giving a man credit for his mentoring. Instead, the most common cartoon theme shows a woman putting down her husband as being unwilling to give her a penny for her thoughts, while ''Now I'm being paid a fortune for them.'' Ironically, the woman is giving her husband the power of depriving her of her identity as a thinking person. One cartoon in *New Woman* (September 1984) pictures a woman reporting her husband to the police for stealing her identity.

What are the hidden messages in the cartoon on the next page?

Imagine a man saying to another man ''I've discovered it pays better to be a public servant than to be my wife's servant.'' The cartoon unwittingly reveals a woman's three-option socialization: income from husband, income from work, or some combination. The anger in the cartoon comes from her husband's inability to pay her enough. A man would never ever feel angry were his wife unable to give him enough income so he could have the option of not working.

In this cartoon, as in all the others, there is no hint of preparation for the job, nor of gratitude. She does not say, ''My husband supported me for ten years while I completed my law degree, ran for state assembly, lost the first time for state senate, and now he's willing to postpone having a child until I run for

"I've decided to run for Congress. I've discovered it pays better to be a public servant than to be my husband's servant."

New Woman, August 1983

Congress.'' There is no picture of her husband on her desk. He didn't, after all, pay her enough to stay at home.

Neither this cartoon nor any of the hundreds of others I reviewed dealt with *disappointed fantasies*—as in a second scene, six months later: "My husband is bailing me out of a hundred-thousand-dollar debt for that run for Congress. And believe it or not, *his* finances are being questioned by the IRS.'' There is no portrayal in this or in any other women's magazine cartoon of a woman sweating it out in the primaries.

Are these just cartoons, not reflections of real attitudes? Think of the American presidential primaries. *Since the beginning of the women's movement, not one white woman sweated out the primaries for a major party nomination.** For the 1984 Democratic nomination eight men killed each other off. The survivor *appointed* a woman as the vice-presidential candidate. When Geraldine Ferraro was questioned about her husband's withholding his records from scrutiny, she responded, "If you live with

---

*Interestingly, during this period both a black woman (Shirley Chisholm) and a black man (Jesse Jackson) made the effort.

an Italian man, you know how they are!'' Mario Cuomo objected to her comment—because it referred derogatorily to *Italians*, not because it was derogatory toward men. Had Mondale or Reagan ever said, ''If you live with an Italian woman, you know how *they* are,'' the comment would have been seen as both an ethnic slur and a sexist slur. Mondale or Reagan would have suffered. A cartoon is not very distant from reality.

Underneath, though, the cartoon hurts women as much as men. The underlying message to a woman is that she cannot have intimacy with a man *and* career goals. We shall see below why this is a false dichotomy.

If I'm Successful, Will He Just Want Me for My Money or Be Threatened That I Have Money?

It's you I'm crazy about, Gloria. The fact that you make $30,000 a year is just frosting on the cake.''

Woman, October 1984

From the above and following cartoon we can observe that if a successful woman rejects a man, she is justified because she knew he only wanted her for her money. On the other hand, if he rejects her, it is because he couldn't handle her success. Another way to avoid introspection.

In these cartoons we can detect a double standard. *When men*

*"Are you passing me because you don't like
lemonade or because you feel threatened by
a career woman like me?"*

Playgirl, December 1982

in relationships have more money, we call it power. When women
in relationships have more money, we say they are being used.
When a woman is sensitive about feeling used, we call her "in
touch with her feelings." When a man is sensitive to his financial
support of her being termed "power," he's called "defended."

What happens when a man is neither competitive nor threatened
by his wife's or woman friend's success? Here is the reaction:

Pooping Out By Eve Babitz

*Why is it that as women become successful,
the men in their lives turn into whiny
dorks who forget their own ambitions?*

Playgirl, December 1981

What is the message behind this message? Could it be that the complaint serves to justify searching for a man who is so successful "he couldn't possibly be threatened or be using me"? Is this all a subconscious way of reinforcing the justification of marrying up?

The cumulative effect of these messages is to reinforce the female fear of success—that success will force her to forfeit men. Yet this contradicts reality. *Contrary to popular belief, husbands with successful wives are happier with their marriages.*[11]

Does the complaint of "pooping out" accurately reflect male behavior—or female behavior? Among wives of executives in large corporations, 87 percent are unemployed.[12] As mentioned above, the more successful the man, the more likely the woman is to not work at all.[13] Conversely, the more successful the woman, the more likely she is to marry an even more successful man.

Daddy Knows Less

Just as "Daddy knows best" is part of the problem called sexism, so "Daddy knows less" is part of the problem called the new sexism.

"Come off it, Daddy—Cinderella's an outdated concept!"

New Woman, October 1983

Not only does Daddy know less than Mommy, but less than child. No, not exactly. Less than *female* child. Among the hundreds of cartoons I looked at in the women's magazines, *all* the put-downs of men by children came from female children. As with the cartoon that shows a girl selling lemonade and telling a man passing her that he was threatened by a successful career woman.

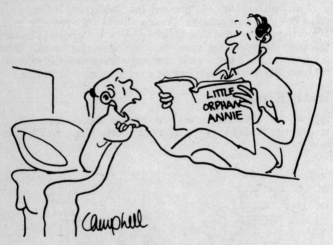

"What does she need Daddy Warbucks for when she's got the movie contract, the personal appearances and the licensed products?"

New Woman, May 1984

What would these cartoons look like in reverse? In the "Little Orphan Annie" cartoon there are two components. The most obvious is that a man is useless except for his money. A reversal of this might suggest the situation depicted at the top of the facing page.

On a more subtle level is the underlying fantasy that even a girl in the most hopeless position might get a man's money, be flash-danced to fame and fortune, and criticize both the man's money *and* the method by which he attained it (Warbucks) *even while she takes it*. The reversal of this (opposite page, bottom) is quite revealing.

"*Why should the Prince marry Sleeping Beauty? Wouldn't she be a drain on his fortune when she got old and fat and wrinkled?*"

Author's role reversal

"*If Annie were a boy would her name be Horatio Alger?*"

Author's role reversal

When we see how the put-down of men (as in Daddy Warbucks) keeps all of us from asking why Little Orphan Annie doesn't make her money the way Horatio Alger did, and when we see *Ms.* readers buying enough Cinderella and heirloom dolls to support hundreds of thousands of dollars' worth of advertising, we see that Cinderella and the Flashdance phenomenon are not outdated concepts.

Yet we would all object to the following cartoon if *Esquire* were to print it.

"Come off it, Mommy—Cinderella's your complex!"

Author's role reversal

We ask why fathers don't participate more in child care. Then, when they do, we criticize how they do it. We call working mothers Superwomen but don't call men who both work and father "working fathers." Instead of Supermen we say they are sexist. If we were to put down working women similarly, *Esquire* might feature cartoons like the following:

"Are we all about prepared for the case?"

Author's role reversal

Kiss Daddy Goodnight . . .

Item: "Don just came into my life. He loves my daughter Carrie and Carrie loves him. On Sunday mornings, Carrie joins us in bed and we frolic around with each other—tickling, kidding, hugging, loving. Last Sunday I left them together while I made French toast and when I returned . . ."

Complete the above item here:_____
_____

Take five seconds to let the images run through the imagination. What were Don and her daughter doing when she returned? If the images involve some version of Don's touching Carrie sexually, think of what that says about the trust level that is built into our psyches about men and male sexuality. Every newspaper article about incest in the past ten years has increased our mistrust of men. Yet we still assign men the responsibility to initiate sexually. This means men have an additional hurdle to overcome—another layer of distrust.

As Carrie's mother Kristin returned to the room she had to deal with that distrust. Don and Carrie may play with each other for ten years without her distrust ever completely disappearing ("She's growing breasts now . . ." "He's teaching her how to dance . . ." "She's modeling a bathing suit for him . . ."). It is one more way men must prove themselves *before they even get to equality* with women. Here's the way the item ends:

". . . When I returned Carrie and Don were in the middle of making a big drawing of me under the heading 'the best mommie in the world.' (Of course Don put a little asterisk after 'mommie' and wrote on the back 'etc.' when Carrie wasn't looking.)"

If Daddy is employed, he is criticized for not taking care of the children. If he is unemployed, he is suspected of molesting them. If he's a biological father, he wants a son to carry on his name. If he's a stepfather, he may be marrying the mother to have access to the daughter. All of these accusations have become commonplace statements about fathers between 1976 and the present. In the past decade liberation has meant fathers going from "Daddy knows best" to "daddies molest."

By 1986 department stores like J. C. Penney routinely allowed mothers into their sons' dressing rooms, but not fathers into even a five-year-old daughter's dressing room. When sued for discrimination, J. C. Penney was able to explain "the public perception is that men are voyeurs and molesters."[13a]

Respect to Suspect

In 1970, a person who spent his or her life earning a Ph.D., attending a decade of staff meetings, helping female and male students on doctoral dissertations and master's theses, spending evenings and weekends preparing articles for publication in the most competitive journals, and spending four summers in a row writing and rewriting a book, might earn respect—as long as she or he became an associate or full professor. By 1977, the professor role took on a different connotation with Philip Roth's *Professor of Desire*.[14]

By the mid-eighties a successful book with *professor* in the title was *The Lecherous Professor*.[15]

This drawing is a precise rendition of the cover of the book.

Like professor, "Daddy" used to be a word that connoted respect. Yet by 1980 *Kiss Daddy Goodnight* was one of the best-selling books in the United States on incest.[16]

The Ultimate Example of Male Dominance Is Battered Women—Especially Battered Wives . . .

Question: What is the ratio of battered wives to battered husbands?

_____ *(a)* 4 to 1

_____ *(b)* 102 to 1

_____ *(c)* 2 to 1

_____ *(d)* 34 to 1

Answer: None of these. These ratios reflect *police* records in different cities. Police records reflect the incidence of complaints. If, instead of turning to police records of complaints, we turn to the only large nationally representative sample of spouse abuse—a sample of 2,143 persons, conducted by Drs. Murray Straus, Suzanne Steinmetz, and Richard Gelles[17]—we find that *12 percent of husbands were violent toward wives and 12 percent of wives were violent toward husbands.* A ratio of 1 to 1. Frankly, when I first read this, I was angry—I didn't believe the findings. It flew in the face of everything I had read. I asked immediately, "How is violence defined? Who inflicts more harm?"

I found the researchers had studied violence in seven areas. Rank these from one to seven according to which would violate you most if it happened to you:

_____ *(a)* Throwing things
_____ *(b)* Pushing or shoving
_____ *(c)* Hitting or slapping
_____ *(d)* Kicking or hitting with fist
_____ *(e)* Hitting with something
_____ *(f)* Threatening with knife or gun
_____ *(g)* Using knife or gun

Compare your rankings with the actual findings as reported by Dr. Suzanne Steinmetz in *Victimology:*[18]

**COMPARISON OF PHYSICAL VIOLENCE
USED BY HUSBANDS AND WIVES (in percent)***

Violence	Husbands	Wives
Threw things	3	5
Pushed or shoved	11	8
Hit or slapped	5	5
Kicked or hit with fist	2	3
Hit with something	2	3
Threatened with knife or gun	0.4	0.6
Used knife or gun	0.3	0.1
Used any violence	12	12

*This study was conducted with 2,143 persons.
Source: Suzanne Steinmetz, *Victimology*, vol. 2, 1977–1978, Numbers 3–4, pp. 499–509.

Although I have been trained in research methods, until doing this book I had never questioned whether the publicized statistics about spouse abuse came from police records and social worker records—indications of who *complained* the most—or whether they came from a survey of a random population sample.

If women and men in fact do batter each other, how is it that only men have gotten the bad reputation?

Look at how we view male and female death differently. We feel horror when we hear that "innocent women and children" are killed. Yet when men are killed they are, as Fredric Hayward puts it, called "soldiers, miners, workers, people, and, often, just numbers, as in 'Scaffold Collapses: 18 Plunge to Death.' "[21]

By calling men who die in war Americans rather than saying "Of Americans who died in Vietnam, 56,886 were male and 8 were female" we cover up male death. We might respond, "Well, men sent these men to war—so it's hard to feel sorry for men who are killed at their own self-destructive games." How would this explain our lack of feeling for men when Margaret Thatcher sent 473 men and no women to their death in the Falklands.[22] *We blame men for doing it to themselves*.

I recently saw the movie *The River*. During the film Sissy Spacek has her arm punctured by a farm machine. The audience let out shouts of shock and revulsion. Several scenes later her husband—isolated from his family behind a picket line, living under conditions of squalor and low wages for weeks to earn enough to keep his family back in the warmth of their home—gets his face smashed in by the picketers. There was absolutely no reaction from the audience at the blood dripping out of the punctures on his face.

By *expecting* men to play life-threatening roles, we are less horrified when their lives are lost. By being less horrified, we can continue the assignment rather than look at our roles in making the assignment, our roles in *sponsoring* violence against men by turning to war films, murder mysteries, westerns, or TV movies in which men are killed routinely for our entertainment.

Women are often killed in horror movies. Why horror movies? Because the very purpose of horror is to break taboos—that is what creates horror. Killing a woman is taboo. Killing a man is not. In westerns and war films men are killed left and right, yet they are not called horror films. When a woman is killed, as in *Death Wish*, when Charles Bronson's wife was murdered and his daughter raped, the sense of outrage was so deep that theatergoers all over the country cheered wildly for the rest of the movie as Bronson shot mugger after mugger in revenge. The energy from the outrage was strong enough to sustain an entire movie. The producers were aware that they could not sustain this level of audience outrage by opening the movie with a scene of a mugger killing a man.

In non-horror films, women are not killed left and right, as men are in war films and westerns. In fact, one way of predicting the outcome of all but three or four non-horror movies is that if the life of a woman *who has appeared in more than two scenes* is threatened, we can safely predict she will not be murdered or shot. With a few exceptions, a woman's murder takes place in the opening scene in nonhorror films, before we can get to know her as a woman. Such is not the case with male characters. As with Alexis of *Dynasty* versus Bobby Ewing and J. R. of *Dallas*, the excitement is women being *threatened*, but men being *murdered* or *shot*. When men are shot, it is not horror, but *excitement* worthy of bumper stickers and guessing games (as in "Who Shot J. R.?").

The most important part of this difference is that when women are killed, they are recognizable as victims. When men are killed, they appear to deserve it. After all, we say, the men are killing each other in war. We do not acknowledge how they are victimized by being assigned the role of protector and hero in war films, westerns, or space movies. *We protect women by not assigning them roles in which they must kill each other; in the process we make violence against their lives more appalling than violence against men's lives*.

Once we are more shocked by violence against women it becomes easy for hundreds of researchers, who would ordinarily know better, to "measure" the amount of violence against each sex by looking at police reports of those who select themselves out to complain.

When we block ourselves from asking questions we are otherwise trained to ask, we know the subconscious is operating. Could it be we have an investment in viewing women as victims and men as perpetrators? If someone protested that the "Who Shot J. R." craze is the glorification of violence against *men*, would he or she be told to go water some pansies?

The Burning Bed

A television event watched by more viewers than the World Series* was NBC's movie *The Burning Bed*, starring Farrah Fawcett and based on a true incident in which a battered wife murdered her husband.

Does *The Burning Bed* ever happen in reverse? What is the reaction when a man retaliates by murdering his wife and is freed? Let's look at a reverse *Burning Bed* that occurred in Florida in 1980.

Betty King had beaten, slashed, stabbed, thrown dry acid on, and shot her husband.[23] Eddie King had not sought prosecution when she slashed his face with a carpet knife, nor when she left him in a parking lot with a blade in his back. *Neither of these incidents even made the police records as statistics.* She was only arrested twice—when she stabbed him so severely in the back and so publicly (in a bar) that the incidents had to be reported.

All these stabbings, shootings, and acid throwings happened during a four-year marriage. During a subsequent shouting match on the porch of a friend's house, Betty King once again reached into her purse. This time Eddie King shot her. When an investigation led to a verdict of self-defense, there was an outcry of opposition from feminists and the media.

Eddie King's response was to an immediate threat; a two-second delay could have meant his death. In *The Burning Bed* the husband was asleep. It is more difficult to claim the only alternative is murder when the "threat" is sleeping. Yet this was the fifth such reverse *Burning Bed* handled by Eddie King's lawyer alone.†

Why do we feel justice is served when a wife murders an abusive husband who is asleep but not when a husband murders an abusive wife who is awake? Why was it important that one of America's most beautiful women (Farrah Fawcett) play the woman in *Burning Bed*? Because the more beautiful the woman, the more "feminine," and the more feminine, the more empathy. The image of a *beautiful* woman being hurt evokes subconscious empathy, just as the man being hurt evokes a reaction similar to that when a criminal is hurt.

---

*The film received an A. C. Nielson rating of 36.2, higher than the World Series for the same week.

†Florida public defender Pat McGuiness.

Woman-as-criminal does not register for us—in part because the image of man-as-complainer does not register. Man-as-complainer never was in style. In post-Renaissance France, a man abused by his wife was ordered to wear women's clothes and parade through the center of town on a donkey—sitting backward.

Recently in Great Britain, Christine English confessed to killing her boyfriend by *deliberately* ramming him into a utility pole with her car, but she gained acquittal by successfully arguing that premenstrual tension had pushed her out of control. Both historically and internationally, images of male as criminal and female as Farrah Fawcett–fragile have distorted our findings, leading us to avoid certain questions and find legal reasons to reinforce our biases.

We have a conscious and unconscious history of protecting women, while men practice killing each other to earn the role of protector. Nobody kills a ladybug.

The Rites of Birth

Until recently circumcision was considered a way of preventing infection, masturbation, and cancer (as if they were equally harmful!). As of 1975, the American Academy of Pediatrics, unable to prove those correlations, advised physicians that "there is no medical indication for circumcision in the neonatal period."[24] Yet it is still done *routinely*. In three extensive research checks I was unable to uncover a single study of the psychological differences between men who are and are not circumcised, with factors such as socioeconomic background and parental attitudes statistically controlled.

Perhaps part of the reason men are the way they are is the trauma perpetrated on males so early after birth—perhaps not. Do men who are not circumcised live longer, other factors being equal? *We have not cared to ask.*

We were outraged at the medical community and blamed its men for not researching the full price of the Pill before allowing women to take it. Thousands of articles claimed that such a thing would never have been done to men. Of course, the Pill should not have been released to women without the risks being more clearly publicized. But the very outcry showed we were concerned about women's bodies.

Let's look at whether we have shown that concern for men's

bodies. Never mind war, boxing, and football—the societal bribes to *pay* for men to damage their bodies. Start with birth. Within moments after infant boys are born, 80 percent undergo surgery.[25] Their penises are taken to the blade of a knife and cut. This is done to the male child prior to the age of consent. If we had not protested the inadequate research on the Pill, our silence would have told us much about our attitude toward women. The fact that we do not know the long-term impact of this surgery and *have not asked to know* tells us about our attitude toward males.

Doesn't lack of circumcision make a boy child feel different? Yes. Which is why, if circumcision creates birth trauma, it needs to be publicized very widely so another 15 to 20 percent of parents can be added to the 20 percent who already do not circumcise infants, thereby minimizing the "difference factor" —once 35 to 40 percent of boys are either circumcised or are not, the numbers on both sides are large enough to minimize locker room ridicule. Parents who have watched a film showing an infant's reactions to circumcision find it is so gruesome that almost all of them decide against it. The issue is not to circumcise or not, but the subconscious lack of caring about men that is displayed when we do not even ask for the information we need to make a decision. No one would say, "We don't know whether the Pill is harmful or not; let's not bother to find out."

Take This Quiz

Fred Hayward, one of the most insightful philosophers of the new sexism, constructed a quiz* to help us stop the "hardening of our categories," as Gabriel Marcel put it. Here are a few questions from that quiz:

Question: Women's organizations have raised our awareness about the high percentage of violence against women. Which do you feel is the main reason so many women are *murdered?*

_____ *(a)* Television and movies
_____ *(b)* Pornography
_____ *(c)* Bias in the legal system
_____ *(d)* Social acceptance of violence against women

---

*For the full quiz and Hayward's other writings, write Men's Rights, P.O. Box 163180, Sacramento, CA 95816.

Answer: None of these. "So many women" are not murdered. Three out of every four victims of homicide are male.[26] Men are also 1½ times more likely to be assaulted. The rules of sexism do not free men from the terror of violence; they only keep men from complaining about it.

Question: The American legal system guarantees that a man is considered innocent until proven guilty. True or false?

Answer: False. A simple allegation of battering or molestation, or even the allegation of potential abuse, is sometimes enough to get a man thrown out of his home and excluded from his family. Divorced fathers frequently report that their visitation rights are not being restored even *after* their successful defense against criminal charges.

Question: The most common child batterer is:

_____ *(a)* a suburban father
_____ *(b)* a middle-class father
_____ *(c)* an uneducated father
_____ *(d)* a divorced father

Answer: None of these. Most abuse occurs in households headed by women.

Consciousness Balancing

Some months ago I was working in an office at the sociology department of the University of California at San Diego. The department's newsletter crossed my desk.[28] A female department worker had filled in eleven examples of sexism in the blank space at the end of a page. The observations of the women's movement were so assimilated that she had no fear of stirring controversy or losing her job by presenting them without presenting "the other side." Perhaps neither to her nor to anyone else in the department was "another side" even possible. In the table opposite some of the most potent of her examples are listed on the left, and on the right some examples of the New Sexism that would have resulted in consciousness balancing.

CONSCIOUSNESS BALANCING

Traditional Sexism	The New Sexism
• Devious men are considered shrewd, while devious women are scheming.	• When women use their power at age twenty it's called a wedding; when men use it at age forty it's called a mid-life crisis.
• Angry men are called outraged, while angry women are called hysterical.	• When women hold off from marrying men, we call it independence; when men hold off from marrying women, we call it fear of commitment.
• When men talk together it's called conversation, but when women talk together it's called gossip.	• A woman who supports a man for a lifetime is called crazy, while a man who supports a woman for a lifetime is called a breadwinner.
• Forceful men are referred to as charismatic, while forceful women are domineering.	• When men die at age nineteen in Lebanon, we call it power; when women live to the age of ninety in La Jolla, we call it powerlessness.
• Obstinate men are called strong-willed, while obstinate women are called stubborn.	• Why is it that we feel more sorry for widows than for their dead husbands?
• When men have pictures of children on their office desk, it's a sign of a loving father; when women do so, it's considered the sign of a woman who doesn't take her work seriously.	• An unemployed mother is called a dedicated parent, and an unemployed father is called a bum.

Comic Relief

To give ourselves some comic relief my assistant and I reviewed one thousand cartoon strips in 1985 issues of the *Washington*

Post, the *Chicago Tribune,* and the *Los Angeles Times*—to examine the incidence of male versus female violence.[29] Here are the findings in summary. Violence was eight times more likely to occur to men. Men were much more likely to do it to each other than were women to do it to men. Strips in which violence was *about* to occur were eleven times more likely to have men as potential victims. The only taboo among the thousand strips was woman-to-woman violence.

The Women's Room

When racism or sexism is discovered, it is woven throughout both the literary masterpieces and best-sellers of the day, as Kate Millett illustrated in *Sexual Politics.* One of the best-sellers of the late seventies and early eighties, Marilyn French's *The Women's Room,*[30] similarly reflects the new sexism. *The Women's Room* could be outlined in five stages:

1. Dependent wife.

2. Wife "realizes" men oppress her.

3. Woman leaves husband, has nothing to do with men.

4. Woman meets Mr. Wonderful.

5. Even Mr. Wonderful is a jerk. Implication: *All* men are jerks.

If we look closely at *The Women's Room* we can see even from the outline how the woman's "realization" that she is oppressed by men leads naturally to alienation from men, which creates a self-fulfilling prophecy that all future Mr. Wonderfuls will become Mr. Jerks. With that approach, "liberation" becomes a room of one's own.

The anger feeds on itself. Writers need to get published to eat, so they write what sells. If there is a growing constituency for the bad rap on men, few writers can afford to buck the tide. So they feed the fire to feed their families.

Are Women Second-Class Citizens?

In the past fifteen years even our portrayal of racism has undergone a transformation—from a system that oppressed both sexes to a system that oppresses predominantly women. The civil rights movement and Alex Haley's *Roots* allowed for both sexes' oppression. But by the 1980s, Alice Walker's *The Color Purple* was portraying four black women oppressed and four black men oppressors. *Despite the time span, which included both World War I and the Depression, not one black male was portrayed as a victim.*

The black males were portrayed rather as rapists, child molesters, child stealers, child sellers, incest perpetrators, wife beaters, and self-serving on the one hand, or, on the other, as wimps. The women were portrayed as victims who, through sisterhood and confronting their black male oppressors, could emerge victorious. In reality, though, the emergence came when the independent Shug Avery married a rich man and flashdanced to wealth and when the dependent Celie was first swept away by the newly flashdanced Shug Avery and then flashdanced via her dead father ("death wish") to an inherited home and business. How were the two black male saviors portrayed? One as a self-serving jerk; the other was never seen.

Could a black male do anything right? Yes. When all three black women unite against the black oppressor he is shown defeated. It is only by defeating him that he will rise again, transformed into a savior (who returns Celie's children and her sister from Africa).

The result? The book received a Pulitzer prize, and the movie, although receiving no Academy Awards, received eleven nominations. Even racism had entered the era of the New Sexism—the portrayal of only one sex's experience of powerlessness.

Women and men are both slaves and second-class citizens in different ways. Just as the traditional woman can be seen as a slave in a man's house, so the traditional man can be seen as a slave in a woman's house. We could portray the woman as a slave master, assigning the role of tilling the field and earning the income to the man, who would then bring it back so she could spend it as she wished to run the plantation. In this version, like the slave or the worker bee, the man brings back his earnings to the queen bee. And like the worker bee, he dies off sooner in the process.

Women are the only "minority" group to be born into the upper class as frequently as men. The only minority group whose "unpaid labor" enables them to buy fifty billion dollars' worth of cosmetics each year; whose members have time to read more romance novels and watch more television than men during every time category[31]; whose members earn one-third what white men earn and outspend them for all personal items combined.[32] Women are the only minority group to systematically grow up having a class of workers (called fathers) in the field working for them; they are the only minority group that is a majority.

Does this mean women have more power than men? No. It does mean the sexes, unlike the classes, have approximately equal numbers of people born into privileged and oppressive conditions. It is in the interests of both sexes to hear the other sex's experience of powerlessness.

8

Why Did the Sexual Revolution Come and Go So Quickly?

During the late seventies and early eighties, the focus of feminist protest shifted. At first feminism was associated with sexual freedom. Germaine Greer talked about having sex with your local cabdriver. By 1984 Greer's *Sex and Destiny*[1] was advocating abstinence and celibacy. By the mid-eighties, U.S. government brochures, socialist feminists, the Moral Majority, and Dr. Joyce Brothers all agreed on only one thing—women should hold back more on sex. As in the "old sex."

Universal Press Syndicate, April 30, 1985

What happened? In the beginning of the sexual revolution, during the late sixties and early seventies, birth control led to a removal of the intellectual rationale supporting female sexual restraint; women earning their own incomes meant there was less of a need to hold out for economic security, and women depending more on themselves were less dependent on orthodox religions that had advocated sexual restraint. For a while, intellectual,

237

economic, and religious reasons for sexual restraint were weakened. *But as female incomes allowed women to be more honest in relationships—without the fear of being left penniless on the street, supporting self and children—marriages broke up.* Suddenly this created a new picture—*economic independence was associated with economic insecurity.* Work as freedom of choice was *much different* from work as necessity—to support oneself and help to support the children.

Once marriages broke up, what started out as a right had become a responsibility. It was no longer sexual freedom *plus* economic freedom. As in the ads for I. Magnin and Wayne Clark (which was "for the woman who has every thing"—including a horse and male sex object) the Ninja ad below portrays a woman as wanting sex from a man for its own sake (without a man's providing security). Women portrayed as wanting sex for its own sake are almost always portrayed as not having to worry about income.

Working Woman, November 1984

This was not women's fault. If, from an early age and for many generations, men had been told they could get their dinners paid for by looking good, being supportive, and not being too sexually free, men would be more supportive and less sexually free. Traditionally, withholding sex until security was guaranteed had worked as a strategy. As women's economic independence was seen to be economic *in*security, there was a quick shift back to a more conservative sexuality.

Whether the development was conscious or unconscious, coincidental or not, as soon as it became apparent that sexual freedom was not coming hand in hand with economic freedom, it was questioned. Erica Jong went from writing about sex with strange men on Amtrak trains to warning against sex without commitment.

The Moral Majority, meantime, had never had any trouble keeping sex and commitment linked via God and morality. Feminists dumped the morality rationale; instead they developed a distrust-of-male-sexuality attitude, which was called upon as a replacement for morality as the rationale for shifting back to a more conservative sexuality prior to commitment.

The issues of the late seventies and eighties increasingly became distrust-male-sexuality issues: protests of pornography, prostitution, sexual harassment, rape, child molestation, and incest. This distrust allowed a woman to return to the position in which a man had to prove trust before she would be sexual. It also created an uneasy alliance between the religious fundamentalists and feminists. Both groups—with different reasons—had arrived at the same role for female sex as the lead article in *Cosmopolitan*: "Make Him Earn It."

By the 1980s, the new sexism and "distrust male sexuality" messages combined so effectively that even magazines like *Glamour*[1a] could advocate female sexuality in ways they would never advocate male sexuality. For example, *Glamour*'s "Sexual Pleasures of Childbirth" article explains how when mothers breast-feed babies, mothers should experience the child's sucking motions in a sexual manner and achieve orgasms from the contact of her nipples with the child's mouth and lips. Yet, in the mid-eighties incest is often defined as any contact with a child *in which a man has sexual feelings*.

A child needs both breast-feeding and bathing, but male parents were being arrested on the mere accusation they had touched a child genitally "for too long" when bathing it—particularly if the child was a daughter. In some areas, doctors literally hooked the father's penis up to a machine and showed him pictures of a female child while the machine registered whether these pictures excited him.[2] If they did, it was considered *significant* evidence against him. Reputations were ruined whether the accused was found innocent or guilty. Divorced fathers were deprived of their rights to their children before they were found guilty and many never had their children returned once they were found innocent.

How is it that, by the mid-eighties, a woman's sexual experience with her child could be condoned whereas a man could be arrested merely on the *accusation* of touching his child for too long while bathing this child? How is it that in *Glamour* the descriptions of sexual pleasure between mother and child are more explicit than the descriptions of sexual pleasure between an adult woman and an adult man?

Why, by 1985, was *New Woman* running a cover feature by Dr. Joyce Brothers entitled "Why You Shouldn't Move in with Your Lover,"[3] explaining that if a woman lives with a man "there is no way she is going to get as much out of the relationship as he does"?[4] Because she provides him with, Brothers explains, "the equivalent of marital sex without expecting much except an orgasm in return."[5] And "that is *all* she is going to get,"[6] Brothers observes (emphasis added). In short, he gets sex and she gets sex. If that is considered unequal, we can see why men are afraid of commitment. We have returned to the old sex in the *New Woman*.

The distrust of men and male sexuality has become so profound that Dr. Joyce Brothers could say, and *New Woman* could headline, that living together is "a phony relationship," that it is as destructive as cocaine, and that the "woman *always* gets the worst of it"[7] (emphasis added).

Look at the cartoon on the next page, which ran under the headline "Why You Shouldn't Move in with Your Lover." Does this man sound trustworthy?

Notice how the *article* condemns *living together* for women, but if the cartoon had said "I didn't mean marriage . . . I meant living together," that would have made the man sound too reasonable for the cartoon to be used as support for the article. By making him sound unreasonable ("playing house from time to time"), living together could be linked to stupidity. That subconscious emotional link is needed to make him appear as an opportunist who gets sex and she as a victim who gets nothing— rather than as equals who both want to know each other before they make a lifetime commitment and perhaps raise children together.

"I didn't mean actually <u>living</u> together, Mitzi; what I had in mind was more like playing house from time to time."
New Woman, March 1985

The emotional association of living together is made to mean for the woman: "It's stupid and meaningless and you are being taken advantage of by an opportunistic cad who just wants your body." By consistently seeing men portrayed in this way, "new women" are learning to combine the Old Sex (sex as a bargaining chip for a lifetime income) with the New Sexism (distrust of men and male sexuality). The effect is to take the focus off equality and self-responsibility.

How can we know when the distrust of male sexuality and the old sex are being used to gain the outcome of income and security? When a lot of excuses that do not stand up are given to marry. In the *New Woman* piece, Dr. Brothers tells us that living together does not help a couple get to know each other because both the man and woman are on their best behavior, putting their best foot forward. Yet obviously a year or two of handling finances, housework, and cooking, of sharing closets, bathroom sinks, and stereo albums, of working out a decorating scheme, coordinating bedtimes, adjusting to moods, work schedules, values, habits, relatives, and perhaps each other's children, tells us a lot more about a person than jumping from evening dates and vacation sex into marriage. How could an intelligent person make such a comment? Only as a *strategy*—an ideology in which common sense is blinded by the goal.

As a strategy for lifetime income, the new sexism and the old sex can indeed be effective. But they are also effective at getting women literally raped. Let's look at how the old sex and new sexism backfire against women, against men, and against love.

The Six-Stage Rape Cycle

"All men are rapists and that's all they are."[8]

Marilyn French, author of *The Women's Room*

I would not be so concerned about the old sex and the new sexism if they did not combine with sex roles to produce many more problems than they solve. The combination of the old sex, the new sexism, and sex roles creates a six-stage cycle. Let's look at that cycle with an emphasis on the role of the old sex.

1. Sex is dirty (the old sex).

2. Initiating sex is men's responsibility (sex roles).

3. Men cannot be trusted since they're just out to get all this dirty stuff (old sex plus sex roles leading to New Sexism).

4. A man must prove himself worthy of trust before a woman has sex with him (she does not need to prove herself worthy of trust before he accepts her sexually).

5. To handle rejection men learn to turn women into sex objects, which reinforces the alienation necessary for women to continue treating men as success objects. The "Sex Object/Success Object Cycle" is established.

6. Turning women into sex objects is a prerequisite to rape, alienation from sexuality, alienation from self, alienation from intimacy . . . which just proves Stage 1: Sex is dirty.

Stage 1: We Used to Think of Sex as Dirty . . . But That's No Longer True, Is It?

Many women end up liking sex and feeling frustrated when they are not sexually fulfilled. By understanding how sex-is-dirty messages have returned, we can get a deeper understanding of what we are doing to create the distrust toward men that leaves women and men sexually unfulfilled.

Item: Backstage at the Merv Griffin show I am preparing for a discussion on sex-role training as divorce training. Merv Griffin is onstage:

Merv:	E.T. has a sister. . . .
Merv's Straightman:	What's her name?
Merv:	E.Z.

"Dear Abby" exemplified the return to the old sex when in the 1980s she reran a column she had run years before on the dangers of premarital sex, saying it was still relevant. I agree with columns that caution both sexes about their psychological readiness for sex—especially the first few times. But "Dear Abby" does not caution boys; she cautions girls only:

Does he love you? Someone who loves you wants whatever is best for you. He wants you to:

Commit an immoral act.
Surrender your virtue.
Throw away your self-respect. . . .
A boy who loves a girl would sooner cut off his right arm . . .
Why not prove your love by sticking your head in the oven
and turning on the gas . . . ?[9]

Imagine the reaction to the reversal of a column like this by "Dear Abbott." Abbott advises, "A woman who wants you to prove your love by fulfilling her primary fantasy—by marrying her—wants you to stick your head in the oven and turn on the gas. . . ." Would we think Abbott had a neurosis about marriage that he was trying to impose on the rest of us? Would we protest the newspapers that were syndicating this neurosis?

By the early 1980s, family planning information and government pamphlets were dispensing advice about intercourse as if it were the same as pregnancy. The back cover of a health education bulletin on "Counseling for Teens: The Consequences of Sexual Activity" answers its own back cover headline "What Happens When You Have Intercourse?"

"8 in 10 dropped out of high school . . .

"their babies are twice as likely to die as other babies . . .

"they are more than twice as likely to die themselves during pregnancy."[10]

Obviously, 8 out of 10 teenagers who have intercourse do not drop out of high school. Many *who do not use birth control* do. Teenagers often get negative messages about sex, one of which is that they should not go around with birth-control devices— because it "looks as if you want it." The message that sex is dirty is reinforced by pamphlets like this—pamphlets that help create the disasters they ideally desire to prevent.

Has our vocabulary about sex really changed in the past twenty years? Most of the words we associate with sex are still swear words. Say "sensuality" and watch the warmth come into someone's eyes as he or she hears its implied contrast to *sexuality;* say "spirituality" and watch for even more warmth as he or she hears a deeper contrast. The dichotomizing of love and sex, sensuality and sexuality, and spirituality and sexuality always puts sex in the "one down" position: making it anti-sensual, anti-spiritual, anti-love. This is "either-or" thinking.

Most people feel that violence is bad and sex is good. Yet parents often will not ask their child to turn off a television that has bullets ripping through male bodies as they fall off horses and get bloodied by a stampede of hooves (in a G-rated western). Yet if we saw our child watching sex on Saturday-morning television, most of us would be outraged, label it "gross" and immoral, and write a letter of protest.

We claim to want our children to be sexually responsible, yet most Americans support the continued television ban on birth-control advertising. When we see what other advertising we ban on television, like guns and cigarettes (with the capacity for death) and alcohol and drugs (considered vices), we understand that we still see sex as such a vice that being *responsible* sexually is also a vice. We would rather risk abortion or protest abortions than hint, via birth-control advertising, that we are suggesting sex might be okay.

While most men have relationships with women who have struggled to conquer the attitude that sex is dirty, many men find its residue playing itself out in thousands of subtle ways. One man was disillusioned to discover that women who scream during sex scream even louder on game shows for prizes.[11] And men who date single mothers often report the extraordinary lengths to which the mothers will go to keep their sexual activity hidden from their children.

"Okay, okay, I'll stay on my own side of the bed."

Cosmopolitan, August 1984

"You know why I'm so fond of you? We can cuddle all night and you never try to force sex on me."

New Woman, February 1984

How do children first pick up these messages? At first we make it unconsciously clear to both sexes that sex should be separated out from the rest of life by separating out their genitals from the rest of life: many parents bathe their children on the entire body, for example, but quickly skip by the genitals. Or, when their child touches her or his genitals in public, they give a disapproving look, or physically remove the child's hand, or publicly humiliate the child. Sometimes the separation is rationalized with the word "private" as we ask the child to put a bathing suit over the genital area, or to change in a separate room. *We separate sex out from the rest of life and then wonder why our children separate sex out from the rest of life.*

Once we've made both sexes' genitals unnatural, we are ready to make the transition from genitals as nature to genitals as commodity.

Both sexes learn genitals are dirty. *During adolescence a girl eventually learns that although her genitals are dirty, for what-*

ever reason, those disgusting men want her dirty genitals. She learns she has possession over something both dirty and valuable.

Is there a way to avoid appearing dirty? Yes. Assign the responsibility for the dirt to someone else. Whichever sex is assigned the responsibility for the dirt will not be trusted. So Stages 2 and 3, "Initiating sex is men's responsibility" and "Men cannot be trusted," go hand in hand.

Stages 2 and 3: Men—They're All Alike . . .

"An erect penis has no conscience"; yet when it is not erect, we call a man "impotent." Men are caught between a rock and a soft place. The impact of men's taking sexual initiatives is enormous in a culture that considers sex dirty.

"Don't play house with him, You'll never get out of the bedroom!"

Playgirl, April 1983

"No way, José—hand-holding just leads to the hard stuff!"

New Woman, July 1984

In these cartoons we see the link between the male role of sexual initiative-taking and the feeling that sex is dirty—even in *Playgirl* and *New Woman*. Notice, in *New Woman*, that the "new woman" does not initiate. So he is vulnerable to being accused of giving the wrong line. *Women often ask, "Why do men give the same lines to different women?" The answer is: for the same reason women wear the same perfume for different men. We all try the things that work.*

In *Playgirl*, the most positive about sex of the women's magazines, we see hundreds of male-sex-as-negative cartoons. Imagine a cartoon in *Playboy* that said, "Don't play house with *her*. You'll never get out of the bedroom." *Playboy* would be more likely to run a cartoon saying, "Don't play house with her. . . . you'll never get *into* the bedroom."

The book *No Good Men* (see cartoon below) illustrates how we ask men to initiate, leading to men activating their sexuality (a prerequisite to initiating), leading to distrusting men as potential rapists:

This cartoon was reprinted in *Playgirl* as part of a feature that put men down more than forty times in nine consecutive cartoons.

If we did a reversal of men's overzealousness for sex, it might look like this portrayal of a woman's overzealousness for her primary fantasy.

Author's role reversal

Why are these antisex and antimale cartoons in the only female magazine that seems open to sex with men? Are we really saying men should take responsibility for this dirty sex so they can be accused of being disgusting and untrustworthy? This does seem like the message, but why?

Stage 4: Reject Men Until They Prove Themselves

The less men can be trusted, the more they have to prove themselves. We have seen that even in the eighties one of the best ways men can prove themselves trustworthy, serious, and responsible (as in "not a Peter Pan") is to promise to transfer the fruits of any success to a woman via commitment and the follow-up diamond. Now that sex is easier to get, has the pressure on men to prove themselves trustworthy diminished? No. *While we loosened up on sex a bit, we tightened up on our mistrust of men, meaning that men still have to prove themselves.* Whether the reason for a woman's restriction is immorality (as in religion), fear of pregnancy, or mistrust, *her restrictions, however legitimate, have become his conditions*—what he must do to prove himself before he is "allowed" to have sex.

I'm not saying sex should be unconditional. I am saying both sexes should have about equal conditions, which will only begin to happen when both sexes equally share responsibility for initiating—which will only happen when both sexes share equal responsibility for earning the income. It would be neat and simple to keep these issues separate—but such a separation has contributed to men's and women's misunderstanding of each other.

Why has the Moral Majority been less harsh on male sexuality than feminists? Partly because the traditional woman needed a man for her security too much to risk being thought of as a man-hater. Her man-hating discussions were with her women friends, behind men's backs, not published in *Ms.* magazine. Instead of overtly speaking out about her distrust of male sexuality, she focused instead on her opposition to birth control, fear of pregnancy, fear of disease, and religious convictions to get a man to prove himself before there was too much sex. Whether these convictions were legitimate or not, their impact on men was the same.

Dr. Kristin Luker, in a nationwide study of women who oppose abortion and those who believe in abortion choice, discovered that the most significant difference was that *women who oppose abortion are almost always likely to perceive their major income source as men*. Therefore, the sacredness of such a woman's role as potential mother must not be tampered with via abortions. Conversely, women who favor the option of abortion almost always want to retain the option of a career.[12] They want the option to choose career or child—an option facilitated by abortion.

This does not make abortion beliefs or religious beliefs insincere or superficial. Our most sincere beliefs are those that emerge from our self-concepts. Ideology, religion, and atheism all have one thing in common: they follow self-interest. And so the seventies and eighties returned to "abortion as fetus-killing" and introduced "herpes as God's message to the sexually promiscuous" to counter the "progress" of those who would separate sex from commitment and recombine them by choice rather than edict. Homosexuals were also to be condemned; they too threaten the notion that marital commitment is a condition of sex. If that notion did not apply to homosexuals, how could we make it apply to heterosexuals? And if we couldn't, we feared we'd be giving sex away again.

Few people prefer sex without love to sex with love. But the male approach tends to follow the old Irish saying: "Sex with love is the best thing possible. Sex without love is the second best thing possible."* For many women "just sex" sounds like "just a housewife." Again, both sexes prefer sex under ideal conditions. Men feel they have to prove themselves by meeting women's nine conditions, while requiring women to only meet their one condition (see Chapter 1).

When we link sex and love we get *making love,* and when we link sex and commitment we get *marriage.* Yet when they are separated, we get *one-night stands, free* sex, *recreational* sex, *casual* sex, *cheap* sex, all implying *sex without conditions.* The people who engage in *cheap sex* are *cheap trash.* The condemnation implies sex should cost and love should cost. Pay-as-you-go sex. Pay-forever sex.

If men still pay to get sex, women still pay if they give it away too easily—the slurs of *promiscuous, whore,* or *prostitute* are not outdated, even though a prostitute is someone who does not give it away for free. The more negative our attitude toward sex, the more men have to pay to "earn" it. And that maintains our unconscious investment in keeping our attitude toward sex negative with the unintended result of making our attitude toward men negative.

*For example: 91 percent of American men do not feel love is necessary for good sex. This statistic is taken from Anthony Pietropinto and Jacqueline Simenauer's *Beyond the Male Myth* (New York: Signet, 1977), p. 230.

In a workshop in Maine, Carly said she felt "used" when a man she slept with for the first time did not call the next day. Carly was expecting something as a result of the sex. She did not question herself for not calling.

Do men suffer bad reputations related to sex? Once they commit, yes. Alan Alda is praised for his fidelity. If a man has sex with too many women without the apparent intention of committing, he, like Ted Kennedy, is seen as a "womanizer" and an "exploiter of women." Why? Doesn't each woman agree to have sex with him? *Or is it assumed she is being used because she gets nothing more than sex? If such men are womanizers, why are women not "manizers"?* What are they doing for him after *he* gives sex? Both sexes can suffer bad reputations.

A man suffers rejection if he does not prove himself worthy beforehand and is given a bad reputation if he does not give more than sex later.

Stage 5: The Sex Object/Success Object Cycle

I have mentioned how men's role of taking sexual initiatives teaches men to turn women into sex objects so rejection will hurt less; and how the longer the period of friendship prior to sex the longer the period of potential rejection. However, men's resistance to friendship prior to sex creates women's alienation from men and increases the likelihood of the woman rejecting the man, which leads him to further objectify her, which leads her to further alienation and rejection of him, which leads . . . And so we are in a vicious cycle.

In the sixties and seventies the solution to this problem was falsely seen as shortening the period of friendship prior to sex. But once a short period became the "in thing," it became part of the problem, since by definition a fad denies individual needs and feelings.

We have begun to see that the real solution to objectification comes with sharing responsibility for earning income so that we do not have a subconscious need to keep men desiring women's sexuality more than women desire men's, in order for men to earn women's sexuality by short- or long-term payments (e.g., commitment).

At this point in our genetic history, much of the gap between male and female sexual desire for the other is doubtless biological. The solution involves that much more effort to use the socialization process to narrow that gap rather than using the socialization process to widen the gap.

On an everyday level this solution includes sharing the 150 stages of sexual initiative-taking between eye contact and sexual contact. We have seen how far from that sharing we are. And of course, as long as women's bodies are advertised more, we will reinforce men's "neediness" for women's bodies and therefore the male incentive to initiate.

The cost of not sharing is remaining in the mire of the "Sex Object/Success Object Cycle": men turning women into sex objects as a prerequisite to taking sexual initiatives; women turning men into success objects as a prerequisite to marriage. The consequences of turning women into sex objects include rape; the consequences of turning men into success objects include war.

Stage 6: Objectification Is a Prerequisite to Rape

Turning women into sex objects is a prerequisite to rape, just as objectifying Vietnamese as "gooks" was a prerequisite to bombing.

The first five stages build a deep-seated anger in women toward men for objectifying, and for not believing women's nos when they do mean no. In men they build an anger toward women that deepens each time a man is rejected. In women they build a contempt for men who brag and give inane lines; in men they build a contempt for women who do not share the adult responsibility for taking initiatives and who cry wolf—saying no at first and later enjoying sex. In women they build self-doubt about what they are valued for even as they apply makeup that reinforces the objectification and self-doubt; in men they build self-doubt about their values even as they attain success that reinforces their objectification as success objects.

The anger, contempt, frustration, insecurity, and self-doubt lead to feelings of powerlessness and violence on the part of both sexes toward each other, to each sex's objectifying and raping the other in its own way. All this will not stop as long as sex is thought of as dirty and one sex is assigned the role of being the dirty one.

I Feel Damned If I Do and Damned If I Don't

"A feminist man is like a jumbo shrimp—neither makes any sense."

Comedienne Cassandra Dans of the High Heeled Women

"Beware of the man who praises women's liberation; he is about to quit his job."

Erica Jong (1980)

A parallel to the Jong quote above would be: "Beware of the woman who likes sex; she is about to press for marriage."

In many books and magazines men are accused of being afraid to say, "I love you" because it will give a woman power[13]; in others, they are accused of saying, "I love you" to get a woman's sexual power.[14] As long as a man is put down no one says, "Wait a minute . . ."

When women make love to men orally it is most frequently described as "servicing"; when men make love to women orally it is often described as "controlling."[15]

In the past two decades the aware man has consistently heard that monogamy is a male invention to control female sexuality and at the same time that men are the advocates of "smashing monogamy" as a way of exerting their male supremacy and emotionally abandoning women.[16]

Dr. Joyce Brothers writes that 100 percent of 40 women she surveyed from a variety of backgrounds *(not* clients going for therapy) had faked orgasms.[17] *All,* she found, fake them at least *half the time*. Yet men are accused of being insensitive to women's sexual happiness. How would a woman feel if a man faked ecstasy about her new dress and then wondered why she continued to wear it, concluding she was insensitive to his dislike of the dress?

It is a sign of male adaptiveness that men haven't gotten in touch with their feelings about being "damned if they do and damned if they don't," and either withdrawn more or fought back. Both sexes fake their emotional responses rather than risk the disapproval of the other sex.

Why Do Men Separate Their Emotions from Sex?

Actually, men get quite emotional about sex. When we say men separate their emotions from sex, we really mean they more often separate sex from emotional commitments. That is, they separate sex from the *types of emotions* women would more often like men to get emotional about. Which is why this complaint usually comes from women.

Dennis gets emotional about sex in much the same way that Dawn gets emotional about being asked to the senior prom. Both are emotional about getting their primary fantasy met for an evening. Neither is necessarily emotional about the person as much as about the experience the person is providing—sex or the prom. If the person is also special, then the emotions increase. But if Dawn feels her excitement will make Dennis feel she is ready for sex before she is, or if Dennis feels his emotional excitement will make Dawn feel he is ready for commitment before he is, they will each be forced to cut off their emotions in order not to mislead the other.

Regardless of our sex, we often separate our emotions from what the other sex would really like us to be emotional about. We do it especially if we feel that the other sex wants us to be emotional about its primary fantasy before we are ready to fulfill it.

When I Take Initiatives Men Seem to Back Off . . . Why Is That?

Many men do back off when women initiate. Just as women back off when men initiate. The more a person initiates, the more rejection she or he will get—and the more likely he or she is to get his or her ideal partner. People who initiate are selecting people *they* want, not necessarily people who have an interest in them. So they get rejected. It is not always because the man cannot handle a woman initiating. Most men, if interested, love it.

There is, though, one reason some men back off even when they are interested. That reason is performance pressure—the feeling that "she wants me; now I must be erect when she wants."

Unfortunately, the closer a woman's publication like *Playgirl* gets to giving its female readers the message "sex is okay," the more its articles and cartoons berate men for poor performance. Note the pressure in the following cartoon.

*"Oh nothing. It's just that you were better
as a fantasy."*

Playgirl, December 1982

Dozens of *Playgirl's* cartoons feature women mocking men who are making jerks of themselves trying to please them. This is distinct from anger toward women in *Playboy* and *Penthouse*, which is usually a defense against rejection, not criticism for a woman who has accepted him but is performing inadequately.

If *Playboy* and *Penthouse* consistently featured cartoons of men who were bored or critical when they were having sex with a woman, *we might get the feeling the men were putting down women to cover up their own sexual aversion.*

*"Oh nothing. It's just that you were better
as a fantasy."*

Author's role reversal

"I'd like to go all the way with Ronald, but he can never last that long."

Cosmopolitan, September 1984, p. 356b

Fantasy versus Fear

The possibility that put-downs of men are covering up female readers' sexual aversion becomes clearer when we look at the difference between cartoons in *Playgirl,* which criticize men for sexual performing at more complex sexual acts, versus those in *Cosmo.* In *Cosmo* the men are criticized for performing inadequately at the basics. A survey of *Cosmo* readers' own sexuality[18] discovered the *Cosmo* woman is afraid of the basics (such as lovemaking in daylight). By putting down men at the level at which she is still making a transition to becoming comfortable, the woman can say, *"I"*m not afraid of sex; it's just that men do it all wrong."

In the *Cosmo* cartoon we get another hint about this need for reassurance by the fact that the woman is talking to another woman behind the man's back.

I Don't Feel Comfortable Having Children See Me in Bed with Him Until I Know He's Not Going to Disappear

Two new situations are making the new sex become more like the old sex: sexually transmitted diseases like herpes and AIDS and the female as single parent. Herpes and AIDS for obvious reasons. But let's look at the dilemma of the female as single parent.

Sophie often had Henry sleep overnight, but leave before the children awakened. Henry didn't like setting the alarm for 4:45 A.M. to shower and shave and leave before the kids might awaken to the sounds of his car pulling out of the driveway; he didn't like eating breakfast out on the way to work, or killing an extra hour before work and being exhausted before the day was half over. Sophie was traditional. *Henry first felt he had to prove himself before he could stay overnight, and now had to prove himself again before he got introduced as Sophie's sleeping partner.* Double jeopardy.

When I met Henry and Sophie at an Atlanta workshop they were about to split over this issue. Henry did not feel he could commit to Sophie before he had a real relationship with Sophie's children and more time with Sophie; he also wanted to continue sleeping with her. Sophie felt she could not afford to have the children see her sleeping with "a lot of men" and therefore needed a stronger statement of desire to eventually commit. Henry felt that was hypocritical; after all, she was sleeping with him: "If it is all right for you to sleep with me, isn't it all right for the children to be told? And if it isn't all right, maybe you shouldn't be sleeping with me at all. . . ." Sophie knew what *that* meant.

By focusing on sex Henry missed the issue of stability. It is often upsetting for a child to get emotionally attached to a man,* and then, when the adults break up, to have the man suddenly disappear. And Sophie had missed how "being introduced to the children" had become her substitute "withhold" now that she was no longer withholding sex until commitment.

---

*This happens much less the other way around because, as mentioned above, women are over nine times more likely to have custody.

Sophie had decided to withhold ''introducing-to-children'' after an experience with her last male friend, Pat. When she and Pat had broken up, the children were shocked and felt left out. (''Why isn't Pat coming to see us tonight, Mommy?'') Could Sophie have minimized her children's disappointment? Yes. Sophie had felt guilty about sleeping with Pat unless she and Pat were serious. So she *overstated* Pat's permanence, leaving her children unprepared for the possibility of Pat's leaving.

As Sophie felt less guilty and less as if she needed to withhold something until Henry proved himself, she was able to introduce Henry to her children without overstating Henry's importance. To do this, she needed to forfeit the expectation that Henry had to prove something in exchange for sexuality. As Sophie let that go, Henry and she became more of a team, rather than working at odds with each other. The team approach seemed like a more natural path to commitment than a modern substitute for withholding sex.

Men Are a Bit Perverted, Aren't They?

''Your secretarial skills are perfect. How are you with a whip?''

Playgirl, July 1983

Even in *Playgirl* male sexuality is associated with the male willingness to make S&M a condition for employment, as in the cartoon above. Is this a realistic portrayal of males?

In the largest nationwide study of singles (by Jacqueline Simenauer and David Carroll), *heterosexual* males were 2 percent more likely to engage in bondage than heterosexual females: 3 percent to 5 percent.[19] Does this mean bondage is a particularly male fetish? Among gay women, almost one-third reported engaging in bondage, compared to 7 percent of gay men. Similarly, Simenauer finds "almost *half* the lesbian population reports indulging in group sex," as compared to 30 percent among gay men.[20] This does not mean men do not objectify, or have anonymous sex in different ways (as in gay men's baths); it means only that when sex is taken out of the male-female context, and therefore away from its economic implications, both sexes engage in quite similar behavior. But the distrust is of men, not women, almost as if the ostensible message in *Playgirl* is to enjoy sex, while the real message is "distrust men and their sexuality." Its effect? To keep men in the "prove yourself" position.

"Male Power Controls Women's Bodies"

Lately, we have all heard the "history" of men controlling women's bodies via male opposition to birth control and abortion. But this ignores the turn-of-the-century feminists' powerful lobbying for the Comstock laws and the statutes opposing birth control and abortion[21]; it also ignores the fact that the most dedicated Right-to-Lifers are almost all women who stay away from their families to such an extent that some of their resentful husbands have dubbed themselves the Right-to-Wifers.

Rape is said to be an extension of male political power and economic power. If that is so, why do women report black men as rapists five times as often as they do white men?[22] Do blacks suddenly have more political and economic power? Maybe rape does not derive from power, but rather from powerlessness.

Men Have a Sexual Double Standard, and I'm Fed Up with It . . .

Every study I have ever seen about the relative number of sexual partners of women vs. men tells us that women have many fewer sex partners than men do. But whom do these heterosexual men have sex with? Could it be prostitutes? The statistics still reflect a huge gap even when prostitutes are not counted. For example, among singles, 61 percent of men have had sex with ten or more women; 31 percent of women have had sex with ten or more men.[23] Is this because married women are having sex with single men? No. All statistics show *every category of woman* to have sex with fewer men than men do with women. And to have sex with less frequency than men. Of course, this is statistically impossible. What the statistics really show is how many partners each sex admits to.*

The double standard is the difference between what men and women are willing to admit, not what they do. This is not women's fault. We give women less permission to admit to having extramarital sex, which makes it understandable that women would admit to it less. So let's acknowledge that, rather than believing statistics that do not add up merely because they reinforce the stereotype of Man the Infidel.

I Have to Keep My Affairs Secret . . . It Would Hurt His Ego to Tell Him

Once we understand that Man the Infidel is a statistical myth, we are ready to understand how such a myth gets reinforced in our everyday lives. Trish and Tom kept their sexual affairs secret from each other. Trish because "Tom couldn't take it; it would hurt his male ego—his male pride." Tom agreed it *would*, in fact, hurt him. Why? "Because Trish told me, point blank, that 'Sex, for me, can't be just sex. I wouldn't just go out and have sex unless there was something wrong with our relationship—or at least unless I had an emotional involvement.' How could she expect it not to hurt if that's the meaning she attaches to it?"

Tom explained he didn't reveal his affairs because Trish had told him clearly, "I can't understand how you can just have casual sex." Since Trish had made it clear she could only misunderstand him, Tom felt telling Trish would accomplish nothing but jeopardize their relationship. And for Tom, an extramarital affair did not mean wanting to hurt his relationship with Trish.

Trish's saying "It would hurt his ego" was her way of

---

*It may be said that men exaggerate the number of partners. In my own research I find men exaggerate in high school, but married men also admit to *fewer* extramarital affairs than they actually have, but the gap between reality and admission is just smaller.

keeping herself from being vulnerable to Tom. *Blaming her silence on his ego transfers the responsibility to him.* In the process, the contempt for his "fragile male ego" is reinforced. Imagine Tom saying, "I didn't tell Trish because it would damage her female identity." We would sense both his contempt and his cover-up. What was Trish covering up? How Tom might be hurt because he was taking Trish at her word—"Sex, for me, can't be just sex . . ."—and how her hurt might stem from not accepting Tom's statement that sex means just sex to him, that it doesn't mean a threat.

Since we don't have a significant difference between the number of male and female sexual partners, no one knows whether we have an *actual* (as opposed to admitted) difference between the number of male and female extramarital relationships. We can see a difference between what both sexes say sex outside of a relationship means. And what both sexes admit to. That is the only double standard that can be validly documented.[24]

"Your Penis Is Bigger than a Gorilla's"

In the chapter on commitment, I discussed the male intuition about a woman's secret agenda—how a man backs off from a woman when he senses subtle contempt but is usually unable to put words on what he is feeling.

One of the most frequent forms of that contempt is felt by a man when a woman "protects his ego." A great deal of the "ego protection" comes in the area of sexuality. What does it say to a man? Usually that she feels sex is for him, not her, and that he can be toyed with. A woman who can catch herself in this can take the first step toward reexamining her contempt. Here's an example of how it comes up in Dr. Joyce Brothers's guide for women. Dr. Brothers shows us how a woman can be "helpful" about a male's penis size; two women are talking.

"I tell him that it's bigger than a gorilla's. That really makes them feel good," she said. "You know how big a gorilla's penis is?"

I had to confess I didn't.

"It's teensy," she giggled. "About the size of my little finger!"[25]

They say they'll call, but never do.

No Good Men, p. 8

When a Man Says "I'll Call You in the Morning" and He Doesn't, Is It Because Men Are Basically Liars?

Many women's magazines run periodic articles about two aspects of men not calling in the morning. First: a woman and man have sex and he neither calls nor promises to call; second, he says, ''I'll call you tomorrow'' and doesn't.

Men who do this with a woman are often unaware that she may be saying to a woman friend before the next day's evening news, ''Why didn't he call me, that bastard.'' Especially if she really liked him. And if they have just had sex for the first time, her feelings are usually intensified.

A man who says he'll call and fails to *is* at fault. As much at fault as a woman who tells a man she'll call and does not—but no more so. If a woman says she'll call and she doesn't, a man is likely to pick up the phone himself and call. He doesn't call another male friend and say, ''Jeannie promised she'd call me and didn't.'' If he called a man with that complaint he would not get empathy, but ''What's the matter with you—lost your fingers, Frank?'' In similar circumstances, we are very harsh on men and empathize with women.

The underlying question is, though, *Why didn't the woman*

take responsibility to promise to call? The societal assumption that the *man* will promise, or fail to promise, is the underlying sexism.

When sex is involved, even more deeply sexist—and shocking— is the frequency with which "liberated" women who during their workday initiate scores of sales calls are quick to blame men for not calling the morning after, even when the man has not promised to do so. *This is clear evidence of the assumption that the man owes the woman for sex.* The unspoken presumption is: "If I *give* him sex, he should *at least* give me a call."

But it goes beyond this. Often the hidden translation is, "He should ask me out again," meaning, "I want him to see a future in this like I do," meaning, "If he had sex with me, he owes it to me to give me the option of accepting or vetoing a future with him—and he should pay for it to boot." *All of which is why men sometimes do not follow through on their promises*—or fail to make a promise to begin with. And the man who feels pressure to make the promise, is buying into the notion that he owes her something more than she owes him.

Would more liberated men like the woman to assume she has just as much right to call? No. Just as much responsibility to call. I find that women who do share that responsibility have a much different experience with men. Such a woman understands how sometimes she does not want to call because she fears it may lead to another time out with him fairly soon, when, in fact, she'd prefer to wait a while longer; although she liked him, she is more interested in seeing Gary next week.

Women who share this responsibility share the male experience, and their empathy is felt by men. Ironically, these women rarely see men who do not call in the morning. Like impotence, not calling in the morning is the symptom—not the problem. Men who blame their penises and women who blame men will find the problem that much deeper the next time around.

His Masculinity Is Threatened—That's Why He's Impotent

Legions of trees have spent their life after death thinly sliced into a *Redbook, McCall's, New Woman,* or *Ms.* Each tells a woman that *she* is the fairest—that *he* is the problem, he with the fragile ego, the male pride, the threatened masculinity, the impotence, the fear of commitment. Blaming him gives her a temporary fix, but it keeps her worried about attracting men and continually anxious about them. From the magazines' perspective, it is necessary for her to retain this anxiety; diet articles and diet products would sell less without it, as would makeup and deodorants.

But blame creates relationships with men that are close to hell. Or, in the case of a *Cosmo* woman, relationships that were better with her magazine.

How does the line "His masculinity is threatened" help a woman—or a man—know what to do to unthreaten it? How does "Men have fragile egos" build a secure ego? How does "The women's movement causes male impotence" help men, or women, or the women's movement? All of these accusations can be accurate in some instances. But *none* is helpful if it stops there.

Sometimes a Man I'm with Is Impotent. Does That Mean He's Turned Off or Threatened?

I define *impotence* as a soft penis at a hard moment. It might be thought of as God's way of keeping a man in touch with his feelings. But even God could not have contemplated we would have created a word that condemned men for their powerlessness to such an extent that they would forget what a soft penis is for.

A man can think of his penis as radar. Its softness is his signal that his feelings are "off." If it did not work by being soft, *then* he would be impotent.

"I think this calls for a moment of silence."
Playgirl, December 1983

By suggesting that a man's power is located in his penis, the word *impotence* reinforces a man's self-consciousness about his penis, thereby reinforcing a likely problem: self-consciousness. In my work with men's groups, I find approximately 90 percent of so-called "impotence" to be catalyzed by some combination of *self-consciousness and fear of rejection* or, on the other hand, simple *distraction*. When the catalyst occurs at a moment when we are expecting a body organ to change its shape, *the body organ cannot concentrate*. Our self-consciousness prevents loving consciousness.

Martin, a Cleveland area sales representative, had not lost his job, but his career was not going as well as he and Glennis had expected when they got married. Martin was becoming "less interested in sex" and occasionally "impotent." Glennis was doing better at work than he, and they both agreed Martin felt "threatened." Which was true. But *why?* They had gotten married with the expectation of Martin's doing better, or their having children by this age, and of getting along better. Martin was accurately sensing that Glennis was disappointed, open to stimulation by a man at her office, and having some doubts about Martin. Martin was feeling more needy of Glennis's support exactly when Glennis felt least desirous of offering it.

Martin's feelings were fear of rejection and *self*-consciousness ("Am *I* disappointing her?" "Is she angry at *me?*" "Does she feel I'm not trying hard enough?"). His self-consciousness prevented loving consciousness.

What was the solution for Glennis and Martin? They had started out as a team—"in it together." They had lost team consciousness. Martin needed to feel they were still a team at a time when he was not shining as the most valuable player. That feeling could not be one of false assurance from Glennis. The penis senses false assurance. It knows when team consciousness has returned. (Just as a woman who finds herself withdrawing from sex—although she may have been told many "I love you's"—may, in fact, have been sensing something fade from the man.) Claiming that Martin's masculinity is threatened was Glennis's and Martin's mutual pact not to explore Martin's feelings.

In *The Liberated Man*, I suggested redefining impotence by using the word "readiness." Implicit in the word readiness, however, is that the man is not sexually ready. This is still inaccurate, since, *if two women can make love without a penis, a man with a soft penis is every bit as ready as a woman.* Perhaps one of the most self-enhancing experiences a man can have is to observe two women making love. To observe the caressing and tenderness that creates fulfillment without a penis—hard or soft. The security that it offers him about the nonessentialness of his penis to sexual satisfaction can allow him to treat his penis as a nice addition rather than a prerequisite to his sexuality.

Once the penis is seen as an *addition* to a man's sexuality, we can see how the expression "he is impotent" would be like saying about a person with a headache, *"He is a headache."* We make no attempt to separate impotence from the total personality, as we do with a headache. All of this gives us little clues about the degree of pressure on men to perform—turning penises into machines, like airplanes. The penis is expected to do what Delta Airlines gets paid to do: "Penis is ready when you are."

Why is this part of the new sexism? When Drew called Susan frigid she called him a sexist. When Susan got together with Sheila, Drew's former woman friend, and the two laughed about Drew's "not being able to get it up" the first time, they didn't think of themselves as sexist. Drew called Susan frigid when he perceived her as both emotionally and sexually unresponsive to him. He would never have called her frigid had she actively kissed him, touched him, and opened up, but had difficulty receiving him because she was not lubricated enough. *He would never have gotten together with a man friend and laughed about how Susan "couldn't get it wet." The issue, for most men, is not women's physiological functioning. It is their desire.* Shouldn't that, in fact, be what concerns us about our loved one—male or female?

If desire and overall sexuality are our real concerns, how do we describe what we formerly called impotence? We can substitute a description of the behavior, as in "He is soft when he would like to be hard." That keeps our mind open to discovering the feelings that create the behavior. Is there a quick word or two, like the word "impotence," that can substitute for impotence while still not blocking access to feelings? Yes. We might abbreviate to "soft penis." If it is chronic, we call it Chronic Soft Penis (CSP); if occasional, Occasional Soft Penis (OSP). As long as we remember: OSP is a penis that is working *for* us. Like our ability to feel pain, it is our body working to give us a message.

The New Sexism, then, is part of our need to make our major

competition the enemy, a need that arose mostly for women who were not being economically provided for by men. It occurred at a point in history when women were getting divorces ftom men and therefore men as their economic support system suddenly became men the major competitor.

Sexual freedom returned to the Old Sex when sexual freedom could no longer be linked with economic freedom, when divorces created economic insecurity for women. Our natural response—to make the competition into the enemy and put down everything about him, from his competence to his penis size—has only created an emotional dilemma for women, the ''Marry the Enemy'' dilemma. It has placed men in so many ''damned-if-I-do, damned-if-I-don't'' positions that even being Superman is no longer a solution. It has left the sexes more blaming than introspective—more at war and less in love. It has also made people who pooh-pooh psychology and communication discount them even further as they sense the gap between the goal of intimacy and the frequent outcome—disappointment. Somehow they sense we are sharpening our tools of blame even more than our tools of love.

9

Dialogues on Sex, Success, and Fragile Egos

*Q:**   Why do men have such fragile egos?

WF: When I submit a manuscript to a new friend—meaning one who does not believe me when I plead for a critical reading—there is a tendency for him or her to give me lots of support. Friends pay a price for rejecting us. But employers pay a price for accepting us. In my business, for example, *Family Circle* cannot accept more than a few dozen of the 30,000 manuscripts it sees each year. The marketplace rejects over and over and over. *An ego on the marketplace needs protection from that rejection.* Women still gain much of their feedback within personal relationships—from people who pay a price for rejecting them.

Q: Now that many women are experiencing the rejections of the marketplace are their egos getting like men's?

WF: Women who depend on reinforcement from the marketplace are beginning to experience a fraction of the male fragile ego in that area. It is rarely as intense, though, because of an important distinction: *Few women have husbands who depend on their wives' acceptance or*

---

*Sometimes the best way to impart information is by responding to questions. But a simple question-answer approach is an insult to the reader— because it does not encourage a person to pursue the answer. It encourages passivity and acceptance of one answer as *the* answer. Q stands for questioner and WF for Warren Farrell.

rejection by the marketplace. It is the provider's ego on the marketplace, with the pressure upon it, that gets internalized to create a fragile ego. And that pressure is his source of love. This creates for men a connection between pressure and love that few women have to face.

For a man to see the person he loves try to cover her disappointment as he tells her he's been rejected hurts. *The more a man sees a woman as fragile, the more he will see his ego as fragile.* The more he senses her dependency, fragility, and disappointment, the more he feels the emotions of the rejection. Which is why women's liberation and men's liberation are so interconnected.

Q: Don't many men really love their work more than their family?

WF: That's a tough question, because of the *inseparability* for men of success at work and feeling loved by a woman. And then, as a couple has children, the man's intensifying act pays him to intensify his commitment away from home so he can pay her to love the children at home. Studies that find "men love their work more than their family" are treating the two *as if they were separable.* For men with families, commitment to work is rarely separable from commitment to family. The exception is the rare family in which both parents share total responsibility for making an equal contribution to all expenses—from mortgages to college education. And they commit themselves to that equal sharing no matter how unpleasant the work gets. Then a woman's fragile ego will be connected to the workplace almost as much as a man's is.

Q: Why *almost* as much? Why not equally, if she is sharing equally? And what about women who earn more than their husbands, and women who are single parents?

WF: All three groups of women are doing things that exceed society's expectation of them. Like a man who has custody of the children and cooks and cleans. On some level, whatever he accomplishes in this realm is beyond expectations. He is not viewed as unmanly for burning the frozen dinner. When we accomplish outside of our expected role our ego is not as hurt by rejection because the failure is not as important to our self-concept as man or woman.

In part, the male ego is as fragile as it is because there is so much that *appears* fragile that depends on it (anything dependent must appear fragile in order to continue getting support).

Q: Even at the moment of men's triumphs they still seem to be searching for approval. Why?

WF: I agree. I began to understand more why this happens when, a few years ago, I took a train from New York City to Philadelphia to surprise a friend of mine who received an invitation to speak at the University of Pennsylvania. I had heard that he was a good speaker, but as I saw his power, control, command, and articulateness, I was overwhelmed. On the way home, in the car with his wife, he begged me to tell him everything I thought about almost every sentence he spoke, about his response to almost every question, about his body language, voice, everything. At first I was a bit put off at this self-centeredness. "After all," I thought to myself, "he's just had three hours of undivided adulation—doesn't he ever get enough?" And then I tried to put myself in his position. I remembered how, when I finished speaking, I also wanted to know the reactions of my friends in detail. He was just open enough to ask for it. I felt I understood a bit more how the more I put my ego on the line, the more I risk, the more I need reassurance, need friends, need home. Fragile egos come from risking rejection.

Q: How does a woman who heads a single-parent family avoid the female equivalent of the fragile male ego, with all the pressures on her?

WF: She often develops an equivalent in the form of anger and the new sexism. She's angry when her primary fantasy is not fulfilled. This and vanity are her equivalents of the fragile male ego. The gut issue of the mother heading a single-parent family is the *multitude* of her pressures *from so many directions*, not the expectation that she must help to provide for her former husband, pay child support, or pay for the dinners of the men she dates. All of her demands require money. And that is what makes "male as wallet" as important an issue as child care, housework, physical attractiveness, and financial competence combined are for many women. In essence, *all men's eggs are in one basket.* Which is why men's egos are all in one basket. *Each person's ego is fragile in the places where his or her eggs are stored.*

Q: If women have fragile egos about their beauty and are then rejected by an "eligible" man, are they like children in these areas of rejection?

WF: Yes. The more of her eggs are in the basket of beauty and male dependence, the more she will be a woman/child. *Women who are beauty-focused have egos as fragile about beauty as men do about success.* Except we call it vanity. An experience I had with a former Miss USA illustrates the parallel dilemma for women. I was asked to facilitate a "men's beauty contest" for "The Mike Douglas Show." The contestants were Alan Alda and the men from the Fifth Dimension, a singing group. The judges included Miss Universe and Miss USA. Miss USA and I arrived early. She wanted me to tell her my feelings about beauty contests. I summarized how I felt they reinforced for women the feeling that their self-worth was wrapped up in their bodies. She appeared to be listening attentively. Six men walked into the room during our fifteen-minute conversation. She asked *all six* something about how she looked: "Does my dress fit okay over my hip area?" "Is my eyeliner smudged?" "Are there any wrinkles in my dress?" "Do I need more blush?"

Here was a woman officially recognized as having one of the two most attractive bodies of any woman in the country. She also appeared the least secure about her body of any woman I had ever met. She was a woman/child, the female version of the man/child. Why? All her eggs were in one basket. So her ego was in one basket. *She was both most developed (woman) and most fragile (child) where all her eggs (source of power over the other sex) were invested.*

Women experience the woman/child dichotomy in other areas as well. The desire to be taken out and paid for is a childlike expectation. And just as we say war is big boys playing with big cap guns, mothering can sometimes be big girls playing with big dolls.

Q: Many women are getting a bit obsessive about success, yet they did not grow up with an "oil crisis,"* with male sex in short supply. Why is that?

WF: When women are obsessive about success, it is often to prove themselves competent in a world in which they were told they were incompetent. This can generate almost as much obsessiveness as among men, but for different reasons. A woman must overcome the subtle and not-so-subtle barriers of sex discrimination *plus* the normal barriers of any hierarchy; she must decide how much to adapt to male values and socialization and when to exert her own—all of which can generate obsessiveness. The nature of female obsessiveness is akin to that of the refugee from another country trying to prove herself or himself in a foreign land.

Even the success-oriented woman is caught between two value systems: one that tells her success is wonderful and one that says a relationship is wonderful. Whichever path she takes will put the other at risk. That's the negative side. *The positive side is her more likely choice of a balanced life.* In contrast, a woman rarely asks a male surgeon, "Have you been communicating well with your wife today?" Nor do his friends blame him for missing his daughter's gymnastics meet because he had to perform surgery. Success is all or nothing for him, his one way of gaining almost everyone's approval for his entire life. The price is the greater likelihood of an unbalanced life.

Q: Do you agree with the theory that women have a fear of success?

*See pages 116–120.

WF: Yes and no. The image of a successful woman still does not enhance "femininity" in most women's or men's eyes. Women fear their loss of their femininity power. But that's really a fear of failure. Women fear that their own success will make them fail to get a successful man.

Q: Well, is the fear based on a reality?

WF: *Some* successful men are highly attracted to successful women, and a woman's success places her among these men. Successful men are taken up by women *more* quickly and are divorced *less* quickly.* So more of her successful colleagues are likely to be both married and supporting a woman and children.

Q: You discuss how women aren't looking for supportive men unless they're also successful. Well, I'm a successful woman who is looking and I'm still finding few. Any suggestions?

WF: Yes. Go to your local supermarket and ask a man how to choose a ripe cantaloupe. Or to a laundromat and ask him his opinion of the difference between all-purpose cleaner and Era detergent, or—

Q: Great! But why aren't they seeking me out? I do some public speaking . . . men are often in my audiences.

WF: Let's look at the "invisible curtain" between supportive men and successful women. Suppose Randy read about a successful businesswoman's desire for an intelligent, loving, sensitive, supportive, yet risk taking and adventuresome single man. Randy feels he fits the bill. The article mentions she lives in Chicago. He decides to try her home phone. On the seventh directory call, checking out seven possible Chicago area phone books, he concludes her home phone is not listed. He is undaunted; he knows the article also reveals she works for AT&T. He asks information for Chicago headquarters. There are six offices listed. He finally makes it through to her secretary. The secretary asks, "Do you

*See Chapters 4 and 6.

know Ms. Arbenz?'' He cannot say he does. ''If not, may I tell her what this is about?'' How does he say, ''Well, I don't know Maria, er . . . Ms. Arbenz, but I'd just like you to tell her that I saw her picture in the paper and . . . well, she looks like the type of person I'd like and I think I'm the type of person she'd like . . . but of course, I don't know for sure, but I'd like to meet her and see . . . would you please leave her that message?''

Then he hangs up and realizes he hasn't distinguished himself from any other jerk off the street. Sending her his picture probably won't do the trick! Being a real risk-taker, he calls again: ''Hi, this is Randy Risk-Taker once again . . . I just wanted you to know I'm not just, er . . . anybody. I'd kind of like to get to-gether with her as . . . as a possible man who might be willing to, er . . . support her work. Yeah. Maybe even raise our children. Ummm . . . Well, would you leave *that* message?''

If Randy should overcome these barriers, Maria would be suspicious: ''Am I being used—does he just want my money?'' (The shoe is on the other foot.) Ambiva-lence surfaces: ''I don't want a puppy dog, I want a *man.*'' The combination of these barriers forms what I call ''the invisible curtain'' that screens out supportive men from successful women.

The invisible curtain is reinforced outside of business— by the successful woman's tendency to frequent social settings in which supportive men are not easily found. Successful women go to fewer laundromats.

Q: Well, maybe it's not that important to have a supportive man. A career-focused man can be just as supportive by understanding my career focus.

WF: If a woman is successful, the importance of attracting a supportive man who is not overly career-focused him-self is becoming increasingly clear in recent studies of dual career couples.[1] Successful relationships almost always have at least one relationship ''gatekeeper.'' Two people highly focused on their own success have difficulty being more than ''economic partners.'' Dual careers *can* work, with effort. Dual workaholism cannot work except to support each other's workaholism.

Q: About your statements that men are addicted to genetic celebrities: If this is true, why do some beautiful women say they sit around on a Saturday night without a date?

WF: Her Saturday-night story is like Burt Reynolds complaining he sat home alone on Thanksgiving. It makes him seem human, vulnerable, and reachable—a nice alternative to provoking jealousy. It spurs a thousand phone calls inviting him for the next Thanksgiving dinner—none of which can make it past his secretaries. Her "secretaries," or screening devices, are, for example, politely "switching the topic," when she senses Joe Average preparing to ask her out. Therefore, many men screen themselves out rather than be screened out, and occasionally this does leave a woman alone on a Saturday night. But no one ever asks if Burt made any attempt to ask anyone if she or he would join him for Thanksgiving. Nor does anyone ask "the beautiful woman who sat home on Saturday night" if she asked anyone out. But it does make her seem human to tell of the times when her screening devices worked too well. And it increases the demand on her—and therefore her power, even though she feels powerless because she has not developed her resources for Saturday nights alone.

Q: What about a handsome man—can't he attract a woman sexually without enduring the 150 initiatives you mentioned?

WF: He can *attract* a woman sexually, but handsome men tend to seek out beautiful women, who, they report, are more likely to hold back their sexuality as a prize—especially if she thinks it will keep the man interested longer. So handsome men can undergo the same 150 stages of potential rejection as less handsome men. Not all the time—but a third of the time is enough to hurt. For the average woman this doesn't ring true—she may even have been rejected by a handsome man. But from the handsome man's perspective, it does ring true because he wasn't interested in the average-looking woman—his sights were on the beautiful woman. That's where he took his risks.

The handsome man is faced with another hazard. An advertisement is likely to remind him of a beautiful woman who may have broken up with him. It's like being reminded daily of a former loved one. The man addicted to a woman's attractiveness is like a former drug addict watching tempting cocaine ads.

Q: What about a handsome gigolo?

WF: A handsome gigolo can*not* use his looks to get his primary fantasy to support him. His primary fantasy is not older women. An attractive woman, though, *can* use her looks to get her primary fantasy to support her. At first a gigolo might appear to have the same primary fantasy as a woman—using his looks and body to gain security from the other sex. But that would be like saying that being a prostitute is the female primary fantasy. Prostitutes of either sex have not achieved the female primary fantasy—long-term security from *one* partner. So even a gigolo cannot do what millions of women can do. Like everyone else, he must compensate for his powerlessness.

Q: If men feel this financial pressure, why do supposedly powerful men turn into boys as soon as a woman offers to pay for dinner on a first date? Why are men such boys underneath?

WF: If a man were rational, he would accept the woman's offer to pay—as an example of a woman who is *really* willing to help a man undo his financial pressure. But he is not rational—he is dealing with fear of rejection. And the more attractive the woman, the greater the odds that she will screen him out, so the more insecure he feels and the more he compensates by paying for her—the better the restaurant needs to be, the better the wine, the more apparent the gold card—and the more she will laugh inside at this man/child. After all, was he worthy of the cheerleader if he didn't make the team?

A secure man will be delighted, and paying on the

first social occasion will make a woman special more than anything she says. It establishes her as her own person. If he's not secure with her paying, he won't be secure with other independent parts of her . . . so she might as well find out before she's hooked.

Q: But it seems many men insist on paying. What can a woman say if she doesn't want to turn romance into a conflict?

WF: She can say, "Can you think of a nicer way for me to tell you you're special?" or, in a playful tone of voice, whisper, "Listen, handsome—if you insist on paying, I'll insist on celibacy!" If he's secure he'll respond, "You win!" immediately and, if he's the type of man she wants, his respect for her will soar . . . especially if she pays without hesitating. From that point on he will be unlikely to think your nos mean maybe. In fact, if women refused to have sex with men who insist on paying for them the first time because they fear getting hooked into men who do not respect their independence, women would gain independence overnight.

Q: So paying for women is what insecure men do to defend against rejection?

WF: Yes, but this defense, a form of quasi-prostitution, alleviates insecurity only temporarily.

Q: Why only temporarily if the man has a dependable supply of sex and an emotionally supportive woman— doesn't that take care of his primary fantasy and his intimacy needs?

WF: It is temporary alleviation because underneath he becomes more insecure that he isn't worthy of a woman like her *unless* he pays. The woman rationalizes, "It's not prostitution—he earns more, it's only fair," or, "He asked *me* out—so he should pay," or, "Being treated is just plain romantic . . ."

Q: Wait . . . what you call women's rationalizations for prostitution don't seem like rationalizations, they seem valid. Men do earn more . . .

WF: They do. But have we ever seen two women go out on a first social occasion, and say "who earns more?" when the check comes? If a woman doesn't ask this question of a woman, why should she of a man? As a rule of thumb, unless a woman is treating the issue of pay with a man just as she would with a given woman, we have to ask "exactly what is the man paying for?"

But more important, *every time a woman assumes a man will pay* (on the first social occasion, that is) *she reinforces the male image of the type of job he needs to keep to earn money to take out women.* The assumption that he will pay puts pressure on him and takes it off her. *She contributes to the mentality that leads to women earning less than men,* and to men feeling that the more they earn, the more they can take out women, and the more "desirable" a woman they can take out (buy). This is all part of what I mean when I say "male power" is men earning their way to equality with women.

Q: Still, if he asks me out, isn't his paying just plain appropriate?

WF: Unless a woman asks men out (the first time) *as often* as they ask her out, then the statement "*He* asked *me* out, therefore he pays" is just *a double jeopardy of the male role:* he must not only do the asking, he must pay. It's two conditions he must fulfill to be equal to her company. It reinforces his feeling that he has to compensate for his powerlessness.

More important, though, *a man asking a woman out has put his ego on the line, exposed vulnerability, shown interest. Isn't there a way she might show a little interest aside from using her body?*

Q: I hadn't thought of it that way . . . but I still find it difficult to shake the feeling that it's just plain appropriate for the person doing the asking to pay.

WF: If a woman said to another woman, "You seem like a nice person, would you like to get together for dinner sometime?" would we *assume* she was paying?

If the woman who asked also drove out of her way to a restaurant in the other woman's neck of the woods, might not the other woman offer to pay for her? Yet if a man did that, would she offer to pay for him (the first time)? If not, what is the man paying for?

Q: What about romance . . . who wants to split a check on a first time out?

WF: Both sexes love to be romanced—to be treated. But "romance" is often a smokescreen for hard reality—*among the more than 600 women's and men's groups I have started, both sexes admit that on a first date women almost never treat a man.* They may split the tab, or he treats—but she almost never does. This is even true among poor college students—*if there is sexual interest.* So again, what are the men paying for? "Romance" is often a cover for prostitution . . .

Q: You keep emphasizing "the first time" or "the first date."

WF: The first time is often when the man is most interested in sex and when the woman is most uncertain. So he is most insecure. Sex is in shortest supply at that point. So it's the clearest indicator of what's being paid for.

Q: Why are some men Don Juans? And why do I find them appealing in spite of myself?

WF: Don Juans, like all women and men, do what works. Because they are usually blessed with good looks by nature, "working the system" is within reach for them. They don't have to repress their instincts to go for it because they can get it often enough without losing their composure in the process. And it is the combination of their acting out their instincts and not losing their composure that is appealing to many women "in spite of themselves."

Q: Then why do I find myself hurt and feeling I got involved in spite of myself?

WF: The woman who enjoys the Don Juan but says "in spite of myself" is, in a sense, blaming herself for a fair trade: her spontaneity, charm, and sexuality for his spontaneity, charm, and sexuality. In fact, she may have chosen him because she feels he is even better-looking or more spontaneous than she. So it can be more than a fair trade. But she has come to expect commitment or the potential of commitment as part of the package of "giving her body away," so she blames herself for "being used" and blames him for using rather than rejoicing in what she enjoyed and what she learned from the spontaneity. She is trapped by her need to impose her fantasy on each man rather than enjoying him for himself and enjoying herself in the process.

Q: Are you suggesting that Don Juans are not insensitive to women?

WF: Don Juans are often quite sensitive to women—not to what women say they want, but *to what their experience with women has taught them women respond to*.

Q: Why is it I can't find a Don Juan type who is also a deep and thoughtful thinker?

WF: They exist. But they're difficult to find because the Don Juan is often an adapter. One kind of Don Juan finds out what women want and adapts—by making money or showing charm. Because he gets so many rewards from adapting to the system, he has little incentive to do the work that is necessary to question society's values—and, in the process, deepen. It is a rare person who questions what works.

Q: But he held out possibilities he didn't keep—that's what hurt. Why did he make those promises?

WF: Want a blunt answer?

Q: Of course.

WF: To get your juices flowing! Just as the woman wears a low-cut dress to get his juices flowing with the implicit promise of the rest of her—if only he plays it right. His verbal promises are part of what he uses to get her juices flowing by holding out the possibility of the rest of him—if only she plays it right. *Only the woman who makes him into a primary fantasy object (who wants to be swept away by someone she doesn't really know) can possibly want what he is promising to begin with.* If she does, rest assured, there will always be someone around to make promises. When women are given promises that aren't kept, we empathize with their hurt. When men are given promises that aren't kept, we deny any promise was implicit. And often feel it serves men right.

Q: With all the problems both sexes have, there nevertheless seem to be more women who have it together by their thirties than men. Does what you're saying account for that?

WF: Yes. Women who had their primary needs taken care of by a man could focus more on developing the other four components of power during this period of their life. Many of the women whose maturity we respect are divorced. Children, divorce, and the need to support themselves have added humility, too. Most men, though, have never had someone providing for their primary needs once they left home. They didn't have a "genetic celebrity" source of power they could exercise to attract an income from women. By their forties, when they've developed their power enough to exercise it, we don't say they "have it together" if they exercise their power. And if they haven't earned their power, they have broken dreams—also not a sign of having it together.

Every day in about half the advertisements, a man sees the constant reminder of the woman he was not worthy of. Yet if he goes for a nineteen-year-old when he's forty-five, he feels like an immature jerk. Which he could handle if his being a jerk weren't so transparent to everyone else. And if he doesn't go for it, the ads are saying, in essence, "What a jerk."

During this whole process men's deprivation is great enough, and therefore their desperation is strong enough that they may never see the forest for the trees—they may never see the extent to which their jobs or their image in the community evolved from directions begun during puberty about how they could best prove themselves to women. And the fact that many perceive their lives as virtually gone by forty-five makes seeing the forest so depressing they would rather avoid it.

Q: So what can a man do?

WF: He has options. He may say to himself, "What I'm doing gives me more internal rewards than anything else, no matter what I was originally motivated by." Or he may decide, "Those original motivations may have gotten me into this, but I'll bet if I looked hard something else would give me more satisfaction." On the other hand, he may decide he likes attracting women enough to keep doing things he doesn't like that much. At least then he's making a conscious choice.

Q: Do you feel women should be helping men through this process, or that men should be getting it together by themselves?

WF: A woman can help by sharing sexual initiatives, by supporting herself financially, and *also* by encouraging a man through the process.* Women's interest in this is obvious, since men's private lives are in their homes and men's political decisions could ruin their homes. And to the extent women do not share initiative-taking and financial burdens, they tempt themselves into loving "success objects" more than full human beings.

*See Part 5.

PART 5

REWEAVING
MASCULINITY

Should I Question My Motivations for Changing Him?

Anyone—woman or man—who wishes to change another person has to ask first whether the desire to change the other is basically a desire to reinforce the "he or she needs help—*I'm* the better one" syndrome. When missionaries want to save natives, the missionaries reinforce the rightness of their own ways of looking at the world. They reinforce their specialness—the natives become conversion objects. The underlying (or is it overlying?) assumption of the missionary position is superiority. Yet *if the missionaries had not needed the "fix of feeling superior," they may never have focused their energies on changing the native*.

Which is why when we're feeling badly about ourselves, and need a "superiority fix," we criticize others. And later, when we're feeling better, the criticism fades.

The focus on wishing a man would change can become so intent it masks the possibility that the woman's underlying mythology has not changed—she is playing the role of wanting to be saved by a man who does it better or makes it better. She may not yet have escaped from the most traditional assumption that "the man is responsible," and therefore to blame. She may not have escaped the myth that she's helpless, that he should have been the savior, but he's messed it up along the way.

What motivation needs to be behind change? Think for a moment about the point in a relationship in which a person feels most open to changing. Usually, it's either at the beginning, when a person feels most loved, and hopes that by changing she or he will secure that love forever, or at the end—when he or she is afraid of losing love. In both cases a person needs to feel the potential for love to be motivated to change; otherwise there's little to lose by remaining the same. So before we can expect a man to change, we have to communicate what we love about him.

So let's look at what there is about male socialization, and therefore very possibly the man a woman loves, that is lovable, or "What I Love Most about Men." A woman who can do this without saying, "But wait a minute, I have that good trait too," or "I wonder if the author's suggesting that men are better than I am," can be certain she is not trying to change a man out of a need to feel superior. Her willingness to seek out the best in men and apply it to the men in her life nondefensively is the acid test of her not wanting to change him merely to get a superiority fix.

10

What I Love
Most about Men

Every virtue, taken to the extreme, becomes a vice. For the past twenty years I have critiqued traditional masculinity because masculinity has been taken to the extreme. And taken to the extreme it creates anxiety, homicide, rape, war, and suicide; not taken to the extreme it has many virtues not to be tossed out with the bathwater.

Praise of men is an endangered species. But the good about men is not. And when something good is being endangered it needs special attention. And so, for a rare moment in recent history, here is special attention to what's good about male socialization. I'll start with a tongue-in-cheek poem I wrote for the occasion. Imagine a woman saying it.

A Man Is Good For . . .

Taking out the garbage
   and carving up the meat;
For driving when he's exhausted
   and I want the passenger seat;

He's good for changing a light bulb
   and, oh yes, for changing a tire;
For taking the top off an uptight jar
   and chopping wood for a fire;

He's good for steering a car through fog and
   fishing with our son;
For raking fallen leaves and
   making up bad puns;

For spinning ghost stories to the kids
  ("Make it scary . . . but not *too* scary!")
For telling the children the quarters were left
  by a magical tooth fairy;

For reaching back into a cupboard high
  while his fanny sticks out far,
(As he removes a rusty waffle iron
  from behind a dusty jar);

For watching Monday Night Football games
  and acting like he's the winner,
For taking me to restaurants and
  reflexively paying for dinner;

For letting me stick a snowball down
  into his private part;
For giving a head start in a race
  (he's really just a kid at heart!);

For riding roller coasters, saying he's
  glad I was born . . .
For coaching the kids at baseball,
  for returning to mow the lawn;

He's good for painting houses
  and for renovating a flat;
For keeping me warm when it's freezing
  despite one less layer of fat;

But most of all he's good for coats
  he puts around my shoulder,
For the way he swings our
  daughter about, for how he stops to hold her;

For the way he says, "I love you"
  with his strong but tender hugs,
And, oh yes, men are good for . . .
  killing spiders and swatting bugs!

Our first reaction to this poem might be that these are all male
stereotypes. A closer look reveals that they are also, for the most
part, verifiable descriptions of male as opposed to female reality,
which can help us see what stereotypes really are. Stereotypes

are reflections of the need to get approval by behaving certain ways or having certain attitudes. Those who say, "Oh, that's a stereotype," by which they mean either "Don't pay any attention to it, it's not true" or "It doesn't match my egalitarian desire for the world; therefore discount it" are encouraging themselves to ignore reality. Instead we should ask a different set of questions. First, *is* it true? Second, if it is, and if we don't like the outcome, how do we change ourselves so we can change the result?

Throughout this chapter, the female reader will see that she has many of these positive characteristics of male socialization, such as being giving. She may have these traits within the framework of female socialization (being giving to her family) or within the framework of male socialization (giving at work so she can provide for her family). Nothing about men's socialization is strong enough to prevent any individual woman from attaining any of the characteristics that men are socialized to have. The value of looking at the best and worst about men is understanding men's pressures. Socialization is pressure. Men are neither better nor worse than women—both sexes respond to the pressures that are aimed at them. In this way we are all equal.

One of the fascinating parts about men is our tendency to subject ourselves to war, physical abuse, and psychological abuse and call it "power." The ability to be totally out of control while continuing to view ourselves as the ones with the power can have certain advantages to a woman. As expressed in this poem:

One-Night Stand

He bought me drinks all evening
    in response to just a wink
Then accepted my invitation to
    repair my kitchen sink
Then I brought him into beddy-bye
    to get a little sex
Then couldn't help but smile
    when *he* called it conquest!

And now, here are "The Thirty-One Best Things about Men"—or, in some cases, the best sides of some bad things. Writing this chapter helped me appreciate men more than I anticipated. I started out telling friends I was doing a chapter on the "Ten Best Things about Men." The most common reply was a half-joking "Oh, yeah, tell me one!"

The Best Parts of Male Socialization
Teach Men:

Giving/Generosity

Why do we think of women as giving of themselves and men as giving gifts? Because women's socialization teaches direct giving—as listening nurturers, cooks of men's meals, and doing more of his wash than he does of hers. He may give by working in a coal mine and contracting black lung so his child can attend college as he never could, but his giving is done at the mine— where we don't see it. The result of his giving is a check. With women's giving we appreciate more than the result, we appreciate the process: we see her cook the meal, serve it, and usually clean it up. We don't see him wading through water in a dark and damp mine shaft, or driving a truck at 2 A.M. on his fourth cup of coffee, behind schedule in traffic and with no time to nap. We see him at home withdrawing from the coffee.

He may spend much of his life earning money to finance a home his wife fell in love with, but we don't think of him as giving when he's away from home nearly as much as we think of her as giving when she cleans up his dishes.

Sometimes a man's giving is reflexive and role-based, such as when he reflexively picks up a tab at a restaurant. We forget this is also giving: fifty dollars for dinner and drinks may represent a day's work in after-tax income. Theater tickets, gas, and babysitters are another day's work. We don't think of his picking up these tabs as being as giving as when a woman spends two days preparing a special meal for him. Both forms of giving are role-based; hers are just more direct.

Men's driving cars is also role-based, and therefore we tend to discount the giving involved when a man and woman are both high and exhausted after a party and he reflexively takes the driver's seat and she the passenger seat. We forget that men's one less layer of fat means men are more likely to "hit the wall" or to suddenly "run out"—be exhausted and colder—because they have fewer reserves of fat to feed off. Yet men never use this as an excuse not to drive. His giving by driving may be role-based, but that is the point—his role stimulates this type of giving. When Ted got arrested for drunk driving his family looked down on him. No one considered Ted as a giving person because he drove when he and his wife *both* had drunk too much.

Every study of executive women has uncovered the generosity (although it is rarely worded this way) of "the man behind the woman"—the male mentor. Like parents, mentors are often not only not appreciated but even rebelled against. Which is understandable. Women, flexing their desire to feel independent after years of not feeling that way, are unlikely to call attention to a man who helped them, which would reinforce the perception of them as a woman who is just dependent on men. The willingness of the male mentor to keep giving despite little recognition can be seen, in part, as generosity.

Men tend to give reflexively in little ways. When I lived in New York and occasionally took cabs, a cabbie would sometimes ask me what I do. When I'd explain that I was researching male-female relations, more than a few volunteered their observations about the difference between the way women and men paid for cabs when there were two or three women together as opposed to two or three men together. "With men, each guy volunteers to pay the full amount; with the ladies, they divide the fare by two or three—right down to the penny; and then, as an afterthought, remember the tip, debate about what they usually give for a tip, and then divide that—also to the penny."

Fairness

The best thing emerging from sports, games, work rules, winning, and losing is fairness. Not necessarily honesty—fairness. In Little League, when I trapped a ball in my glove just after a bounce, the umpire credited me with catching a fly. I volunteered to the umpire that I hadn't. The umpire, embarrassed, changed the decision. The angry coach bawled me out. The other coach bawled out my coach for bawling me out. They disagreed on honesty. But neither would have disagreed with the fairness of a neutral umpire making the decision.

Male socialization teaches the value of a careful system of rules, within which anyone can work to gain advantage, and some of which can be gotten around (with possible consequences). Once mastered, the rules give everyone a much more equal chance than they would have had without the rules. To men, mastering these rules feels like survival—survival of themselves and their family. A lifetime of practicing these rules gives many men a sixth sense for fairness. Groups of men and women who have disregarded these rules as "too male" or "too establishment," as did the Students for a Democratic Society in the sixties and seventies, soon evolve into backstabbing elites which self-destruct.

Nurturing

Carl wasn't great at expressing feelings. And he didn't understand fully that sometimes Cindy just needed a listening ear. His way of supporting her was to volunteer to help Cindy with the problem that was making her upset. For Carl, taking Cindy seriously meant taking Cindy's problem seriously, and taking Cindy's problem seriously meant trying to find a solution. To him this was an act of love. Anything less, like just standing around when she was hurting, was an act of cruelty. "If Cindy's bleeding," he'd say, "find a solution. . . . Don't just stand there with that sickening supportive smile on your face while the woman I love is bleeding to death!" *Solutions are male nurturance.*

The other two forms of male nurturance are not usually thought of as nurturance. The first actually emerges from what men do badly: expressing feelings. *One good thing comes out of men's expressing fewer feelings: there is more "air time" for women to express theirs.* Since we all feel time to express feelings is nurturing, let's appreciate how nurturing it's been not to have had that time taken up.*

The second type of nurturing that is not referred to as nurturing can be appreciated most by women like Fay. Fay was one of 45 percent of women who went directly from the nurturance of her parents to the nurturance of her husband.[1] Like her parents, Gregory nurtured by offering a security blanket in which Fay could choose among a wide range of options. Fay sensed that Greg loved her so deeply that his encouragement of her, no matter whether she chose to work part-time, full-time, or have

---

*Better listening would, of course, lead to less "air time" needed for everyone.

children, would be backed up by his commitment to working however much she needed him to so she could choose among her options and either succeed or fail. Greg was like a nurturing parent who would provide the nurturance through which Fay could discover herself. But Fay paid a price—Greg wasn't available as much as she wanted for direct nurturance. So she thought of her women friends as being more nurturing than Greg because she did not appreciate the indirect nurturance she received from having the "financial womb" provided. She blamed Greg for it. Now they are divorced; Fay now provides her own financial support. Part of her now wishes she had understood the indirect nurturance provided by Greg's financial womb.

Fathering through Coaching

We don't usually think of a father coaching a soccer, Little League, or Bobby Sox team as sharing in child care, but he is, and he's doing it in a way that creates a special memory for the child. Children feel nurtured by "my dad" caring enough to be "the coach." A dad coaching is more vulnerable than he's seen as being: any idiosyncrasy is quickly noticed and subject to mockery within earshot of his daughter or son. Dad never knows what his child has heard behind his back. Coaching pushes all his "compulsive-win" buttons; he suddenly sees how the game teaches fairness, responsibility, loss, the importance of attitude, and so on. Is Dad trying to overteach and neglecting just plain fun in the process? But if he treats the game as mostly fun and his kids lose, will his child see him as a "nice guy loser" and lose respect? How does he give his child that little something extra without playing favorites?

Leadership

Accusations that "men have the power" have appeared more frequently in the past decade and a half than appreciation for the billions of hours sacrificed by men to give themselves the leadership training to get that power. Or the benefits of the leadership itself. For example, few articles explain how male socialization has trained millions of leaders to lead thousands of businesses that are now providing millions of women with opportunities for leadership that might not exist were it not for male leadership.

Outrageousness

While women are socialized to get male attention by being "good girls" or not offending male egos, men are being socialized to get female attention by standing out. One way a man can stand out is to be outrageous. The best part of outrageousness is the barriers it breaks to allow all of us more freedom to experiment with discovering more of ourselves. The Beatles' hair, considered outrageous at the time, permitted a generation to experiment with their hair; Elvis the Pelvis allowed a generation to experiment with their sexual selves; the Wright Brothers were told it was scientifically impossible to fly—and suicidal to try; and Salvador Dali, Picasso, and Copernicus looked at the world in ways considered outrageous in their time; in retrospect, we can see that they freed us to live in it in a way we could not have dreamed of before.

To Keep Emotions under Control

Although in relationships, this tight lid leads to a "male volcano" after months of repressed emotions, the flip side is our dependence on this male trait in crisis situations. Dirk recalls a head-on collision. "Five cars crashed. There was glass and blood everywhere. Four of us guys ran from car to car, following the screams and preparing tourniquets. We stopped two cars to recruit passengers to redirect traffic, called the police, and removed a woman and her son from a car that burst into flames a minute later."

The newspapers reported the accident. But no headlines read "Men Control Their Emotions in Order to Save Lives of Women and Children." They ran a picture—not of four men standing next to the women and children they saved, but of the five *cars* that collided.

Ego Strength

When women reevaluate what goes wrong in a relationship the unspoken assumption is that this takes ego strength. When men compete fiercely to be number one, we see it as a reflection of their fragile egos (which it can be) and call it strategizing, *rather than recognizing the ego strength required to conduct a self-reevaluation immediately after a loss*. A man needs to ask,

''What did *I* do wrong?'' And then, when he finds the answer, rather than credit himself with his introspection, he must focus immediately on correcting it before the next game.

If he doesn't learn how to correct himself reflexively when he's younger, the price will be one of not meeting sales quotas and never making it to district manager when he is older. Because the male training for quick recovery from a bad situation has been labeled in macho terms (''when the going gets tough, the tough get going''), we have missed the self-reevaluation implicit in this recovery. It happens so quickly we focus on the process of the game rather than on a man's introspection—just the way people who lose all the weight they desire in a week get less attention than the ones who are forever on a diet. Doing rather than talking takes ego strength.

If a career woman fails to get a promotion, she can turn to a woman friend or her husband for emotional support. *A family man (someone whose career supports the family) can also turn to his wife, but his wife is the person second most devastated by his failure. So her support is almost always connected to pressure.* Because a businesswoman's failure rarely devastates her husband, she does not have to turn to a husband she has just failed to feed and ask for his emotional support at that moment. Her husband may listen less effectively in part because it matters less to him. The positive part of this poorer listening is the smaller amount of pressure attached.

All of this can help us understand why even though most women work, the pressure on them to make a quick change—or else—is rarely as great. The pressure on men creates both fragile egos, of which we are well aware, and strong egos, of which we are less aware.

To Separate the Issue from the Friendship

From grammar school to high school, every school-day lunch hour meant gulping down a cafeteria lunch and running outside to ''choose sides'' for the game. Along with the bad that came out of the compulsive competition came much good: today's opponent was tomorrow's teammate; we reflexively called close plays ''out'' if it was the other team's runner, ''safe'' if it was our team's runner. We were emotional for the moment—but we gradually learned that the Steve Garvey or Reggie Jackson we cheer in 1986 we would boo should he switch teams in 1987. We were slowly learning there are few inherently bad or good persons, but that everyone takes on roles.

My woman friend Anne describes a court scene between her lawyer and the lawyer of her former husband. "They both called the evidence of the other lousy, and each other's preparation 'incompetent.' In public. Then the judge offered the decision. A second later, my lawyer yelled across the courtroom, 'Hey, Bill, how about some tennis Saturday?' "

We see this separation even when an entire career is at stake. George Bush attacked Ronald Reagan's policies as voodoo economics in July 1980; in August 1980, Reagan offered Bush the vice presidential nomination. The best part of the intensity of male competition is insight into the game of life—a philosophical distance allowing men to separate the roles they play from their friendships. Allowing for the gentleness of judgment that comes when we experience in our own lives that "Where I stand depends on where I sit." The man who does not separate the issue from the friendship soon finds enemies on his way up the ladder.

To Express Anger

"One minute we were shouting and calling each other names. A minute later we were concentrating on the next play." The male tendency to take sports seriously combined with the willingness to express feelings intensely leads many adult men to say, "I lose my temper for a minute, then it's done with." The positive side of male anger is the quick, intense release of emotions, with the subsequent calm that follows the storm. If the intensity is understood, and not exacerbated, grudges are rarely held. The intensity, like all powerful energy, can be harnessed—and channeled into powerful lovemaking.

To Keep His Complaints about His Relationship within the Relationship

In my travels I frequently sit alone in a restaurant, café, or cafeteria—and make a point of sitting a table away from same-sex groupings. I am struck by the observation—which has not changed in seventeen years—that two women are roughly ten times more likely to be talking about the problems with the men in their lives as are two men to be discussing their problems with women.

The positive side of a man's being less "relationship-focused" is that his luncheons with other men rarely find him talking behind his female friend's back. He gets most of his information about her from her.

By seldom repeating private conversations out of context to a male friend who judges a woman through the filter of his own hang-ups, a man gets less negative feedback about her, and he therefore generates less distrust toward her.

I remember working with a couple—Tim and Iris. Iris often complained, "Every time I have lunch with Julie, Tim makes some snide comment like 'Didn't you see her last week?' in one of his negative tones of voice. It makes me feel: 'If he can't even handle my getting together for lunch with another woman, what can he handle?' "

Tim had not articulated well enough what led to this feeling. Finally he was able to say, "The last few times you returned from Julie's I felt you were distrustful of me." That led us to understand how the distrust was generated. He felt Iris's feedback about him from Julie was based exclusively on the image Iris had created about him—from Iris's vantage point.

As Iris began to see that occasionally she distorted Tim to feel closer to Julie (she and Julie both felt closer to each other when they could laugh and concur about the problems they had with men), she began to work on discussing her problems more assertively with Tim and less frequently with Julie. In the process, she came to appreciate Tim for not airing his complaints about their relationship behind her back.

To Save Her Life at the Risk of His Own

I described in the introduction how my younger brother Wayne died in an avalanche as he ventured ahead to check out a dangerous area alone rather than have his woman friend share the risk or do it herself. No news account of his death discussed this as an example of men's willingness to forfeit their lives for the women they love. We read of accounts of women lifting automobiles to save the life of a child, but not to save the life of a husband. Frequently, a woman who hears about this difference gets defensive even though she says she wants to appreciate men more.

There is nothing to be defensive about. It is not a statement that men are better. Members of each sex do what they are socialized to do both to give themselves the feeling of being part of a whole and to deviate a bit to feel like an individual. This makes both sexes equal—with different programming. A man's dying for a woman he loves doesn't make him better at all, but part of his socialization leaves him vulnerable. My brother was quite vulnerable.

To Give Up His Life for His Beliefs— or to Support a Family

Some men give up their lives at war because they believe in their country; others do it because if they cannot be a hero they'd rather not live; others do it to support families. Others risk their lives in war so that if they live, they will earn enough money and status to "earn" a wife. Men with different class or ethnic backgrounds do the same in the CIA, FBI, State Department, and Mafia: their beliefs or their willingness to support their families are as important as their entire existence.

For these men, these are not empty words. While the worst part of this is an extraordinary statement of male insecurity and compensation for powerlessness, the best part is the extraordinary conviction men have for their beliefs and their families. It is a statement (within their value system) of the importance of values, responsibility, and quality of life: theirs and their family's.

To Sort Out Our Own Values

Myron Murdoch and I used to debate values in the seventh grade. Was there a God? What was the difference between Myron's Judaism and my Christianity? We didn't know then that this debate of our values was a sorting out of our values, which was more important than the outcome. We didn't know that whatever the outcome we'd end up providing money for women's socialized values—that our values might become largely a way of earning mortgage money. In the process we did learn to sort out values of our own—even though "of our own" meant choosing from among those in style. Both sexes learned values. Women learned to type up men's values so he could provide money for her values. The difference in our values was more than substance; it was the process. We valued debating the values. The best part was a sorting out, a first step to a clarity and the start of a philosophy of life.

Self-Sufficiency

We don't call men "career men," because the word *career* is built into the word *man*. Self-sufficiency is built into masculinity. I can remember a prerequisite to becoming a second-class Boy Scout was being dumped on the shores of the icy Hudson River. With the evening turning dark, I was told to fix myself dinner in the snow. There was a catch. I had to dig up branches from the snow and start my fire without paper and with only two matches. Each time I used up two matches without starting a fire, the Scoutmaster told me to bury the branches back into the snow and start over again. I cheated a little (I was bad at counting matches), but the lesson in self-sufficiency was clear.

Most male self-sufficiency messages are not so direct; they are implicit. Implicit in the imagery of Superman and the man on the white horse is self-sufficiency. Male socialization is an overdose in self-sufficiency. There are no fairy tales of a princess on a white horse finding a male Sleeping Beauty and sweeping him off to a castle; no fairy tales glorifying a man who is not self-sufficient. When the going gets tough, he doesn't talk it through, he gets going.

How do these fairy tales translate into reality? Liberation has been defined as *giving* women the "right to choose": to choose the option of being at home or being at work. *Men do not learn they have the right to choose to be at home. That would imply someone else would have to take care of him at home.* A man doesn't learn to expect that. He learns, instead, "The world doesn't owe you a living." Self-sufficiency implies *earning* rights. The right to choose, he learns, comes from choosing, for example, to take a job that pays a lot so he has more choices when he is away from the job. As a result of a man's training to take care of himself, millions of women have been freer to look at their own values—and to criticize men—than they would be if they had to support them.

Self-Starting

If a man is in a bar feeling insecure, and he's interested in a woman who is talking to someone else, he learns that if he cannot self-start nothing will happen. If he feels underpaid on his job or undervalued in his position, he doesn't feel he has a right to better pay or a better position unless he makes himself noticed. That takes self-starting. He must self-start to create the change or self-start to prepare for a competitive job that pays more or self-start to search for a job. He does not expect to be discovered like Cinderella, or passive like Sleeping Beauty. He learns that being the discoverer means perpetual self-starting. Self-starting to get money, women, sex, jobs, and promotions.

Risk Taking

The male socialization to take risks on the playing field prepares a man to take risks investing in stocks, businesses, and conglomerates. To invest in his career with years of training, and then extra training. A plastic surgeon may have risked from age five to thirty-five as a student or part-time student, underpaid and overworked, in order, during the second half of his life, to be able to earn a half million dollars a year.

James Joyce received 200 rejections before he got one acceptance for publication. George Washington risked his life in numerous battles and *lost* most of them as did Dwight D. Eisenhower. Winston Churchill risked and lost numerous elections. Thomas Edison failed at dozens of inventions, and Ty Cobb, one of baseball's greatest base-stealers, was also one of the most "tagged-out" baseball players of all time. Babe Ruth was a home-run king because he risked being a strike-out king.

On numerous levels, male socialization teaches men to risk a lot and be willing to fail a lot—and all for the hope of being rewarded a lot. (Conversely, if he doesn't risk, he doesn't expect the rewards.) If he survives, he will then be able to provide a security for his wife and children that he never had for himself.

To Challenge Authority

Although Myron and I debated values as peers, Walter O'Conner and I took our tentatively sorted-out values and challenged our parents, relatives, and even Sunday school teachers. We would challenge our Sunday school teacher with our questions about God, or about whether people should be allowed to be nude in public. "God created humans, not clothes," we'd say. "No," the clothed Sunday school teacher responded, "God created modesty to punish Adam and Eve for disobedience." Whatever the real answer, the class accepted the challenge from us boys. If a girl had questioned whether clothes were God's invention, all we boys would have wondered about her, as the girls would have—for different reasons. And so we all contributed to the pressure on the girls not to challenge the laws established by authority. In the process, Walter and I were learning to question authority and risk authority's rejection by challenging it.

To Invent

In the process of sorting out values and challenging authority, we occasionally stumbled on ideas we thought were original. They were rarely, if ever, original, but that made little difference—we were learning how to invent.

To Develop Identity

The pressure on men to be more than self-sufficient, which forced them to take risks and self-start, to sort out their values quickly, to learn how and when to challenge authority, and to invent, resulted, at best, in the development of *identity*. Identity arises out of seeing both how we fit in and how we don't fit in—but especially how we don't fit in. The foundation of society is here before we arrive and after we pass. Identity is discovering our uniqueness in that continuity. As we take risks, and challenge what exists, the friction between ourselves and society makes all the boundaries clearer. Which is how we develop identity, and why the best parts of male socialization are helpful in developing identity. Of course, most men sell a good portion of their identity out to institutions just as most women sell out to a man. But the part of a man true to the values he has sorted out still challenges, still takes risks, still benefits from the development of identity.

Humility

The stories a man reads of men who succeeded may have told him to try, try again (or risk, risk again), but did not tell him how often even the "greats" failed. But he knows when *he* fails. So a gap develops between the image of success and the reality of his own vulnerability—even if he is successful. And if he is part of the masses at the pyramid's bottom, he deals with his failure every day. Moreover, he cannot give into this image; that is bad strategy. *This silent, internal confrontation of his own vulnerability and failures, of the gap between image and reality, creates the male version of humility.* For many women the parallel is when they compare their pimples to the commercial models of airbrushed beauty. Reality versus ideal creates humility. It also creates vanity—or the male parallel of vanity, the fragile ego.

We get a good understanding of male humility when we contrast the attitude of someone who has never raised a child with the attitude of a parent. A person who has never raised a child is quick to tell us how to raise one. The parent is often humbler. The person who has not had to succeed to the point of supporting herself or himself, a spouse, a mortgage, and children is like the know-it-all without a child—or the recent college grad who feels he or she can conquer the world. Humility time is approaching.

What happens to create this humility? In the areas of both raising a child and success, life's a compromise. A politician who is honest about lung cancer soon sees himself or herself out of a career in a district where tobacco employs the voters. Should the politician give in on that one issue? If the politician is a man who is supporting a family, the choice is to compromise, or to let his children and wife suffer the consequences; if the politician is a woman who is married and knows her husband's income will support her if her honesty results in failure, little confrontation with her ideal is necessary. The male success role, because it encourages supporting more people, also encourages more compromise. *The humility of compromise is intensified because a man spends his prework lifetime sorting values and developing ideals, only to spend a work lifetime compromising those ideals.* A parent of either sex can understand this as he or she faces parallel compromises with ideals. "I want a child with a sense of responsibility" leads to "Clean your room." "I want a child who knows the consequences of not taking responsibility" leads to letting the child live in his or her own pigsty. For the person who must be a success to survive, as for the person who must be a parent, every day involves the compromising of ideals which creates a humble soul.

Responsibility

Male socialization is a recipe book of taking responsibility. From the responsibility of getting a job at age fourteen so he can pay for his first date's food and tickets, to performing adequately within view of the girl he wants to ask out to increase his chances of acceptance, to actually asking his first date out, to arranging for his parents to drive, then, in later years, to borrowing the car, then driving himself, then taking initiatives—all of these are responsibility.

As my research assistant, Paul, read this section, he laughed. "When I asked Cathy out for the senior prom, I not only drove, I arranged to borrow the car from Dad *the night before* as well so I could *rehearse* the route from my house to her house to the dinner place before the prom, to the prom after dinner, and to two alternative places I thought it might be nice to go after the prom." As he was laughing at himself the woman sitting next to us at the University of California at San Diego library laughed too, then said, "I didn't even get a license until a year after I was of age." Why? we asked. She blushed. "Well, guys always picked me up—there was no big urgency."

I can remember how once, when I wolfed down a meal with the appetite of a six-foot-one-inch adolescent male, my mother said, "If you cooked it, you wouldn't inhale it." My dad might have added, "If you paid for it, you wouldn't have inhaled it." I can remember thinking, shortly after, what it would be like to have to pay for the groceries every week. And the toilet paper, soap, Kleenexes, everyone's shoes and coats, pants and dresses, our carpeted floor, couch, car, gas, oil, and so on. This was before I knew about mortgages. It was a shocking five minutes. And perhaps my vision of that gave me a different view of the jobs I took from the view my sister had.

When I mentioned this to my assistant, Paul, he asked me what jobs I had held. I was surprised at how many flashed back into my mind. During high school and the first year of college alone, I could recall golf caddy, milk boy, paper boy on three different routes, post office worker and mail carrier, and high-school newspaper columnist for the *Ridgewood* (New Jersey) *News,* meat wrapper at Grand Union, cabin boy on the Seine River (age fourteen and fifteen), running a mini baby-sitting business and a mini lawn-mowing business, and, by first year of college, running a used bookstore.

Paul rattled off a similar list. Then I observed how the jobs after those—to help put myself through college and graduate school—forced me to integrate risk taking with responsibility (like selling encyclopedias door-to-door). They were jobs in which I often received no money unless I performed, but received a lot if I did. In our attempt to understand the changing nature of female responsibility from home and children to "juggling act," we have paid less heed to the male·equivalent: If a man increases his responsibility for home and children, he is still expected to work, and therefore has his own juggling act.

My study of male-female language-pattern differences reflects the male training to take responsibility. Men are much less likely to use phrases like "This happened to me," and much more likely to use phrases like "I did this."

Sense of Efficacy

In the process of learning to take risks, men get especially strong training in learning what is and what is not effective—a sense of efficacy. In the process of trying a wide variety of jobs, we learn what we are effective at. We are socialized with a different attitude toward lost investments—as experiences that fine-tune us to the questions we must ask to prevent the next loss. We see the loss as an investment in investing. Tinkering for hours under a hood teaches him by trial and error how to be effective with a car (I said teaches him—it hasn't taught me!).

Once again, this is reflected in male-female language differences. Men are much less likely to say, "Maybe we can get Bill to do that," and much more likely to say, "Maybe if I try . . ."

Doing Rather than Complaining

To become effective, men learn to make the unarticulated distinction between two types of complaining: "I'm helpless" versus "This is the complaint, now here's the solution." Men are not tolerant enough of other men complaining, "I'm helpless." But the best part of this intolerance is the pressure it exerts on a man to get rid of the problem that created the complaint.

Pushing the Limits of One's Talents

Doing may be better than complaining, but doing is not enough. A man's pressure to earn as much as he can with his talents means a constant pushing of the limits of each and every talent to discover which one can support him best. When people hear "pushing the limits of one's talents" they think of talents as raw capability; they feel that job advancement involves an expansion of talents and an application of talents toward an appropriate job and frequent promotions. Successful people learn that pushing the limits of one's talents also means balancing the politics of everyone else's egos while making themselves shine; balancing façade with personal integrity; and selling themselves repeatedly without appearing as if they're selling. The struggle to master the complex politics of advancement is the real pushing of the limits of one's talents.

The recent focus on discrimination has made us feel that the formula for success is qualifications plus lack of discrimination. That one-two approach has limited our appreciation of the extraordinary subtlety and range of talents required for advancement.

Creativity and Problem Solving

In my research on male-female listening patterns I have found that when both sexes are together in mixed groups, women ask questions while making eye contact with a man much more frequently than the other way around. A man feels the opportunity to get acceptance from a woman by coming up with good answers. His mind races to solve the problems her questions pose, which helps him become a problem solver; since he does not always have the answer directly, he becomes creative. At its best, his creativity stimulates him to piece together the information he has in ways he has not thought of before. At its worst, it allows him to piece together imagined "information" he doesn't have in ways that make him look foolish—the flip side of the same coin.

The practical result of this on an interpersonal level is men's particular form of nurturing: solving problems. On the business level it is the development of washing machines, dishwashers, electricity, and microwaves that have made women's roles more flexible; the development of more effective birth-control measures and medical breakthroughs that have led to many fewer women dying at childbirth and all of us living longer; the development of telephones that keep us in touch with our families and airlines that take us home for the holidays. By focusing on all this as male power, we have forgotten the creativity male-female listening patterns stimulate in men.

Sense of Humor

Whether it's Woody Allen's ability to laugh at the schlemiel in himself or George Carlin's ability to laugh at masculinity itself, one of the best things that emerges from men's training to see life as a game is the ability to laugh both at our own roles in the game and at the game itself. Even the most traditional and serious of male systems are mocked, such as Bill Murray in *Stripes* mocking the military. It is difficult to find movies similarly mocking the traditional female role—for example, a movie mocking motherhood.

Resourcefulness

Learning to turn nos into maybes and maybes into yeses has its negative side in the sexual arena—I call it rape training. But in the world of business it is called resourcefulness: in finding a way around every "no" a salesperson gets—from the first secretary to the final closing. Women are currently learning to do this in the business arena, but it's not yet being incorporated into their sexual socialization. They may take initiatives, but that's different from resourcefulness.

The best part of football, more than any other sport, is resourcefulness training: "Which of forty-two options can we use to advance this ball as far as we can, given the constantly changing circumstances?" Chess is like that, too. In all these areas—sex, sports, and chess—men are socialized to expand their resourcefulness.

To Enjoy the Woman . . . Not the Potential

The positive side of men's being less focused on commitment is a willingness to enjoy fully the here and now rather than postponing a full emotional and sexual "letting go" until he is persuaded she is "Ms. Right" and then only as long as things are going right. A man's male friends don't innocently ask if he feels used, making him view women as users. This allows him to enjoy a woman without making her feel she has to prove herself first; because his socialization teaches him to enjoy *her,* she is less likely to feel pressure from him to choose between making a decision or losing the chance to enjoy him.

To Play with Kids on Kids' Terms

As playmates, many dads provide a combination of physical risk taking with physical protection—allowing their sons or daughters to test physical boundaries and limits without risking their lives. When Paul and his daughter Amy went to the park, Amy would climb trees she would never have climbed alone, because Paul would stand under her, always ready with a helping hand should her foot slip.

At home I often play horsey with Megan. She lets me know how hard I, the "bronco," should "buck" to give her the right balance between physical challenge and physical protection. I let her know when horsey is exhausted.

Playing with kids on kids' terms often moves to points at which many mothers are uncomfortable. When Carl raced his son and daughter down the icy street on their sleds, they all crashed near the bottom. Some of the mothers looked a bit askance, but the kids loved the fact that Dad let them crash. And that Dad didn't just let them win—although they didn't like Joey's dad, who never let them win. Most of all, they loved the fact that Dad, *un*like kids their age, had a keener sense of when things were going too far. And so they came back for more. They liked that he played with them on their terms. That's the best part of men's being kids at heart.

Change without Blame

Although men have made fewer changes than women, what changes they have made—as in fathering—have occurred without movements that blamed women. Fifteen years ago, few men were sensitive to orgasms or clitorises. Few had heard of the ERA. Few fathers-to-be joined their wives in the delivery room, in the preparation for the birth of their child. But soon, men had changed in all these ways.

The changes that occurred happened without attacking women with equal-but-opposite rhetoric, such as "Women hold a monopoly of power over the child," or "Women have a fragile mothering ego perpetuated by a quiet matriarchy that sends men into the field to die while women conspire to sleep in warm beds at home." Nor did men respond to blame by labeling it psychological abuse.

When we hear the phrase "the battle between the sexes,"

there is an unspoken assumption that both sexes have been blaming equally. The battle, though, could easily be called "the female attack on men," not "the male attack on women." There is a distinction between responding to blame and initiating it. Men have changed less, but they have also blamed less.

I'll end with a tongue-in-cheek poem about what male socialization does *not* teach men to do that indirectly amounts to a good thing or two about men.

Our Mascara Doesn't Run

When we cry (if we cry) our
    mascara doesn't run;
We don't stand at the mirror
    asking, "Who's the fairest one?"

You can kiss our lips and
    never send your collar to be cleaned;
We rarely disappear to prepare
    for being seen.

You can beat us at a bet and
    we won't offer to "pay in kind";
We can meet you at a restaurant
    and not leave our cash behind.

So if male socialization
    is mostly what we've got
Maybe what we're good for
    is also what we're not!

11

How Can I Change a Man (Without Just Getting Him Ready for the Next Woman)?

A woman in love will do almost anything for a man, except give up the desire to improve him.

Nathaniel Branden, author,
The Psychology of Romantic Love, in an interview

These days a guy can't have his neuroses in peace.

Vic, forty-nine

The Politics of Change

Item: In Greek mythology, Pygmalion is a gifted sculptor who, disliking real women, tries to create a perfect woman in the form of a statue. Years of practice result in the perfection of every nuance, until the statue appears like the most perfect and beautiful woman. He has created art so beautiful it no longer appears to be art. Yet his kisses and caresses are met with the response of stone.

After years of fruitless attempts to make the statue respond, he beseeches the goddess Aphrodite to assist. She does. The coldness of statuesque stone melts into the softness of human flesh, into tender lips, responsive kisses, and a pulsating heart.

Which just goes to show, with the help of a god, you can change anybody!

While Greek mythology often reflected a desire to change women—and a subsequent frustration at its impossibility—American reality reflects a desire to change men, and a similar

309

frustration about its apparent impossibility. *The New Yorker* cartoon below illustrates the American Plan.

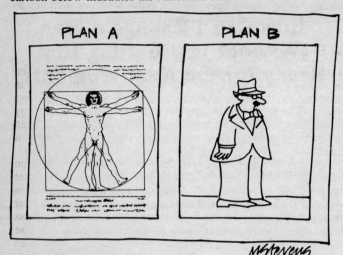

The New Yorker, September 12, 1983

Until recently, the question was "Why can't a woman be more like a man?" It should have been changed to "Why can't both sexes be more like the best parts of each other?" Instead, the pendulum swung to the 1960s feminist lapel button "Adam Was a First Draft." True enough. So are we all. Now, one of the jokes floating about college campuses is:

Question: "Why do men have fewer hemorrhoids than women?"

Answer: "They're more perfect assholes."

I shared this joke with a large midwestern audience. Gales of laughter. Suppose I had asked the question the other way around?

If that's the state of the war, is there a path to peace? Yes. But whether it is worth traveling with any one man—or men in general—cannot be determined until we know if change is possible. If it is, do you want to change a man or change yourself? Hopefully, the introduction to this part helped with that question. If it's a man you want to change (as well as yourself), the next question is, do you want to change your man or change men? Then, if it's your man you want to change, does he want to change? If he's really open, do you know what you want him to change to? No use traveling a path to nowhere.

Is Change Possible?

I have discussed how men spend their lives adapting to women as much as the other way around. We just do it indirectly—as in adapting to our bosses to support a woman we love. We have seen how this performing makes men successful in attracting women and unsuccessful with the women they attract. So men are torn: what we did to *get* intimacy is the opposite of what it takes to *have* intimacy.

Are men willing to adapt to new expectations? Yes. Men adapt all the time—to the different expectations of different bosses. How do we get men to adapt to new expectations from women? By giving men different cues—cues that make it clear they will get more love from intimacy behavior than success behavior. Why are men able to respond to love cues? Because men have learned to provide for their own primary needs, and are able to adapt to their primary remaining need—love. Performing creates an intimacy deficiency; when men are convinced that deficiency will be met, they are great adapters.

Adapting to expectations is not the best reason for change— internal approval is—but the former is the most common. And if the changes themselves are healthy, and the relationship better, why fight it?

In a sense, of course, *we can only change ourselves*. But that changes *the relationship formula*. For this reason I will make suggestions about what a *woman* can do differently even though her question is about how to change a man. A woman might say, "Why should *I* change—what about him?" If either sex wishes to change its partner, he or she can start the process only by doing something differently himself or herself. Only because women have posed most of the questions about how they can change men do most of my suggestions concern how women can start the process by doing something differently themselves. When the complaints come from men—about changing women— the suggestions will be to men.

Unfortunately, men change the most after a relationship ends—or after a career failure. And few men—or women, for that matter—

easily change personality patterns that are *fundamental* to them. For example, a non-self-starter rarely becomes a self-starter. But it is possible to redirect that self-starting energy into a different area. For example, a neglectful father, such as in *Kramer vs. Kramer,* redirected his "giving" energy from work to a balance between work and home. If, then, a woman is not working or if she is not changing a fundamental personality pattern, and is not just into getting a "superiority fix" by convincing herself that helping him implies it is his problem, the next question is: Do you want to change *your man* or change *men*?

Do You Want to Change Your Man or Change Men?

I remember going to a tailor and asking for so many alterations in a sport jacket the tailor said, "Perhaps you want a different jacket." If the jacket were a person with feelings, he might have said, "It would be easier on the jacket for you to make a decision first about whether you really want *that* jacket or a fundamentally different one." Because changing relationships, unlike changing jackets, involves the fear of hurting feelings, acknowledging failure, and so on, we can justify not confronting our secret desire to change partners by saying, "We're letting him/her down slowly." In fact, we're sometimes altering our jackets to buy ourselves options—to see what the altered jacket looks like while keeping an eye out for other possibilities.

When a partner keeps upping the ante, someone usually gets more hurt than necessary. Vicki said she wanted Frank to change. He changed. She upped the ante. He changed more. She still felt frustrated. Vicki, it turned out, was not in touch with her feelings. She wanted out. Somewhere, somehow, she had turned off to Frank. Frank's changes left him humiliated and ultimately bitter toward Vicki, toward himself, and toward the women he later attempted to date. At the point he most needed security, "to make the transition to the meat market," he felt most insecure. And Frank reinforced the problem. He was changing for her—not for himself. Frank was slaving, not changing.

For a long period Vicki did not understand she was upping the ante. Neither she nor Frank understood perhaps the most important basic dynamic of change, what I call "The Toilet Seat Analogy."

The Toilet Seat Analogy

"You agreed to put the toilet seat down and you still always leave it up," Vicki complained.

"I almost always put it down," Frank retorted.

In fact, Vicki could recall half a dozen times she had almost fallen into the toilet in the past month alone. And Frank could recall at least two dozen times he had put it down. Change is like that. The person changing is aware of each time the toilet seat is put down. The person living with her or him notices only when the toilet seat is up. The person who wants his or her partner to stop burping still hears the burps, but not the effort to repress the burp; still experiences the interruption, but not the effort made to refrain from interrupting; still sees the clothes left around, but not those picked up.

The best way to encourage change? Actively notice when your partner completes a meal without burping, or when you complete a sentence without being interrupted. *Assume* your partner made an effort; thank your partner for the effort.

If It's Your Man You Want to Change, Does He Want to Change?

Most men do not want to change. Not much, anyway. Why? For the same reason few women wanted to change prior to the breakdown of marriage as an institution. Both sexes' socialization defines our "wants," and until we feel we are getting more approval by changing what we want, we remain the same and usually want to. But once the approval cues change, we both change even what we feel we want. One day we want wide lapels and miniskirts and the next, thin lapels and maxiskirts. Some people rebel, but usually just with a different uniform, seeking approval from a different source. *Our biology, it seems, wants approval. Our socialization tells us how to get it.* Again, this is true for both sexes. Men have changed less, then, because their approval cues have changed less. We still get more approval than women for succeeding and more disapproval than women for desiring to be full-time homemakers. Even among rebels, artists, punks, and individualists, it's the leaders who get approval, not the homemakers. Men will change when their approval cues change.

We think of men as having many options: president, astronaut, etc. But all those options are really subsets of one option: to *earn income*. Earn income for everyone we ever expect to have an emotional relationship with. Think about that message. No love until we pay for it. So we earn income to get everything from promotions to job satisfaction, from survival to love. For love and money, earn income. One option.

When men want more approval we intensify doing what we are already doing. We learn to "change" by doing more of the same.

Approval is a tricky subject. It kept our grandmothers in the kitchen baking brownies and bread. Approval can keep the slave a slave. Much of what men do is self-destructive. We might say men get more approval than women for self-destructive behavior. *If approval keeps the slave a slave we know why heroes are often slaves.*

What do men's approval cues need changing to? To defining maturity as sorting out values rather than as commitment—a dichotomy poignantly depicted in Somerset Maugham's *The Razor's Edge*. It's only when a man takes the time to sort out values (now this is called a mid-life crisis) that he sees the incentive for changing the core of his relationship to women. Why? Few working-class or middle-class men can afford to arrange their lives according to their values and still support the lives of a woman and children. But if a man believes he cannot get a woman he is attracted to to *share* the financial responsibility for herself, him, the children, and the mortgage—for better or worse, he will stick with the socialization he has learned rather than risk a life without approval. Most men never feel worthy of asking women they are deeply attracted to to share that. So we never allow ourselves even to want it.

Men won't change until we have a perspective on how powerless power makes us. A woman cannot help a man change until she has a perspective on how powerless power makes men. Men will not change as long as we convince women to marry up and men to marry down.

Do You Know What You Want Him to Change To?

Item: *Newsweek*. Front cover. Househusband. Complete with apron. *Time*. Front cover. Clint Eastwood and Burt Reynolds. Complete with steely eyes. *Time* and *Newsweek* appear the same week, same time.

The above "item" illustrates the mixed messages men receive daily. But the mixed messages are less damaging than the "damned if you do, damned if you don't" messages in which men feel damned no matter which part of the mixture is chosen. "Women," men are beginning to articulate, "want us to be successful without the traits it takes to succeed." Perhaps Natasha Josefowitz expresses this best in "The New Etiquette."[1]

> *The New Etiquette*
>
> He hires her
> It is reverse discrimination
> He doesn't
> He's not complying with affirmative action.
>
> He promotes her
> He's playing favorites
> He doesn't
> He's sexist.
>
> He opens the door for her
> She doesn't need his help
> He does not open the door
> He's a boor.
>
> He lights her cigarette
> He's old-fashioned
> He doesn't
> He's rude.
>
> He picks up the dinner check
> She's offended
> He doesn't
> He's stingy.
>
> He greets her with a kiss
> He's unprofessional
> He doesn't
> He's cold.
>
> He gives her a raise
> He has ulterior motives
> He doesn't
> He's a bastard.

This new etiquette—a lose-lose etiquette—is especially effective in getting men to shut up about their feelings. But if a woman is reasonably clear about what she wants, or at least open to confronting the "damned if he does, damned if he doesn't" messages, then she is ready for the next step: the "one-way street boomerang."

Is There an Overall Approach to Change That Works Best?

Change Is a Two-Way Street

If you think he is changeable, the big problem arises: creating the change without sacrificing the romance. *If only one of you is changing, you become the therapist. Therapists who sleep with their clients take grave risks.* Kramer *and* Kramer became Kramer *vs.* Kramer.

If change is a two-way street, does that mean men and women should be working on helping each other with each and every problem? Not quite. In some areas men will tend to need help from women; in others women from men. Changing a partner in one particular area is a legitimate one-way activity, as long as there is an overall balance in the changing that occurs over a period of, say, a year or two.

I'm Sick of Playing Earth Mother . . . Let Men Change Themselves

"I'm sick of playing earth mother," Allison exclaimed. "When I got married to Paul, I wanted a man, not a boy." Allison's attitude toward Paul represents a growing and understandable feeling among women toward men. Understandable because, after a decade in which women have grown and changed significantly, it is frustrating now to be expected to "mother" men. Yet there is more to this "mothering" than meets the eye.

Traditional male-female relationships are much like that of a producer to a star. The producer takes care of the star; the star takes care of the producer; the star feeds the producer; the producer feeds the star. The producer's "mothering instinct" and willingness to provide stability only continue as long as enough of the star's risks pan out; the star's risk taking, then, provides a type of mothering that allows the producer the luxury to mother. It is fair for the producer to say, "I want to be a star too"; it is unfair to think she is the only one who has been mothering.

Executive women have also been mothered by men. Because the mentors of successful female executives are men, no one dares suggest they are mothering, or even nurturing. They are seen as advisers and mentors. I would suggest that just *as women who make it in the world of business need male business mentors, perhaps men who make it in the world of emotions will need female emotional mentors.*

Resistance to mothering can be quite complex. Allison wanted Paul to be more emotionally vulnerable, yet when he was, she lost respect for him. "I'm tired of playing earth mother" was actually her defense. Yet, asking men only to help themselves is like the male chauvinist business executive who says, "If women want business success, they can help themselves. No one helped *me* get here." The truth is *everyone* helped him get there—every man who was successful was a role model who helped him get there. The images not only helped him get there, they left him little choice but to get there or to drop out. In a parallel manner, women were also *born into* a more emotionally supportive environment.

The resistance to helping men is deeply embedded. Lois Lane, after all, was swept away by Superman, not Clark Kent. Clark Kent was emotionally vulnerable. . . . If Clark Kent and Superman represent two sides of a total man, perhaps Allison was falling in love with only one side of Paul.

Allison and Paul, like most women and men, were caught in a transition period. If each sex does not share its power, it will remain in the prison created by that power. The traditional man who protests "I don't want to give away my secrets of power" will find himself alienated from his wife and children even though he supposedly has the power; the woman fearful of helping men change will find men will remain the same. We all need mentors.

I'm Working . . . How Can I Get Him to Share the Housework?

How does this balance between one-way change and mutual change operate in practice in a nitty-gritty area like housework?

Jia and Kirk are good examples. Jia felt she had a *right* to a professional career. And, therefore, a right to have the housework shared. Kirk felt that was fair. Over time, though, he found himself very supportive of Jia's career but not as supportive about sharing the housework. Jia felt she had to nag him and treat him like a child. She began to feel it was easier to do it herself than to remind him. She eventually stopped reminding him, did the housework (and her career), and filled her vacuum with resentment.

What went wrong? For a long time Kirk could not articulate that he did not feel that the responsibility for producing the income was shared. He felt he was taking on more of the psychological responsibility of thinking about how to earn enough for the children's college education, the mortgage, and so on. Jia talked of working or not working. He did not. Since he could not articulate this, he just withdrew from certain parts of the housework, waiting to be asked, acting as if he could do it or not do it. The way Jia did with work.

I consistently find in my work with couples around the country that good news in changing men requires a different formula from bad news.

Here are the two major formulas: First, if the woman demands her independence largely as a *right*, and she persists, either she or he eventually splits; *or* she stays, but largely for his income; *or* he conforms and stays. In what is probably the only acceptable one of the three alternatives (he conforms and stays), there is a price. If he conforms to her demands without getting in touch with his own demands, *her* respect and sexual interest in him usually decrease. Ironically, his respect for her, and sometimes sexual interest, too, increase.

Is this the good news? Fortunately, no. The second formula for change is.

If the *couple* sees their *responsibilities* as *shared*, and *both* undergo a simultaneous reexamination of their roles, dealing with both of their gaps between theory and practice, then they both have the *potential* for increasing respect for each other, intimacy, and sexual energy. Depending on how they conduct the reexamination. The increase in respect for the woman alone is replaced more by mutual pride for their accomplishment as a couple. If they do separate, they are more likely to remain friends.

These formulas may need a second reading. It's ten years of research in one page.

Back to "rights" versus "responsibilities." Don't most rights entail responsibilities, and don't most responsibilities engender rights? Yes. So why the big distinction? Simply, as in the phrase "fight for rights," *rights, like anger, motivate. But they motivate the seeker of rights. It rarely motivates the person dealing with the rights seeker.* Not for long, anyway.

What happens if the couple does try to *share responsibility* for both the income and housework? They muddle through together. A difference from "me-bad-guy-if-I-fail, good-guy-if-I-follow." A woman often finds she has difficulty fully sharing responsibility for the income. He finds, often, he has difficulty fully sharing responsibility for the child care and housework. They both find that the system discriminates against deviants. And they both find their own childhood socialization is as difficult to undo as syrup is from a pancake. And sometimes not worth the effort. The differences with this approach? They *both* laugh, both cry, and both compromise with ideals.

Are There Specific Steps to Changing Men?

We're already beginning to see that the very question, "Are there specific steps to changing men?" gives us a hint that the underlying assumption may be that the man is the problem, and that such an approach backfires more than the joint responsibility approach. However, if the question's intent is to look at the *initiatives* a woman can take that also incorporate looking at her part in the relationship, then we're ready for Rick and Andrea.

Rather than learn from someone's failures, let's look at a couple who made changes that worked. Rick was in a men's group I was part of when I lived in Manhattan. He had joined the group only after Andrea had threatened to leave their relationship unless he joined. He told the group she had previously threatened to leave unless he changed, but he sensed that this time she meant it. Let's become a fly-on-the-wall in the group.

Rick explained, "She's been doing better at work than ever before. That seems to be making a difference. I don't know whether it's self-confidence or just plain having the ability to leave me—financially, I mean."

Rick said he promised her and himself he would change. Yet, he said he also sensed she loved the lifestyle they were sharing: his income was still paying for about two-thirds of it. When he tried to change, he found it hard, on a daily level at work, to stop short of doing the extras that would allow him to be rewarded with an assurance of higher income. Why was it hard to stop? Behind his pride in his work rested his *fear that if he stopped providing the better lifestyle, he would lose Andrea.*

About a month later, in a joint group of men and women, Rick and Andrea stumbled on the dilemma during an argument: "You want me to work less, but you admire all these homes we can't afford, you talk about couples going on great vacations, and the other day you mentioned an old boyfriend who had become a big film producer. You should have seen the awe in your eyes . . . like you missed the boat because you didn't stay with him."

"I told you, Rick, that all that makes no difference. I'd rather be with you any day."

"Somehow, that's not too convincing. It feels like me telling you I'd rather be with you than the beautiful woman I'm ogling as we're walking down the street. . . ."

Andrea retreated. The parallel hit home. Andrea responded by agreeing to put out fewer hints about ideal homes, gorgeous vacation spots, special places she would like to eat, extra drinks she would like to order, and so on. And Rick promised a renewed commitment to discover and explore each other's interests and souls.

Gradually, though, Andrea complained the old patterns were returning. Rick retorted that her hints were returning. "And they're not all verbal hints. When we share the check at a less expensive restaurant, even if we have a nice dinner conversation, you're often too 'tired' to have sex. Yet, when we have a 'romantic' evening out—which translates into expensive evening out that I pay for, you're almost always sexually responsive."

Could anything work? One of the group members suggested an experiment—all of us were good at suggesting experiments for others! Since Andrea and Rick had little to lose, they agreed to experiment by *splitting every expense* for a six-month period. Here's the rub. To do it and still be able to afford the rent in the apartment they were sharing meant cutting back their lifestyles to a level at which Andrea's smaller income could adjust. The result? *Andrea's demands were fewer, since they became demands on herself.*

Rick reported that without the pressure to pick up the extras, he gradually became more his own person at work. "I'm still producing—but I feel freer to produce what I know best, rather than always please my boss. *I always thought women were the 'adapters.' I never realized I was spending my life adapting, too—to a boss."*

Andrea experienced a different impact. "I feel our sexual time is less planned and contrived. It grows out of our time together rather than being an expectation."

Rick and Andrea's experience contained a number of ingredients crucial to influencing men to change.

- Andrea was coming closer to sharing (as opposed to "helping with") the financial burden. At that point, as Rick put it, "I was forced to alter my perception of how I could keep her. *I had to become sensitive and attentive, and share the housework, because I had nothing else."*

- Andrea avoided one of the most destructive of the "female change fallacies"—*substituting* discussions with women friends for discussions with Rick. (Yet she did not avoid *discussions* with women—avoiding same-sex discussions is one of the biggest *male* flaws.) Nor did she agree to keep any part of her conversation that had to do with Rick confidential—or "just between us." She recognized that perspectives gained in confidence (for example, "between you and me Rick really can't be trusted") are often the most haunting—they create a filter through which everything else about Rick is experienced. So she cleared up everything that might affect her attitude toward Rick immediately. This step contains more than meets the eye. (The eye can meet more on this below.)

Cathy Guisewite, *A Mouthful of Breathmints and No One to Kiss, p. 17*

- Andrea used her newly found financial leverage (which made it easier to leave) to get Rick talking with other men. (A woman who is the only change agent rarely succeeds without exhausting herself and the relationship. She usually just prepares the man for the next woman.)

  Most women suggest counseling or a men's group, but if the man resists, they either back off (with a corner on the virtue market) or continue complaining until the point is made but the soul of the relationship is unmade. The "soul of the relationship unmade"? Yes. *As a rule of thumb, relationship excitement diminishes when the ratio of criticism to stroking is more than 1 to 4.* When that point is reached, get help or get out.

  If you think this is a "great idea, but impossible for *my* man . . . (he'd resist therapy and freak out at the thought of a men's group)," read on.

- Rick and Andrea negotiated a practical, concrete experiment that allowed them to "walk a mile in each other's moccasins." The experience addressed their particular issue directly. They did not do what most couples do when a temporary change of roles is suggested—manufacture a hundred reasons why it won't work.

Do Men and Women Change Differently?

Rick and Andrea's case illustrates a fundamental difference between the ways I have found that women and men change. When it comes to relationships, as opposed to business, men seldom change until they have to. But when they do, they often change quite quickly. Once a man believes a woman might leave, he is not as resistant as his appearance might imply; any more than the traditional woman's appearance of financial ignorance accurately symbolizes her newly found ability to enter MBA programs in droves.

Women, on the other hand, often relish the process of relationship change. They soak it up watching the *Donahue* show the way men soak up other men performing while watching Superbowl. *Donahue* is to women what football is to men. Why? Because the more traditional the woman, the more men (or relationships) are her source of income or survival. And the more traditional the man, the more sports is the first symbol of how he performs.

This prepares him for performance—his source of income or survival.

Just as watching football does not necessarily mean a man is good at it, so discussing relationship change does not necessarily mean a woman is good at it.

The Politics of Honesty

What prevents a woman from being good at it? Let's look at Mary. "I was married to Jeff five years and during the first two or three, everything was okay. Then we had Joshua. I stopped working. I love that kid. But the more dependent I became on Jeff, the more I was afraid to confront him. I kept picturing him getting mad at me. Then I had fantasies of me and Joshua being in some small slumlike apartment. By comparison, no issue seemed worth the confrontation. So I didn't confront Jeff. I talked with Mom and read books and magazine articles. But the more I learned, the more my silence gave me a lump in my stomach. I kept telling myself Jeff couldn't handle it. *It seemed the more dependent on him I got, the more fragile I thought his ego was.*"

For Mary, "relationship" increasingly meant survival. Once she had Joshua, honesty became more and more a high-risk operation. More needed, yet more feared. Each day she adapted more herself, and feared more asking him to adapt. She protected him from anything that might create the risk of an explosion to protect herself from his leaving. Ultimately, Mary will save enough to leave, or it will get unbearable enough that she will have to leave earlier. When she is ready to leave she might explode; he will finally get a sense of the problem's importance to her, and *amazingly, he will be prepared to change* (because he has made the male commitment shift and gotten hooked on intimacy) but for her, in her soul, she will already have left.

I find in my work with both sexes that the less a woman supports herself the more she tends to fear honesty with her man. Why? She fears alienation from her bank account. Yet she often maintains the belief that she is the one most interested in relationship change because she talks more about it. Much of that talk, though, occurs with women friends. If a woman understands exactly how female talk can be a substitute for intimacy, she will have conquered the most common of "female change fallacies."

Avoiding the Four "Female Change Fallacies"

The "Substitute Woman Friend" Fallacy

Andrea avoided substituting discussions with women friends for discussions with Rick. Exactly why is substitution harmful? *Substitution often leads a woman to believe she's communicated more with the man than she has.* How? *The woman rehearses her complaints about him dozens of times in her mind's eye. By the time she verbalizes it directly she feels as if it's already been said.* She feels that getting a man to talk is like pulling a thread on a sweater. She fears unraveling the whole thing for a small alteration. So her first attempt is often a "probing initiative" —slipping it in during an argument about something else. Since men tend to listen less than women to innuendoes concerning relationship change, she feels hurt when he responds minimally or not at all.

Frustrated, she airs her complaint with a woman friend. The tones of frustration, though, signal to her sensitive woman friend the need for support, nurturance, and empathy, which often come in the form of *"You* don't deserve *that."* (Translation: "What's a beautiful person like you doing with an insensitive shit like that?") By the conversation's end, the woman is angry. Not just at the man, but at herself for staying with such an "insensitive" man.

Cathy Guisewite, *A Mouthful of Breathmints and No One to Kiss*, p. 5

Back home, the man does not benefit from the energy his woman friend pours into retelling the story to other women friends. Especially if a woman friend wants her negative comments kept confidential. He has not absorbed the level of significance the change has for her. He experiences only her mood changes. Or her sexual withdrawal. And they confuse him. When she ultimately announces she's going to leave, he's astonished. And she's astonished that he's astonished. Which reinforces her conviction that he's not only "in another world," but hopeless. She wonders why she didn't see this before.

Talking to a woman friend occasionally presents yet another complication. The woman friend may empathize, for example, by sharing similar problems she has had with men. This reinforces their feelings of intimacy. One woman put it this way:

"I used to share everything with Marlo—what I liked and hated about Tony. But then things got better between me and Tony, and Marlo said she felt I wasn't sharing as much as before—that she didn't feel as close to me. I felt a type of pressure from Marlo to discuss Tony's and my problems—so I even exaggerated some so she and I could feel intimate again."

Unfortunately, this also reinforces the focus on "the problems with men" and not on her role in contributing to the problem. A setup to repeat her part of the problem with the next man. And ultimately to develop a "need-hate" (sometimes called "love-hate") hostility toward men.

This dilemma has its equivalent in the dilemma a successful man who fails has when he tells a less successful man of his failure: he sometimes sees a *surface support that masks an internal smile*. Unfortunately the socialization of many women to overvalue a man (sometimes *any* man) can lead an unattached woman to harbor a perverse investment in having her woman friend return to the unattached status—thereby making her feel less isolated, less lonely. In this sense, the friend may harbor an unconscious joy in adding to the dumping on the man. A joy masked by surface support.

Cathy Guisewite, *A Mouthful of Breathmints and No One to Kiss*, p. 7

The "I'm Too Adaptive" Fallacy

Andrea knew she was often adaptive. Too adaptive. But she worked on her adaptiveness by becoming competent enough at work to create the ability to not adapt to Rick. She understood adaptation was a way of getting power—or financial security—and one way to avoid adapting was to avoid the underlying need for someone else to provide financial security. Finally, she did not defend herself against hearing Rick by saying, "I'm already too adaptive," "I'm tired of adapting," or "I've adapted all my life, and I've had it."

The "I Need to Be More Assertive" Fallacy

One of Andrea's self-criticisms was that she was not assertive enough. For some women, that "self-criticism" can become an excuse to focus energy on preparing the next assertion rather than carefully listening—which is, ironically, precisely one of men's biggest problems. Andrea asserted herself by asking for the time she needed from Rick, talking her issues through in a women's group, *bringing the issues back to Rick directly,* and asserting herself to attain a position at work that offered her more self-respect. All were positive uses of assertion.

The "Protect His Ego" Fallacy

Systematic ego protection (as opposed to well-placed tact) generally backfires. Why? *To protect a fragile ego is to preserve it.* And to preserve fragility is to make it vulnerable to exploitation and ridicule. *Just as the "fragile, defenseless woman" men protect is also raped by men, so the "fragile male ego," which women protect, can be raped by women.*

I call this a law, because it is true on an international political level as well as an interpersonal level. Internationally, the Soviet Union "protects" Soviet-bloc countries, then invades Czechoslovakia and Afghanistan. The Monroe Doctrine "protected" Latin America. Yet much of Latin America feels that we exploit what we promised to protect. Unfortunately, the two often go together. Interpersonally, *each woman who protects the fragile male ego is doing her part to reinforce the fragility of the male ego,* a fragility she can exploit. The fragility we protect, then, is the vulnerability we can rape, the underdevelopment we can ridicule, the ego we can exploit. What we protect is what we preserve.

Am I Financially Able to Leave? Four Litmus Tests

The self-help and feminist movements have helped millions of women look inward to the point that most women are emotionally capable of leaving a poor relationship. In fact, women's competence at expressing emotions, while interpreted by men as dependence, actually creates their emotional independence. However, we have seen that the movements have done little to dent women's desire for a man to provide security—even if security means having a career she can leave if it proves unfulfilling. How can a woman tell if she is "putting up with him" in exchange for a safety net? Here are four increasingly challenging litmus tests.

Test One

Are you willing to try a Rick/Andrea–type experiment of sharing all expenses—even if it means cutting back the lifestyle so the sharing can be done?

Test Two

Have you looked for an apartment or home you could afford on your own income? Would you be *as willing* to live in that place? If the answer is "If things got tough enough, yes . . . ," that's a sure hint you're willing to put up with a certain amount because of the monetary advantages. To that extent you will tend to shy away from honesty and confrontation until it gets close to that borderline. To that extent there's prostitution in the relationship—an exchange of monetary advantage for tolerance.

Financial ability to leave does not mean merely the ability to support oneself financially. Rather, it means the ability to support yourself in a style not drastically different from the one you are presently sharing with him—unless the style means absolutely nothing to you. But this is as rare as a man with a beautiful woman who doesn't care if she gets fat.

If this is getting too confrontational, avoid it. Skip to the next section. If it is not, here's litmus test three.

Test Three

Reflect back on the househusband versus Clint Eastwood role models in *Newsweek* and *Time*. (Notice that the househusband has no name.) Imagine going home to your parents at Christmas. You've met a man who is slightly more tender, warm, sensitive, and vulnerable than you imgine Clint Eastwood to be. As a househusband he has plenty of time for you. How do you feel in your gut about telling them ''I've fallen in love with a househusband. We're going to be married''? Does that sound better or worse than ''I'd like to introduce you to Clint Eastwood. We're going to be married''? The degree to which your gut would prefer to introduce a less sensitive Clint Eastwood is the degree to which you value fame and fortune over tenderness and sensitivity.

Test Four

Think of how long you would be comfortable with a man's doing something he wanted to do and earning *half* your income doing it. Anne Goshen, a San Diego–based therapist and a business consultant with a broad range of clientele, distinguishes between two types of working couples: the dual career couple and the career/job couple. The true dual career couple is one in which both sexes match their career goals with their lifetime financial goals and share responsibility. With the career/job couple one spouse does this and the other does not. Goshen finds most working couples are actually career/job couples: ''Whenever one cuts back and voluntarily works half-time, in my experience with couples it is *always* the woman.'' An individual, however, may be an exception. The test: Would you feel as comfortable with your partner working half-time as you would working half-time yourself?

Six Creative Change Techniques

What are some creative alternatives women and men can work on together to create change? Here are six exercises. They will seem a little artificial; everything is artificial until it becomes a part of us. If constructive change were easy, everyone would have done it already. However, as a male might put it, "The downside potential is nil." And the upside potential is intimacy.

Ask Your Man to Play Your Woman Friend

One of my own favorite ways of hearing a woman friend more fully is to ask her to talk with me as if I were her best woman friend. I actually pretend (role-play) to be her woman friend. I ask her questions like, "How are things going between you and Warren?" "Are there any things you've been telling him that he doesn't seem to be hearing?" "Are there any things you're having difficulty telling him?" Sometimes I play a friend who is critical of Warren: "It must be a bit 'much' to be involved with a so-called expert on male-female relationships. I bet he thinks he has an answer to everything." Then I reverse to an overenvious friend, "Boy, how did you luck out, getting a guy like him?" The implicit put-down of "luck out" usually draws out some inadvertent remark like "Wait a minute, he's not so perfect . . ." How daring I get depends on how secure I feel that day.

I learn an enormous amount about myself from these sessions. They can take as little as a few minutes. It's like being a fly on the wall in a private conversation, and it's surprising how detached from my ego I get when I'm playing my friend's friend—an improvement over playing myself!

It's pretty easy to get a man to try this experiment, as long as he's not approached with "*I* have something I'd like *you* to try." Try, rather, "I'd like us to understand each other better. I read about an exercise I think will help me understand more about what you were telling me the other day." Each of the experiences that follow is best introduced in this manner. In fact, a bad introduction can be a passive-aggressive way of setting up a partner to be the one to reject the experience, giving the introducer yet another corner on the virtue market.

Tape-Record Your Conversations

Rose and Sal used to fight a lot. "We have Mediterranean blood—we fight with passion and love with passion." Their passion for fighting, though, was beginning to take a toll on their passion for loving. "So we took a tape recorder—one I had bought Sal for his birthday—and placed it in the bedroom, which seems to be where all our passion begins. The moment we felt tension breeding, one of us turned the tape recorder on—usually the one who thought the other was being ridiculous. But later, when we listened to ourselves—well, it was a real eye-opener.''

Taking this a step beyond what Rose and Sal did, write down what you each feel you did to escalate the argument, what you might have done differently, and what you feel your partner might have done differently.

Role-Reversal Conflict

Sal and Rose took a tape of their conflicts to a workshop I started near my home in San Diego. They then did a "role-reversal conflict"—each acting out the other's role. They took the passion they normally used to argue *against* each other and channeled the passion into taking the other person's position. Soon they were arguing passionately—but the opposite arguments to those they had been arguing at home—until they and everyone at the workshop broke down laughing.

How did they do this? They tried not to mock each other. They imitated, but did not caricature, each other's body language, silence, dominance, and passive-aggressiveness. How did they reverse passive-aggressiveness? For example, Sal loved Rose in a particular skirt; he told Rose; Rose agreed to wear it more often, but Rose "never got around to lengthening it." In the role reversal, Sal played passive-aggressive by pretending not to be able to "find time" to get his hair cut, as Rose preferred it.

Sometimes Rose, while playing Sal, was able to say things like, "I feel hurt because . . ." and come up with a reason Sal had never been able to get in touch with. They tried to get themselves in touch with their partner's underlying hurt. They both had to give up power to do this. And in the process they both gained power.

Role-Reversal Date

My favorite experiment to try personally and also to do in workshops is a personal, private version of the role-reversal or "insight-reversal" date. When I've done it personally, it's been with a woman I already know. We exaggerate *traditional* roles in reverse—she formally asks me out, makes dinner reservations, buys me flowers, drives, picks me up, and makes passes at me all evening. In an exaggerated female role, I show a strong interest in her career, listen attentively, ask her questions, draw her out, dress appealingly, never make passes, am receptive— but not too receptive—gently change pace when she comes on too quickly or too soon, and fight very hard against anything overtly sexual on our "first date." The experience is a hilarious, sometimes tiring, process allowing each of us to undo some of the ruts our relationship may be falling into. It's also an amazing turn-on.

Wipe the Slate Clean (or "If I Met You for the First Time, I'd Fall in Love with You All Over Again")

Many couples have difficulty undoing a relationship's history. Each partner feels changing would do little good because, after all, the other partner would retain old perceptions. How can we get new perceptions of our loved ones? How do we "wipe the slate clean"? One way is to spend a fun evening picking up our partner all over again. Here is how I ask couples in my workshops to "wipe the slate clean."

Each person is instructed to bring separate cars to the workshop on Saturday. That evening they plan to arrive at a restaurant about five minutes apart. They find a way of eventually "discovering each other" at the restaurant—introducing themselves, asking basic questions about values, what they do, and what they want out of life. The process helps a couple remember why they chose each other, and to feel acutely how deep the loss of the other would be. When we fear loss most, changing is put into perspective before it is too late.

Design Your Own Experiment

Once a couple understands how to reverse roles, they can create their own experiments. For example, most relationships reach a "sexual initiative imbalance."[2] That is, one person may be moving too quickly sexually for the other's moods. So they both contract for a one-month experiment in which only the person who normally initiates least does *all* the initiating. It changes the dynamic, relieves the pressure, and even when it doesn't solve the sexual problem, it deepens the understanding and therefore the love.

Do you still feel he'll reject these experiences as games? Maybe he will. But each time a woman assumes that of a man, she increases her contempt for him while remaining nice on the surface. If he doesn't like your suggestions, try this approach which works for a friend of mine. "I say to him, 'I'd like to understand you better—can you think of some way you can help me do that?' "

Summary

In summary, how can a woman change a man? Without just getting him ready for the next woman?

1. If you want to change a man who is resistant, be certain you are not dependent on him for providing a lifestyle you're not willing to forfeit. He'll be torn between putting the energy into changing and putting the energy into providing for your lifestyle. And most men intuitively perceive a woman's dependence on the lifestyle he provides as gut-level fundamental. A man must perceive that his changing is more important than his providing; that you are willing to leave if he is unwilling to listen.

2. Remember that while the ability to leave is necessary, it's not sufficient. Leaving is to a relationship what nuclear war is to the world. It is the trump card. Once it's used, there's little left. Unless a woman who asks, "How much can I change my man?" *is willing to ask the same question of herself* she will find herself using nuclear power before she has focused on her own contribution to the war.

3. Distinguish rights from responsibilities. If you approach him with the idea of your sharing his responsibilities, he'll owe you. If you approach him with demands for rights, he'll soon want his rights (e.g., his right to quit work). Few people remain motivated on a gut level if they are only being asked to give something up.

4. If either his or your criticisms outpace your compliments by a ratio of more than one criticism to four strokes, implement this chapter immediately, get help, or get out.

5. Practice doing simple "insight-reversal" experiences with him by reversing roles. Get into his moccasins and ask him to get into yours. Introduce this to him by explaining you are willing temporarily to give up the power of holding on to your perspective—by understanding his experience more thoroughly. Let him know that you're offering this as a way of deepening the relationship. That you want to deepen it so that the question of leaving will never arise.

12

How Can I Get Him to Express Feelings?

Myths about Feelings

Item: In an experimental setting, the Condreys asked observers to comment on the feelings expressed by a nine-month-old infant. If the observers were told the infant was a boy, they labeled the crying "anger." If they were told it was a girl, they labeled the exact same crying by the same child at the same time "fear."[1]

By interpreting the same behavior as anger if we're told it is a boy, and fear if told it is a girl, we do more than reinforce the stereotype of boys as angry and girls as fearful. Since we tend to associate anger with people who are powerful and oppressive, and fear with victims or potential victims, our images of "man the oppressor" and "woman the victim" get reinforced—even when the behavior is identical. Even when the feelings are identical.

In similar ways we have arrived at the myth that women are good at expressing feelings, and men are bad at it. Women *are* better at expressing *some* feelings—but we shall see why *both* sexes are very bad at expressing feelings of vulnerability. That's the feeling that's usually implied when we ask, "Why can't men open up?"

The Male Volcano Versus the Female Volcano

In what ways do both sexes have problems expressing feelings of vulnerability? Men's suppressed anger often leads to the "vol-

Nicole Hollander, *Sylvia*, Rockport, Maine

cano effect''—an explosion characterized by a viciousness that could not have been caused by the incident that supposedly triggered it. Because we eventually see lots of anger, we tend to think of it as evidence that a man is able to express at least one feeling—anger—instead of seeing that the volcano came as a result of the man's suppressing his anger. Because the male volcano is so powerful at the moment it happens, we sometimes forget both the feeling of powerlessness that stimulated it and the humiliation and powerlessness involved in the subsequent apologies at having ''lost control.'' Sometimes those apologies last for days.

Women's suppressed anger is likely to lead to the female volcano: either ''the suddenly leaving effect'' or ''the anger phase of feminism.'' These both erupt after long periods of playing ''the good wife.'' He experiences her suddenly leaving as a volcano, not only because the explosion may follow years of relative silence but also because she may keep the anger from him until she has psychologically prepared herself to leave. In this sense, her volcano has an impact which his anger is unlikely to have for him. For him, it is more likely to be an outlet, preparing him for peace and apologies after the storm; for her, the explosion doesn't prepare her for anything with him—it is the symbol of her having accomplished the preparation to be without him.

Many women get as upset as they do about male anger because they subconsciously feel it must mean to him what her anger means to her. That is rarely true. Similarly, many men don't take female anger to heart because they interpret it the way they interpret their own anger—as an outlet, a passing phase.

The ability to understand the male and the female volcano can allow us to use the volcanoes to communicate rather than miscommunicate.

Both male and female volcanoes reflect the tendency on the part of *both* sexes to suppress feelings.

Why Do Both Sexes Suppress Feelings? And Exactly How Do They Do It?

Women fearful of losing economic security rarely express negative feelings if they sense the feelings will result in the loss of the security. This is their area of vulnerability. We all suppress feelings in the areas in which we are vulnerable. Men fearful of having affection, nurturance, and sexuality withdrawn rarely express feelings they feel will jeopardize that nurturance. Since a woman's most unfulfilled primary need (financial security) is also her fantasy, and since men often supply a lot of both, we can see why she is tempted to withhold her negative feelings from men—and express them instead to other women.

The areas in which both sexes repress their feelings tell us much about their unfulfilled primary needs—the areas where they consciously or subconsciously feel their partner has a "hold" over them. How does this work in practice?

I recently called the home of one of the veteran leaders of the men's movement. "Dwight isn't here anymore. We've separated, Warren—I've asked him to leave the house."

"Oh." I was more taken aback than usual. I had known Eleanor and Dwight well—and knew that she had thoroughly experienced some of the ways he might be difficult to live with during their years together. She had pressed for commitment and he had agreed. Their wedding was beautiful.

"I knew Dwight was never as committed as I was, Warren, but he always denied it. Last summer he fessed up, admitted he had not felt as deeply committed as he wanted to, but said he felt a real change now. My anger at having my feelings discounted for two and a half years just came pouring out. Now he wants to stay. He says it's history—that he can forget it—but it's my history, and it hurts too deeply for me to forget it."

I felt sad after the phone call. I knew they both had wanted very much to make it. I felt her hurt at having her feelings denied. And I also felt sad that those few sentences reflected much about the male and female dilemma concerning feelings. On the first level, she was able to express her feelings and he was not. On the second level, when he did, she left him—which may tell us a lot about why he held back his feelings to begin with. His feelings of ambivalence came into conflict with a second set of feelings: the fear of losing Eleanor. Dwight was withholding his feelings about lack of full commitment while working on himself to increase his commitment.

But it goes deeper than that. Eleanor did not want Dwight's feelings—she wanted feelings *different* from his. She wanted him to have the feelings she felt he should have. Or else. As when a man asks a woman, "How many lovers have you had?" and she says, "Fifty or so," and he disappears, she knows he really did not want the answer to his question. He wanted reassurance. The next time she's likely to lie: "Just enough to appreciate you." Both sexes withhold the feelings they feel will lose them the love of the other sex. Ironically, Dwight's denial of feelings was actually a statement of his commitment.

Dwight and Eleanor illustrate another common myth about feelings: that all feelings are equal. For example, by telling Dwight she doesn't feel enough commitment from him, Eleanor is likely to get him to do things to demonstrate his commitment. Eleanor's feelings are her power—they get Dwight to do things. But when Dwight admits he does not feel as committed as he would like, he is giving power away. He risks losing her—psychologically and physically. Just as a woman who says, "I don't feel committed to this relationship" gives power away.

When we ask our partners for feelings that might result in their expression of ambivalence, and they offer those feelings with love, we are both vulnerable. Such feelings are only productive if we are secure enough to hear them and focus our energies on resolving the problems that led to the feelings. Otherwise, we learn the lesson that reflected Jesse Owens's contempt for white society while he verbally praised it: "You don't get nowhere giving people the low-down on themselves."

Negative feelings are the emotion both sexes express when we feel our security will not be jeopardized by expressing them. In the "civilized world" both sexes treat feelings as a luxury—

secondary to their primary unfulfilled needs. *Detecting the feelings we suppress is the Geiger counter to our vulnerability*.

If we recognize this, can something be done? Yes. Six months after Dwight and Eleanor separated I got a call from Dwight. He and Eleanor are back together.

If both sexes have difficulty expressing feelings, why do we think women are so much better at it? In part because they are *somewhat* better at it. And this leads us to label other behavior— behavior that is quite similar to men's business behavior—as "feeling" behavior (similar to the anger/fear labeling in the Condrey experiment). Let's see how this works in everyday life.

Joyce and Sheila meet for coffee. Sheila asks, "How are you, Joyce?"

"I'm feeling wonderful—all over."

"You look wonderful. Okay, tell me. What is it? Something with you and Frank?"

"Would you believe it? Frank flew in from Chicago last week and said he wants to spend his vacation with me in June!"

"Do you think that means he'll get a divorce after all?"

"I think so. . . . I sense a different feeling from him this time."

"I'm *so* happy for you. But do be careful. A similar thing happened to me a year ago when . . ."

Six months later:

"How *are* you, Joyce?"

"Terrible. You were right—I should have known about married men. Frank told me he felt he had to stay with her. I let myself get so close to him. I think when it comes down to it, he just can't handle me. He wants a nice, subservient wife. He's threatened by me."

Notice that the two women are discussing feelings related to success or failure in achieving their primary fantasy—a commitment.

Now for two men:

"What you been up to, Jack?"

"A bunch. Harvey flew in from Chicago last week and said he wants me to take a job at Headquarters. He wants me and the family to move out there in June."

"Does that mean they're gonna dump Sam and clear you for the next promo?"

"Looks that way."

"Great shooting, kid! Be sure to cover your ass, though, Jack. Bank of America did a similar thing with me a year ago, and . . ."

Six months later:

"How's the new job, Jack?"

"Terrible. You were right—Harvey's afraid to get rid of Sam. I move the whole damn family out there for a promotion I would have gotten the equivalent of six months later right here. When push comes to shove, Harvey wants a nice subservient yes man. He's threatened by me."

While Joyce seemed to be expressing feelings and Jack discussing business, both Joyce and Jack were discussing the same thing: success or failure at achieving security. In neither of these conversations did either discuss feelings toward the other. Sheila didn't tell Joyce, "Your self-centeredness bores me"; Jack didn't say, "I felt hurt you didn't say you'd miss me when I move." Both talked about being recognized as special by someone who could add to their security; and both attempted to assure their friend someone else was to blame when the source of their security fell through. Neither took the opportunity of failure to reveal his or her deepest doubts about herself or himself to the friend. But because we associate relationships with intimacy, we assume women are being more intimate and vulnerable than men.

While both sexes avoid feelings, men do it by focusing instead on one or more of the "five male crutches":

- Business
- Women (in a sexual sense)
- Issues
- Sports
- Equipment (cars, stereos, guns, etc.)

What are the female equivalents to these five male crutches?

- Discussion of their primary fantasy (commitment, children, home, men)

- Discussion of the means to achieving their primary fantasy (diet, cosmetics, clothes, men)

A man's happiness about a business event or a woman's about a wedding date are feelings—but not the feelings that create intimacy and trust by risking vulnerabilities. *Both* sexes avoid the feelings they feel will make them vulnerable in the area of their primary needs or primary fantasies.

Are Women or Men More Willing to Express Negative Feelings?

Wendy and Todd walk into a party on an evening they have a couple of invitations. After a few minutes they both conclude, "No one here seems interesting, eh?" They have both made negative judgments about twenty people within a few minutes. They have both ruled out the potential for friendships with twenty people. Millions of decisions are based on similar instantaneous judgments based on the underlying feelings (such as uncomfortableness or fear of rejection) that created these judgments.

Are women or men more willing to express such feelings or judgments to the person being judged so they can be cleared up directly? I received some insight to this when I asked workshop participants to pair off at random and express their first positive and negative feelings toward each other—so they could get in touch with the feelings that led to attraction or avoidance of each other before they were conscious of it. Before they expressed their negative feelings, their partners had to volunteer "I definitely want to hear the negative feelings as well." I then built in additional safeguards to avoid the damage of unsolicited criticism. (Unsolicited criticism in the name of honesty can be like a punch in the stomach for which we are unprepared. The great magician Houdini died of such a punch from a fan who didn't allow Houdini time to prepare himself.) In this context—the beginning of a relationship—women were more hesitant to share negative feelings *directly* (to the person about whom they felt the feelings). When we discuss women's hesitation to confront—or share negative feelings—we call it the "good girl syndrome." *We rarely discuss it as part of the difficulty women have discussing feelings*. If we hear two women talking negatively in a restaurant about a man in their lives, we don't say, "There's another woman who has difficulty expressing feelings directly to a man.'' We focus more on how beautiful it is that two women can be intimate. Should a woman fail to express her feelings directly to a man, we talk about her adaptiveness and how she's been trained to please men. We reinforce our view of her as adaptive victim.

But what happens when a man expresses negative feelings directly to a woman? For example, if he initiates talk about ending a relationship, do we credit him with the courage to initiate those feelings—or put him down as afraid of intimacy? Many books and articles add salt to the wound by condemning men because they take a woman to a fancy French restaurant to end a relationship, calling this sly, guilt-expiating behavior,[2] rather than seeing it as an act of generosity added to an act of courage from a man who is in touch with his feelings of disappointment, hurt that the relationship didn't work out, yet willing to pay to make the transition time as loving as possible rather than use the money to take out another woman. When men do express feelings, as in the Condrey experiment, we tend to find ways of reinforcing our view of men as insensitive, unfeeling jerks. Put simply, this is sexism. The new sexism.

How Can I Get Him to Express Feelings?

The best way to get a man to express feelings is to choose a man who already expresses them and avoid men who don't—which means making an active choice, rather than passively being chosen. It also means that a woman must reexamine her values. *Our choice of partners is one of the clearest statements about our choice of values*. If a woman values feelings, but values security more, the man she chooses probably reflects that.

Suppose a woman's choice is already made? How can she be certain she is doing what she can to facilitate his feelings? And why should she take any responsibility? As I've said, men need emotional mentors just as women need business mentors. Just as many women don't know where to begin on the stock market, many men don't know exactly what is meant when they're told to get in touch with feelings. On a physical level, she can encourage him to look at the five barometers of his feelings: muscle tension, breathing patterns, sweat, his penis, and his dreams. His penis and his dreams are like computer printouts of his unconscious, and his muscle tension and sweat are a good link between his conscious and unconscious. Getting in touch with them or listening to his feelings means experimenting with them, as he would with a radio he wanted to repair: just keep testing until he sees what goes with what.

When he starts getting in touch with his feelings he'll be able to ask for what he really needs from her—which may be a different type of fidelity.

The Worst Infidelity

> *"Whenever we get into a fight she's on the phone to her girlfriend or her mother, complaining about me. But if we've had a great day, she doesn't excuse herself to call them to say how great she thinks I am."*
>
> Mel, twenty-two

One reason men are afraid to express feelings is that they fear the one-sided distortion of these feelings to everyone else the woman they love cares about. Once men become sensitive to these conversations (many remain ignorant of them), the feeling of betrayal runs deep. Why is it such a betrayal that I would label it the *"worst* infidelity"—worse than her having sex with someone else?

The more successful a man is, the more mileage people get out of discovering his real vulnerabilities and discussing them behind his back. One discovery can lead to the loss of a promotion to a close competitor—which any successful man knows implies the virtual plateauing of a promising career. The more successful he is, then, the more a man has learned to cover his real vulnerabilities—and fake a few endearing ones.

Yet intimacy requires *real* vulnerability. And the more a man protects himself at work, the more he needs someone with whom he can be totally vulnerable at home. All his eggs of intimacy and vulnerability are in one basket.

When a woman reveals those vulnerabilities to a woman friend a man may experience that as infidelity: he has opened himself to her in an area that was as closed off by his socialization as sexuality was by hers. *When he senses that she is using his vulnerabilities to build a relationship with a woman friend, he feels like a high school girl who has finally opened up sexually and discovers that she is being casually talked about by her boyfriend to a "buddy."*

Just as a married woman may value the sexual exclusivity of her marriage, many men value the confidentiality of their vulnerabilities. They are exclusively for his "one and only." It is what the man "buys" to gain intimacy when he commits. For men who are struggling with opening up—and who associate that with a "bad reputation" that leads to failure, a woman who talks about what he has privately revealed to her commits the worst infidelity.

Sometimes the worst infidelity is exacerbated when a woman agrees to talk confidentially with a woman friend—with the confidences including negative things about a man. She then sees him through a filter *she can never clear up* because the confidentiality requires her to not share it with him. It therefore becomes the worst category of the worst infidelity—because her intimacy with her friend becomes a clear substitute for her intimacy with him.

Is there a way you can share negative feelings about a man with your woman friend and not betray confidentiality? Yes, by doing two things: First, clear with him ahead of time anything involving him that you sense you would not share with your woman friend if he were present. Check with him whether he would mind its being shared. If he wouldn't, share it. Second, make it clear to your woman friend that nothing will be kept in confidence if it concerns you or your relationship—no perceptions, no feelings, no "in confidences," no "just between you and mes." It's fine to keep in confidence what concerns the woman friend and anyone or anything else—but not what concerns you and your partner. That is salt on the wound of the worst infidelity. It creates a self-fulfilling prophecy of inhibiting men from revealing their vulnerabilities and opening up.

Creating an Atmosphere for Feelings

When a woman discusses feelings about her partner with her woman friend, she is not being vulnerable; when she discusses feelings directly with him, she is. The direct expression of feelings—feelings she fears may distance him—before she is psychologically prepared to leave him creates an atmosphere of vulnerability that a woman can initiate if she really wishes to facilitate his discussing his most vulnerable feelings. If she wishes to prevent male withdrawal and male volcanoes. Once she has explored her own vulnerability, the next task is to accept his vulnerabilities.

I Want to Accept Him, but Somewhere I Seem to Get Stuck . . .

There is little incentive for a man to remain closed if he feels understood when he opens up. But how can a woman tell what he might not feel understood about? First, she can check every place in this book in which she felt defensive. That's a good hint that if he revealed his real feelings about those areas he would encounter defensiveness. Remember, *men are great adapters.* The reason we don't know that about men is they've adapted so well even they are not in touch with the feelings to which they are adapting.

For example, men are rarely in touch with their own sexual powerlessness. The woman who responds to the chapter on sex and success with *"I'm* the one without power" will never find a man in touch with his feelings of powerlessness. Conversely, the woman who hears his feelings without being defensive will rarely find herself with a man who is living "The Secret Life of Walter Mitty." A secret life is merely a better alternative than rejection. Male socialization, like female socialization, has an ugly side. And, as with female socialization, the two sides are connected. A man who feels someone understands how the part of him that is most admired creates the part of him that is least admired can release his defensive energy. That's the change we're all awaiting—the change that releases a man's energy to love himself and love a woman.

Second, she can be aware of which part of her listening skills encourage and discourage men from expressing feelings. One part is especially good for drawing men out, the other especially good at cutting men off.

How Can I Get Him to Be Less of a Male Volcano?

A woman often feels in a dilemma about male anger. She does not wish to choose between his anger and his condescending verbal niceties. She would like to be able to get him to express without exploding. How does she prevent the build-up?

Many women have told me, "My husband says I push him into a corner. But I don't know exactly what I do to do that." Here are a few checkpoints both sexes can use to determine if they are pushing their loved one out of love, to see if they are indirectly provoking the male or female volcano.*

When your partner gets angry, do you:

_____ (a) Criticize the style ("You exaggerated"; "You called me names"), or
_____ (b) Look beyond the style to the pain?
_____ (a) Point out shortcomings (especially if yours have been pointed out), or
_____ (b) Empathize?
_____ (a) Look for the flaw, or
_____ (b) Look for the fact?
_____ (a) Sidestep the issue and counterattack, or
_____ (b) Ask for an elaboration of the cause of the anger?
_____ (a) Say "It's hopeless" and begin to cry, or
_____ (b) Recognize the grounds for hope in the fact that feelings are emerging?
_____ (a) Wait for an apology, or
_____ (b) Apologize for the specifics you feel you contributed?
_____ (a) Become more caring, or
_____ (b) Emotionally withdraw?
_____ (a) Become more affectionate, or
_____ (b) Sexually withdraw?

I almost eliminated "sexually withdraw" since it is perfectly legitimate for someone to feel sexually distant after anger. There is, however, a price for that—the repression of anger. This price should be understood even though the feeling is legitimate. The possibility that sexual withdrawal is being used as a way of regaining power at the point where a person feels criticized and therefore powerless should not be discounted. Many women withdraw sexually after an argument, while many men want even more intensely to make love—for acceptance after rejection, a compensation for lost power.

Is there a way to withdraw sexually without encouraging your partner to withdraw from angry feelings? Yes. You can make a special effort to initiate sexually after you are feeling sexy again. And you can help yourself feel sexy by having a better feeling about the anger to begin with. Part of that will come with using

*Use this in conjunction with the guide to listening to a complaint in Chapter 5.

the two listening exercises; for a woman, part of that will come by understanding the male style of anger and what anger means to a man. But before we look at the male style of anger, let me confront a touchy issue: making love after making war.

Many couples feel funny making love after making war. Even if the passion is not a substitute for communication. My response? You didn't repress the negative feelings, so why repress the positive ones? They all come from the same deep well. In fact, go one step beyond not repressing the passion. After a fight, seek it out. Couples who punish bad communication with bad passion have "civilized" themselves into a lose-lose situation. They soon find themselves in the mire of the "Marital Incest Taboo." In brief, when it comes to making love after making war, love it; don't leave it.

Don't You Ever Call Me a Bitch Again!

Just as the male and female volcanoes have different meanings, they also have different styles. What does a man's swearing and name-calling mean to him? Part of male socialization is to swear, call names, fight it out, and forget it. Profanity was not censored as being "unboylike," so profanity has a different meaning to the adult man than to the adult woman.

Not holding back his anger means he's treating a woman as he would a man under similar out-of-control circumstances; he's no longer protecting her with verbal niceties; he's unconsciously treating her as an equal. An equal he may be angry at, in a style that is not very endearing, but that's part of equality male-style.

Not understanding this style leads many women to make a big thing out of these angry moments ("Don't you *ever* call me a bitch again . . ."). She withdraws because she takes it in. She demands an apology for being called a name. He sees her point, apologizes, but now builds up real frustration because she has used his name-calling to sidestep the issue that created his anger. So he never feels heard. The message he gets is that if he lets his feelings out *he* will be attacked.

Few men have educated themselves to put their fingers on what's happening, so they feel helpless and out of control. Which increases the intensity of his explosion and convinces her that he's all-powerful—not that he feels as helpless as she does. From his perspective, the very moment he cries out helplessly he has to withdraw quickly, become strong again, and pay attention to her feelings. Now she senses he is a bottomless pit of anger without understanding how or why he got that way.

The solution? First, remember we are asking him to adapt to the female style of expressing anger—no name-calling and swearing. I consider this male adaptation preferable; name-calling and swearing are degrading, humiliating, and objectifying and therefore predictably lead to the substance of a discussion being ignored. The easiest way to get a man to adopt the female style is first to pay attention to the substance of what's bothering him. In real life terms, here's how it might work:

He: God damn you, you're not listening!

She: Sorry. I'll listen.

In three words she's deflated his anger. She follows the listening guide* and then it's her turn to be heard. Now:

She: John, when you say "God damn" and shout, I feel like you don't even like me. I agreed to listen and then listened; I want you to agree to give me a chance to hear what's bothering you without swearing or shouting.

She has done three things: (1) told John how she feels, (2) reminded him how his need was addressed, and (3) given him something specific he could do to replace what he should not do. It is a fair exchange, which taps into his socialization for fairness. A solution is within reach, which taps into his socialization to *do* something. He has felt heard, so he is in a more receptive mood than he would be if he had not felt heard.

The biggest block for many women in getting a man to drop his swearing and name-calling style is letting the style pass by her for that first minute—until she has addressed the substance. This is where it helps to internalize repeatedly where that style came from—to remember that thirty seconds after he and a member of another team had called each other all sorts of names they were both concentrating on the next play.

*See Chapter 5, "What Makes a Man Successful at Work That Makes Him Unsuccessful at Home? Or Why Can't Men Listen?"

How to Draw Out His Feelings: The Politics of "Awe Training"

Female socialization has taught women an efficient process for soliciting from men what they want men to say. It might be called "awe training." I have mentioned that in my research on male-female listening patterns, women in mixed groups are more likely to ask a question, often with their eye contact, on a man in whom they are interested, thereby drawing him into the center of attention. He notices the woman, which magnifies any possible interest he might already have felt about her and makes him secure enough to pursue this interest because of the decreased likelihood she will reject him. She increases the look of awe in her eyes when she is impressed, and decreases it when unimpressed. Like a Pavlovian dog, if he is interested, he picks up the cues: "She likes it when I talk about my feelings," or "She likes it when I talk about computers."

If she has the skills to draw out from him much of what she wants, why isn't she getting to his feelings of vulnerability? Why does a man seem to open up more at the beginning of the relationship than later?

Let's look at how he opened up at the beginning. If he was interested in her, he responded to her cues—her awe training. If she responded well to feelings, he gave her feelings. If he thought she wanted vulnerability, he gave her feelings of *"safe* vulnerability." A contradiction in terms? Exactly. Why? Because he felt she wouldn't respond well to real vulnerability. By definition, real vulnerability would have made her distant from him ("I would have preferred to ask out Michelle, but I was afraid of being rejected by her, so I asked you out"). He sensed she didn't want him to be really vulnerable, so he gave her statements full of feelings like "and then my dad died when I was four . . ."; or past mistakes: "I got so into my work, I paid no attention to my former wife . . . when she left me I learned the most important lesson of my life."

Because he has learned his lesson, he appears willing to learn. Because he admits his mistakes, he appears vulnerable. Because he is discussing a hurt, a relationship, and feelings, he appears sensitive. And, he has simultaneously left the impression of being a dedicated worker ("I got so into my work") who doubtless built a firm foundation. In brief, he's rapidly becoming primary fantasy material. None of his feelings of "safe vulnerability'' violate her security; all of his feelings offer her hope. So she has no problems drawing out his feelings more and more deeply.

While awe training is like a biofeedback machine that actively *encourages* selected feelings, most women have also been social-ized to subtly discourage a man from expressing other feelings. When, in discussion groups, I observe a woman who fears her man is going to say something that might threaten her security, she often signals him not to continue by using either withdrawing body language, a disapproving distance in the eyes, or watering eyes. The opposites of awe training. If he says it anyway, a frequent response is ''sidestep-ignore'' or ''sidestep-counterattack.'' If the sidestep leaves the man feeling unheard, the counterattack also leaves him feeling acutely discouraged. The man responds to cues to suppress feelings that would make her feel less secure just as he responds to the awe training that solicits from him feelings that make her feel more secure. The same woman who started the relationship with a finely honed awe training when she perceived her security as unthreatened now uses her relation-ship skills to cut off other feelings she feels might be threatening to her security.

Since almost all relationship dynamics are symbiotic, a man must take responsibility for the awe training he feeds into by being hooked into a woman's supportive expressions. If she ''sidestep-ignores,'' he must take responsibility for not pursuing the sidestep (as he would with a man) out of fear of being called too logic-focused and out of touch with his feelings.

His adaptiveness to her supportiveness blinds him to the pres-sure he feels when she tells him, ''I just *know* you can beat Stu—you're a hundred times better than he is.'' It appears supportive to the man because he is not aware of how it discour-ages him from expressing fear of failure, feelings like, ''I feel Stu is more qualified.'' The flip side of support is pressure to perform. He has become addicted to her supportiveness and may adapt by unrealistically discounting his competitors and therefore overworking, and feeling even worse if he loses to an unworthy competitor. Eventually he may turn to drinking or use women, religion, or success symbols to relieve the pain. All these are ways a man suppresses his fears of failure—by not understanding that the flip side of the support to succeed is pressure to succeed.

How can a woman actively draw out his feelings? By using her awe training and body language to solicit his fears of failure and the portions of his feelings that do not enhance her ego or immediate security. The incentive for her? Intimacy—and a man who will stay with her because his primary needs that he cannot meet by himself are being met by her. Female socialization taught her the tools to solicit his feelings; the underlying question is deciding whether she really wants his truly vulnerable feelings.

Big Boys Don't Fear a Tear

Crying is an excretory process, like urinating, sweating, and exhaling, all of which remove impurities from our body. The results of not crying are now well-documented. Dr. Margaret Crepeau, a Marquette University behaviorist, studied a control group of people who were healthy versus those who had colitis or ulcers. All 150 participants were the same age and of similar backgrounds. She found that the healthy group cried significantly more than those who had either colitis or ulcers.

Children born with a genetic disorder that prevents them from crying (familical dysautonomia) respond to even mild anxiety by a rise in blood pressure, breaking out in red blotches, perspiring, and salivating excessively, according to Dr. William Frey, a biochemist at Saint Paul–Ramsey Medical Center.

It is likely that the more men cry, the less we will need to relieve tension by compulsive sex. Our role of taking almost all of the 150 sexual initiatives that comprise the anatomy of a sexual experience creates extraordinary tension; the fear of crying seals in that tension. The more we cry, the less we will seek out women as an outlet and release of tension, the less pressure we will exert on women, the more relaxed both sexes will become, and the less a man will become like a puppy dog wagged by his penis.

How can a man get himself to cry more often? For me, it was mostly an attitude shift. As I made that transition, instead of holding tears back if I felt sadness or hurt I told myself that crying will "cleanse my hurt." I imagine myself preventing an ulcer. This imagining encourages tears. Because crying is an excretory process, like urinating, it can either be held back at will or encouraged by relaxing our attitude toward it. Telling a man "Big boys don't cry" is like telling him "Big boys don't urinate."

New-Age Feelings

Who can be "politically correct" about abortion and in touch with *all* of her or his feelings? Being in touch with feelings requires being in touch with what does not conform to either the age-old or the new-age. Feelings have no constituency. To be politically correct is to be a constituency conformer. In a sense, to be politically correct is to be emotionally constipated. It requires the suppression, not the expression, of feelings.

The expression of feelings can be misused to conform to new-age expectations. I remember a man in a Manhattan men's group who exclaimed, "I cry more than anyone in this group." By turning crying into competition he had turned it against itself. He had become the "biggest jock in the sensitivity group."

When Men Get in Touch with Their Feelings . . .

When and if men ever get in touch with their feelings on a mass level, they will be venting anger and hurt both at their own socialization and at women who go for heroes while saying they want vulnerability. They will be asking, "Why are women threatened by *un*successful men?" Women who accuse men of being wimps or worms will be seen with as much anger as men who call women dykes or ballbreakers.

When a man recalls how his first sexual feelings may have been rejected with "no, no, no . . . ," he will wonder how he expresses any feelings at all. When he hears a woman say she feels used, he will wonder whether that meant she was expecting something in addition to sex. He may feel used by being expected to pay for dinner or call afterward.

When a man gets in touch with his feelings of powerlessness by seeing the extent to which the roles he played—which were labeled "power"—were actually bribes that kept him from choosing how he wanted to balance his five components of power, he will experience a mid-life crisis. And *he will welcome it because he is directing it—rather than being directed by it.* If he is in touch with his feelings early enough it will be an early-life crisis—a time to sort out his values and direct his life by creating his own values.

As a man looks at what he was told about whom he can and cannot touch, he will feel anger at the message not to touch or kiss men while women get permission to touch and kiss women.

Each time he touches the wrong person the wrong way it could mean his life's work—career, income, and salary—down the drain. And his family, his daughter or son, lost forever. Instead of feeling his external reward power as power, he will feel the powerlessness of accepting a preprogrammed definition and seek to create his own. Instead of feeling guilt at his privilege to initiate, he will feel the impact of being worse than America's second-class citizen—an untouchable.

Dialogues on Feelings

Q: Some men I know seem really in touch with their feelings—both my therapist and a minister I know, for example. How did they get this way?

WF: Male clergy and male therapists are experts at listening to the feelings of others, but rarely at expressing vulnerabilities of their own. They are "feeling professionals," who may only be "feeling heroes." The reason people come to them is that they maintain an image of respectability. A woman plays into a man's being a "feeling hero" if she is not giving him respect for the feelings he expresses about himself that lead her to admire him less.

Q: How can I respect what I admire less?

WF: By respecting his courage to reveal what is not admirable.

Q: For example?

WF: Suppose a Catholic woman goes to confession and tells her priest she and her husband are having marital difficulties. She asks the priest for advice. Imagine him saying, "Well, I can't help you. The only human relationship I've ever had is with my parents and, to be honest, one short-term relationship in a monastery—with a man."

Q: That's ridiculous. Why would he say such a thing? She didn't ask for that type of revelation.

WF: That's the point—his role makes the expression of real vulnerability ridiculous—and inappropriate. She didn't go to him for his role as an expresser of feelings, which is why when these men are mentioned as examples of men in touch with their feelings, we must question what she wants out of men's feelings. At most he has shown himself to be in touch with *her* feelings. A woman who considers a man in touch with his feelings because he listens to hers is likely to select a man who plays advice-giver but keeps to himself the things he feels she will not approve of. Male "feeling professionals" do that as a matter of professional role as well as of male role. It is a very rare "feeling hero" who is truly vulnerable with feelings he believes will be disapproved of by the people he needs for his security. Even feminist men limit most of their feelings to those feelings they believe will be approved of by feminist women.

13

Conclusion:
Clearing the Way
for Love

One morning, the phone rang.

"Hi, Warren, this is Rosemary. . . . Remember when you spoke with Lynette Trier's women's group some months ago and encouraged us to look at men differently? Well, I decided to do it, and the weekend after that I went up to San Francisco . . . saw this guy at a disco and I thought, 'I wish a guy like *him* would come my way.' I kept remembering your saying, 'Some of the happiest relationships I've ever seen are relationships in which the woman originally approached the man . . .' and so I went up to him . . .''

"Great! What happened?"

"Well, we had a terrific evening and the next day he didn't call. Normally I would have said, 'And the next day he didn't call, *of course.*' My gut response was still to call Lynette and bitch about men, but I took a different attitude and called *him* instead."

"And . . . ?"

"And, well, to make a long story short, it's blossoming into one of the best relationships I've ever had. Because I've shifted my approach and attitude every step of the way."

"Fantastic! . . . What made you call me about it now?"

"Last night we told each other what we loved about each other, and one thing he said was, 'I feel so understood by you—maybe because you're willing to take the risks I take.' Well, when he said that I knew I had to call you!"

"What a beautiful gift to give me, Rosemary," I said.

A few hours later, I realized Rosemary had given me a second gift—a beginning for my conclusion. For certainly few examples better represent how only when a woman shares male risks can she really begin to understand men; how empathy without sharing is intellect without gut; how sharing male risks is part of becoming independent of men and *with* men rather than independent and without men; and how the woman who shares male risks stops categorizing men as heroes or jerks because she is sharing that responsibility herself—sometimes being her own hero, sometimes her own jerk.

Clearing the Way for Love

Item: Sun Up San Diego. Christmas 1984. Jerry G. Bishop, the host, asks each woman in the audience, "in the spirit of Christmas," to list the things she loves about men—or even what is good about men. Not one woman comes up with one thing.

When we are asked to list what is good about women we can reflexively think of "warmth," "cooperativeness," "nurturing," "gentleness," "commitment," "love," and "struggling for independence." This doesn't mean we can't come up with negatives as well, or that women are this way all the time, or that these characteristics do not have their flip sides—it only means our gut is so in touch with this side of women that it provides a filter of love through which the less endearing qualities of women can be seen.

Just twenty years ago feminists helped us understand that when we heard the word *femininity,* we reflexively thought of words like "incompetent," "irrational," "inferior," etc. Today the word "woman" incorporates more than femininity; it incorporates struggles for independence on the one hand, combined with victimization by divorce, battering, rape, pornography, sexual harassment, and incest. While the focus on independence has given women a good name—beyond femininity—the focus on battering, rape, and pornography has increased our view of men as oppressors.

We have seen, though, by looking at the fantasy-not-yet-fulfilled magazines, that the more the magazine focuses on independence and equality the greater the anger toward men; that, in fact, at least part of the new focus on age-old issues like battering, rape, and pornography has really derived from the underlying feeling that women have been victimized by, and are no longer taken care of by, men. This could not be admitted directly. So the focus on women as independent and men as even more oppressive had to be established *before* there could be an emphasis on blaming men as too immature to commit. Hence the popularity of books playing on the women-who-can't-get-a-man-to-commit theme in 1983 to 1986: *The Peter Pan Syndrome; Smart Women, Foolish Choices;* and *Women Who Love Too Much;* all of which were on *The New York Times* best-seller list for long periods. These books, as we have seen, could not have made it far with reverse titles. So we entered the period of ''Marry the Enemy.''

What was the larger picture behind the way we got from ''Daddy knows best'' to ''Daddy molests,'' or ''marry the enemy''?

During the past two decades, women have been caught between the traditional method of having their specialness confirmed by the fact that a hero-type male discovered their specialness, thereby confirming it, and, on the other hand, creating that feeling of being number one via their own achievements. As women as a group strove more to confirm their number-one status by their own achievements, it became functional to define their major competitor—white men—as an enemy, just as the United States and the USSR define their major competitor as the enemy. The more men were the enemy, the more special women were. The more men were the enemy, the more women could feel solidly aligned and ''sisterly'' with other women. The more men were the source of all evil, the more energy it stimulated in the woman to see her specialness as defined in put-downs of this source of evil. These, then, are some incentives against change. And they are part of human nature.

However, the part of many women that still desires a hero-type man to confirm her specialness is in conflict with the man-as-enemy approach. For many a woman this creates a constant hero/asshole dichotomy in her approach to men. And this can wreak havoc on her personal life.

Some women, though, like feminist authors Robin Morgan and Sonja Johnson, try to resolve this conflict. The Robin Morgan resolution: ''Men are the enemy, except a few special men; one of these few, of course, chose me.'' Or the approach of Sonja Johnson, author of *From Housewife to Heretic*, as spoken before the profeminist National Organization for Changing Men in 1984: "I make you 'honorary *women*.' " To extricate himself from enemy status, a man need only deny he is a man. And then we ask "Why are men so resistant to changing?"

How can we love men without making men into "honorary women"? It can start with developing a willingness to associate reflexively some positive images with the word *men*. Images like "mentor"—which would let us feel some warmth toward men for their willingness to act as mentors even when they are preparing women to compete with them, images like "doer" (as opposed to "complainer") or "self-starter." We can praise men for their refusal to use words like *love* when they mean "security," for "playing with kids on kids' terms," for their willingness to make themselves the butt of self-effacing humor, for keeping complaints about a relationship within the relationship, for separating issues from friendship, for having enough ego strength to risk being confronted by the cruelty of the marketplace (even when they're feeling as scared as a child on the first day of school), for a man's willingness to give his life for a woman he loves, to assume responsibility, to confront himself with the immaturity of his male socialization enough to forfeit his primary fantasy of many women for one woman whom he really loves.

Is there any fundamental switch in consciousness that must precede our willingness to make parallel positive associations with *men?* Yes. It requires looking within—and seeing how, underneath it all, the reason we are different is because we are so much the same. We all start life hoping everyone will approve of us; we all adapt in order to get that approval, but each sex still adapts to fundamentally different messages in order to fulfill an identical need for approval. As we have seen, each sex gets many of its cues about how it should adapt from the messages the other sex gives it.

Both sexes' dependence on approval is obscured by our delight with the courage we muster to make the little deviations. We call this our individuality. But when looked at closely, these deviations are often derived from an assessment of whether our weaknesses and strengths would allow us to "make it" in the approval system—according to the values of our parents, friends, and class background. In this underlying way almost all humans are remarkably identical.

Applying this understanding to men coincides with the pragmatics of change: "The more we make men the enemy, the more they will have to behave like the enemy."

As a man, I know we must take much of the responsibility for almost two decades of attacks, without expressing our own feelings. I have mentioned how, in my case, my stake in female approval kept me from doing that for years. As did my tendency to just do things rather than express feelings that were making it difficult for me to carry that out. For example, I can recall Megan being depressed at dinner. After some prodding she explained how her ''old girlfriend,'' with whom she had been ''best friends,'' was now beating her up because she had a new ''best friend.'' It seems Megan had already tried some self-help solutions, like alternately ignoring her old friend and spending time with her. She was afraid if she told the teacher or principal she'd get beaten up on the way home.

We eventually discussed the possibility of my calling her friend. Megan felt the girl would pay attention to me. I explained I would be willing to call if she was okay with my just talking with—not lecturing—her ''friend.'' In fact that was Megan's desire too—we both understood that anything else would result in her friend calling her ''chicken'' for having me do her dirty work.

Frankly, I had never made a call like that before. It seemed strange to call a twelve-year-old out of the blue. And I was deeply touched that Megan trusted me to call.

After the call Anne came up to me and took my hand. ''Honey, your hand's all clammy.''

''Hmm . . . I guess I was nervous about making that call.''

''Really . . . ? Why is that?''

''I don't know. . . . I guess I didn't know what to say, or where to begin.''

It took me a while to let myself know that it was exactly because I was touched by Megan's trust that I didn't want to ''mess it up.''

The next morning Anne mentioned, ''I told Megan about your nervousness about making the phone call. She was really surprised. I think it was good for her to know that.''

Yes. It was good for her to know that. But I hadn't told her. Nor did I tell her for a while how touched I was that she trusted me to call. I was still defining love by doing. And then was wondering why it took her so long to love me.

Both sexes use the other sex to feel special. One way is by feeling needed. As we looked at the ''five components of power,'' we saw how each sex develops deprivation in different areas (women, in things economic; men, in sex and intimacy). Both sexes tend to feel needed—or special—in the area where their *partner* feels most deprived. Which gives each sex a short-term investment in keeping its partner less than fully powerful.

Women and men both need intimacy. But when asked to name the people toward whom they feel close or intimate, women often name children or other women, and men often say women. Why? We have learned to think of ourselves as intimate with those who need us. Men have learned to feel okay about getting the "intimacy" of feeling needed by a woman who is financially deprived; in contrast women have received a conflicted message in their attitude toward men: *they want men to need them yet feel neediness is unmanly*. They "turn off" to a man they feel they must "mother"—so only a little leeway is allowed between his showing neediness and being "too needy." This also creates a dilemma for men: he looks bad if he lets himself feel needy and looks bad if he doesn't let himself feel needy.

How do many women satisfy this basic human need to feel special to someone by feeling needed? By letting children need them. So one incentive for women to have children is for women to get part of their "power" of feeling needed from the "appropriate" outlet of children rather than from the inappropriate outlet of a needy man.

A needy man creates a fundamental void for a woman: he does not confirm her specialness as a woman to her peers, to her parents, or to herself; he does not confirm that she is able to attract a hero man. On the one hand she wants a man to need her, as Lois Lane wanted Superman to need her. But she wants that neediness to fall within a framework: if his self-examination or neediness develops to the point where he is no longer able to provide her a security blanket should she fail, she often feels it has gone too far.

A needy woman does not create such conflicts for a man in American culture. But if his feelings of "intimacy" *derive* from her neediness, he then has an investment in her continued neediness. This inhibits a woman from developing sufficient independence and inhibits a man from developing sufficient dependence. How much dependence is sufficient? Enough to fail. The freedom to fail is a prerequisite to internal freedom. A prerequisite to personal power.

Men's feelings of intimacy that are dependent on feeling

needed keep women in their place and keep women loving children more than men.

This difference allows us to understand why women with children have been known to lift a car off a child's body to save the child but never to lift a car off a husband's body to save a husband. The woman allows herself the power that comes from feeling needed by the child but not the power that comes from feeling needed *by* her husband. Especially not in the areas of physical strength or fiscal responsibility.

The alternative? Helping our partners develop a balanced sense of power in each area of the five components of power, redefining intimacy to include helping our partner *increase* his or her power in each area. If we do that, we will be getting our power of feeling needed by promoting growth rather than nurturing deficiency. And we will be allowing women to come close to men as well as to children.

Understanding the Male Experience of Powerlessness

Show me a hero and I will write you a tragedy.

F. Scott Fitzgerald

Our love for children is so immediate in part because we feel their powerlessness immediately; conversely, part of the way we deny our love for men is by denying men's powerlessness. Too often we have confused love for men with respect for them, especially for their power to take care of us—which is really just love for ourselves. Let's review a bit and then enter into a new way of loving men.

A girl of thirteen sees male power, and thinks of it as her boyfriend's birth*right*. Her boyfriend sees male power and sees it as his birth *obligation*. In fact, it is *not* his birthright; it *is* his birth obligation. Until he gets it he gets told he is nothing without it. So ''Men have the power'' translates to the adolescent boy, ''You, boy, have to try to get the power *from* men.'' It is *other* men who have the power, not him. He must compete to get power. A woman can then marry a survivor. *Or* get it herself.

''Men make the rules to benefit men'' means little to the

eighteen-year-old boy who must register for the draft while his sister does not. (If registering for death is a benefit, he'd like to see the punishment.) It means little to Phil, a thirty-five-year-old veteran of Vietnam, who is just one of the estimated 1 to 1.5 million Vietnam War veterans to suffer post-traumatic stress.[1] And it means little to Tony, who every morning looks at his seven-year-old son, deformed without a right hand, try to pick up a fork at the breakfast table, feeling guilty because, "Agent Orange gave *that* to him." To Tony, "Men make the rules to benefit men" misses something. Tony never made any more rules than his nine-year-old daughter. "Men make rules to benefit men" seems to tell Tony, "It's your fault you got that Agent Orange. It's your fault your son is deformed." To Tony, it is blaming the victim.

By glorifying male death and calling it "power," we have been able to justify having men sacrifice themselves to save others and then blame them for causing the war.

Our response is, "Well, they do cause the war . . ." as if it were *part* of their power, rather than understanding that it is, in fact, part of women's power to be able to be in a warm home while men are sent off to die. But is it not men—*some* men—who cause the wars? And don't most men behave in warlike fashion? How can a sex that puts us all in danger be lovable?

To clear the way for loving men we must look carefully at our unquestioned assumption that "men cause wars—therefore . . ." If our larger image of men is distorted, it will distort the way we look at individual men. And the way we love them.

But Don't Men Cause Wars . . . ?

Men do not cause wars by fighting in wars any more than women cause wars by raising the boys who fight in wars. Both sexes carry out their sex-role obligations. And what we assign both sexes is the responsibility of both sexes.

War is the competition for territory, money, and resources—the competition for external-reward power. Most cultures have assigned the gathering of external-reward power to men. The assignment is to men. But the benefactors—or losers—are both sexes.

The psychology of war comes from the neediness and greediness for the approval, recognition, and respect that cultures have made a by-product of external-reward power. Ferdinand Marcos was greedy; Imelda Marcos was also greedy.

Both sexes are needy and greedy for this approval, recognition, and respect. Both sexes give approval, recognition, and respect to those with more external-reward power. Men are assigned the role of dying to compete for this neediness and greediness.

But aren't men the key decision-makers? *It is both women and men who socialize our sons to be decision-makers and our daughters to marry them.* And women and men teachers who reinforce that socialization. It is both women and men who choose to get their approval, recognition, and respect by either making decisions or blaming others for decisions they did not even make an effort to be elected to make. And it is both women and men who cast the votes that elect the decision-makers.

Margaret Thatcher, Golda Meir, and Indira Gandhi are often cited as proof that women in leadership positions can make decisions that involve their nations in war. That is true. But to blame the female leaders misses the point as much as to blame the male leaders. Blaming the decision-makers is both sexes' escaping the responsibility for electing them. And both sexes' escaping responsibility for the neediness and greediness that supports their leaders—of either sex—in the use of violence. In a nation in which only 50 percent of the people vote in national elections and 25 percent in most local elections and many national primaries, a concerted effort on the part of either sex could produce significantly different decisions about war. Blaming men because they fulfill the responsibility we assign them to take is part of the problem. It is the same problem as assigning men the sexual initiative-taking.

Equality implies equal responsibility for what does and does not happen. Our mutual responsibility for war happens on an everyday level in our hometown. Both sexes give scholarships to encourage our sons to enter a "den of molestation"—called a football team—prior to the "age of consent." We take our family to see this molestation on Thanksgiving. And to see the most attractive girls give their attention to the boys who win at this molestation.

Both sexes reinforce this association of glory and power with male death every day as we create—via our choices—TV programming and films that feature a ratio of over 200 males to 1 female shown actually being killed on television or in the movies.[2]

For our entertainment. We call male death heroism. Or villainism. One minute we encourage it, the next we condemn it. And yet this entertainment doesn't touch the reality: the ratio of actual violent death in the Vietnam War was almost seven thousand males to each female. And still we protest the violence against "innocent" women more than the violence against "guilty" men. We even care more about the death of whales than the death of males. Because the underlying assumption is "Males cause war—whales don't"; and "Males cause war—females don't," which is all a reflection of the stereotyped sex roles that males take responsibility and women don't.

How do we get men less involved with war? We stop worshipping them for performing. There will be fewer heroes. And fewer wars. When the American officer or Nazi officer is no longer the hero of romance novels, there will also be fewer performers and fewer wars. And when men take responsibility to stop performing for beautiful women, and confront the mechanisms that addict them to beautiful women—from *Glamour* to *Penthouse*—they will have less need to play hero to get the genetic celebrity's attention. Performers will always come into conflict with each other, and the more holy their causes the greater will be their wars (the Holy Wars were Christian wars, and Hitler's crimes came from a Christian nation which, like the United States, declared *"Gott mit Uns,"* or "God is with us"). Women and men both cause war and both cause peace.

When we accept that mutual responsibility, we will do a lot to end sex-role training (the assumption that men are responsible), end divorce training, minimize war, and maximize women as equals. As both sexes acknowledge our roles in reinforcing the symbiosis of the sex-role dance, we will begin to see men as part of *us*—rather than as "them."

The Politics of Making Men Our Friends Again

It becomes easier to make men our friends again if we recall that our choice of partners is one of the clearest statements about our choice of values. Both sexes were socialized to seek some of these values through others (as in financial security or tenderness or innocence). We may thus have chosen a partner to balance out our deficiencies. So our choice of partners can reflect *both* our choice of values *and* our area of inadequacy, immaturity, or dependency. Which is why making either sex the enemy is merely an escape from introspection.

We are more likely to make men our friends again when we remember that both sexes often want results, but are intolerant of the process. Men want women's beauty, but not the time in the bathroom; women hate the male locker room, the Superbowl preoccupation, the western shoot-'em-up mentality, and the mafia-type corruption. Yet they marry the performance orientation that breeds these characteristics.

We can see men less as "them" when we see how both sexes pursue our primary means to our primary fantasies in a competitive and aggressive manner. In the competition for the female primary fantasy, women have their own Superbowl (Miss America), locker room (the Red Door), western (watch any soap opera), and mafia ("Protect Your Reputation").*

Put-downs—like the "gender gap" when it is used to imply "Women vote for peace and social issues, men vote for missiles and war"—also alienate us from men. We could have chosen to view the gender gap as the gap between the 99 percent of readers of romance novels who are women and the 1 percent who are men. Does this gender gap involve many women in absolute numbers? It involves, we saw, over 25 million women, which is 4500 percent larger than the fewer than 500,000 subscribers to *Ms.* magazine. And these women purchase an average of ten romance novels per month versus one *Ms.* per month. So we can begin to make men our friends again if we begin to be a bit fairer.

When we look at the whole gender dance we see how every time a woman assumes a man will pay, she reinforces the man's calculating the type of job he needs to earn money to take women out. The assumption he will usually pay puts earning pressure on him and takes it off herself. Which contributes to the mentality that leads to women earning less than men. In a similar vein, the more a woman experiences a man as not sharing housework, the more she tends to take it on as her responsibility and the greater the chance of her becoming obsessive. And similarly again, the more a man experiences the woman as not sharing responsibility for the first kiss or genital touching, the more he tends to activate his sexuality until we blame him for sexual obsessiveness. Overall, *the area in which we blame the*

*See Chapter 2 for all of these.

other sex reflects the area in which we need to look at our own responsibility.

What tempted us away from seeing this gender dance, and into saying "Men have the power"? In part, it was that the Western world has overvalued the one component of power which men are assigned to gather—external-reward power.

We also viewed male adaptation to their jobs quite literally—as if men were adapting only to their jobs. Men did, of course, adapt to their jobs—and their bosses, which is why IBM could be called "I've Been Moved." But we tended to forget that male adaptation to jobs was *also* male adaptation to women (as in taking that responsibility to provide 76 percent of the average family's income). We therefore thought of books on "relationships" and "love" only on the literal level, as if women were the sex concerned with love, forgetting that books on love served a second purpose for the married woman earning 24 percent of the family income—they were the equivalent of what business school was to men.

In this atmosphere of forgetfulness in which men become more and more our enemy, it was forgotten that male adaptation to women was also quite direct. A restrained kiss was male adaptation; or his saying, "I'd like to make love" rather than "I'd like to have sex"; or "Would you like a foot massage?" rather than "I'd like to make love." Or his willingness to give up a lifetime's stimuli of beautiful women in every commercial to commit to sex with one woman exclusively, and less of it than he wants. This is perhaps the most unappreciated adaptation in all human behavior. And almost as unappreciated is what this willingness to adapt implies about men's desire for intimacy and love.

How Can We Change the System That Creates This?

Todd's parents—Jeanne and Tom—believed Todd should be able to cuddle with a teddy bear for as long as he wished. But when Todd's seventh-grade classmates visited his home one afternoon and saw a teddy bear and a little stuffed sheep on his pillow, they rode him mercilessly at school, calling him "Toddy Bear," going "Baa-baa" every time they passed him in the hall, and making rhymes like "Toddy Bear, Toddy Bear, bet he wears pink underwear." Soon "Toddy Bear" was forced to "show the boys his pink underwear . . . or else."

When Todd buried his teddy bear and stuffed the sheep into the garbage can with his dinner over it, Todd's parents finally put two and two together. They blamed themselves. Had they allowed their beliefs to make Todd into a "social guinea pig"? In their attempt to allow gentleness had they fostered their son's self-hatred? They felt themselves to be in a dilemma—they wanted their son to have options they didn't have when they were children, including the option of gentleness, but they couldn't change the school system.

Or could they? Tom and Jeanne invited to dinner two couples they respected who also shared their feelings about options. They decided to run four of them for the school board over a period of two years. Three of the four won. A year later, they influenced the choice of a new school superintendent, arranged for special staff training for the teachers, and perceived the impact as filtering down to their own children. Jeanne and Tom took a route considerably distinct from most parents—who play victim to "the system," rather than understanding that the inactive parent is also part of the system. The "educational system" is quite easily influenced, because schools are locally based; the child is home-based; her or his peers are neighborhood-based; and the television is bedroom-based. To suggest we cannot create change because we cannot "change the whole educational system" is usually an escape from changing the most resistant system: ourselves.

How to Make a Living Changing the System

We cannot expect the system to change if people cannot make a living changing the system. So how can a living be made? By starting with a useful "rule of thumb": For every societal dysfunction there is an equal and opposite potential for profit. That is, every time we complain about something that's "wrong with society," and others are nodding their heads, that is a sign of a potential market. The complaint, in brief, often signals a need waiting to be filled. For example, when women started working, many complained of a lack of time to cook. Business-oriented people—who knew how to turn others' complaints into their profits rather than be one more complainer—tuned into this change (with fast-food restaurant profits doubling and tripling) and responded by quadrupling the number (and quintupling the profits) of fast-food restaurants and by creating gourmet frozen dinners and more luxury restaurants—all of which brought profits to the doers and filled the mouths of the complainers.

For years we complained about overcompetitiveness, which produced everything from stress to alcoholism. The dysfunction —stress—soon created the need for seminars on stress management; drug and alcohol addiction produced everything from community to corporate rehab programs; male socialization to "find the flaw" has already spawned the *One-Minute Manager* ("Catch him or her doing something *right*").

What will happen in the future? The problems of self-listening have already begun to lead to business consultants in listening; role-reversal techniques are beginning to be applied to listening skills in business, government, academia, and international politics; the need for paternal involvement in child care is currently producing consultants in paternity leaves, which have recently become part of many institutions' benefits packages; women's socialization to choose fields that pay less can lead to jobs for school consultants to train guidance counselors to help girls make the selections that create financial independence; the same consultants can help boys question the human costs of choosing only from careers that allow a man to single-handedly support himself, a woman, and children.

The reality of dual careers creates the reality of dual parenting, which is now increasing the need for corporate consultants on flexible job arrangements. Companies are finding that many forward-thinking and secure employees are the same types who are forward-thinking and secure enough to want to work twenty to thirty hours a week for five or six years while sharing child-rearing. Joint custody, which has evolved out of the desire for dual parenting, has led to mediators rather than lawyers in the 1980s and will lead to follow-up work with joint-custody families in the 1990s.

The imbalance in sex-role analysis has already led to over one hundred courses in men's studies, to changing university departments of women's studies into departments of sex roles. In at least five states[3] proposals have been introduced to develop commissions on the status of men. It will soon mean consultants on male abortion rights, new experts on the multiple roles of pornography; experts on everything from the two sides of job discrimination to the complexities of sexual harassment. It implies more columns on men's issues (like those in *The New York Times* and *Los Angeles Times)*, developing television and radio programming on men, and developing video and audio cassettes on topics from male life expectancy to female sexual initiative-taking and draft registration laws.

Perhaps the most profitable and useful way of making a living changing our sex-role training for divorce is by starting a small advertising firm whose specialization is advertising free from dependence on the old sexism or new sexism. The development of ads like the ingenious, nonsexist series of old Volkswagen ads, rather than "Love is Lenox."

Are There Ways Women's and Men's Movements Can Work Together?

Is loving men contradictory to feminism? Hardly. Every true feminist, I believe, is deepened and matured by being also a masculinist—a person who understands the male search for equality and approval *as the male experiences it*. As is every masculinist deepened by being a feminist (a person who understands the female search for equality and approval *as the female experiences it*).

That is the point of this book—what most needs changing is the neurotic need to see ourselves as "right" and someone else as "wrong." That change is the deepest "paradigm shift," the deepest shift in our world view. Understanding the male experience of powerlessness is only a paradigm shift to the extent that the understanding of men is not brought about by the blaming of women. This does not mean blaming is *verboten*—that would only be a new artificial rule of liberation. It means blaming as a defense mechanism against looking within is part of the problem.

Minimizing blame and enemy creation is such a crucial prerequisite for preventing nuclear war that the shift must be considered our next step evolutionarily. If our attitudes are win-lose and our technology is destroy-to-win, we are destroyed.

Exactly how do we go about doing this? It is worth looking at three methods of bringing about equality without blame:

- Alliance building
- The listening matrix
- Reversing roles

Each of these can help us both on an international level and with our loved ones.

First, alliance building, or alliance creation. How could alliance creation have been applied to pass an Equal Rights Amendment? Partly by changing the incentives. For example, change Equal Rights to Equal Rights *and Responsibilities* and we suddenly acknowledge that the male-female relationship is a written and unwritten contract of rights and responsibilities combined— *un*like civil rights. The new attitude—reflected in the new language—creates new allies.

How can alliance creation be applied to the strongest opponents of Equal Rights (and Responsibilities), like pro-family women? Statistically, "pro-family" women are much more likely than ERA supporters to be receiving their economic support and emotional acceptance from men and marriage.[4] Therefore, portraying men as oppressors does not serve this woman well. Even if she recognizes his oppressive characteristics, for this woman the man is her source of income and emotional acceptance. She fears divorce. *Pro-family is pro-self-interest.* So what can make *her* an ally? The focus on sex-role training as divorce training. *That* focus puts an Equal Rights (and Responsibilities) Amendment in her terms.

Alliance creation is applicable to almost everything in our life—to the unnecessary adversaries of good versus bad, us versus them, nature versus nurture, holistic versus traditional (as in medicine), democracy versus communism, logic versus emotion, and women versus men. And it is at the core of gossip (they're bad; we're good).

But how can we listen carefully enough to want to create alliances with "the enemy"? The first step is the listening matrix, which is also necessary to create love.

Love Is in the Balance

The women's movement has offered us part of a four-part listening matrix: the female experience of powerlessness. And its corollary—the female experience of male power. We have seen how when only one part is heard, there is a tendency to arrive at false assumptions, such as "Men have the power that women do not have." This reinforces the old adversarial win-lose approach that looks like the illustration on the following page.

Author's drawing

Listening only to the female experience of powerlessness has resulted in the new sexism. In *The Liberated Man* I helped to fill in this first part of the matrix by interpreting to men some of the female experience of powerlessness as I had come to know it from my position with NOW in New York City and from my work in workshops. In this book it is my hope that I have added the three dimensions to this matrix I proposed in the introduction, creating, in total, a full matrix:

Female Experience of Powerlessness	Male Experience of Powerlessness
Female experience of power	Male experience of power

There are no boundaries to the matrix. The moment we begin to argue "my powerlessness is greater than yours" or "me the biggest victim in the self-help group" we have an investment in making ourselves look helpless. At that moment we cease hearing the other sex's experience. Nor must we deny that one group has more or less power. So, for example, when we apply this matrix to male-female relations, we find a much different outcome than we do in relationships between classes of people, or between ethnic or racial groups. The ghetto Irish, Italians, and blacks did not share the homes, income, or children of the people on the other side of the tracks. Women and men have traditionally shared homes, income, and children—our futures have been bound together in ways those of different class, ethnic, and racial groups never were or will be.

By hearing each person's experience in each of these four quadrants we are able to keep love in the balance.

We are able to love blacks, whites, Jews, Arabs, Russians, Americans, males, females, gays, straights, holistic medicine and traditional medicine, nature and nurture, and, ultimately, because we diminish the need to defeat another to make ourselves appear special, we can therefore relax and love ourselves. Which is why love is in the balance.

I have mentioned how the adversarial approach of assigning males to kill each other off so the winners can breed with the culture's most attractive women was what Darwin discovered as the sexual selection that was integral to the survival of the fittest. And how suddenly, with nuclear technology, this approach leads to the survival of nobody. What was once functional has become dysfunctional.* This forces us to employ the adaptive part of our human nature—to adapt to the technology that has made our win-lose adversarial system into a destroy-all system rather than a destroy-the-"weakest" system. Suddenly problem-solving methods like role reversal, alliance creation, and hearing the four sides of a problem become more than topics of study—they become studies of survival.

We think of ourselves as a generation in transition. But we have also seen how our situation is more in transition than our approach to each other; how our technology is in transition and challenging our psychology to keep apace; how our survival needs are in transition and challenging our problem-solving methods to adapt.

For the first time in human history the psychology that is a prerequisite for intimacy has become the psychology that is a prerequisite for species survival. Our need to find men as the enemy in our interpersonal relationships is part of our need to find an enemy in our international relationships. Our need to look at only one sex's experience of powerlessness is only the first of four quadrants in survival problem-solving. One quadrant

---

*See Chapter 3 for part of this discussion.

developed alone reinforces the old method—which technology has transformed into the annihilation method.

The part of our human nature that wants to find an enemy, then, is in tension with another part of our human nature—the capacity to adapt to changing circumstances to survive. For this reason, love is in the balance; and love *is* the balance.

Is there a precedent for humans taking such a radically different approach to each other to survive? Darwin and Galileo did lead the world to look at itself from a totally different perspective. And Darwin was trained as a clergyman and Galileo was originally a professor of the Ptolemaic view of the earth as the center of the universe.

As long as Galileo retained the Ptolemaic view and kept his telescope away from the heavens, he was applauded with lifetime tenure by the Venetian senate. As soon as he took his telescope to the heavens and described what he saw as well as he could, the special interests who were offended perceived their interests as unreconcilable with his findings: "The church has said *we* are the center of the universe. It is blasphemy to question this. . . ."

It is not important that Galileo was eventually deemed correct. Because the telescope of human relations reflects varied human experiences, each human peers at objective phenomena through a different telescope. We view the world through the filter of our special interests. Therefore, the best we can do is not prevent ourselves from trying each other's telescopes out of fear it will hurt our special interests. Somehow, the church and the heliocentric way of looking at the world co-exist in peace today. If we co-exist in peace tomorrow it will not be due to new Galileos; it will be due to a willingness to share each other's telescopes.

Notes

CHAPTER 1

Men Have the Power—Why Would They Want to Change?

1. U.S. Bureau of the Census, *Current Population Reports*, "Marital Status," Table P2, in press.
2. U.S. Bureau of the Census, *Statistical Abstracts of the United States, 1984*, p. 79.
3. U.S. National Center for Health Statistics, *Vital Statistics for the United States*, cited in *Statistical Abstracts of the United States, 1973*, pp. 57–59.
4. Ingrid Waldron and Susan Johnson, "Why Do Women Live Longer than Men? Accidents, Alcohol and Cirrhosis," *Journal of Human Stress*, vol. 2, June 1976, pp. 19–30.
5. U.S. National Center for Health Statistics, *Health Statistics from the U.S. National Health Survey: Vital Health Statistics*, ser. 10, no. 72, and unpublished data cited in *Statistical Abstracts of the United States, 1973*, p. 81.

INTRODUCTION TO PART 2

Women Have Changed—Why Aren't Men Changing Too?

1. "Circulation of Leading U.S. Magazines," *The World Almanac 1985* (New York: Newspaper Enterprise Association, 1984), p. 426. The *Almanac*'s source is FAS-FAX Reports, Audit Bureau of Circulations.
2. *Forbes*, November 19, 1984.
3. *Good Housekeeping*, July 1984.

CHAPTER 2

What Women Want: The Message the Man Hears
1. *Ms.*, April 1982.
2. *Ms.*, March 1984.
3. *Harper's Bazaar*, August 1982.
4. *Seventeen*, January 1985.
5. Joanna Steichen, *Marrying Up* (New York: Rawson Associates, 1984).
6. A. C. Nielsen, 1984.
7. The December 1984 issues of *Seventeen, Teen,* and *Young Miss,* and January 1985 issues of *Seventeen* and *Young Miss.*
8. Television advertisement for Weisfield Jewelry, Christmas 1982.
9. *Cosmopolitan*, October 1984, p. 51.
10. *Ms.*, September 1985.
11. *Woman*, October 1984.
12. *Self*, August 1984.
13. *The Ladies' Home Journal*, September 1984.
14. *Working Woman*, November 1984, p. 194.
15. *Good Housekeeping*, July 1984.
16. *Woman*, December 1983.
17. *New Woman*, October 1984.
18. *Romantic Times*, New York Office estimate, February 12, 1985. This estimate is also the agreed-upon figure of the publishing industry in New York.
19. *Los Angeles Times*, September 26, 1984.
20. John Markert, "Romancing the Reader: A Demographic Profile," *Romantic Times*, no. 18, September 1984.
21. Interview, February 18, 1985, with John Markert, independent researcher and contributor to *Romantic Times* and author of "Marketing Love," dissertation in progress.
22. Lawrence Heisley, president of Harlequin Enterprises, quoted in *Los Angeles Times*, September 26, 1984, p. 5.
23. See Carol Cassell, *Swept Away* (New York: Simon & Schuster, 1984), p. 128.
24. *Playgirl*, October 1983, p. 53.
25. Ibid.
26. See Bob Greene, "Words of Love," *Esquire*, May 1984, for each quote from the letters.
27. *Rolling Stone*, January 31, 1985.
28–29. *Penthouse*, December 1984, p. 87.
30. Jacque Lynn Foltyn, "Feminine Beauty in American Culture," doctoral dissertation, University of California at San Diego, in progress.

31. M. Beck, "A Controversial Spectator Sport," *Newsweek,* September 17, 1984, is the source for the data in these paragraphs.
32. Interview with Jean Kilbourne, producer of *Killing Us Softly.*
33. *Newsweek,* September 17, 1984.
34. *Newsweek,* September 17, 1984, p. 56.
35. Ibid.
36. *Ms.,* December 1983.
37. *Good Housekeeping,* February 1985.
38. In-person interview, June 25, 1985, Perth, Australia.
39. *Seventeen,* January 1985.
40. *Cosmopolitan,* September 1984.
41. *Seventeen,* January 1985.
42. *New Woman,* October 1984.
43. *New Woman* (cover), August 1984.
44. *Woman's Day,* August 1; 1984.
45. *The World Almanac 1985,* based on FAS-FAX Reports, Audit Bureau of Circulations.
46. *Playgirl* magazine's estimate is that their subscribers are 50 percent male and 50 percent female. Telephone interview, February 15, 1985.
47. *Time,* January 28, 1985, p. 76.
48. Joyce Jillson, "The Art of Meeting Men or Flirting," *Glamour,* May 1984.
49. *Newsweek,* May 23, 1983.
49a. *MS.,* February 1986.
50. *Seventeen,* December 1984.
51. *Teen,* December 1984.
52. *Glamour,* November 1983.
53. Jacqueline Goodchilds and Gail Zellman, "Adolescent Sexual Signaling," in Neil Malamuth and Edward Donnerstein, eds., *Pornography and Sexual Liberation* (New York: Academic Press, 1984).
54. *Cosmopolitan,* February 1985, p. 150.

CHAPTER 3

The Flashdance *Phenomenon*

1. Herbert Hildebrandt and Edwin Miller, *1983–1984 Newly Promoted Executive,* University of Michigan, Graduate School of Business Administration, Management Succession 14th Survey (Ann Arbor: 1984).
2. William Novak, *The Great American Man Shortage and Other Roadblocks to Romance* (New York: Rawson Associates, 1983).

3. Donald Symons, *The Evolution of Human Sexuality* (New York: Oxford University Press, 1979).

CHAPTER 4

Why Are Men So Preoccupied with Sex and Success?
1. Leslie J. Friedman, *Sex Role Stereotyping in the Mass Media: An Annotated Bibliography* (New York: Garland, 1977). See, for example, Kirsten Amundsen, "The American Woman, Myth and Reality," *The Silenced Majority, Women and American Democracy* (Englewood Cliffs, N.J.: Prentice-Hall, 1971), and Warren Farrell, "Masculine Images in Advertising," *The Liberated Man* (New York: Random House, 1974).
2. Susan Goldberg and Michael Lewis, "Play Behavior in the Year-Old Infant: Early Sex Differences," *Child Development*, vol. 40, no. 1, March 1969, p. 29. Data are drawn from children of parents from all classes, but limited to Caucasians.
3. Ibid.
4. Karen Shanor, *The Shanor Study: The Sexual Sensitivity of the American Male* (New York: Dial Press, 1978), p. 253.
5. Joyce Brothers, *What Every Woman Should Know about Men* (New York: Simon & Schuster, 1982), p. 103.

CHAPTER 5

What Makes a Man Successful at Work That Makes Him Unsuccessful at Home? Or Why Can't Men Listen?
1. Herb Goldberg, *The New Male* (New York: William Morrow, 1979), p. 56.
2. Lee Benham and Alexandra Benham, "Employment, Earning and Psychiatric Diagnosis," in Victor Fuchs, ed., *Economic Aspects of Health* (Chicago: University of Chicago Press, 1982), pp. 203–220.
3. Fernando Bartolome and Paul A. Lee Evans, "Must Success Cost So Much?" *Harvard Business Review*, March-August 1980.

CHAPTER 6

Why Are Men So Afraid of Commitment?
1. David Hellerstein, "The Peter Pan Principle," *Esquire*, October 1983.

2. New York: Dodd-Mead, 1983.
3. U.S. Bureau of Census, *Current Population Reports*, ser. P25, no. 965, "Estimates of the Population of the U.S. By Age, Sex, and Race, 1980–1981," Table 1, 1985, p. 9.
4. See William J. Lederer, in Harold Hart, ed., *Marriage: For and Against* (New York: Hart, 1972), p. 135.
5. Abraham Maslow, *The Farther Reaches of Human Nature* (New York: Viking, 1971).
6. Karen Shanor, *The Shanor Study: The Sexual Sensitivity of the American Male* (New York: Dial Press, 1978), p. 253.
7. *U.S. News & World Report*, April 15, 1974, pp. 59–60, cited in Herb Goldberg, *The New Male* (New York: William Morrow, 1979), p. 236.
8. Joyce Brothers, *What Every Woman Should Know about Men* (New York: Simon & Schuster, 1982), p. 249.
9. U.S. Bureau of the Census, *Current Population Reports*, ser. P23, no. 136, "Lifetime Work Experience and Its Effect on Earnings: Retrospective Data from the 1979 Income Survey Development Program," 1984, pp. 6–7.
10. See, for example, Marjorie Shaevitz, *The Superwoman Syndrome* (New York: Warner Books, 1984).
11. William Iverson, "Love, Death, and the Hubby Image," *Playboy*, September 1963, p. 92, cited by, Barbara Ehrenreich in "The Male Revolt," *Mother Jones*, April 1983.
12. *Los Angeles Times*, September 10, 1984, p. 2.
13. Howard Hayghe, "Working Mothers Reach Record Numbers," *Monthly Labor Review*, December 1984, pp. 31–34.
14. Herbert Hildebrandt and Edwin Miller, "The Newly Promoted Executive," monograph, University of Michigan, Graduate School of Business Administration, Ann Arbor, 1984.
15. Philip Blumstein and Pepper Schwartz, *American Couples* (New York: William Morrow, 1983), p. 320.
16. Jacqueline Simenauer and David Carroll, *Singles: The New Americans* (New York: Simon & Schuster, 1982), pp. 229, 392.
17. Colette Dowling, *The Cinderella Complex* (New York: Pocket Books, 1981), p. 5.
18. Ibid., p. 8.
19. See Ruth Moulton, "Women with Double Lives," *Journal of Contemporary Psychoanalysis*, vol. 13, January 1977, p. 64, and Judith Bardwick, The *Psychology of Women* (New York: Harper & Row, 1971).
20. See Judith Bardwick, Ibid.
21. Simenauer and Carroll, op. cit., p. 15.
22. Blumstein and Schwartz, op cit., pp. 307–308.

23. Ibid.

24. Brothers, op. cit., p. 103.

25. Blumstein and Schwartz in a lecture given at the department of sociology, University of California at San Diego, May 24, 1984.

26. Ibid.

27. Blumstein and Schwartz, op. cit., p. 125.

28. Ibid., p. 265.

29. Simenauer and Carroll, op. cit., p. 205.

30. Blumstein and Schwartz, op. cit., p. 195.

31. U.S. Bureau of Census, *Current Population Reports,* ser. P20, no. 389, ''Marital Status and Living Arrangements,'' March 1983, Table 5 (Washington, D.C.: U.S. Government Printing Office, 1984), p. 32. According to Table 5, 12.7 million children under 18 live with just a mother; 1.2 (or 1.3) million children live with just a father.

32. National Center for Health statistics data, cited in S. B. Garland, ''Divorce Easier Second Time Around,'' *Los Angeles Times,* October 28, 1983, part V, p. 23.

33. Dowling, op. cit., p. 141.

34. See Lynette Trier and Dick Peacock, *Learning to Leave* (New York: Warner Books, 1983).

35. See Jacques Ellul, *The Technological System* (New York: Continuum, 1980).

CHAPTER 7

The New Sexism

1. Philip Blumstein and Pepper Schwartz, *American Couples: Money, Work and Sex* (New York: William Morrow, 1983), p. 22.

2. See Shere Hite, *The Hite Report* (New York: Macmillan, 1976).

3. Blumstein and Schwartz, op. cit., p. 227 (emphasis mine).

4. Compare the relative circulations in *The World Almanac 1985,* total average paid circulation six months prior to December 13, 1983, based on Fas-Fax Reports, Audit Bureau of Circulations, 1984.

5. Nanci Hellmich, ''Why Smart Women Make Dumb Choices,'' in *USA Today,* review of Connell Cowan and Melvyn Kinder, *Smart Women, Foolish Choices* (New York: Clarkson N. Potter, 1984).

6. Robin Norwood, *Women Who Love Too Much: When You Keep Wishing and Hoping He'll Change* (Los Angeles: J. P. Tarcher, 1985).

7. Dan Kiley, *The Peter Pan Syndrome: Men Who Have Never Grown Up* (New York: Dodd-Mead, 1983).

8. Dan Kiley, *The Wendy Dilemma: When Women Stop Mothering Their Men* (New York: Arbor House, 1984).

9. Sonya Friedman, *Men Are Just Desserts* (New York: Warner Books, 1983).

10. Elissa Melamed, *Mirror, Mirror* (New York: Simon & Schuster, 1983).

11. Blumstein and Schwartz, op. cit., p. 161.

12. Herbert Hildebrandt and Edwin Miller, ''The Newly Promoted Executive,'' monograph, University of Michigan, Graduate School of Business Administration, Ann Arbor, 1984.

13. Ibid.

13a. *Los Angeles Times,* February 24, 1986. Suit brought against J.C. Penney in Canoga Park, Calif.

14. Philip Roth, *The Professor of Desire* (New York: Farrar, Straus & Giroux, 1977).

15. Billie Wright Dziech, *The Lecherous Professor* (Boston: Beacon Press, 1984).

16. Louise Armstrong, *Kiss Daddy Goodnight: A Speak-Out on Incest* (New York: Hawthorn Books, 1978).

17. See Suzanne Steinmetz, ''The Battered Husband Syndrome,'' *Victimology,* vol. 2, nos. 3–4, 1977–1978, pp. 499–509.

18. Ibid.

19. Murray Straus, ''Wife Beating,'' *Victimology,* vol. 2, November 1977.

20. Observation is made by Suzanne Steinmetz in *Victimology,* op. cit., about Richard Gelles's *The Violent Home* (Beverly Hills, Calif.: Sage, 1974).

21. Fredric Hayward, ''Another War—And Only Men Die,'' *The Washington Post,* June 5, 1982.

22. Ibid.

23. See Paul Dean, ''Husbands Too Ashamed to Admit Abuse by Wives,'' *Newsday,* January 20, 1981.

24. Committee on the Fetus and Newborn, *Standards and Recommendations for Hospital Care of Newborn Infants,* 5th ed. (Evanston, Ill.: American Academy of Pediatrics, 1971).

25. *American Health,* September 1984, p. 54.

26. Federal Bureau of Investigation, *Crime in the United States: 1983. Uniform Crime Reports for the United States* (U.S. Department of Justice, Washington, D.C., 1984).

27. Hayward bases this on his interviews with prison officials.

28. UCSD Department of Sociology, *Newsletter,* fall 1984.

29. The 1,000-strip total came from the *Washington Post,* 44 daily

strips, ten days; the *Los Angeles Times*, 23 daily strips, ten days; and the *Chicago Tribune*, 33 daily strips, ten days. No one day was the same so that no strip was duplicated. My assistant was George Lewis Singer.

30. Marilyn French, *The Women's Room* (New York: Summit Books, 1977).

31. A. C. Nielson ratings, 1984.

32. Jacque Lynn Foltyn, "Feminine Beauty in American Culture," doctoral dissertation, University of California at San Diego, in progress. Foltyn measured square footage of departments offering male versus female items in shopping malls and boutiques, on the assumption that if women's departments were not creating enough profit per square foot, they would be forced to give way to men's or general departments. *Foltyn found seven times as much square footage was devoted to female personal items as to male personal items.*

CHAPTER 8

Why Did the Sexual Revolution Come and Go So Quickly?

1. Germaine Greer, *Sex and Destiny* (New York: Harper & Row, 1984).

1a. *Glamour*, March 1984, "Sexual Pleasures of Childbirth," excerpted from Diana Korte and Roberta Scaer, *A Good Birth, A Safe Birth* (New York: Bantam, 1984).

2. See *The Champion: Official Journal of the National Association of Criminal Defense Lawyers*, Jan./Feb. 1986, Vol. X, No. 1, pp. 16–18.

3. Dr. Joyce Brothers, "Why You Shouldn't Move in with Your Lover," *New Woman*, March 1985, pp. 54–57. Excerpted from *What Every Woman Should Know about Marriage* (New York: Simon & Schuster, 1982).

4. Ibid., p. 56.

5. Ibid.

6. Ibid., p. 54.

7. Ibid.

8. Gail Jennes, "Out of the Pages," *People*, February 20, 1983.

9. "Dear Abby," New York *Daily News*, May 15, 1982, and syndicated throughout the United States.

10. National Clearinghouse for Family Planning Information, Health Education Bulletin, "Counseling for Teens: The Consequences of Sexual Activity," June 1981, no. 22. Cited in Carol Cassell, *Swept Away* (New York: Simon & Schuster, 1984), p. 188.

11. John Gordon, *The Myth of the Monstrous Male* (New York: Playboy, 1982).

12. Kristin Luker, *Abortion and the Politics of Motherhood* (Berkeley: University of California Press, 1984).

13. Cassell, op. cit.

14. Steven Naifeh and Gregory White Smith, *Why Can't Men Open Up?* (New York: Clarkson N. Potter, 1984).

15. Philip Blumstein and Pepper Schwartz, *American Couples* (New York: William Morrow, 1983), p. 304.

16. Barbara Leon, ''The Male Supremacist Attack on Monogamy,'' in Redstockings, *Feminist Revolution* (New York: Random House, 1978).

17. Dr. Joyce Brothers, *What Every Woman Should Know about Men* (New York: Simon & Schuster, 1982), pp. 175–176.

18. See Linda Wolfe, *The Cosmo Report* (New York: Arbor House, 1981).

19. Jacqueline Simenauer and David Carroll, *Singles: The New Americans* (New York: Simon & Schuster, 1982), p. 198.

20. Ibid., p. 199.

21. John Gordon, op. cit., p. 194.

22. Ibid., p. 57.

23. Simenauer and Carroll, op. cit., p. 150.

24. The most recent extensive documentation is in Blumstein and Schwartz, *American Couples*.

25. Brothers, op. cit., p. 165.

CHAPTER 9

Dialogues on Sex, Success, and Fragile Egos

1. See, for example, Philip Blumstein and Pepper Schwartz, *American Couples: Money, Work and Sex* (New York: William Morrow, 1983).

CHAPTER 10

What I Love Most about Men

1. Philip Blumstein and Pepper Schwartz, *American Couples: Money, Work and Sex* (New York: William Morrow, 1983).

CHAPTER 11

How Can I Change a Man (Without Just Getting Him Ready for the Next Woman)?

1. Natasha Josefowitz, *Is This Where I Was Going?* (New York: Warner Books, 1983).
2. See Ken Druck, *Secrets Men Keep* (New York: Doubleday, 1985).

CHAPTER 12

How Can I Get Him to Express Feelings?

1. John Condrey and Sandra Condrey, "Sex Differences: A Study in the Eye of the Beholder," *Child Development*, vol. 47, 1976, pp. 812–819.
2. See, for example, Carol Cassell, *Swept Away* (New York: Simon & Schuster, 1984), pp. 60–61.

CHAPTER 13

Conclusion: Clearing the Way for Love

1. Roger Melton, Westwood, California, Vietnam Center, quoted in the *Los Angeles Times,* November 14, 1983.
2. My own count of prime-time and daytime television from January to September 1985 and of movies released from 1984 through September 1985.
3. Illinois, Maine, Maryland, Massachusetts, and New Hampshire.
4. Kristen Luker, *The Politics of Abortion* (Berkeley: University of California Press, 1984).

Bibliography and Resources

Perhaps the most important resource we have is the sharpening of our observation of reality. To understand how women are objectified as sex objects, study *Playboy* and *Penthouse*—the pictures and the ads. To understand how men are objectified as success objects, read the women's magazines and romance novels, and watch soap operas. To understand the current roles the two sexes still play, read *Forbes* and *Sports Illustrated*, and compare them with *Better Homes & Gardens*, *Family Circle*, and daytime television. Observe the differences in advertising and make a quick list of the articles or TV programming in two columns. Then go to an informal restaurant and listen to conversation differences, or to a schoolyard and watch the boys' and girls' play patterns during lunch hour. Keep these realities—your own research—in mind as you study the broader perspectives discussed in the works listed below.

Baumli, Francis. *Men Freeing Men*. Jersey City, N.J.: New Atlantis Press, 1985.

Bloomfield, Harold, with Leonard Felder. *Making Peace with Your Parents*. New York: Random House, 1983.

Blumstein, Philip, and Schwartz, Pepper. *American Couples*. New York: William Morrow, 1983.

Brothers, Dr. Joyce. *What Every Woman Should Know about Men*. New York: Simon & Schuster, 1981.

Cassell, Carol. *Swept Away*. New York: Simon & Schuster, 1984.

Diamond, Jed. *Inside Out: Becoming My Own Man*. San Rafael, Calif.: Fifth Wave Press, 1983.

Dowling, Colette. *The Cinderella Complex*. New York: Pocket Books, 1981.

Druck, Ken, with Jim Simmons. *Secrets Men Keep*. New York: Doubleday, 1985.

Ehrenreich, Barbara. *The Hearts of Men*. Garden City, N.Y.: Anchor Press, 1983.

Ellis, Albert. *Sex and The Liberated Man*. Secaucus, N.J.: Lyle Stuart, 1976.

Farrell, Warren. *The Liberated Man*. New York: Bantam, 1975.

Friedan, Betty. *The Second Stage*. New York: Summit Books, 1981.

Garfinkel, Perry. *In a Man's World: Father, Son, Brother, Friend, and Other Roles Men Play*. New York: New American Library, 1985.

Gerzon, Mark. *Choice of Heroes: The Changing Faces of American Manhood*. Boston: Houghton Mifflin, 1984.

Goldberg, Herb. *The Hazards of Being Male*. New York: Nash Publishing, 1976.

Goldberg, Herb. *The New Male*. New York: William Morrow, 1979.

Gordon, John. *The Myth of the Monstrous Male*. New York: Playboy, 1982.

Hapgood, Fred. *Why Males Exist*. New York: William Morrow, 1979.

Harrison, Jim. "Warning: The Male Sex Role May Be Hazardous to Your Health." *Journal of Social Issues*, 1978, 34(1):65–86.

Maccoby, Eleanor, and Jacklin, Carol Nagy. *The Psychology of Sex Differences*. Stanford, Calif.: Stanford University Press, 1978.

Money, John, and Erhardt, Anke. *Man and Woman, Boy and Girl*. Baltimore, Md.: Johns Hopkins University Press, 1972.

Money, John, and Tucker, Patricia. *Sexual Signatures: On Being a Man or a Woman*. Boston: Little, Brown, 1975.

Naifeh, Steven, and Smith, Gregory White. *Why Can't Men Open Up?* New York: Clarkson N. Potter, 1984.

Novak, William. *The Great American Man Shortage and Other Roadblocks to Romance*. New York: Rawson Associates, 1983.

Pleck, Joseph H. *The Myth of Masculinity*. Cambridge, Mass.: M.I.T. Press, 1981.

Schenk, Roy U. *The Other Side of the Coin: Causes and Consequences of Men's Oppression*. Madison, Wis.: Bioenergetics Press, 1982.

Sexton, Pat. *The Feminized Male*. New York: Vintage Books, 1970.

Shanor, Karen. *The Shanor Study: The Sexual Sensitivity of the American Male*. New York: Dial Press, 1978.

Simenauer, Jacqueline, and Carroll, David. *Singles: The New Americans*. New York: Simon & Schuster, 1982.

Trier, Lynette, and Peacock, Dick. *Learning to Leave*. New York: Warner, 1983.

Zilbergeld, Bernie. *Male Sexuality: A Guide to Self-Fulfillment*. Boston: Little, Brown, 1978.

Resources

Coalition of Free Men
PO Box 129
Manhasset, NY 11030

Joint Custody Association
10606 Wilkins Avenue
Los Angeles, CA 90024

Men's Organizations & Publications Directory
68 Deering Street
Portland, ME 04101
(Directory costs $7.00; updated monthly)

Men's Rights, Inc. (MR)
PO Box 163180
Sacramento, CA 95816

National Congress for Men
68 Deering Street
Portland, ME 04101

National Organization for Changing Men
PO Box 451
Watseka, IL 60970

Index of Questions Women and Men Ask

The questions below are the questions each sex most frequently asks about the other. These questions are asked so frequently in part because the answers normally given are rarely answered in the numerous contexts which constitute life. By referring to each page in the book in which the question is addressed, the reader or researcher can view the answers from a number of different contexts.

Pages in *italics* indicate the most *direct* answers. Other pages give relevant background from which the reader may draw different conclusions from my own.

Page numbers with descriptions in parentheses (e. g., Analogy) indicate that the question is addressed in that particular section of that page.

Questions like ''When women do 'make it' in business, why do they seem to become like men?'' imply that, in fact, they *do* become like men. The pages to which I refer the reader do not always agree with the underlying assumptions (that women *do* become like men), or the underlying critique (that it is completely bad to be like a man). Instead, pages refer the reader to a number of considerations related to the question.

Questions Women Ask:

Questions Men Ask:

Acknowledgments

I wish to acknowledge my dad, Tom Farrell, whose sensitivity gave me permission; my mother, Muriel, whose life and loss of life prompted me to look at women's lives; my new mother, Lee, whose energy and independence stimulate respect; my sister, Gail, who has fought the battles between dependence and independence on many fronts, and whose capacity for love reaches me wherever I am; and my brother, Wayne, who taught me that the best thing I could give him was to learn from him.

One woman, Anne Goshen, has grown with me through each draft of this manuscript, testing each idea against her own life experience—listening, adding, refining, eliminating—until a synergistic relationship emerged among the three of us (me, Anne, and the manuscript—the manuscript sometimes remembered what I had forgotten by the next chapter!). Into that threesome often entered Anne's daughter, Megan Hubbard, thirteen, who became my consultant on youth while quietly teaching me a new type of love.

A handful of people have offered me support at crucial turning points of my life: my former wife, Ursie Fairbairn, a true Superwoman who taught by example but never by rhetoric; Jim Crown, Ziva Kwitney, Harold Bloomfield, Ken Druck, and the San Diego author's group, who taught me the meaning of supportiveness; and Ted Becker, who pressed me into a ''mid-life crisis'' in my late twenties. These people will be part of whatever I write.

Ellen Levine juggled the role of agent, critic, supporter, editor, and wise negotiator through each stage of the manuscript over almost half a decade; Tom Miller's line editing clarified and streamlined thousands of sentences in the book (with the exception of a few in which I insisted on "my way"). Toni Burbank's contributions during the manuscript's proposal stages and Jacque Lynn Foltyn's insights throughout the writing of the book proved invaluable.

Lin Richardson devoted thousands of hours to word-processing all three drafts of the book, beginning with tens of thousands of handwritten index cards, meeting deadlines, pasting up art, and deciphering instructions. Her contribution was remarkable.

George Lewis Singer, Steve Fineman, and Paul Evans all not only capably assisted me in research but sparred with me over dozens of ideas in their embryonic stages.

Especially careful and insightful editing and commentary were offered by Fred Hayward, Annetta Mauch, and Richard Haddad throughout every paragraph of the book. Careful readings were also done by Ken Blanchard, Al Crespi, Albert Ellis, Gail Farrell, Holly Forcier, Alan Garner, Harley Hahn, Natasha Josefowitz, Gayle Kimball, Jane Navarre, Nena O'Neill, Dick Peacock, and Lynette Trier. The contributions of the cartoonists I commissioned, John Ashley, Doug Dohrer, Michelle Fournier, and Bob Lee, are in evidence throughout the book, as well as those of the cartoonists who gave me permission to reprint their cartoons. Jim Francis Miley is credited with the back cover photo.

The reference staff of the Central University Library at the University of California, San Diego, and especially Sue Galloway, offered generous support for over four years and three drafts. The 106,000 women and men who were willing to "walk a mile in the moccasins" of the other sex during workshops were the pioneers who created the core research base for *Why Men Are the Way They Are* and hopefully grew a little in the process. The National Organization for Women, National Congress for Men, National Organization for Changing Men, and Herb Goldberg have all made significant contributions to my thinking on gender roles and sexual politics.

I acknowledge the late John Lennon, who, when he joined a men's group I had formed, gave life to my hope that successful men could be sensitive too.

At various stages I benefited from the contributions of Pat Chawla, Jim Cook, George Corey, Letty Cottin Pogrebin, Karen DeCrow, Tom Dembofsky, Diana Finch, Lori Glazer, Frank Goodall, Ron Graff, Joan Hennebury-Corrales, Spencer Johnson, Lyn Lindsey, Joyce McHugh, Joe Pleck, Alix Olsen, Ruth Rogin, Gloria Steinem, Deborah Sundmacher, Chris Wimpey, and the professional staff of McGraw-Hill, from administrative assistants to Gladys Justin Carr, chair of the editorial board, all of whom sought to make this book better than it would have been without them.

General Index

About the Author

Warren Farrell, Ph.D., is the author of *The Liberated Man*, which UPI called "the most important and incisive piece of social commentary in more than three decades." Over a period of twenty years, Warren Farrell has formed over 600 women's and men's groups and has worked with more than 106,000 men and women from all walks of life. Dr. Farrell is the only man to have been elected three times to the Board of the National Organization for Women in New York City; he has also served on the boards of the National Organization for Changing Men and the National Congress for Men. He has been described as "the Gloria Steinem of Men's Liberation" by the *Chicago Tribune*.

Dr. Farrell was chosen by President Johnson in 1965 as one of the nation's outstanding young educators. He has taught political science, psychology, sociology, sexual politics, and public administration at Georgetown University, Rutgers, Brooklyn College, American University, and the California School of Professional Psychology. He received the highest honor at New York University for his Ph.D. thesis on changing men's roles and behavior in response to women's roles. Dr. Farrell has appeared seven times on *Donahue*, and has also appeared on *Today*; *Good Morning America*; *The CBS Morning News*; and *Tomorrow*, among other nationally broadcast shows. He has written for publications ranging from *The New York Times* to *The World Book Encyclopedia*, from *Cosmopolitan* to *Ms.*, from *Glamour* to journals of sociology and psychology. Dr. Farrell is now teaching at the School of Medicine, the University of California at San Diego. He lives in Leucadia, a suburb of San Diego.